The World of the
JOHN BIRCH SOCIETY

The World of the

JOHN BIRCH SOCIETY

Conspiracy, Conservatism,
and the Cold War

D. J. MULLOY

Vanderbilt University Press

NASHVILLE

© 2014 by Vanderbilt University Press
Nashville, Tennessee 37235
All rights reserved
First printing 2014

This book is printed on acid-free paper.
Manufactured in the United States of America
Book design by Dariel Mayer
Composition by Vanderbilt University Press

Frontispiece: Former major general Edwin Walker is led
away at bayonet point by U.S. troops after refusing to move
from the courthouse in downtown Oxford, Mississippi,
during the attempt to prevent James Meredith from
registering at the University of Mississippi, October 1, 1962.
© Bettmann/CORBIS

Library of Congress Cataloging-in-Publication Data on file
LC control number   2013039765
LC classification number   E740 .J6M86 2014
Dewey class number   322.4'4—dc23

ISBN 978-0-8265-1981-8 (cloth)
ISBN 978-0-8265-1983-2 (ebook)

To my grandparents
Catherine "Kitty" McCabe (1906–1986)
John Mulloy (1905–1951)
Edith King (1922–1980)
and Thomas Telford (1921–1987)

Contents

List of Illustrations

Acknowledgments

M any people have contributed to this book and I am extremely grateful to all of them. Much of the initial research for it took place in the wonderful archives of the Wilcox Collection for Contemporary Political Movements in the Kenneth Spenser Research Library at the University of Kansas. Because of the expertise and generosity of all the staff there, including Tara Wenger, Karen Cook, Letha Johnson, Sherry Williams, Deborah Dandridge, Meredith Huff, Toni Bresler, and especially Rebecca Schulte and Kathy Lafferty, the time I spent in Lawrence was immensely rewarding and productive. I am very grateful for the short term research grant I received from the Research Office of Wilfrid Laurier University for enabling that trip, as well as for a book preparation grant. My thanks also to the dedicated librarians of my own university who have helped with this project in countless ways, especially Patti Metzger, Angela Davidson, and Hélène LeBlanc, as well as to the outstanding administrative assistants in the History Department at Laurier, Colleen Ginn and Cindi Wieg. I would like to thank my editor at Vanderbilt University Press, Eli Bortz, for his enthusiasm for, and commitment to, the project, as well as all the people at Vanderbilt who worked so hard to bring it to fruition, including Susan Havlish, Betsy Phillips, Joell Smith-Borne, and Peg Duthie. Adam Crerar and David Monod read the manuscript at various stages: their careful attentiveness and insightfulness—as well as that of two anonymous reviewers—improved the book beyond measure. Thank you. Thank you also to Sarah Cracknell, Jónsi Birgisson, Neil Halstead, and Mark Hollis for keeping me company during the writing process, and to my friends and colleagues in the History Department at Wilfrid Laurier University, where I have the great pleasure to teach. Above all, though, I would like to thank the two other writers in my family, Pamela and Esme Mulloy, for their love, support, and considerable patience.

Fantastic? Of course it's fantastic. . . .
We are living in fantastic times
and a fantastic situation. . . .
We are in circumstances where
it is *realistic* to be *fantastic*.
　　　—Robert Welch, *The Blue Book*

A conspiracy is everything
that ordinary life is not.
　　　—Don DeLillo, *Libra*

Introduction

It was an extraordinary claim. The thirty-fourth president of the United States, Dwight D. Eisenhower—the widely beloved war hero, the man who had helped save the world from fascism during World War II—was a traitor, a "dedicated, conscious agent" of the Soviet Union and of the whole "Communist conspiracy." Nor was he the only American political figure apparently in thrall to the nation's deadliest enemy. U.S. secretary of state John Foster Dulles and his brother, Central Intelligence Agency director Allen Dulles, were similarly indicted, as were numerous other senior members of the Eisenhower administration and the wider political establishment. In fact, in what might have been the most fantastical claim of all, Dwight Eisenhower—"Ike," as he was almost universally known—was not even the ringleader of this cunning group of plotters. That accolade went to his younger brother Milton (who, when not busy directing the conspiracy, bided his time as the president of Johns Hopkins University in Baltimore).

The allegations had been circulating around the conservative anticommunist network in the United States since the mid-1950s in the form of a privately printed letter called *The Politician*.[1] They were the work of Robert H. W. Welch Jr.—a retired candy manufacturer, former board member of the National Association of Manufacturers, and poetry aficionado. They are obviously easy to ridicule—as indeed they were when they became much more widely known in the summer of 1960, and have been ever since. Yet Welch was also the founder, in 1958, of what was to become the largest, most important, best organized, and most formidable "radical" or "ultra" right-wing group of the period, the John Birch Society—although members of the Society preferred the terms "conservative," "anticommunist," or "Americanist" to describe themselves—which at the height of its power in the mid-1960s was taken very seriously by considerable swaths of the American population, as well as leading politicians, journalists, academics, and cultural commentators of all kinds. So seriously, in fact, that the "Birchers"—as they were called—were feared to be on the verge not only of taking over the Republican Party and propelling a dangerous "extremist" into the White House, but also of being a threat to the very foundations of American democracy itself, and perhaps even enabling the rise of fascism in the United States. "The political extremism of the Radical Right and of The John Birch Society," wrote Benjamin Epstein and Arnold Forster of the Anti-Defamation League in one notable and widely read report on the organization in 1967, "is no minor surface rash on the body politic. It can be a creeping malignancy that would destroy the vital centers of the American political organism. And it is still spreading."[2]

As it turned out, just as Epstein and Forster were publishing their report, the heyday of the Birch Society was fast approaching its end. With an estimated peak membership of one hundred thousand in 1965–1966, Birchers had played a substantial role in—and, initially at least, had also benefited from—the energizing and enormously consequential 1964 presidential campaign of the Arizona Republican senator Barry Goldwater. By 1968 the number of Birchers had declined to between sixty thousand and seventy thousand, and by the mid-1990s the figure was down to fifteen thousand or twenty thousand (estimates are all that are available because the Society declined to release its official membership rolls).[3] Such figures, while not inconsiderable, are a long way from the million members Welch set out to recruit when he first established the Society—or even his revised goal of four hundred thousand, announced on the occasion of its tenth anniversary in 1968—and the Birch Society's relatively small size, its sudden appearance and precipitous decline, and the tendency of many of its key figures to "believe the unbelievable," as one of its contemporary critics put it, meant that there has long been a tendency to dismiss the significance of the organization and its concerns.[4] If the Society is remembered at all, it is generally as just another example of the marginal, esoteric, and exotic groups that have always existed on the abundant and historically deeply rooted "lunatic fringe" of American life.

But the significance of an organization is to be found not only in the number of its recruits, or how long it manages to command attention on the political scene. Seemingly small groups can still have a powerful impact on a society, and they can also provide a meaningful window through which one can better understand and come to terms with that society at a particular moment in its history. Such organizations can generate new ideas, or give a renewed lease of life to old ones; they can pioneer innovative modes of political activity or communication; they can embody—and give voice to—some of the central tensions or conflicts of the time, and through their actions and beliefs they can compel opponents and observers to defend and sharpen their own positions, policies, and practices; they can attract millions of sympathizers and supporters to their cause; and they can leave behind a substantial legacy—positive and negative—for others to examine and learn from. As we shall see, all of this applies to the John Birch Society in the years between 1958 and 1968. It also applies to contemporary political movements (whether of the Left or the Right). Indeed, many of the key lessons to be drawn from an examination of the John Birch Society are more than applicable to the various forms of "extremism" that have been such a prominent feature of American political life during the opening decades of the twenty-first century.

Far from being an irrelevant or easily dismissible footnote to the politics and history of the late 1950s and 1960s, the John Birch Society was actually closely involved in—or at least had much to say about—many of the major issues and controversies of the period, such as the rise of the civil rights movement, the role of the military in American life, the assassination of President John F. Kennedy, the Cuban missile crisis, the Vietnam War, and a host of others. Opinion polls taken by Gallup in January 1965, for example, showed that 79 percent of Americans of voting age were aware of the Society, which, in the view of one scholar, was "very close to the saturation point of knowledge of contemporary political organizations among the American public."[5] (By way of comparison, the figures for the American Communist Party, the National Association for the Advancement of Colored People, and the Congress of Racial Equality were 80 percent, 82 percent, and 70 percent, respectively.)[6] Moreover, the appearance and activities of the Birch Society during this time speaks to the broader context in which it operated: it reveals a great deal about the Cold War culture and politics of the United States, about its rapidly proliferating conspiracy culture (which was given further impetus by the tragic events of November 22, 1963), and about the newly emerging—and soon to be triumphant—conservative movement's challenge to the previously dominant "liberal consensus."[7]

Robert Welch would do all he could to deny any direct connection between his "privately" expressed views in *The Politician* and the "official" policies and beliefs of the Birch Society, but his disavowals were not successful. Even though the extent to which ordinary Birchers shared their leader's views about President Eisenhower in particular is by no means clear—and one must also raise the possibility that Welch himself may not have believed his own charges literally, seeing them more as a hyperbolic warning about what he regarded as the deeply lamentable state of American politics at the time and about the extraordinary dangers the United States faced from the unrelenting communist threat—his allegations haunted the Society throughout its controversial spell in the political spotlight. And whether or not all Birchers believed that Eisenhower was a secret communist agent, there was no escaping the fact that conspiracism and an implacable hostility to communism were the central components of the Society's worldview.

This was made abundantly clear in *The Blue Book of the John Birch Society*, the organization's foundational text, a transcript of the two-day state-of-the-world seminar Welch gave to potential new recruits personally in the early days of the Society's existence. All subsequent members were expected to be familiar with the text. "Communism, in its unmistakable present reality," Welch wrote, "is wholly a conspiracy, a gigantic conspiracy to enslave mankind; an increasingly successful conspiracy controlled by determined, cunning, and utterly ruthless gangsters, willing to use any means to achieve its end."[8] These included: "bribery, lies, bluff, brutality, the countless tentacles of treason, murder on a scale never before dreamed of in the world," and above all, "patience."[9] In fact, the tentacles of the communist "octopus" were so extensive, Welch asserted, that they

> now reach into all of the legislative halls, all of the union labor meetings, a majority of the religious gatherings, and most of the schools *of the whole world*. It has a central nervous system which can make its tentacles in the labor unions of Bolivia, in the farmers' co-operatives of Saskatchewan, in the caucuses of the Social Democrats of West Germany, and in the class rooms of Yale Law School,

all retract or reach forward simultaneously. It can make all of these creeping tentacles turn either right or left, or a given percentage turn right while the others turn left, at the same time, in accordance with the intentions of a central brain in Moscow or Ust' Kamenogorsk [a city in Kazakhstan]. The human race has never before faced any such monster of power which was determined to enslave it. There is certainly no reason for underrating its size, its efficiency, its determination, its power, or its menace.[10]

Not underrating the size, efficiency, determination, or power of the Soviet Union provided the raison d'être for the United States' entire national security apparatus during the Cold War, of course. What distinguished the Birch Society's approach to the subject from those actually charged with the responsibility of keeping the nation safe was its emphasis—constant and insistent—on the *internal*, as opposed to the external, threat posed to the nation by the communist menace. As the reference to legislative halls, union meetings, religious gatherings, and schools in the preceding quotation make clear, Welch's overwhelming concern in this area was with the subversion of the United States from *within*: with infiltration, treason, weakness, and betrayal. These were the recurring themes of *The Politician* as well.[11] It was this preoccupation with the internal threat of communism that, in the eyes of its critics at least, made the radical Right so "radical"—in the pejorative sense of the term—in the first place. Other notable radical Right organizations of the period include: Dr. Fred C. Schwarz's Christian Anti-Communism Crusade; Rev. Billy James Hargis's Christian Crusade; Dr. George S. Benson's Harding College, based in Searcy, Arkansas; Rev. Carl McIntire's American Council of Christian Churches; the family-run operation of Phyllis, Fred, and Eleanor Schlafly's Cardinal Mindszenty Foundation, which was named for József Mindszenty, who was imprisoned by the Hungarian government in 1949 for his anticommunist activities; Kent and Phoebe Courtney's Conservative Society of America; Willis Carto's Liberty Lobby; and a host of smaller groups and one-man operations with historically evocative names like We, The People!, Moral Re-Armament, Let Freedom Ring, and The Freedoms Foundation at Valley Forge. Dan Smoot, the radio and television presenter—and former FBI agent—was also a radical Rightist, as was the ex-dean of Notre Dame Law School, Clarence Manion.[12]

The activities and beliefs of the radical Right—its unremitting pursuit of the "enemy within"—provided, for many Americans, a distressing reminder of the only too recently concluded traumas of the Second Red Scare: the wild accusations; the destructive atmosphere of secrecy, suspicion, and fear; the diminutions of freedom; the cultural and ideological straitjacketing; and the political excesses that had so often resulted.[13] For most, the censure of Senator Joseph R. McCarthy (R-WI) in 1954—his death followed three years later—had brought the Second Red Scare to at least a symbolic close, and there was a great deal of anxiety at the prospect of any revival of the phenomenon. Much of this anxiety and a great deal of hostility was directed—at times unreasonably, but perhaps inevitably—toward the John Birch Society and its leader, as the spearhead of the new anticommunist Right in the United States, and eventually just as much from "fellow" conservatives as liberals. Which raises the question: who was Robert Welch and what exactly did he hope to achieve with his new organization?

Before the Society: Robert Welch and the Story of John Birch

Robert H. W. Welch Jr. was born on a farm in Chowan County, North Carolina, on December 1, 1899. Something of a child prodigy, he could read by the time he was three, had learned his multiplication tables before he was four, and began to study Latin at the age of seven.[14] He was twelve when he enrolled at the University of North Carolina and sixteen when he graduated. He entered the United States Naval Academy at Annapolis, Maryland, in 1917, but resigned two years later in order to attend Harvard Law School in Cambridge, Massachusetts. Having met his soon-to-be-wife, Marian Probert, who was a student at Wellesley College, and clashed repeatedly with one of his instructors, the future liberal Supreme Court justice Felix Frankfurter—the "young man from North Carolina recognized . . . H-O-G-W-A-S-H when he heard it," writes his hagiographic biographer G. Edward Griffin—Welch left Harvard in 1922, a year short of graduating, intent on making his fortune in the candy making business.[15]

Initially things did not go well. Despite a prodigious work ethic and his canny invention of the "Papa Sucker," a caramel lollypop that wouldn't melt in the heat of summer, Welch walked away from his first venture, the Oxford Candy Company, in June 1929, following a dispute with his board of directors over its desire to reduce the quality of the products the company was selling. He set up business again in Brooklyn, while supplementing his income—he now had two children to support—by working as a part-time salesman for E. J. Brach and Sons in Chicago, one of the largest manufacturers of confectionery in the country. Selling candy at the height of the Great Depression proved no easier the second time around, however, and Welch's new business folded in 1933. Welch worked for Brach and Sons full time until 1934, when—indefatigable as he proved to be all his life—he started a third company, the Midwest Candy Company of Attica, Indiana. This too failed, and in 1935, after filing for bankruptcy, Welch returned to Boston to work for his younger brother's much more successful candy venture, the James O. Welch Company (James had left the Oxford Candy Company to go out on his own in 1927).

As the James O. Welch Company prospered, so, finally, did Robert Welch. In addition to being vice president in charge of sales and advertising for his brother's company—a role that saw him traversing the country, managing its sales offices in Atlanta, Pittsburgh, Chicago, Houston, Los Angeles, and Seattle—he quickly became a director of the Boston Chamber of Commerce, the Cambridge Chamber of Commerce, a national councilor of the U.S. Chamber of Commerce, the director of a local bank, and a member of his local school board, in Belmont, Massachusetts. He published his first book, *The Road to Salesmanship*, in 1941, and served on the board of the Office of Price Administration as well as the War Production Board during World War II. During the war years, Welch also became chairman of the National Confectioners Association's Washington Committee. In 1947 he received the "Oscar" of the confectionery world, the Kettle Award from the magazine *Candy Industry*.[16] Three years later, his achievements were further recognized when he was appointed to the board of directors of the National Association of Manufacturers (NAM), a prestigious position he would hold for the next seven years. During this time, Welch also spent three years as one of the NAM's regional vice presidents, three years on its executive committee, and two as the chairman of its education committee. Needless to say, all these wealthy and well-placed contacts would prove extremely useful once the Birch Society was established.

Welch first became involved in politics in 1946, when he volunteered to work on Republican Robert Bradford's successful campaign to become governor of Massachusetts; he was appointed vice chairman of the state's Republican finance committee two years later. In 1949 Welch went a major step further, however, when he announced his intention to become the next lieutenant governor of the Bay State. Like many other conservatives and businessmen of the time, reducing government "interference" in the economy and turning back the "creeping collectivism" of Franklin D. Roosevelt's New Deal were among Welch's principal concerns, as he made clear in an interview with Courtney Sheldon of the *Christian Science Monitor* on the eve of the election. "Our first and most important job," Welch explained, "is to keep us from going any further than we have already gone in extension of government ownership of business, operation of business, interference with business, control of business, and control of the details of our daily living." He was also "very strongly opposed," he said, to "socialized medicine at the national or at the state level," to "federal aid to education in any shape, manner or form," and to "federal housing plans."[17]

What were to become two of the more pronounced features of Welch's approach to the world as head of the Birch Society—a tendency toward melodramatic, if not apocalyptic, rhetoric and a firm belief in the revelatory power of the conspiratorial—were also both evident, albeit in embryonic form, during his first foray into partisan politics. In a speech in May 1949, for example, Welch argued that it was "no secret" that there was a "war" going on in the United States between "collectivism and individualism," a war that was being waged on many fronts. "In the field of commerce and industry the battle is between free enterprise and state socialism," he said. "In politics it is between the people's ownership of the government and the government's ownership of the people. In sociology it is between self-reliance and dependence on a welfare state. In international relations it is between a brutally aggressive tyranny and the remains of an independent civilization." And the outcome of this war depended on "whether we are going to leave our children and our grandchildren a world at least as good as the one we have inherited, or one that is already plunged into the incipient shambles of a new Dark Ages."[18] Even more explicitly, in a fund-raising letter of July 17, 1950, Welch wrote:

> The strategy of the socialists is to divide and conquer; call all businessmen crooks so that nobody will speak up for them, and strangle them with controls

and taxation; bribe all the farmers with their own money into a selfish pressure group for more bribes; infiltrate the labor unions, and convert them into political tools; discredit the medical profession until the rest of the public clamors for "government medicine"; attack every segment of our population with tactics which alienate the support of all other segments. . . . The forces on the socialist side amount to a *vast conspiracy* to change our political and economic system.

It was, says Griffin, the first time Welch had used the word "conspiracy" in a public statement.[19]

Welch placed second in the Republican primary for lieutenant governor by a margin of over one hundred thousand votes, but the defeat didn't seem to overly concern him. As he put it in a letter to his campaign workers and contributors dated September 21, 1950, it was his hope that the almost 60,000 people who had voted for him—the figure was 59,238—would become "a far stronger, more militant, and more effective force of political strength in other campaigns to come." Indeed, as far as Welch was concerned, "*this crusade has just started.*"[20] Two years later Welch failed again, this time in his attempt to be elected as a delegate, pledged to the Ohio senator Robert Taft, for the 1952 Republican national convention. Eisenhower's defeat of Taft to secure the Republican Party's presidential nomination was even more significant, however. Welch regarded it as the "dirtiest deal in American political history," and along with the censure of Senator McCarthy in 1954, it seems to have been the key event that convinced him of the need to move beyond conventional party politics as a means to secure America's salvation.[21]

Nineteen fifty-two was a banner year for Welch in at least two other respects, though. First, it saw the publication of his first explicitly political book, *May God Forgive Us*, a powerful critique of American foreign policy in Asia, a conspiratorial denunciation of what he called the "almost unbelievable combination of trickery, chicanery, and treason" at work in the administration of Harry S. Truman, and a heartfelt cry of support for Chiang Kai-shek and his Nationalist struggle against Mao Tse-tung's communist hordes.[22] And second, it was while he was in a committee room of the Senate Office Building in Washington, DC, following up on his research for *May God Forgive Us*— to check some facts that had been the subject of dispute—that Welch first encountered the name John Birch.[23]

Born in India in 1918 to missionary parents, Birch was raised on a farm near Macon, Georgia. After graduating from Mercer University in Macon and the Bible Baptist Seminary in Fort Worth, Texas, he went to China in 1940 as a missionary. During the Second World War, he volunteered for General Claire Chennault's Fourteenth Air Force—better known as the Flying Tigers—and was involved in the rescue of several of Lieutenant Colonel James Doolittle's "Doolittle Raiders" who had been forced to ditch their planes over China following their attacks on Tokyo and other targets in Japan on April 28, 1942, the first air raids on the Japanese homelands. Ten days after V-J Day, on August 25, 1945, while on a secret mission with American, Chinese Nationalist, and Korean officers and soldiers, near Hsuchow on the Shantung Peninsula, Birch and his party fell into an altercation with a group of Chinese communist guerrillas. There is some dispute about what exactly happened next—some accounts have Birch insulting the leader of the guerrillas while trying to bluff his way out of the situation; others, most notably Welch's, find nothing remiss in Birch's conduct. Whatever actually took place, the result of the confrontation was that Birch was shot and bayoneted to death. His last words, reported by Lieutenant Tung, a liaison officer with the Nationalist forces who was a member of Birch's party, were said to be: "It doesn't make much difference what happens to me, but it is of utmost importance that my country learn now whether these people are friend or foe."[24]

These were the words that caught Welch's attention seven years later in the committee room of the Senate Office Building. *The Life of John Birch: In the Story of One American Boy, the Ordeal of His Age*, published in 1954, was the result. As the book's subtitle suggests, as interesting as the specific details of Birch's life were, it was the wider resonance of his story that really appealed to Welch. Indeed, as far as Welch was concerned, Birch was the first American casualty of World War III—brutally murdered by the communists—and the fact that so few of his fellow countrymen knew about it illustrated just how deeply the "conspiracy" had penetrated the nation. Birch would not die in vain, Welch said. Rather, Welch hoped that "even now his story may still serve to throw one more needed beam of light on the nature and the aims, the strategy and the tactics, of the conspiracy that will destroy us unless we expose and destroy it first."[25]

In 1954 Welch also began work on *The Politician*. He did so, he later recalled, at the prompting of a traveling companion who, during a car ride to New York, had listened to Welch complaining about how Eisenhower had "double-crossed" conservative Republican candidates in that year's congressional elections. (Welch revised this initial "letter" to his friends in 1956 and again in 1958, by which time the manuscript was running at eighty thousand words.)[26] Preparing to commit himself completely to his political endeavors, in February 1956 Welch launched a new magazine called *One Man's Opinion*—later to be retitled *American Opinion*—and in June he formally resigned from the James O. Welch Company (effective January 1, 1957). In an already eventful career, the stage was set for the creation of the John Birch Society.

Organizational Mechanics and Ideological Fervor

As the end of 1958 approached, Robert Welch sent out letters to seventeen of his friends and associates, inviting them to join him in Indianapolis on December 8–9, following the conclusion of that year's NAM Congress of Industry in New York, which about half of the invitees would be attending. Welch did not specify the purpose of the meeting—he indicated only that it was a matter of the "utmost importance"—but eleven of the seventeen accepted his invitation, and all but one of them became founding members of the John Birch Society as a result.[27] They were: T. Coleman Andrews, a former commissioner of internal revenue of the United States; Colonel Laurence E. Bunker, the former personal

Figure 1.1. Robert Welch at his desk in the Birch Society offices in Belmont, Massachusetts, May 1966. A portrait of John Birch hangs on the wall behind him. © Bettmann/CORBIS

aide of General Douglas MacArthur; William J. Grede, the head of Grede Foundries in Milwaukee, Wisconsin, as well as a former president of the NAM; Fred C. Koch, the president of Rock Island Oil and Refining of Wichita, Kansas, and one of the wealthiest men in the state (as well as the father of Charles and David Koch, who would become two key backers of the twenty-first-century Tea Party movement); W. B. McMillan, the president of the Hussmann Refrigerator Company of St. Louis, Missouri, and the first official member of the Birch Society after Welch himself; Dr. Revilo P. Oliver, a committed conspiracist and a distinguished professor of classical languages and literatures at the University of Illinois; Louis Rothenberg, one-time president of the Indiana Chamber of Commerce; Fitzhugh Scott of Milwaukee, although he apparently never became an "active" member of the organization; Robert W. Stoddard, another former president of the NAM, as well as the head of the Wyman-Gordon Company of Worcester, Massachusetts; and Ernest Swigert, who was yet another past NAM president, and the head of the Hyster Company in Portland, Oregon.[28]

These men and many like them in the years to come—businessmen, ex-military officers, intellectuals, publishers, and physicians—would form the National Council of Welch's new organization, which, as he explained in *The Blue Book*, had three basic functions (the hint of paranoia and mischievous sense of humor in the description are typical Welch touches):

(1) To show the stature and standing of the leadership of the Society; (2) to give your Founder the benefit of the Council's advice and guidance, both in procedural or organizational matters, and in substantive matters of policy;

and (3) to select, with absolute and final authority, a successor to myself as head of The John Birch Society, if and when an accident, "suicide," or anything sufficiently fatal is arranged for me by the Communists—or I simply die in bed of old age and a cantankerous disposition.[29]

Yet Welch was also clear, in what would become another of his statements (alongside those in *The Politician*) to attract considerable criticism and condemnation, that the Birch Society was to be "a monolithic body." It would "operate under completely authoritative control at all levels," he said. A "republican form of government or of organization" had many "attractions and advantages, under certain favorable conditions," Welch conceded, but "under less happy circumstances"—the circumstances then facing the United States—it lent itself too readily to "infiltration, distortion and disruption," while democracy he dismissed as "merely a deceptive phrase, a weapon of demagoguery, and a perennial fraud."[30]

Accordingly, the Birch Society was to be organized through a series of small local chapters—critics would sometimes refer to them more sinisterly as "cells"—usually made up of ten to twenty members, each with a chapter leader appointed either by the Birch headquarters (based in Belmont) or by an officer of the Society "in the field, who [had] themselves been duly appointed by headquarters." Monthly dues were initially set at $24 a year for men and $12 for women, although a life membership could be bought for $1,000, and chapter meetings were expected to take place at least once a month. When a local chapter reached the maximum of twenty members, the "extra" members were expected to break off and form a new chapter of their own, but there was also a "Home Chapter" for those unfortunate enough to live in an area without a Birch group to join. Paid coordinators supervised the work of the volunteer chapter leaders and helped to form new chapters, and above them stood regional major coordinators.[31]

All in all, it was a hierarchical structure derived not just from the many years Welch had spent in the world of business, but also from his openly, if perhaps surprisingly expressed, admiration for the organizational tactics of his communist foes. Acknowledging the similarity between Lenin's notion of "the dedicated few" and his own plans for the Birch Society in *The Blue Book*, for example, the always-capitalized Founder explained that he was "willing to draw on all successful human experience in organizational matters, so long as it does not involve any sacrifice of morality in the means used to achieve an end."[32]

This approach was reflected clearly enough in some of the specific actions Welch had in mind for how the John Birch Society might resist the depredations of the communist conspiracy while "awakening" the apathetic and "brainwashed" American people to what was actually going on around them, including the use of front organizations—"little fronts, big fronts, temporary fronts, permanent fronts, all kinds of fronts"—as well as the deployment of petitions, massive letter-writing campaigns, and other methods of "exposure." It was time, Welch believed, for an "organization which has a backbone, and cohesiveness, and strength, and definiteness of direction" to put its "weight into the political scales in this country just as fast and as far as we could" in order to "reverse . . . the gradual surrender of the United States to Communism." But because Welch always saw the Birch Society as an educational organization as much as a political one, he also wanted to establish a speakers bureau and a national network of reading rooms where the best anticommunist works (including his own) could be purchased or consulted, and to expand the reach of conservative periodicals such as *American Opinion*, the *Dan Smoot Report*, and William F. Buckley Jr.'s *National Review*, as well as that of conservative radio broadcasters such as Fulton Lewis and Clarence Manion. Certainly no one could accuse him of lacking ambition.[33]

"Communist conspiracy" may have been the most conspicuous and oft-deployed term in Welch's—and the Birch Society's—arsenal, but to a certain extent this was because it functioned as a kind of rhetorical shorthand, encapsulating within it a broader—and perhaps deeper—concern with collectivism in all its forms and "big government" in particular. As "important and absolutely vital as our stopping the Communists has become," Welch argued in *The Blue Book*, "even throwing the Communists completely out of the picture would not stop the fatal deterioration in our sense of values which is now in process," given the "extent to which the cancer of collectivism has weakened and endangered us."[34] The "*increasing quantity of government, in all nations, has constituted the greatest tragedy of the twentieth century*," Welch maintained: the "greatest enemy of man is, and always has been, government. And the larger, the more extensive that government, the greater the enemy."[35]

Acknowledging this perspective helps to explain the appeal of the Society not just to those fearful about communists secretly taking over the American state but also to those worried about high taxation rates or the expansion of workers' rights—industrialists and businessmen, for instance. The Society also attracted those resistant to attempts to "legislate equality," whether through income redistribution or the termination of the rule of Jim Crow in the South, as well as those who just wanted to get government "off the backs" of the American people, to employ a phrase popularized during a later period.[36] Indeed, in these terms we can see the Birch Society as a kind of bridge between the older Right of the 1940s and 1950s—including the McCarthyite Right—and the New Right of the 1970s and 1980s, and on into the Tea Party Right of the twenty-first century, to a time when "anti-government" rhetoric and attitudes have become so central to American conservatism they almost seem to provide it with its sole reason for existence.[37]

Studies of the membership of the John Birch Society show that overwhelmingly it was the ideology of the organization—its core beliefs about American society, politics, and the nation's role in the world—that caused people to join it: in a national survey of Birchers in 1965, for example, 62 percent of respondents gave this as their reason for becoming members.[38] And contrary to the stereotypical image of the radical Rightist as "an older, less well-educated individual . . . of lower-income and occupational status," research by

Barbara Stone, among others, later revealed that "typical Birchers" were in fact relatively young (the median age was forty-four), reasonably well-educated men and women with "substantial incomes."[39]

Nor were the Society's "supporters"—people who were "sympathetic" to, or "approved" of, the Society, but who had not actually joined it—irrational or suffering from some type of "social strain" that would account for their "strange" ideas, which was the predominant explanation for the organization's appeal when it first emerged on the American political scene.[40] Rather, as the political scientist Clyde Wilcox discovered when he examined the data on the Birch Society in the late 1980s, for the most part its supporters were (in the language of social science) simply "conservative Republicans who were . . . dissatisfied with government, and negative toward Communists, symbols of the Left, and the eastern establishment."[41] In terms of geography, Birchers could be found across the United States, but they were most prominent in the South and the West of the country, especially in California, Oregon, Tennessee, and Texas.[42] And although Welch claimed that Catholics accounted for 40 percent of the organization, while others believed that Protestant fundamentalists predominated, in truth religion—except in the most general sense—was never central to either the Society's makeup or its appeal.[43]

The late 1950s and early 1960s was a confusing and difficult period for many Americans, and the Birch Society offered guidance on how best to navigate these troubled times while maintaining, if not extending, the nation's preeminence in the world. It did so within the context of a clear and coherent institutional and ideological framework, albeit one that aroused the considerable ire of its many opponents and critics. But it also encouraged its members to actually *do* something to help turn back the collectivist tide that seemed to be engulfing them. Each issue of the Society's monthly *Bulletin* contained a list of specific activities for Birchers to engage in, for example, and this too was part of the organization's appeal.[44] It also offered hope. Birchers belonged to a movement of "historical importance," Welch claimed. They were the "moving force of a new age."[45] The "very purpose" of the Society, he wrote in 1965, was to "blaze a path of truth through the darkness of deception and immorality and cruelty and corruption, which now hovers over our whole earth" in order to reach a new "plateau of light and sanity and freedom and kindness, and honesty and peaceful labor, which other men may then behold with longing and with hope."[46] Prosaic yet grandiose; practical but conspiracy-laden; reassuring if fearful; radical and conservative: this was the world of the John Birch Society.

Partly in response to the rather belated recognition, as expressed by Alan Brinkley in 1994, that "twentieth-century American conservatism has been something of an orphan in historical scholarship," a number of historians, most notably Lisa McGirr, Jonathan M. Schoenwald, Eckard V. Toy Jr., Rick Perlstein, Geoffrey Kabaservice, and Michelle M. Nickerson, have begun to give the Birch Society a renewed, closer, and more sophisticated look.[47] In her detailed examination of Orange County in California, McGirr has shown, for example, how the Birch Society and other grassroots activists and organizations "became the ground forces of a conservative revival" in the United States, "one that transformed conservatism from a marginal force preoccupied with communism in the early 1960s into a viable electoral contender by the decade's end."[48] Similarly, in a chapter on the Birchers in his history of modern American conservatism, *A Time for Choosing*, Schoenwald has argued—correctly, in my view—that although it has generally been "ignored or belittled," or otherwise "dismissed as a collection of 'kooks,'" the Birch Society "performed much like a third party" during the 1960s, forcing the "GOP, the Democrats, and conservatives of all types to respond to its agenda." It helped to create a "new kind of conservative activism" and "conservative movement culture," and also functioned as a kind of "protest movement, which challenged the status quo through its demands to revise foreign and domestic policy." The Society, Schoenwald concludes, "was far more complex, played a historically understated role as a faction in the conservative movement, and helped to chart the course of postwar conservatism in America."[49] Toy has explored the origins of the Birch Society in the Pacific Northwest. Perlstein incorporates the organization into his larger examination of the significance of the Goldwater campaign of 1964; Kabaservice considers it as part of his study of the decline of moderation in the modern Republican Party; and Nickerson discusses it within her study of grassroots women's activism in Southern California during the 1950s and 1960s. Yet despite all these fine works, as Kim Phillips-Fein pointed out in a roundtable discussion of conservatism published in the *Journal of American History* in 2011, much still remains to be done on the Society.[50]

Outside of academia, interest in the Birchers has also been revived by the appearance of the Tea Party movement in the United States (of which the twenty-first-century John Birch Society is a small part). There are certainly interesting and suggestive parallels that can be drawn between the activities and ideology of the Tea Party and those of the Birch Society of the 1950s and 1960s, including their keenly expressed hostility toward "big government," their conspiratorial tendencies—up to and including suspicions about the "real loyalties" of the president of the United States—and the concerns each have generated about their attempts to "capture" the GOP and turn it to their own particular purposes.[51] I do not pursue these parallels explicitly in the pages that follow, however.

Instead, this book focuses on the critical ten-year period between 1958 and 1968. The first extensive study of the Birch Society to appear since the 1960s, it is divided into two parts. Part I—Chapters 1 through 3—takes a narrative and chronological approach, beginning with the storm of controversy that greeted the first widespread exposure of the Society's ideas and activities in the summer of 1960 and ending with its expulsion from the broader conservative movement (of which it considered itself a key part) in the wake of Barry Goldwater's seemingly catastrophic defeat in the 1964 presidential election. In between these two events, the Society also became deeply embroiled in the case of Major General Edwin A. Walker, who was accused of indoctrinating troops under his command with Birch propaganda, amid widespread fears that there might be a military or fascist putsch in the United States. This is the subject of Chapter 2.

The second part of the book—Chapters 4 through 6—is more thematic: Chapter 4 examines the Society's response to the rise of the civil rights and black power movements in the United States during the 1950s and 1960s, as well as the issue of rights in American society more generally. Chapter 5 considers the Birch Society's understanding of, and proposed solutions to, the problems posed by the Cold War, Fidel Castro's revolution in Cuba, and the war in Vietnam, among other foreign policy issues of the time. And Chapter 6 explores the Birchers' promotion of conspiracy theories as explanations for all the ills believed to be plaguing American society during the 1950s and 1960s.

This is not an organizational history of the John Birch Society, although one certainly needs to be written (and I hope the organization will open up its records to interested researchers in the near future). Rather, it is an examination of the Society's key ideas and beliefs, the articulation and dissemination of those ideas and beliefs, and the reaction to them within the broader political culture of the time. It is a story of argument and contestation: about the rise of conservatism in the United States, about the impact of the Cold War on American society, and about the place of conspiracy theories in American life. Indeed, in many respects, the reaction and response to the Birchers is as revealing of the United States during this period, exposing its many rifts and fissures, as is the emergence and activities of the organization itself.

My aim, then, is to provide a much fuller and more complex portrait of the John Birch Society than has appeared to date. Doing so requires more than simply identifying the centrality of conspiratorial reasoning to the Society's worldview and then dismissing the organization and its members as irrational fantasists unworthy of any further serious consideration (the unfortunate hallmark of an earlier generation of scholarship on the Birchers). It requires engaging with those ideas, attempting to understand where they came from, and exploring the role they played in the Birchers' ideological system. It also requires looking beyond the Society's conspiracism to the more conventional conservative beliefs and principles that were also animating it. None of this means endorsing the Birchers' views, of course. But in order to properly come to terms with the world of the John Birch Society—the world it created, as well as the world it was part of—we need to see the organization and the historical period in which it existed more completely and with a great deal more clarity.

PART I

Chapter 1

Exposure

For eighteen months following its formation in December 1958 the John Birch Society operated in relative obscurity. This period of initial calm was brought to an abrupt end in July 1960 when the *Chicago Daily News* published the first significant exposé of the Society, including the contention of its founder, Robert Welch, that President Dwight D. Eisenhower was a "dedicated, conscious agent" of the communist conspiracy in the United States. For the next few years Birchers found themselves at the center of a storm of controversy. This chapter examines the period in which the Birch Society and its leaders first came to widespread public attention, focusing especially on the crucial years of 1960 and 1961.

There had certainly been criticism of the Society before the *Chicago Daily News* articles appeared, but it had largely been confined to fellow conservatives and other members of the anticommunist network. For example, the Society's Committee Against Summit Entanglements had protested—and attempted to prevent—Soviet premier Nikita Khrushchev's visit to the United States. In the December 1959 issue of *American Opinion*, Welch reflected on the negative reaction this had generated in some quarters. "Most of these critics are sincere, and all of them are wrong," Welch stated. "It is of vital importance to the Communists to split Americans into all kinds of groups, snarling at each other." This would not be the Birch Society's approach, however. "We are fighting Communists. Period. Nobody else," he said.[1]

Similarly, in "An Aside to the Squeamish" in the June 1960 issue of the *Bulletin*, Welch acknowledged the "lack of enthusiasm" some of the Society's members had evidenced for the slogan it had deployed in the hope of dissuading Eisenhower from attending the planned follow-up summit with Khrushchev, British prime minister Harold Macmillan, and French president Charles de Gaulle, in Paris in May 1960. The summit collapsed in the aftermath of the shooting down of Gary Powers's U-2 spy plane on May 1, but the Birch Society's message to Eisenhower, "If you go, don't come back!," delivered by means of telegrams, postcards, and letters, had been too much for some Birchers.

In "charting the course of the Society we are at all times torn between two forces tugging in opposite directions," or "tugging in the same direction at very different speeds," Welch noted. There were members of the organization who wanted it to be "much more outspoken or even belligerent" in its statements and letters, and those who wished it to be "more restrained." In this case "the number applauding the slogan ran about four to one against those who disliked it," but Welch hoped the dissenters would bear with him "in the assurance that we do not intend to 'run wild,' nor to indulge in any dramatics just for the excitement." At the same time, though, he also sought to remind them that the Birch Society as a whole was not engaged in a "cream-puff war" or "a pillow fight" and that, as another of its slogans had it, "we do mean business every step of the way."[2]

As we shall see, internecine conflicts and internal tensions of this kind never disappeared, but for the next couple of years they were greatly overshadowed by all the externally generated attention directed toward the Society.

A "Vicious Attack"

Timed to coincide with the Republican national convention taking place in Chicago that year, the Birch Society's first taste of more widespread exposure occurred in the summer of 1960, with two articles by Jack Mabley in the *Chicago Daily News* on July 25 and 26. Describing the Birchers as an organization of "ultra-conservatives" who had banded together to fight communism in the United States, Mabley noted that while "not a secret society in the normal sense of the word," it did try to "avoid publicity"—and indeed had been largely successful in that endeavor until now. In Mabley's view, however, the prominent conservatives and thousands of ordinary people who had been attracted to the Society "should know the thinking of the man to whom they are pledging their energies and loyalty."

Setting the tone for much of the criticism that would follow, Mabley quoted Welch's "dim view of democracy" from *The Blue Book* as a "deceptive phrase, a weapon of demagoguery, and a perennial fraud," and characterized the Society as authoritarian, monolithic, and dictatorial, with Welch functioning as its "absolute and unquestioned head." Mabley's real journalistic coup, though, was that he had managed to obtain a copy of *The Politician*, which he described as "a 302-page black paperbound book . . . intended for secret distribution only to the leaders of the society." It was in the pages of *The Politician* that the most damning evidence against the Birch Society was to be found.

This "fantastic document," Mabley reported, "accuses President Eisenhower of treason. It flatly calls him a Communist, and for 302 pages attempts to document the charge." And he provided "an exact quote" from the book to prove his claim—one that would haunt Welch and the Birch Society for years to come, but which was mysteriously—although understandably—absent when the book was "officially" published in 1963. It was: "While I too think that Milton Eisenhower [the president's brother] is a Communist, and has been for thirty years, this opinion is based largely on general circumstances of his conduct. But my firm belief that Dwight Eisenhower is a dedicated, conscious agent of the Communist conspiracy is based on an accumulation of detailed evidence so extensive and so palpable that it seems to me to put this conviction beyond any reasonable doubt."[3] Mabley also noted the other significant figures Welch accused of being part of a communist conspiracy to take over the nation, including U.S. secretary of state John Foster Dulles and his brother, Allen, the director of the CIA; Chief Justice Earl Warren; former defense secretary Neil McElroy; and "dozens of others." It might be tempting to dismiss all of this as the work of a "crackpot," but "the circumstances of Welch's position and influence"—together with his persuasiveness as a public speaker—as the Society tried to reach its goal of a million members, necessitated "further examination," Mabley contended.[4]

Other articles followed in the wake of the revelations contained in the *Chicago Daily News*, including in the *Milwaukee Journal*, the *Chicago Sun-Times*, and the *Boston Herald*—all essentially repeating Mabley's critique and focusing on the allegations made in *The Politician*—but the Society was able to weather this first wave of attention relatively easily. Welch reported to the Society's members in the August 1960 issue of the *Bulletin* that the negative publicity the Society had attracted would only make it stronger, and that such attention should be understood as part of the "growing pains" of a new organization that was "rapidly gaining stature."[5] He did, though, also feel the need to address some

Figure 2.1. President Dwight D. Eisenhower (center) and his brother Milton (left), who were both accused of being communist agents in *The Politician*, work on the president's 1955 State of the Union address at his Key West headquarters in Florida, in the company of the president's chief speechwriter, Kevin McCann. © Bettmann/CORBIS

of the issues raised by *The Politician* for those Birchers who had not previously been aware of its existence.

Welch explained that its origins lay in December 1954 in the form of "a long letter to a friend" in which he had "expressed very severe *opinions* concerning the purposes of some of the top men in Washington." Carbon copies of this letter had been sent to a "few other friends, who in turn asked for copies for their friends." By 1956, through various revisions and additions, the length of the letter had grown to sixty thousand words. It was only at this point, Welch said, that "we had begun to refer to [the letter] as the manuscript of *The Politician*." By 1958, another twenty thousand words had been added. Welch having decided not to make any further amendments, this "final version" was typed up, and a "limited number" of copies were prepared "for the convenience of any other readers to whom it would be sent."[6]

"A majority of these more formalized copies of the long letter was sent to various friends during the summer and early fall of 1958," Welch went on, the crucial point of this being that this was "before The John Birch Society was even founded." Thus, in what was to become the crux of his defense whenever its status was raised, as far as Welch was concerned, "the document had, and still has, no connection with the Society in any way except that: (1) it was written by your Founder; and (2) as the Society grew I sent copies to some of those new acquaintances who had now become my good friends through their work for the cause." For Welch, the nature and form of the letter/manuscript/document was of crucial importance. "The introductory page to this manuscript states clearly that this is *not a book*, has never been intended for publication, and is still of the nature of a long letter to a friend," he told his readers. No copy had ever been sold, and those that were loaned out all contained a covering letter explaining that the views expressed in the accompanying manuscript were simply "this writer's opinions, and a collection of facts . . . on which those opinions are based."[7]

Because of "new forces and new leaders now appearing on the scene," it had been his intention, Welch said, to allow "this whole 'letter' to fade out of the picture," but then Mabley's columns appeared—although Welch refused to identify him by name, referring to him only as "a columnist of the *Chicago Daily News*." Through "some violation of confidence," someone who had been sent the letter in 1958 had passed it on to Mabley, and the journalist had naturally "selected for quotation the most extreme statements he could find, without the benefit of any of the explanation or modifying import of the context around them." This was only to be expected. "What was categorically unfair," in Welch's view, however, "was that this column quoted me as stating *as fact in a book* sentences which the whole document clearly revealed were expressions of *opinion in an unpublished confidential manuscript* of the nature of a letter."[8]

In other words, it was not just the uncertain ontological status of the letter/manuscript/document/book that was important, but also the epistemological caveats embedded carefully within it. After all, it was just Welch's "firm *belief*" that Eisenhower was a "dedicated, conscious agent of the Communist conspiracy," and the evidence on which this belief was based—although "extensive" and "palpable"—only "*seemed*" to put his "*conviction*" beyond any reasonable doubt.

Welch also contested Mabley's assertion that the "book" was intended for secret distribution only to the leaders of the Society. Given the "history of the document" he had outlined, and "since at least two-thirds of our Chapter Leaders had never even heard of *The Politician*," any "attempted tying of the Society to the manuscript, or vice versa, is entirely unsupported by the facts," he said. Moreover, if Mabley had "expected to do serious damage to The John Birch Society he must by now be badly disappointed." The "total net effect" of the *Chicago Daily News* articles had been that three new members of the Society had asked for their membership applications to be "'held in abeyance' until they could find out what was what." (Welch allowed that Mabley's "only real purpose may have been to make his column exciting," in which case he was prepared to concede him "a certain measure of success"—presumably on the basis that the revelation of any kind of secret is always exciting to a certain extent.)[9]

Some members of the Society may "feel that I made a mistake by being so outspoken, even in a confidential statement of opinions," Welch confessed, but he questioned whether anyone really knew what was right "in this gathering nightmare of our times which none of us have wished?" Treason was still to be found in the United States' government, he reminded his readers, and he illustrated the point with "a horrible truth which most people seem determined to avoid," insisting that the forthcoming 1960 presidential campaign was really a contest between two puppets: Welch viewed John F. Kennedy as the "longtime stooge" of Walter P. Reuther, the leader of the United Automobile Workers union, and Richard M. Nixon as the "newly acquired stooge" of Nelson Rockefeller, the liberal New York governor. The election would determine whether Reuther or Rockefeller would "be the boss of the United States under a one-world international socialist government." In a formulation that pointed to the dark heart of the Society's metaphysical understanding of American politics and world history, Welch explained that "we have no clear grasp of what is going on, or how near we are to the end of American independence. But of course it is so much nicer to accept the surface appearances as themselves the realities of the contest."[10]

The Founder's defense of the Society ended with a prediction that the "recent vicious attack, in Chicago, is undoubtedly only the forerunner of many more, of many kinds, to come."[11] He was right. The events of 1960 paled in comparison with the attention the Society received in 1961.

The "Attack" Intensifies

The second and much more widespread exposure of the Birchers began on the West Coast. In January 1961 the *Santa Barbara News-Press* published an investigation of the Society by its reporter Hans Engh. The organization had begun its "semi-secret existence" in the county the previous year, but had already developed several chapters, with membership in the hundreds, and the rumors were "flying," Engh said. His account outlined the origins of the Society and Welch's background, but not surprisingly it focused on Welch's statements in *The Politician*, his critical views of democracy, and his more recent recommendation—made in the September 1960 issue of the *Bulletin*—that Birchers should work to "take over" their local parent-teacher associations.[12]

The paper's stand on the Birch Society was made abundantly clear in a series of highly critical editorials written by its editor and publisher, Thomas M. Storke. In "Statement of Principles," published on February 26, for example, Storke acknowledged that "communism's advance" threatened democratic institutions around the world, but argued—in what would become a common-place contention in discussions of the Birch Society—that democracy could be endangered as much by "extremists of the right as by those of the left," that it could be strengthened only through the open discussion of ideas, and that "secret or semi-secret political organizations" had "no place" in American society. Evoking the memory of the McCarthy years—although not by name—Storke also argued that "democracy suffers when fear of communism leads to irresponsible, unsubstantiated charges of treason or evil connivance against our political, religious, educational or cultural leaders," and that "traitors should be dealt with by the courts, not by vigilante groups."[13] Condemning the "adoption of totalitarian organization or tactics to fight the Communist danger," the publisher urged all Americans to "keep our balance in what we do."[14]

The *Los Angeles Times*'s coverage of the Society ran in March 1961. Written by Gene Blake, the five-part series covered much the same ground as Engh's and Mabley's articles had done, but in greater detail and with more extensive quotations from both *The Politician* and *The Blue Book*.[15] The connection with McCarthyism was made explicit, however—the late senator had become "almost a patron saint of the John Birch Society," Blake noted—and the overall tone was considerably harder.[16] *The Blue Book*, for instance, was introduced in the following terms: "Communism has Karl Marx's 'Communist Manifesto,' nazism had Adolf Hitler's 'Mein Kampf,' and the John Birch Society has Robert Welch's 'Blue Book.'"[17]

As with the *Santa Barbara News-Press*, some of the strongest criticism came at the end of the series in the form of an editorial—signed not by the paper's editor, Nick Williams, but by Otis Chandler, its new publisher—entitled "Peril to Conservatives." Chandler took the view that the extensive quotations from Welch and his "lieutenants" had "nail[ed] down the treacherous fallacy that an honorable or noble objective justifies any means to achieve it." Every conservative "must adhere to the general purpose of the society," Chandler argued. Every loyal American "must agree devoutly" with its intention of stopping the communists and their "blood-soaked" conspiracy—which included "sowing distrust among us, aggravating union and racial disputes [and] entering without conscience into any course that will serve the purpose of Moscow." And every informed American "must agree" with the Society's tenet that the United States was engaged in a struggle with the USSR for the "survival of our system." The problem, as Chandler saw it, was that Birchers were adopting the very "techniques and the rules of conspiracy to fight Communists in Communist fashion."[18]

In addition, Chandler argued that the Birchers were actually weakening "the very strong case for conservatism" they were trying to promote. "The *Times* believes implicitly in the conservative philosophy," he wrote. "But the *Times* does not believe that the argument for conservatism can be won—and we do believe it can be won—by smearing as enemies and traitors those with whom we sometimes disagree." He concluded, "Subversion, whether of the left or the right, is still subversion," echoing Storke's comparison of left- and right-wing extremism, which had appeared a couple of weeks earlier.[19]

The week of the *Los Angeles Times* series saw both the publication of "The Americanists" in *Time* magazine and a stinging denunciation of the Society in the United States Senate by the North Dakota Republican Milton Young. Any lingering hopes that Welch might have had of continuing to build up his organization with a minimum of outside interest were clearly gone. The Birchers were now operating in the full glare of national attention.

Time's coverage was the most critical yet. "Among the U.S. brotherhoods dedicated to the fight against communism, nothing is quite like the John Birch Society," it began. "Except for an elite corps of leaders its members shun personal publicity and their names are held by the society in strictest secrecy." Referring to the organization's chapters as "cells" whose members accept the "hard-boiled dictatorial direction of one man," the article argued that because of the Birchers' use of fronts, their aggressive letter-writing campaigns, and their attempt to impeach Earl Warren—a high-profile campaign of the Society, launched in January 1961—they could not be dismissed as simply "tiresome" or as some "comic-opera joke."[20] "Welch's 'Mein Kampf' is a masterpiece of invective called 'The Politician,'" it was pointed out, and the article noted that while Welch attracted some praise as a "freedom fighter" from right-wingers like Clarence Manion, the actor Adolphe Menjou, and the former U.S. diplomat Spruille Braden, many other conservatives objected to the Society's "contempt for dissent from its views," feeling that "its militant words and thoughts are barely a goosestep away from the formation of goon squads."[21]

Milton Young denounced the Society from the floor of the Senate on March 8. For the "past year or more I have been deeply concerned about the increased membership and spreading influence of a relatively new organization called the John Birch Society," he began. Birchers had "gained considerable membership" in several major cities in North Dakota, the senator reported, pointing out that in "one city alone," it had "at least four cells."[22] Describing the Society as "ultraconservative in nature," Young found it very strange that most of its criticism was leveled not against liberal public officials, but at "more middle-of-the-road, and even conservative, Republicans" like himself. "They have accused me of being about every kind of scoundrel, including a Communist or pro-Communist," he said, but this gave him little concern as he was certain that "no sane person would believe there is the slightest substance to such a charge." Indeed, in an indication of the extent to which the very word "conservative" was still a source of opprobrium at the time, Young's view was that such accusations were actually a "sort of medicine to some liberal thinking people who have often accused me of being a reactionary conservative."[23]

At the heart of Young's concerns—once again—were Welch's allegations against Eisenhower and other government officials in *The Politician*, which, he said, went "far beyond anything the late Senator Joe McCarthy ever thought of." Quoting from Mabley's original article in the *Chicago Daily News*, Young explained that he had been reluctant to give further publicity to Welch's "dastardly attack," but he felt it was his duty to provide much-needed information on the Birchers to the citizens of North Dakota and elsewhere "who may be influenced" by them.[24]

Despite the "unbelievable" nature of Welch's allegations, Young, like Storke and Chandler before him, still felt the need to invoke the anticommunist pieties of the early Cold War period and to turn them back against the Birchers. Communism was "the same international conspiracy it has always been, seeking to enslave the entire free world," he declared, but Welch and his cohorts were not helping to defeat this menace. On the contrary: "To label some of our most loyal and dedicated people as Communists plays right into the hands of the Communist movement."[25]

The *New York Times* made its first mention of the Birch Society in an article reporting Young's speech in the following morning's edition ("Senator Scores Group Calling Eisenhower a Red") and the political floodgates opened.[26] Senate majority leader Mike Mansfield (D-MT) praised Young's courageous denunciation of the Society, church groups and leaders began denouncing it, and calls for an official investigation gathered pace.[27] An elite consensus was quickly forming around the organization. As Richard Nixon put it in a letter to the *Los Angeles Times*, in which he endorsed Otis Chandler's criticisms of Welch on March 12: "One of the most indelible lessons of human history is that those who adopt the doctrine that the end justifies the means inevitably find the means become the end." Decrying the Bircher's "totalitarian methods," the former vice president argued that "it may at times seem unrealistic and naïve to follow the rules of the game when our opponents are so unscrupulous and completely devoid of morality. But, in the end, refusing to resort to methods that are wrong not only is right but in the long run is the most effective way to combat an evil doctrine like communism."[28]

Investigation Fever

Not surprisingly, given the extensive coverage the Birch Society had received in Santa Barbara and Los Angeles, the first calls for an official investigation of the organization appeared in California. As the end of March approached, the Golden State's Democratic governor Edmund G. "Pat" Brown, responding to the concerns of legislators and local educators, ordered Attorney General Stanley Mosk to look at the activities of the Society—"because fascism is just as dangerous as Communism." The State Assembly Rules Committee began deliberations over whether Robert F. Kennedy, the new attorney general of the United States, should be asked to investigate the Society nationally, and the California State Senate Un-American Activities Committee set a date in June for its own hearings.[29]

At the same time, Milton Young was getting additional support within Congress for his own campaign against the Society. On March 28, Senator Gale McGee (D-WY), a Kennedy administration ally, called for "the searchlight of truth and the daylight of publicity to be brought to bear" on the Society. Senator Stuart Symington (D-MO), an arch-opponent of Joe McCarthy who had played a key role against him during the Army-McCarthy hearings—McCarthy referred to him dismissively as "sanctimonious Stu"—contended that whatever Birch supporters "have on their mind, especially with respect to this book [*The Politician*], the more the American people know about it now, the better for the country."[30]

Other senators, including Democrat Thomas Dodd of Connecticut and Republicans Thomas Kuchel of California and Jacob Javits of New York, soon joined in the calls for more exposure of the organization. Commending the recent outpouring of articles on the Birch Society, Dodd noted that the press had "a tremendous weapon for public good in the power of exposure," and that it had been used "effectively in the case of the John Birch Society." (In the interests of balance, Dodd hoped it would be deployed just as effectively in the months ahead against the Fair Play for Cuba Committee, other "Communist-front operations," and the whole "subterranean operations" of the Communist Party that were at work in the United States.) Denouncing Welch's "incredible libel" against Eisenhower and the campaign to impeach Earl Warren in particular, Kuchel demanded to know whether the American people and the attorney general were willing to let such "vile spleen" pour down on the heads of people who had given their whole lives in dedicated service to the United States, and called upon the Senate Government Operations Committee to summon Welch before it to "ask him the basis upon which he makes these fantastic charges."[31]

Over in the House, Wisconsin Democrat Henry Reuss had written to the chairman of the House Committee on Un-American Activities, Francis Walter (D-PA), asking for an investigation of the Society. Walter ordered a preliminary inquiry by his staff but informed Reuss that based on the information he had about the Society, he didn't think his committee had the jurisdiction to launch a full investigation.[32] A similar view was evident at the Justice Department, with a spokesman telling the *New York Times* on April 1—significantly, the paper's coverage of the Birch phenomenon had now moved to its front page— that although the "ultra conservative society was a 'matter of concern'" to the attorney general, the department was doubtful that there were grounds for an investigation of it.[33]

The attempt to subject Birchers to the "searchlight of truth" did produce some immediate results, however. Representative Edgar Hiestand (R-CA) identified himself as a member of the Society on March 30.[34] The next day, he "outed" his fellow Californian, Republican congressman John Rousselot, as a member too. Contrary to expectations, both men said they would welcome an official investigation of the Society. Rousselot, indicating that he knew of "several" other members of the Society in Congress (unlike Hiestand, he was not willing to identify them without their permission), argued that "full and clear hearings on both the national and state level should be held so that the mysticism of the society—the cloak of darkness—can be cleared up."[35] Likewise, Hiestand believed that hearings would dispel the charges that it was a dictatorial or fascist organization.[36]

Such views merely echoed those of the Founder himself, who had responded to the initial calls for an investigation of the Society in California by sending a telegram to the State Senate Un-American Activities Committee indicating the eagerness of Birch members to testify on the record. Welch had assured the committee's chairman, Hugh Burns (D-Fresno), that "unlike our Communist enemies, none of our members will take the Fifth Amendment."[37] Rather than seeking to avoid such hearings for fear of negative publicity, the leaders of the Birch Society seemed to welcome the opportunity to get their message out. Convinced of the righteousness of their cause, and faced with an avalanche of attention that could not simply be ignored, Welch in particular quickly realized that his initial strategy of working quietly behind the scenes to build up support for the Society and its causes would have to be abandoned. As he informed readers of the *Bulletin* at the start of 1961, soon after stories about the Society began appearing in the *Santa Barbara News-Press* and the *LA Times*: "The John Birch Society does not seek publicity. But we have given up all hope of avoiding publicity, either good or bad."[38]

On April 1, 1961, Welch sent a telegram to the chairman of the Senate Internal Security Subcommittee, James O. Eastland (D-MS), asking him to open an investigation into the Society because of "the charges now being so widely circulated about us, some of which are extreme distortions of fact and many of which are sheer fabrications." Repeating the assurance he had made to Burns about the willingness of Birch Society members to testify under oath, Welch told Eastland that far from being a secret society, the organization was merely "a group of men and women of good character, fervent patriotism, religious ideals, and excellent standing in their respective communities," one whose "materials" were "wide open for anybody to purchase." The Society "has broken no law and violated no moral principles," Welch said. "Our only 'crime' is fighting communism and that we intend to continue until our side wins."[39]

If Welch was looking for a sympathetic forum to present "the simple truth" about the John Birch Society to the American people—as he was—he couldn't have made a better choice than the Internal Security Subcommittee. Eastland, a staunch conservative and committed anticommunist, had already made public a letter that he had written on the subcommittee's behalf, responding to questions about the Society, on March 20. It read, in part: "The John Birch Society, about which you asked is known to be a conservative anti-Communist organization. . . . We are happy to state that it seems to be, from our records, a patriotic organization."[40]

In fact, the question of which congressional committee or committees were best suited for an inquiry into the Birch Society was a matter of some debate.

Speaking in the House at the end of April, Congresswoman Edith Green (D-OR) indicated she could not join with those of her colleagues who were demanding that the House Committee on Un-American Activities (HUAC) should hold hearings on the Birch Society. She was, though, in favor of the House Ways and Means Committee and the House Administration Committee doing so—the former to see if Birchers were operating in violation of the ban against tax exemptions for political organizations or other violations of the Internal Revenue Code, and the latter to see whether they were selling "free" public documents that had been prepared by the Government Printing Office. "Legislative investigation, with an eye to specific legislative recommendations in the area of action—yes," Green declared. "But investigation of what even the Birchers believe—no."[41]

Irrespective of the venue or the form of "official" inquiries, and whether they should be taking place at the local, state, or national level, the tensions raised by the possibility of having institutions of the state undertaking such inquiries into the Birch Society were the same. On the one hand, the power of investigation was one of the most important functions of Congress. Helping to inform the public—and members of Congress themselves—about the urgent issues of the day, and making policy and legislative recommendations concerning those issues—this was what congressional committees were supposed to do. Democracies depended on such activities. Citizens could only make informed and rational decisions about their self-governance if they had accurate information to help them. And wasn't it also the job of law enforcement agencies like the Justice Department and the FBI to root out potential threats and dangers before they could become major problems?[42]

On the other hand, was it not also the case that democracies protected the rights and freedoms of citizens? Were not the freedoms of speech and association—the right not to be persecuted because of one's political beliefs—the sacred values upon which the United States was founded? The very rights it brandished unrelentingly against the Soviet Union as part of the ongoing Cold War struggle?

Then there was the question of whether official investigations of groups like the Birch Society might not legitimize their concerns, encourage more people to become members, and lead to the spread of their "extreme" ideas rather than the discrediting of them. Recollections of the "witch-hunts" of the Second Red Scare were also fresh in the minds of many people, as Green's reservations about a HUAC investigation indicated. Nor could partisan political concerns be ignored; indeed, they were intimately connected to memories of the McCarthy years. Who might benefit most from an investigation, the Republicans or the Democrats? Both, or neither?

Opposing any formal investigation of the Society, the *New York Times'* "critic at large" Brooks Atkinson commented sarcastically in his April 25 column: "Apparently, the House Committee on Un-American Activities and the Senate Internal Security Committee are not sure that their jurisdiction extends to a Right-wing organization like the Birch Society. They are more concerned with the iniquitous thinking of citizens who do not approve of them. Investigating the

Birch Society would be a little like investigating their own political attitudes—always a painful process."[43] And the prominent conservative senator Barry Goldwater (R-AZ) warned that there would be "a lot of embarrassed people" in Congress if the Society were to be investigated, as he knew members of both parties who belonged to the organization.[44]

Those giving voice to these issues often took counterintuitive positions. For example, even as many Birchers pushed for an investigation, some of their harshest critics—including Milton Young, who had done so much to propel the Society into the limelight in the first place—opposed one. During the course of an especially acerbic attack on the floor of the Senate on April 3, in which he denounced the Society as a "Fascist group" of "rightwing crackpots" led by a "little Hitler," Young argued that it was nonetheless "legal for a man to be a Fascist . . . and to express opinions no matter how distorted, fantastic, and extreme they may be," and that given how "busy" he and his colleagues in the House and Senate were, he knew of "no valid reason for any congressional investigation" of it.[45] The "conscience of the Senate," Democrat Philip Hart of Michigan, also cautioned against any congressional investigation of the Society, urging liberals to be consistent on that issue, and arguing that the practice would make people afraid to express unpopular views.[46] The prominent liberal anticommunist pressure group Americans for Democratic Action opposed an investigation on the basis that it served "no legislative purpose," and because, to that point at least, the Birchers "posed no threat to the nation's internal security."[47]

Speaking in the House on April 19, New York congressman William Ryan argued that any congressional investigation of the Birchers "would be just as antithetical to our heritage as some of the views of the society." "What would be accomplished by such an investigation?" he wanted to know. "An investigation into the political beliefs of citizens for the sake of exposure achieves the same results whether one is exposing the beliefs of the extreme left or the extreme right. Freedom of dissent, expression and association is curtailed in an atmosphere of suspicion and fear." All that was needed to defeat the Birchers, in Ryan's view, was widespread public discussion and a little faith in the "intelligence and good sense" of the American people. The opinions of Birchers would not stand up to "examination and objective analysis," he predicted. Like the ideas of their predecessors, the Know Nothings of the 1850s and the America Firsters of the 1940s, they would "wilt and die in the glare of public exposure and debate."[48] Yet the Rabbinical Council of America had taken exactly the opposite view, arguing in a telegram to Robert Kennedy on April 18 that, because of the Society's violation of American ideals and principles, which could "ultimately eventuate in a breakdown of democracy and fair play in our national dealings," it was essential that the attorney general's office begin "an intensive study . . . to find out if the society should be placed on the subversive list."[49]

Four days before the Rabbinical Council's telegram, however, news had broken that Major General Edwin A. Walker, the commander of the Twenty-Fourth Infantry Division based in Augsburg, West Germany, may have been "indoctrinating" his troops with John Birch Society material. The allegations, the extent of Walker's connection with the Birch Society, and his subsequent resignation from the army—as well as the wider significance of the case—are all examined in detail in the next chapter. What is important to note here is that the allegations against Walker were examined by the Special Preparedness Subcommittee of the Senate Armed Services Committee from January to June 1962, and that one of the effects of this inquiry was to divert attention away from the demands of those who wanted a more direct and full-scale investigation of the Birch Society.

At the heart of the problem for those opponents of the Society who were in favor of a formal investigation was the question of what exactly it had *done* to justify one. Certainly Birchers had been accused of holding "strange" views, of conducting well-organized letter-writing and postcard campaigns, of agitating for the impeachment of the chief justice of the Supreme Court, of trying to get themselves elected to local PTAs, and of generally operating in a secret or "semi-secret" manner. But from one perspective, all this looked a lot like functioning as active—if somewhat troublesome and contentious—citizens in a free republic. Would the cost of investigating them be worth the trouble? And what would such investigations say about the state of American democracy? As Percival E. Jackson from Sea Cliff, New York, put it in a letter to the *New York Times* on April 11:

> It seems from the newspaper reports that Robert Welch of the John Birch Society advocates Chief Justice Warren's impeachment because Chief Justice Warren would defend Mr. Welch's right to advocate Chief Justice Warren's impeachment.
> Shouldn't this make further investigation of Mr. Welch unnecessary?[50]

It was a response and a question that pointed toward another way of dealing with the Birchers, one some distance away from the great fear being expressed in some quarters: mockery and ridicule. It was an approach Robert Kennedy had employed during his first press conference as attorney general on April 6, 1961, and it was one that would be deployed against the Birchers on a regular basis in the years to come, often as a way of attempting to diminish the Society's concerns and importance.

The Art of Mockery

Reflecting the general allure of the Kennedy presidency, Robert Kennedy's first press conference as attorney general of the United States attracted considerable media attention, airing live on the radio and drawing 174 news reporters— "more than the Justice Department usually sees in a month," the *New York Times* noted. On the issue of the John Birch Society, Kennedy was clear that he would not be launching an investigation into the headline-grabbing Society. "Under the Constitution, people can say pretty much what they want to," he noted, and as far as he was concerned, Birchers had not been doing anything illegal. Kennedy conceded that he had not actually met any Birchers, but based on what he had read about them, he found the Society to be "ridiculous," "an organization that's in the area of being humorous," and one that made "no contribution to the fight against communism." The situation might be improved, he suggested, if people simply stopped paying so much attention to it.[51]

The *New York Times* columnist Arthur Krock advocated a similar strategy. Ridicule was becoming "a lost art in American public controversies," he lamented in the paper on April 7. Reminding readers that Franklin D. Roosevelt had achieved the "emasculation" of the anti-New Deal Liberty League in the 1930s by "making the general public laugh at it," Krock suggested the art's revival against the Birchers would be relatively straightforward since "no citizens, however well-meaning, have made their movement and its followers a more vulnerable target to destruction through ridicule" than Robert Welch and other prominent members of the John Birch Society's leadership.[52]

Newspaper cartoonists found rich material in the Society. "Herblock" (the pen name of the cartoonist Herbert Lawrence Block), who had famously coined the term "McCarthyism" in a cartoon in the *Washington Post* in March 1950, depicted two suited figures representing HUAC and the John Birch Society. As they lean in conspiratorially toward each other, one whispers, "They're all Communists except thee and me—." "Mauldin" (the pen name of William Henry "Bill" Mauldin) drew on the Mad Hatter's tea party for his "Malice in Wonderland" cartoon in the *St. Louis Post-Dispatch*. The John Birch Society was the Mad Hatter, the U.S. Nazi Party a particularly malevolent-looking dormouse, the Ku Klux Klan a hooded snake emerging from a kettle on the table, and the White Citizens Council—inevitably, perhaps—the White Rabbit (although in actuality it is the March Hare and not the White Rabbit who attends the tea party in Lewis Carroll's story). Alice, alas, was nowhere to be seen.[53]

The *St. Louis Post-Dispatch* sought to coin a new word with which to counter "Comsymps," which the Society employed to denote "Communist sympathizers." "It would be a pity if sympathizers with [Welch's] views were to have to struggle along without proper means of identification," the paper noted. To "start thought flowing on the subject," it offered the "tentative suggestion" of "Birchsaps."[54]

The gentler humor of the *New Yorker* was deployed against the Birch Society in two separate articles on April 15 and May 20, 1961. In the first, the magazine's editors argued that the Birch Society's discovery that such highly placed figures as Dwight Eisenhower, Earl Warren, and the Dulles brothers were actually communist agents was the "best news" they had heard in the past couple of weeks, since even with the "executive and judicial branches of the Government safely in their hands [these communist agents] were utterly unable to make their designs effective upon, or even apparent to, the rest of the Nation." America, it seemed, was "able to absorb any number of such conspirators with no ill effects whatever." Grateful as the editors were for this revelation, though, they went on to express irritation at the "upstart" nature of the Birch Society. "As it happens," the editorial continued, "we are a member of a sort of semi-secret organization ourself—one that has been in continuous existence for nearly 200 years."

To be sure, the attention of this organization had not been "wholly fastened on fighting communism," but it had, the editors believed, nonetheless done "quite a lot of good work, in its way." Membership was said to be "impressively large" and unlike that of either the Communist Party or the Birchers, it was "not composed of secret cells." Rules were few, and there were no "gaudy uniforms— not even so much as an armband," but each member did receive a title. "It is not an imposing title, we suppose," the editorial read, as it moved toward its climatic payoff, "but it makes up in homely dignity whatever it may lack in romance, and to some members, at least, it has a certain glamour of its own." And then it came—in words seemingly intended to call to mind Edward R. Murrow's famous televised denouncement of McCarthyism in 1954: "The title, dear John Birch Society, is Citizen."[55]

A month later, A. J. Liebling's review of the Birch Society's *Blue Book* appeared in the *New Yorker* under the title "The Candy Kid." The review begins with Liebling imaginatively reconstructing Welch deep in his candy factory, immersed in his readings of world history. (Welch's former occupation as a manufacturer of candy was a ready target of ridicule in much of the coverage of the Society at the time, as it has been ever since, inspiring critics to portray him as some kind of maniacal Willy Wonka.) Liebling wrote:

> And while the peppermint popped and the popsicles purred, he [Welch]
> became so impressed by the analogies he discovered in his reading that,
> like Mohammed, he heard a voice saying to him, "Recite." Accordingly, he
> summoned a number of disciples to meet him at a hotel in Indianapolis, where
> there are always rooms (except during auto-race week), on December 8, 1958.
> "The Blue Book" . . . is a record of what was said at the ensuing meeting, as
> fraught with consequences as a chocolate bar with peanuts.

This candy-based tone of mockery was lovingly sustained throughout the review, with Welch's analytical eye described as being equipped to "decipher surface appearances as easily as it does the creme fondant within the walnut imperial," his plans for defeating the communist menace as "a program for eating your jelly beans and having them," and his overall understanding of the world, if taken seriously—which Liebling obviously didn't—as being "more destructive than the nerve gas that all up-to-date chemical-warfare branches are now supposed to possess, which paralyzes the will to resist. Only this gas, instead of being carried over borders by ICB missiles, is a native product, for home consumption, like coconut bars."[56]

Mockery of the Birch Society wasn't confined to politicians and journalists. Artists, writers, comedians, and musicians all joined in the fun.[57] A previously apolitical folk group, the Chad Mitchell Trio, had a surprise hit with its song "The John Birch Society" in the early part of 1962, for example.[58] The liner notes to the LP on which the song subsequently appeared, *The Chad Mitchell Trio at the Bitter End*—a live recording of a March 19, 1962, performance at a Greenwich Village coffeehouse—jokingly noted that there were "undoubtedly more discussions about their 'Birch Society' tune today than possibly any other folktune since the Elizabethan days of yore." But the controversy surrounding the song was real enough: the *Chicago Daily News* ran an approving editorial on the song, while some radio stations refused to play it. As far as the trio was concerned, though, this was all good news, because "Americans[,] in laughing at themselves, tend to see the situation in a different and many times better light."[59]

Set to a jaunty, banjo-driven, up-tempo tune, "The John Birch Society" satirized the organization in a tone of slightly bemused incomprehension as it recounted the strange beliefs of the Society from the supposed perspective of the Birchers themselves. The chorus provided the sing-along element as the trio repeatedly declared, "We're the John Birch Society, the John Birch Society / Here to save this country from a communistic plot."[60]

Bob Dylan, the new great hope of the folk revivalist movement in the early 1960s—and later, for many, its great disappointer—also addressed the subject of the Birch Society from the perspective of a putative insider in his song "Talkin' John Birch Society Blues." Written in January 1962, the song was first published the following month in the inaugural issue of *Broadside*, a folk magazine created in New York to recognize and promote the work of topical songwriters.[61] Employing the "talkin' blues" style most closely associated with his hero Woody Guthrie, Dylan's satirical take on the Birch Society, while not without its lighter moments, was much more biting than the Chad Mitchell Trio's: the song connects the Birchers with fascism, the Holocaust, and the American Nazi Party leader George Lincoln Rockwell, before ending with the narrator, having "run outa things to investigate," pathetically sitting at home investigating himself.[62]

It is not surprising that contemporary folk singers were drawn to the Birch Society. As one of the most prominent and controversial news stories of the day, it would have been surprising if those in search of fresh material for their topical songs had not been attracted to the subject. Moreover, if the Birchers represented a revival of McCarthyism, as many of the Society's critics claimed, then left-wing folk singers, having already been a significant target of anticommunist activism during the Second Red Scare, had very good reason to be concerned.[63] (Indeed, an article in the Birch Society's *American Opinion* had already expressed grave suspicion about the folk boom then going on in the country. "Along with the handclapping, the guitar strumming, the banjo picking, the shouting and the howling, comes a very subtle, but highly effective, presentation of standard Communist Party propaganda," the article's writer pointed out.)[64]

Intended for his second album, *The Freewheelin' Bob Dylan*, "Talkin' John Birch Society Blues" had been motivated in part by the singer's concern about the threat the Birch Society posed to freedom of speech in the United States. There is some irony, then, that his record company, Columbia Records, found the track to be potentially libelous and forced its removal from the LP (even though promotional copies and some advanced copies had already been distributed).[65] Nor was this the end of the matter. In May 1963, having been booked to make his first nationally televised appearance on the *Ed Sullivan Show*, Dylan was prevented from playing the song by an executive from the CBS

Standards and Practices department worried about its controversial content.[66] Rather than be censored, Dylan refused to appear on the show at all, with the result that, as one of the singer's biographers recounts, "Talkin' John Birch Society Blues" had a second life as a "cause célèbre in folk circles, confirming the capricious nature of corporate America," while Dylan himself "felt obliged to champion the song in concert" for the next eighteen months.[67]

If folk music wasn't your thing, however, there was always *The John Birch Coloring Book*. Riding the wave of a coloring book phenomenon that had already seen the publication of *The JFK Coloring Book*, *The New Frontier Coloring Book*, and *The Bureaucrat's Coloring Book* during the previous twelve months, one aimed at the John Birch Society appeared in August 1962. Published by the Serious Products Company with the price of $2.98, the book contained images such as a box of crayons above the instructions, "These are my crayons. I use them a lot. Color them scarlet, crimson, red and pinko"; a stereo system with both speakers on the *right*; and a Birch Society member reading a newspaper with the front-page headline, "Normans Invade England!," alongside the legend, "This is my newspaper. I like to keep up," all waiting to be colored in. The final page featured a black dot at its center with the message: "This innocent-looking black dot is a miniature, self-powered, transistorized, highly sensitive, long-range radio transmitter (made in U.S.A.). We have been listening to you while you were reading this book. Too bad if you laughed."[68] Although it was obviously an attempt to ridicule the Birchers, the last joke in particular also pointed toward the wider level of anxiety and paranoia existent in American society at the time.

The Files Project

On July 1, 1961, Robert Welch made an announcement that provided support both for those who considered the Birch Society to be a serious threat to American democracy and those who regarded it as essentially ridiculous. It was a "project of considerable size and great importance," Welch informed readers of the *Bulletin*:

> We wish to build up, and have available for all future research needs, the most complete and most accurate files in America on the *leading* Comsymps, Socialists, and Liberals—on those who are trying to change the economic and political structure of this country so that it could be comfortably merged with Soviet Russia in a one-world socialist government. And since we do not yet see any chance of putting a sufficiently sizable staff to work on this job, we have decided to make use of the energy, knowledge, libraries, pamphlet collections, determination, and dedication of our members instead.[69]

Welch noted that "the largest file of this kind in America, outside of the government, is reported to contain 1,500,000 name headings."[70] On the basis, however, that there were only three hundred thousand to five hundred thousand communists in the country—"about 1/4 of 1% of our population"—and "not more than a million allies, dupes, and sympathizers whom they can count on for any conscious support," he did not believe that the Birch Society's own "files project" needed to be quite so extensive.[71]

What was needed, Welch explained, was "as complete factual information as possible on the background, connections, and activities of all the leading Liberals (including of course both Comsymps and Dupes)," and he furnished detailed instructions for how Birch Society members were to provide the information they had collected: they were to use an 8 1/2" x 11" sheet of paper for each entry; the subject's name should appear in the upper left corner of each page; pertinent facts were to be supported wherever possible by direct quotations; and the information was to be returned—carefully folded—in the same envelope made available to members for their "Monthly Messages" to the Society. Just dealing in published sources would be a "colossal job," Welch acknowledged—indeed, as in some Borgesian short story, it was one that would "never be completely finished"—but in time he hoped to have "hundreds of . . . cabinets, constituting the most complete, most accurate, and *most useful* file in America on the personnel of the whole Liberal Establishment."[72]

Reaction to news of the files project was not favorable. "What kind of nonsense is this?" thundered the *New York Times* in an editorial on July 14. "Like Ko-Ko in 'The Mikado,' the Birchers have 'got a little list'—or at least they're trying to get one—and with just about as much reason." The whole idea of private groups in a democracy drawing up such lists was "abhorrent," the editorial argued, because their "little list" would "inevitably turn into a little blacklist, a true symptom of the totalitarian mindlessness that judges individuals by their class, their label, their category, not by what they are, what they say or what they do."[73] Some members of the Birch Society itself were equally uncomfortable with the project. In addition to the thoroughly expected "hue and cry from the Liberal press" about the Society's supposed "witch-hunting," protests had also been received from "an even dozen of our members (including resignations from two)," and this probably meant that were "other objections which we never heard about," Welch reported in the August issue of the *Bulletin*.[74]

Although quick to attribute his members' protests to "distortions in the press," Welch nonetheless set out to clarify the exact nature of the project he had asked Birchers to embark upon. Contrary to "some of the loudest accusations" being made against it, the Society had "no intention of publishing any 'list'" based on the information it was collecting, Welch said. Nor had the Society given approval or even "offered the slightest encouragement" for either the publication or the preparation of "any lists by any individual members." Neither was the Society "seeking to make super-dooper snoopers out of our members, or put them to spying on their neighbors." The Society had made it "crystal clear," Welch explained, that all it was asking members to do was to gather material from already published sources, "primarily in government documents or the best of the anti-Communist historical books of the past two or three decades."[75]

"There is nothing whatsoever wrong with what we have asked our members to do," Welch contended. It was all a matter of effective research and efficient information gathering. Once the "planned master-index file" was in operation it was simply intended to facilitate the work of the Society—when, for example, it had to check the accuracy of a statement, or the past record or the connections of "a Dean Acheson [the former U.S. secretary of state] or a Ralph Bunche [a political scientist and the first African American to win the Nobel Peace Prize]." "I am sure that every Left-Wing newspaper in the United States has a file on me," Welch said, "and so long as they stick to the truth in what they publish I don't mind in the slightest degree. It merely simplifies their legitimate work."[76] He added, "Why should not we in turn have files on the now famous triumvirate, Eleanor Roosevelt, Walter Reuther, and Milton Eisenhower, if we can find some way, without the resources of a large newspaper, to accumulate such files? We can assure our readers, and anybody else interested, that *we* shall stick to the truth—which is *exactly* what worries some of our prospective subjects so much!"[77]

Welch's defense of the files project was indicative of his—and by extension, the Society's—overall political and rhetorical approach. "Facts" and "evidence" were simply to be gathered and deployed in the service of "truths" that were otherwise hidden by "surface appearances" (as Welch had written about the two "stooges" of the one-world government who had contested the 1960 presidential election). And because he was on the side of "Truth," the seemingly Orwellian nature of his endlessly proliferating filing cabinets—the fact that they called to mind the very totalitarian regimes he opposed so strenuously—did not concern him. Nor was he concerned about the memories of the McCarthy years the project was stirring up for his opponents—the Security files, the FBI files, the HUAC files, McCarthy's personal files, and so on. On the contrary, Welch and his supporters looked back fondly to the politics of the Second Red Scare; it was a period of American history they wanted to return to, or somehow revive.

That Welch still had some way to go to convince his many detractors of the legitimacy of his strategy of collecting information on the nation's leading liberals, socialists and Comsymps, however, is well illustrated by "Song of a Modern Vigilante" by Bradley Morison, a satirical poem published in the *Catholic News* on February 24, 1962. Introducing it, the paper's editor, William F. Fanning Jr., argued that the form of society advocated by Birchers was "wholly antagonistic to Catholic social philosophy . . . and above all the words of the Popes over the past seventy years." More intriguingly, the *New York Times* reported that the poem had first been brought to Fanning's attention as "an accurate insight into extremist groups" by an unidentified FBI official.[78] As the Chad Mitchell Trio and Bob Dylan had done, the poem's author assumed the perspective of a Birch Society member (if not Robert Welch himself), with the narrator busy "making little lists" of people he or she believes are communists, including college professors, proponents of foreign aid, UN supporters, and "integrationists." The poem ends with the narrator rejoicing in his own and his good friend's loyalty, before issuing a warning that "before my work is through / You may, good friend, be listed too."[79]

The Mosk Report

On July 7, 1961, California's attorney general, Stanley Mosk, submitted his findings on the Birch Society to Governor Edmund Brown. As was only appropriate for a report that had been commissioned in large part by the allegations made in Welch's non-book/letter/private manuscript *The Politician*, Mosk explained that while it might be "assumed by some that I am officially passing on the merits or demerits of the John Birch Society; that I am permitting or proscribing the propagation of their dogma; or that I am 'investigating' them to determine whether they should be silenced or put in jail," nothing could be further than the truth. No official investigation of the Society had taken place, Mosk said, nor did his office intend to conduct one.[80] The views he was expressing were his "personal observations" alone, not those of the "chief law officer of the State," and they were based only on material that had "been in the public press or was voluntarily submitted by interested citizens." Mosk was conveniently ignoring the fact that he had only been asked for his "personal observations" on the Society *because* he was the "chief law officer" of the state of California, of course, and despite his demurrals when the report was made public in August, it was quickly taken up as an authoritative—and government approved—statement on the Society and its activities.[81]

The opening paragraph of the fifteen-page report made Mosk's views on the Society abundantly clear (and contains its most oft-quoted phrase):

> The cadre of the John Birch Society seems to be formed primarily of wealthy businessmen, retired military officers and little old ladies in tennis shoes. They are bound together by an obsessive fear of "communism," a word which they define to include any ideas differing from their own, even though these ideas may differ even more markedly with the ideas of Marx, Engels, Lenin and Khrushchev. In response to this fear they are willing to give up a large measure of the freedoms guaranteed them by the United States Constitution in favor of accepting the dictates of their "Founder." They seek, by fair means or foul, to force the rest of us to follow their example. They are pathetic.

Elsewhere, the report, which had been prepared by Assistant Attorney General Howard H. Jewel, examined the views both of those who saw the Society as comical and those who regarded it as a deadly menace. It recounted the origins of the Society and its Founder (with Welch described as "an embittered candy maker of Belmont, Massachusetts"), quoted extensively from *The Blue Book*, critically examined some of its principal strategies and beliefs—its "Alice in Wonderland thinking"—and found the organization to be paranoid, authoritarian, and totalitarian in character.[82]

Drawing specifically on a recent speaking tour Welch had made of Southern California—and in sharp distinction to Jack Mabley's description of Welch as a "persuasive speaker"—the report pointed out that not only did he give "virtually the same speech . . . and in some instances [use the same] precise expression and phrases" at every place he visited, but according to a number of editorial writers, "wherever [he] makes his speeches, he loses rather than gains popular support." Yet perhaps the most interesting feature of the report was its comparison between the actions of the Communist Party and those of the Birch Society. The similarities were "irresistible," Mosk noted, since both groups readily employed infiltration, intimidation, fronts, and other "mean and dirty" tricks to further their political agendas, and he warned that there was a real danger that the Birchers would "attempt to take over all or some part of one of the existing political parties" in the near future, with the Republican Party seeming to be the most likely target in this regard.[83]

The Great "Smear"

The Birch Society's response to the enormous level of exposure and criticism it received, beginning with Hans Engh's articles in the *Santa Barbara News-Press* in January 1961 and continuing through the rest of the year and into 1962, took a number of different forms. On the most highly publicized charge against it, for example, Welch simply denied that he had ever called Dwight Eisenhower a "card-carrying Communist." "I never had that opinion, I never thought it then with firmness enough to publish it or to say it in public and I don't today," he informed an interviewer on March 31, 1961, falling back again on his argument about the uncertain ontological nature of *The Politician*, which he had already set out for readers of the *Bulletin* back in August 1960, following Jack Mabley's initial "attack" on the Society. Faced with the avalanche of attention that was descending on the Society during the opening months of 1961, Welch made essentially the same argument in the public statement he felt compelled to issue on the subject.[84] And to combat the charges that he was running a secret society dedicated to the destruction of American democracy, he also released a list of the National Council's members and an explanation of its functions.[85]

Three months later, to further alleviate what he called the "absurdity of all the charges about ours being a secret organization"—but also as "a mere matter of courtesy"—Welch announced that although the Society had already been sending its monthly *Bulletin* to press associations and "the few individual newspapers which had specifically requested us to do so," its Executive Committee had unanimously decided on a trial basis to send a copy of the *Bulletin* to *all* daily and weekly newspapers in the United States, beginning with the August issue.[86] In October, Welch also tried to clarify his position as "the Founder" of the Society. "Some of our more mentally destitute critics, straining their inadequate cerebral equipment to try to find nasty things to say about us, have been making snide remarks about the fact that we always write 'founder' . . . with a capital F," he wrote in that month's *Bulletin*. (It had been one of the criticisms made in the Mosk Report, but it was deployed more widely by opponents of the Society to indicate its authoritarian and dictatorial nature, and because by some alliterative alchemy it also called to mind Nazism and "The Führer.") "Well, it just so happens to be my title in the Society, and the only one I have," Welch explained. "We always write all other titles, such as Chapter Leader, Coordinator etc., also with initial capitals. And we just hope that our custom of following good typographical practice in this matter has not given any of our Chapter Leaders any more delusions of grandeur than it has myself."[87]

Individual supporters and members of the Society also came to its defense. The Democratic South Carolina congressman L. Mendel Rivers praised Welch as "courageous and perceptive" and described the Society as being composed of "patriotic Americans" who were dedicated to their country, in a speech in the House on March 22, 1961, for example. (Although the action was little noticed at the time, Rivers also entered a list of National Council members, as well as a list of people who had joined Committees of Endorsers around the country, into the *Congressional Record*.)[88] Similarly, in a statement released to the public on April 3, John Rousselot argued that the organization was just a study and letter-writing group. "It is basically made up of individual study groups in which the members read about and discuss communism in an effort to understand fully the menace it presents to America," Rousselot said. Based on these studies, members of the Society "write friends and public officials and discuss their thinking on political issues."[89] Daniel J. Downing, a Bircher from Stamford, Connecticut, in a letter to the *New York Times* of April 30, 1961, disputed the contention made by Robert Kennedy, among others, that the Society wasn't making any contribution to the fight against communism. Returning to the politics of the Second Red Scare, Downing argued (erroneously) that Presidents Kennedy and Eisenhower and Vice President Nixon had all opposed the loyalty oaths that were needed to keep the United States free from communist infiltration, and that Robert Kennedy himself "had got the charges against a Communist spy in the U.N. dismissed." "If that isn't giving aid and comfort to the criminal Reds," Downing asked, "please set me right."[90]

Underpinning such specific attempts to rebut its critics, though, was a broader analysis of, and explanation for, the problems the Society was facing: the Society believed it was the victim of a well-coordinated "smear campaign" being directly orchestrated by the Communist Party itself. The notion that there was a plot against it was nothing new—the same explanation had been offered in 1960 in response to the first wave of criticism the Society had faced.[91] The notion, however, returned with much greater emphasis after the renewed "attacks" against the Society at the start of 1961. "The smear campaigns against us increase in size, number, and viciousness," Welch noted in the March 1961 issue of the *Bulletin*, and he warned members "not to believe *anything* you hear about us or our policies or views until it has been unmistakably confirmed by this office."[92] By the following month's newsletter, Welch was referring to the "present all-out attack" taking place against the Society.[93]

"The attack was apparently set off, and the signal given, by an article which appeared in the official Communist paper, the *People's World*, in San Francisco, on February 25, 1961," Welch explained. Other "little guns . . . started firing at once," he continued, but "the next big boom in the barrage . . . was the article in *Time* magazine, issue dated March 10." By far the most interesting aspect of *Time*'s coverage—the most damning evidence of the communist-directed plot against the Birch Society in Welch's view—were the similarities between it and the "mother article" in the *People's World*, as Welch called it. Both, for example, referred incorrectly to the Society having "cells" rather than "chapters," and both had focused on the same three or four members of the National Council— out of the twenty-six "good and great Americans" available to them—as did "almost every other magazine and newspaper throughout the country" that had participated in the attack. (The four National Council members in question were Clarence Manion, T. Coleman Andrews, Spruille Braden, and Adolphe Menjou, although *Time* had reprieved Andrews, the former States' Rights Party presidential candidate, "for some reason of its own.") "Somebody issuing orders for the Communist command had decided that they could get more mileage per gallon by driving the propaganda juggernaut over those four than any others," Welch noted gravely.[94]

Many of the subsequent articles appearing about the Society "followed slavishly the line that had been transmitted to them" in the original article in the *People's World*, Welch continued—a notable exception being Gene Blake's *Los Angeles Times* series, which, Welch said, while "bitterly critical," was at least "honest" and based on "comprehensive research."[95] Welch saw the "second stage" of the "all-out nation wide attack" as being conducted by Stanley Mosk, Governor Brown, and all the others who were "casting aspersions" on the legality of the organization's activities, the loyalty of its members, and calling for "an official investigation" of the Society.[96]

In the May issue of the *Bulletin*, Welch tried—somewhat awkwardly—to incorporate the *Santa Barbara News-Press*'s critique of the Society into his conspiratorial narrative, suggesting that the paper had somehow managed to "anticipate" the *People's World*'s attack against the Society in its own coverage back in January.[97] By the end of the year, he had traced the origins of the whole campaign back to a secret "directive from Moscow" from December 1960 that had made the "destruction of anti-Communist groups a major task for the international conspiracy during 1961."[98]

There *was* a story about the Birchers in the February 25, 1961, issue of the *People's World*. It was entitled "Enter (from Stage Right) the John Birch Society." But as its brief two columns largely repeated—and indeed were almost entirely drawn from—already existent newspaper stories about the Society, it seems an unlikely source for all the negative attention it was to receive in 1961 and 1962. Beginning by noting that suburban newspaper columnists had recently been "devoting uneasy attention" to the Birch Society, it dutifully gave a brief overview of Welch, and quoted his views on the "perennial fraud" that is democracy, as well his allegations about Milton and Dwight Eisenhower. It *did* identify Manion, Andrews, Braden, and Menjou as members of the National Council, and it *did* refer to the organization as having "cells" rather than chapters, but overall its depiction of the Society was rather benign. "Letter writing to public officials and to newspapers has been the main activity of the Society but lately its attention has turned to the PTA, which Welch feels is too much to the left," it concluded, for example.[99]

Moreover, the implication that the Communist Party was behind the leaking of material from *The Politician* that was the main source for so many of the problems Welch and the Birch Society had been encountering was more than a little disingenuous on Welch's part as he had already identified the person he thought responsible for this "breach of confidence" back in 1960, after Jack Mabley's article had first appeared. In September that year, in a nine-page letter to Dr. Fred Schwarz of the Christian Anti-Communism Crusade, Welch told him that he knew that over the past few months Schwarz had "repeatedly been making extremely derogatory remarks about myself and the John Birch Society, to various groups and audiences" and that he had "been reading from my private manuscript, called *The Politician*, to support your disparaging remarks." Furthermore, Welch said he also knew Schwarz had been talking in private to "important conservative leaders" and that this was causing those leaders to "discontinue" their support for the Birch Society. Most important of all, though, Welch informed Schwarz that "it was one of your men in Chicago, a close associate of yours and a life member of your organization, who deliberately set off the publicity about *The Politician*, which has caused such furore in several Midwestern papers and some other points in the country."[100]

This man, Welch alleged, had attended several chapter meetings in the Chicago area on the pretext of joining the Society, and at one particular meeting in Glenview—"at the psychological time to do the most possible damage"—had stood up and "read at length from *The Politician*, exhibited the copy he had with him, and otherwise tossed as harmful a bombshell as he possibly could into the proceedings." Welch believed that Jack Mabley was at the Glenview meeting by "previous arrangement," but, whether or not this was true, there was little doubt, he said, "that the copy of *The Politician* which your man displayed at that meeting was turned over to Mabley as the basis of the vicious part of his two articles [on the Society] . . . and [was] then sent by Mabley to Alexander Dobish of the *Milwaukee Journal* for the articles that followed." None of this could have taken place, Welch told Schwarz, "without your knowledge and consent." The "whole smear campaign against myself, so many of my good friends, and The John Birch Society was . . . the result of your attitude and of your wish to harm us."[101]

The question that remained of course was: Why? What had the Society done to deserve such treatment from a fellow conservative and supposed ally in the anticommunist cause? Welch had uncovered the case of a volunteer coordinator of the Birch Society who had once been a "dedicated member" of Schwarz's Anti-Communism Crusade who had "turned against" the minister and made "some critical remarks" about Schwarz during a question-and-answer session at the end of a recent Birch chapter meeting in West Texas. But Welch was hard pressed to believe that "a Christian minister would carry vindictiveness so far, to the point of doing so much harm to completely innocent people, over so isolated a piece of personal criticism." Perhaps, then, professional jealousy was the motivating factor? With the Birch Society "looming as one of the most effective obstacles to the Communist take-over of America," Welch wondered whether Schwarz was attempting to "spike" his organization before it became even stronger. Welch did not believe this either, though. The real explanation, he thought, must lie in differences between the two leaders over the best *way* of fighting the communist menace—the approach to be taken, the means and methods to be employed—together with a misunderstanding on Schwarz's part concerning the "monolithic structure" of the John Birch Society.

Welch disagreed with Schwarz's emphasis on the need for individuals and groups to "fight the Communists in our own various ways," preferring "unity of purpose *and of action*," he wrote, and he sought to assure Schwarz that any "fears" he had about how the Birch Society conducted itself were unwarranted. Foreshadowing the defense of the organization he would make much more widely the following year, Welch told Schwarz that in order to minimize communist infiltration and avoid becoming bogged down in internal disputes, the Society had simply insisted from the start on having the right to "drop anybody from membership without having to go through a lot of explanations and 'proofs' that would interminably drain our energies." Members were free to act according to their own consciences in deciding which of the Society's "recommended actions" to carry out, and could "drop out of the Society at any time, without the slightest objection from us" if they disagreed sufficiently strongly with anything the Society was doing, or was asking them to do. Birch Society members "all know," Welch explained, that "we can exercise control and want to exercise control . . . only by persuasion."[102]

Despite Schwarz's betrayal—his "very culpable breach of confidence"— Welch tried to leave open the possibility of the two men working together again in the future. The letter ended with Welch expressing his hopes that Schwarz would decide that the Birchers were "worthy allies, instead of rivals, or dangerous 'storm troops,' or whatever you may have considered us to be during the past few months," and that rather than trying "to undermine us, for whatever reason you may have had," he would acquire a more "thorough knowledge of our own background, methods, and purposes" and recognize that the Society deserved his support in turn.[103]

On the Uses of Exposure

The intense exposure of the John Birch Society during 1960 and 1961 obviously revealed much about the organization, but it also revealed a great deal about the United States. As we have seen, memories of McCarthyism were never far from the surface of the politics of the period as editors, newspaper columnists, congressmen, law enforcement officials, and ordinary citizens struggled to come to terms with this new face of "ultra" conservatism. Should the Society be investigated and its members placed on the attorney general's list of subversives? Were Birchers simply exercising their rights to freedom of speech and association, or actively undermining the democratic system that guaranteed them those rights? Were they a dangerous threat or a ridiculous joke?

The answers to these questions were still been widely debated as 1961 turned into 1962, yet the unrelenting spotlight of attention and criticism that had been turned on the Birch Society for almost two years had certainly not cowed Welch or the Society's other leaders. In August 1961, for example, as controversy rained down on it from all directions, the Society announced its latest idea in the campaign to impeach Earl Warren: an essay competition for the best under-graduate essay on the subject. Offering $2,500 worth of prizes, the competition was intended "to stir up a great deal of interest among conservatives on the campuses on the dangers that face this country," Welch informed the *New York Times*. It also seemed designed to generate even greater amounts of attention for the Society, which duly came, including from new critics such as the American Bar Association.[104]

Looking back on the first three years of the organization in December 1961, Welch congratulated Birch members for having "held together, in one effective body," despite all the "sniping . . . knifing and criticisms" that had been directed against them. If the Society, in conjunction with "all of the other wonderful groups and individuals working to save America can grow in strength at the same geometrical rate for the next three years that they have for the last three," he said—though declining to reveal the exact "numerical strength" of his own organization—then members would see "the movement well under way, and the whole issue coming to a crisis, by the time of the elections in 1964." There had only been one chance in a hundred of saving the country from communist tyranny back in 1958, Welch explained; now, because of the great efforts they had undertaken, the odds had improved to one in ten.[105]

Many different interests and agendas were at work or were served in the initial attempt to expose the Society and its activities. For example, Otis Chandler, the new publisher of the family-owned *Los Angeles Times*, used Gene Blake's five-part series on the Society as a means of repositioning his paper in a crowded marketplace by distancing it from its own ultraconservative past, as well as a way of asserting his independence from some of his own Birch-supporting family members.[106] Senator Milton Young's ardent opposition to the organization, while doubtless sincere, was also partly motivated by concerns about his own political future.[107] Dramatic stories about the Birchers sold news-papers and magazines, attracted listeners to radio stations, and brought viewers to television programs about them.[108]

They also garnered awards. On November 5, 1961, Thomas M. Storke, the editor and publisher of the *Santa Barbara News-Press*, received the Lauterbach Award of the Nieman Foundation for Journalism for the "defense of civil liberties" in his coverage of the Birch Society.[109] Nobody seemed concerned about Storke's implicit endorsement of vigilante actions against the Birchers in the editorials for which he was being honored. The eighty-four-year-old had written in "The News-Press Stand on the John Birch Society" that his early years had been lived when "West was West and men were men," and if "slanders" of the kind that had been made about President Eisenhower had come to light during this time, they would have "called for a visit from a courageous and irate group which brought with them a barrel of tar and a few feathers." Such visits, Storke said, "were particularly likely to occur if the slanderer came from New England," where Welch had set up home, of course.[110]

Overall, there was an interesting tension at work in much of the early coverage of the Birch Society, manifest most frequently in the tendency of its opponents to condemn vehemently the leaders of the Society, especially Welch, while sympathizing with the frustrations and fears of its ordinary members. It was a tension reflective of the fact, as Barry Goldwater had put it on March 29, 1961, that many of those who had joined the Society were exactly "the type we need in politics"—seemingly sincere, certainly dedicated and, above all, (extremely) active citizens.[111]

Chapter 2

Putsch

On April 16, 1961, the *Overseas Weekly*, a controversial tabloid newspaper sold mostly on U.S. military bases in Europe, published an article entitled "Military Channels Used to Push Birch Ideas."[1] The article alleged that Major General Edwin A. Walker, a decorated war hero of both the Second World War and the Korean War, and since October 1959 the commander of the Twenty-Fourth Infantry Division, based in Augsburg, West Germany, had been indoctrinating his troops with John Birch Society material as part of a program known as "Pro-Blue." On April 17, Secretary of the Army Elvis J. Stahr relieved Walker of his command, pending a formal investigation of the charges against him. As a result of this investigation, Walker was officially "admonished" for his activities. This, though, was far from the end of the matter.

Spurred on by the Walker affair and also by broader concerns about the kinds of anticommunist propaganda and educational programs the military was engaged in, on June 28, 1961, the chairman of the Senate Foreign Relations Committee, J. William Fulbright (D-AR), sent a private memorandum to President Kennedy and Defense Secretary Robert McNamara, expressing his worries about the seemingly increasingly close relationship between the ultraright and the U.S. military, and asserting the need to maintain civilian control of the military in the United States. "If the military is infected with [the] virus of rightwing radicalism, the danger is worthy of attention," the senator wrote. He pointed to the April 1961 attempted coup d'état against Charles de Gaulle in France by retired generals who were opposed to his policies in Algeria—and who had intended to create an anticommunist military junta—as an example of the "ultimate danger" the nation faced.[2]

Walker resigned from the army in November 1961 and entered the political fray, running for governor of Texas in 1962 and becoming a target for assassination by Lee Harvey Oswald a year later. He was also the star witness at hearings undertaken by the Special Preparedness Subcommittee of the Senate Armed Services Committee, "Military Cold War Education and Speech Review Policies," which ran from January to June 1962 in the aftermath of the Fulbright memo, largely as a result of the urgings of Democratic South Carolina senator Strom Thurmond and other conservative members of Congress.

This chapter examines the Walker affair and its significance for the John Birch Society in detail. It explores concerns that the rise of the Birchers heralded either a fascist takeover of the United States, or given their—and other right-wing groups'—apparent connection with members of the armed forces, a move toward military dictatorship in the country. It also considers some of the wider social and cultural anxieties of the time, including fears of brainwashing and the frustrating realities of the early Cold War period.

Pro-Blue

The *Overseas Weekly* article of April 16, 1961, reported that Walker had established a Special Warfare unit within the Twenty-Fourth Infantry Division in October 1960 to conduct a "Pro-Blue" campaign, designed (in Walker's words) to give a "new and vital approach towards anticommunism" and a "positive approach toward the defeat of open Communist subversion of the American way of life." It noted the connection between the name of Walker's "indoctrination" program and the Birch Society's *Blue Book*, informed readers that Robert Welch's *The Life of John Birch* was being distributed to the division's company and battery day rooms, that the Society's magazine *American Opinion* was on sale at army newsstands, and that the division's own weekly paper, the *Taro Leaf*, had published "at least one article" from the Birch magazine. It also alleged that before the creation of the Pro-Blue program in January 1960, Walker had given a speech to a parent-teacher association in Augsburg during which he described legendary newsman and current director of the U.S. Information Agency Edward R. Murrow, newspaper columnist Walter Lippmann, and CBS commentator Eric Sevareid as "confirmed Communists," and former president Harry Truman, former secretary of state Dean Acheson, and former first lady Eleanor Roosevelt as "definitely pink." He was also said to have claimed that communism had "infiltrated every institution in the United States in an attempt to overthrow our way of life," and that communists had control of 60 percent of the American press, TV, and radio industry.[3]

After news of the allegations against him broke, Walker issued a statement denying their accuracy and defending his program. "The Special Warfare section of the headquarters staff of the Twenty-fourth Infantry Division coordinates the Pro-Blue Program, which is original and extensive in source material," he explained. It was not "associated or affiliated with any organization or society," and was designed simply to "develop the understanding of American military and civil heritage, responsibility toward that heritage, and the facts and objectives of those enemies who would destroy it."[4] As already noted, despite his statement Walker was swiftly relieved of his command and a formal investigation of the allegations—to be conducted by Lieutenant General Frederick J. Brown, commanding general of the Fifth Army Corps at Frankfurt—was launched. Walker was transferred to the U.S. Army headquarters in Heidelberg, pending the results of Brown's investigation.

Given their nature and the fact that they appeared in the midst of the storm of controversy already swirling around the Birch Society, the allegations against General Walker quickly became a major political issue. California Republican and Birch Society member Edgar Hiestand was in no doubt, for example, that the ongoing "smear campaign" against the Birch Society and the allegations about Walker were connected. Speaking on the floor of the House of Representatives on April 19, he asked: "Since when . . . is it proper procedure to relieve a military officer of his command for distributing the information of a patriotic society? Since when is it wrong to advance the cause of Americanism?" The move against Walker was clearly "made as a result of the vicious attacks on the Society in this country," he said.[5]

Hiestand's colleague, the conservative Democrat Thomas Dale Alford (AR), was also "deeply disturbed" by what had happened to Walker—and this despite the fact that Walker had been involved in what he called the "unfortunate episode" in 1957, when federal troops had "occupied" his hometown of Little Rock.[6] It was "shameful" that Walker had been "accorded such shortsighted and unfair treatment merely because he dared to carry out the fight against atheistic communism," Alford declared. "Obviously there is a conspiracy of harassment of all patriotic individuals and organizations." He wondered whether Walker would have received the same treatment had he been speaking out on behalf of "one-worldism or other left wing ideologies."[7]

Alford was particularly concerned by the "highly questionable" source of the attack on the general, describing *Overseas Weekly* as a "salacious . . . pink sheet" that routinely published pictures of "half-nude showgirls" in its pages. He proposed that the Armed Services Committee investigate the suitability of the tabloid for the nation's servicemen.[8] Texas Democrat Ovie Clark Fisher picked up the theme in the House on May 24. Noting that the troops themselves often referred to the newspaper as "Over*sexed* Weekly," he urged the Department of Defense to investigate it and its owner, Marion von Rospach. Fisher believed he had uncovered the reason for the paper's claims against Walker in a prior dispute between him and an *Overseas Weekly* reporter called Siegfried Naujocks (whom Fisher cast in an especially unpleasant light by asserting that he had "once worked in the propaganda ministry of the Nazis" before being dispatched to the Eastern Front during the Second World War). The congressman explained that Walker had caught Naujocks attempting to procure an informant within the army's headquarters and as a result had barred the reporter from all the bases under his command, an act which had "hurt the feelings" of von Rospach and prompted her charges against the general. "Surely, General Walker's military career is not to be jeopardized . . . by unfounded and insignificant charges made by a highly questionable get-rich-quick-tabloid publication—the notorious *Overseas Weekly*," Fisher concluded.[9]

Others were not so sure. Representative Frank Kowalski, a Democrat from Connecticut and himself a former serviceman, hoped that Walker would be court-martialed if it was proven, in the words of the *New York Times*, that he "had been conducting a campaign of vilification against the newspaper."[10] Kowalski's fellow Democrat William Proxmire, who had taken over Joe McCarthy's Wisconsin Senate seat in 1957, denounced both Walker's "crass stupidity" and his "idiotic attack" on such "great Americans" as Murrow, Lippmann, and Truman. "How can we expect to instill into our troops a fighting spirit if their own commanding officer tells them that their Government and their country's institutions are already rotted with communism?" Proxmire wanted to know.[11]

Significantly, it was in the context of the Walker affair that President Kennedy made his first public comments on the Birch Society. Speaking at a press conference on April 21, in the immediate aftermath of the Bay of Pigs debacle—itself a source of considerable disquiet for the Birch Society and other conservatives and anticommunists in the United States, as we shall see in Chapter 5—Kennedy revealed that he had been personally involved in the decision to relieve Walker of his command. Having seen the stories about the affair in the press, the president explained that he had called Robert McNamara to tell him to look into the matter, and that once the resultant investigation had been completed he would also be reviewing any decision made by his secretary of defense. A reporter followed up by suggesting that the president's ordering of an investigation into Walker indicated that he must also "look askance at the teachings of the John Birch Society." What were his views of the organization? the reporter enquired. Kennedy's reply indicated the extent to which the Birch Society was creating a problem for the administration and its attempt to sustain some kind of consensus around its Cold War policy. He said: "Well, I don't think their judgments are based on accurate information of the kinds of challenges that we face. I think we face an extremely serious and intensified struggle with the Communists. But I am not sure that the John Birch Society is wrestling with the real problems which are created by the Communist advance around the world." Birchers and others, the president continued, should spend their time addressing the "internal subversion" that was going on in places like Vietnam and Laos—although in actuality this was a key area of concern for the Birch Society and had been ever since its formation in 1958—rather than concerning themselves "with the loyalty of President Eisenhower, President Truman, Mrs. Roosevelt, . . . myself or someone else."[12]

In an editorial on the "fantasies" of the Society the following day, the *New York Times* commended Kennedy with regard to both the specifics of his statement on the Birchers and his wider handling of the Walker affair. Members of the armed forces were as entitled as any other American citizen to have political opinions, the paper declared, but it was "obviously wrong for any officer . . . to attempt to indoctrinate his subordinates with the ideas of a particular group." It was a "fundamental of our political traditions," the editorial went on, getting to the heart of the issue as it would develop in the weeks and months that followed, "that the armed forces serve all of the American people and play no independent political role in our national life."[13]

Having been reviewed and approved by the president, Lieutenant General Brown's report on the Walker affair was made public on June 12, 1961. Brown found that the Pro-Blue program was not in fact attributable to the John Birch Society. (The program's title apparently had been derived not from *The Blue Book*, but rather from military maps, which depicted the "free world" in blue and communist nations in red.)[14] He did find, though, that Walker had made "derogatory remarks of a serious nature about certain prominent Americans, the American press and television industry and certain commentators, which linked the persons and institutions with communism and Communist influence," and that he had also "failed to heed cautions by superior officers to refrain from participating in controversial activities which were contrary to the longstanding customs of the military service and beyond the prerogatives of a senior military commander." Announcing the results of the enquiry, General Bruce C. Clark, commander in chief of the U.S. Army, Europe, declared that while no one doubted Walker's "sincerity of purpose," he had exceeded the limits of propriety for an army officer, and as a result—and with a thirty-year record of outstanding service taken into account—was being officially "admonished" for his actions.[15]

The punishment was the lightest Walker could have received—it was essentially a reprimand and would not even appear on his military record—but the fact that he was punished at all was too much for his supporters, while critics were concerned that it didn't send out a strong enough signal to the military or the nation as a whole. Hiestand, for example, wanted the Pentagon to issue a complete report on the case, while Kowalski argued that at a time of "military revolts in many parts of the world"—an allusion to the recent attempted coup d'état in France in particular—Walker's activities should be "very seriously examined by the American people."[16] Indeed, it was the reaction to Walker's punishment and the tensions within American society with respect both to political extremism and the relationship between the military and civilian society it encapsulated that make it such a revealing window into the United States at this time.

Propagandizing the Cold War

Cabell Phillips of the *New York Times* provided a partial, if somewhat ironic, explanation for Walker's seemingly lenient treatment in an article entitled "Right-Wing Officers Worrying Pentagon" published on June 18: Phillips wrote that, whatever its excesses, the Pro-Blue program had actually been operating in accordance with a secret Cold War policy paper issued by the National Security Council in 1958. Faced with the mounting international tensions of the time, the Eisenhower administration had decided that the Cold War could not be fought as a series of separate and independent actions on the part of the various agencies of the government. Rather, it required the mobilization of all parts of the government—military, diplomatic, and civilian—acting in a unified way, and "with the full understanding and support of the civilian population." In particular, Phillips reported, the administration had decided that the military should be used to "reinforce" the Cold War effort. Implemented through a series of still classified directives and guidance papers to the "top civilian and uniformed authorities," these officials, Phillips revealed, had been instructed to take "positive measures to alert the troops under their command and the public at large to the issues of national security and the 'cold war.'"[17]

The major problem with the directive, the Pentagon was now coming to realize, was the wide latitude individual officers were given in determining how to apply the policy within their commands. In addition, there were further concerns about the participation of high-ranking officers in the various anticommunist and national security seminars, forums, and schools within the United States that were connected to right-wing groups and organizations like the Reverend Billy James Hargis's Christian Crusade, Dr. Fred Schwarz's Christian Anti-Communism Crusade, Dr. George Benson's Harding College, and, of course, the John Birch Society itself.[18]

These were issues that had been troubling the Arkansas senator, Kennedy administration ally, and powerful chairman of the Senate Foreign Relations Committee J. William Fulbright for over a year. Born in Sumner, Missouri, to well-to-do parents in 1905, Fulbright grew up in Fayetteville, Arkansas, attending the university there and at Oxford before becoming president of the University of Arkansas in 1939. Trained as a lawyer, he was elected to the Senate for the first time in 1944, where he served for the next twenty-nine years, during which time he became one of the most influential voices in U.S. foreign policy-making circles (and a vocal opponent of the Vietnam War in particular).[19]

Fulbright had first become concerned about the seemingly increasingly close relationship between the U.S. military and elements of the American Right in April 1960 when an employee of *Stars and Stripes* wrote to him to complain that members of the U.S. command in Germany had prevented the paper from reporting on a recent Senate Foreign Relations Committee hearing in which Fulbright and others had criticized aid to Turkey.[20] On April 19, 1961, just after the Walker affair had broken, Fulbright then received a letter from an air force reserve officer who had recently attended a screening of the film strip *Communism on the Map*, a production of Harding College. (Together with the HUAC-produced *Operation Abolition*, a film about the anti-HUAC "riots" that took place in San Francisco in 1960, it was a mainstay of the anticommunist circuit at the time.) The officer's complaint was less about the film itself or its depiction of the United States standing almost alone in a world engulfed in communism and socialism—a situation the film blamed on Franklin D. Roosevelt and George Marshall, among others—and more about the discussion that took place afterward, which, he said, had suggested that the policies of the Kennedy administration were themselves leading the nation to communism.[21] That same week the senator also received disturbing reports of three Strategy for Survival conferences that had just been held in his home state, where speakers, including active-duty military personnel, had equated liberalism with socialism and criticized members of the Arkansas congressional delegation.[22]

Fulbright raised his concerns with Robert McNamara at a party for the Pakistan president Ayub Khan onboard the presidential yacht on June 11. In the heightened atmosphere of the Walker affair, McNamara encouraged the senator to submit a written statement outlining his worries to both himself and the president, which Fulbright did on June 28. The "Fulbright memo," as it became known—although it was drafted with the considerable aid of his legislative assistant Jack Yingling—drew the president and his defense secretary's attention to the NSC's 1958 directive, suggesting that as currently being implemented it was running counter to the administration's strategies for dealing with the problems of the nuclear age. Fulbright cited eleven instances of programs that were "closely associated" with military personnel and which "made use of extremely radical rightwing speakers and/or materials, with the probable net result of condemning foreign and domestic policies of the administration in the public mind." They included the recent Strategy for Survival conferences in Arkansas, a Fourth Dimensional Warfare seminar sponsored by the Chamber of Commerce of Greater Pittsburgh that had included the screening of *Operation Abolition*, and the programs of Dr. Fred Schwarz and Harding College.[23]

Fulbright conceded that the exact content varied from program to program, but running through all of them, he said, was the "central theme that the primary, if not exclusive, danger to this country is internal Communist infiltration." Moreover, the "thesis" of the nature of this internal threat was often developed by "equating social legislation with socialism, and the latter with communism." As such, Fulbright warned Kennedy that much of the administration's domestic legislative agenda—including the expansion of social security, what would become Medicare, federal aid to education, and the continuation of the graduated income tax—could be characterized "as steps towards communism."[24]

The American people were not well suited to the frustrating realities of the Cold War—the "long twilight struggle" Kennedy had described in his inaugural address—the memo continued. "In the long run, it is quite possible that the principal problem of leadership will be, if it is not already, to restrain the desire of the people to hit the Communists with everything we've got, particularly if there are more Cubas and Laos." And it pointed out that "pride in victory and frustration in restraint" during the Korean War had led to both "MacArthur's revolt and McCarthyism." Fulbright argued that the appeal of the radical Right was understandable given these circumstances because it offered "the simple solution easily understood: Scourging of the devils within the body politic, or, in the extreme, lashing out at the enemy." But the combination of right-wing extremists and a disaffected military was especially dangerous:

> If the military is infected with this virus of rightwing radicalism, the danger is worthy of attention. If it believes the public is, the danger is enhanced. If, by the process of the military "educating" the public, the fevers of both groups are raised, the danger is great indeed.

> Perhaps it is farfetched to call forth the revolt of the French generals as an example of the ultimate danger. Nevertheless, military officers, French or American, have some common characteristics arising from their profession and there are numerous military "fingers on the trigger" throughout the world. While this danger may appear very remote, contrary to American tradition, and even American military tradition, so also is the "long twilight struggle," and so also is the very existence of an American military program for educating the public.[25]

Contrary to the apparent underlying premise of the 1958 NSC directive, Fulbright saw no special or privileged role for the U.S. military in alerting the public to the menace and dangers of the Cold War—other than its "specific, technical competence"—and the six recommendations contained in his memo were all designed to help bring the military back under clear civilian control. Indeed, his first recommendation was that the 1958 NSC policy "should be reconsidered from the standpoint of a basic error, that military personnel have the necessarily broad background which would enable them to relate the various aspects of the cold-war effort, one to the other," as Eisenhower had intended.[26] His second recommendation was that the White House and Defense Department should stop treating the propaganda activities of military personnel as individualized problems of discipline or better public relations management, and begin "formulating directives which will bring such military [propaganda] activities under effective civilian control."[27]

Recommendations 3 and 4 dealt with the roles of the National War College, the Foreign Policy Research Institute, the Institute for American Strategy, the Richardson Foundation, and the Joint Chiefs of Staff in carrying out these activities. The fifth recommendation was that "promising" military officers be exposed to broader educational opportunities—preferably ones "dominated by a board of civilian educators"—requiring the completion of graduate studies in history, government, and foreign policy before their appointment to "high ranks." The final recommendation dealt with the specific problem illustrated by the Walker case. It was for "a civilian committee [to] be appointed to review troop education activities of military personnel from the standpoint of their necessity and, if found to be, to develop procedures for bringing the content of such programs and, if possible, their actual operation under civilian control."[28]

Details of Fulbright's memo—although not the senator's identity as its author—were leaked to the *Washington Post*, where they caught the particular attention of Strom Thurmond, the conservative, segregationist, and virulently anticommunist senator from South Carolina, one-time Dixiecrat presidential candidate, and major general in the army reserve.[29] Outraged by Fulbright's analysis and recommendations—which were revealed by follow-up articles in the *Post* and the *New York Times*—and looking for an issue that might enhance his national political profile and reputation, Thurmond undertook a relentless campaign for a thorough investigation of the matter by the Senate Armed Services Committee of which he himself was a prominent member.[30] Both General Walker and the Birch Society were now entwined in wider concerns about what Thurmond termed "insidious" and "dastardly" attempts to "muzzle the military" in the United States.[31]

Muzzling the Military

As far as Thurmond was concerned the Walker affair and the Fulbright memo—which had now acquired an additional sobriquet as the "muzzling the military" memo—were evidence of a "concerted attack" that was underway against "the anti-Communist indoctrination of the American people and our troops in uniform." Drawing on the Birch Society playbook, Thurmond argued that the attack had been initiated by the *Worker*, the official news organ of the Communist Party USA, but was now "taking the form of a widespread movement from innumerable sources." It was imperative, Thurmond said, that an investigation take place as soon as possible into the ongoing "conspiracy to discredit and intimidate the military leaders of our country in their efforts to provide to their personnel and the public the facts—all the facts—needed to assess the total Communist menace for what it is—a deadly threat to our liberties and our survival as a nation."[32]

Before any investigation could take place, though, there was the small matter of getting access to the memorandum in its entirety. Thurmond had stormed down to Fulbright's Senate office demanding to be given a copy after reading the summary of it published in the *Times* and the *Post* on July 21, only to be informed by Fulbright's legislative assistant Lee Williams that he didn't have one to give to him. (Thurmond apparently told Williams that he wanted it on his desk within an hour, but when Williams informed Fulbright of Thurmond's demands, Fulbright's response was that Williams should tell the South Carolinian to "go to hell.")[33] Rebuffed privately, Thurmond went public, issuing a news release later that morning, and speaking repeatedly on the subject on the floor of the Senate in the days that followed. Nor was he alone. Senators Karl Mundt (R-SD) and Barry Goldwater (R-AZ), for example, both reported that they too had been unable to get their hands on the infamous memo despite their own, separate requests to the secretary of defense. Goldwater also revealed that he had contacted McNamara on several occasions over the Walker affair—indeed, he went so far as to describe Walker's official admonishment as "one of the most dangerous things that has ever happened in the history of [the United States]." It was a very sorry situation, Goldwater believed, if the country had reached the point "where we have a bunch of namby-pambies as our generals, men who cannot use a little strong language once in a while."[34]

Inevitably, the pressure became too much to resist. On August 2, Fulbright formally inserted a copy of his memo and its recommendations into the *Congressional Record*. Pointedly, he did not provide a copy directly to Thurmond. Nor did he let the occasion pass without some withering sarcasm. He was surprised by the intense interest the memorandum had been attracting, he said, since it was based on his strong belief in the principle of military subordination to civilian control, a constitutional tradition he had previously understood to be uncontroversial. The memo was also a personal one, he explained, and he had been equally unaware that it was "the custom, the practice, or the right of Senators to demand access to the private correspondence of their colleagues." It was because he had now been disabused of these misapprehensions, Fulbright explained, that he was releasing the text of the memo—as well as to "dispel the fears of those who have persuaded themselves that the memorandum contains material which is sinister, subversive, or sensational."[35]

Fulbright was missing the point, Thurmond responded in the Senate two days after the public release of the memo. The issue was not civilian control of the military—which was indeed "firmly rooted" in both the Constitution and the nation's traditions. The "real issue" was whether the American people should be "given the facts whereby they, themselves, can exercise the sovereignty which is theirs." The memorandum was clearly an "attack" on the country's military leaders and their ability to educate and inform the nation about the "total nature of communism and the history of its many tactics of aggression," but underpinning it, Thurmond believed, was a fear—evidenced by the memo's references to the revolt of the French generals and the inability of Americans to come to terms with the "long, twilight struggle" of the Cold War—"not of the military, but of the American people themselves." This could be the only explanation, he contended, for the attempt that had been made to protect the memo's secrecy.[36]

Playing on Fulbright's reputation as an elitist, Thurmond argued that while few American citizens were given the opportunity to study at Harvard or Oxford (as Fulbright had done as a Rhodes scholar), formal education was not the "sole source of knowledge and commonsense," and he cast himself as part of the "'uneducated public'" who still believed that "our enemy is communism." And finally in possession of "proof" of the conspiracy he had been denouncing so vociferously, the senator introduced a formal resolution (S. Res. 191) calling on the Senate Armed Services Committee to undertake a "comprehensive investigation" of the whole affair in its entirety.[37]

Kennedy came to Fulbright's defense in his weekly press conference on August 10.[38] Meanwhile, the *New York Times* attempted to connect Thurmond's call for an investigation with California attorney general Mosk's report on the Birch Society, which had been made public the same week. Its editorial cautioned that "Senator Thurmond might like to take a look at how foolish the John Birch Society looks before he goes in for more of his own brand of folly."[39] In September, McNamara testified on the Fulbright memo and the new directives that had resulted from it before the Senate Armed Services Committee. The defense secretary also revealed new details about the Walker affair from Lieutenant General Brown's report, including that Walker had tried to influence the votes of soldiers in the Twenty-Fourth Division in the 1960 elections.[40]

Much to Thurmond's irritation, the Armed Services Committee decided not to hold full hearings into any attempts that might have been made to "muzzle" the military. Instead, a subcommittee was appointed to "study and appraise the use of military personnel and facilities to arouse the public to the menace of the cold war and to inform and educate armed services personnel on the nature and menace of the cold war," with the hearings to begin in January 1962.[41]

Thurmond was the indefatigable driving force behind the push for an investigation of the Fulbright memo and the broader issues related to it, but it was by no means a one-man campaign. The South Carolinian was supported by a host of his fellow congressmen, including—in addition to those already mentioned—Styles Bridges (R-NH), Dale Alford (D-AR), Thomas Dodd (D-CT), Robert Sikes (D-FL), Carl Curtis (R-NB), Homer Capehart (R-IN), and Jack Miller (R-IA), as well as a wide swath of conservative and anticommunist publications and organizations in the United States, including the *Dan Smoot Report*, Hargis's Christian Crusade, Kent and Phoebe Courtney's Conservative Society of America, *National Review*, and the Birch Society.

Dale Alford, for example, was not only chair of the Congressional Committee for Justice for General Walker, he was also a key sponsor of an organization called Voters for the Constitution, which had the aim of "retiring" from public office Fulbright and all those like him who were making "a clandestine assault on the very foundations of our system of government."[42] Former FBI agent Dan Smoot put all the resources of his would-be media empire into urging every American who cared about their country to oppose Fulbright's efforts to gag "anti-communist patriots in the armed forces of America" by writing their elected representatives to demand they "do *something* to reinstate and exonerate Major General Edwin A. Walker who was crucified, for being a patriot, by the very scurviest of scurvy leftwing forces."[43] Hargis took to calling Fulbright the "red-wing Senator from Arkansas" in his weekly broadcasts, and the husband-and-wife team of Kent and Phoebe Courtney—publishers as well as New Orleans Birch Society chapter leaders—issued a seemingly endless series of pamphlets, articles, leaflets, and books about the affair, especially in their newspaper, the *Independent American*.[44]

The editors of the more respectable if no less fiercely conservative *National Review* ran four articles on the Walker case and its aftermath between May 6 and December 16, 1961. In "Let the Generals Beware," published on July 1, they argued that because liberals had never grasped "the scope or nature of the Communist enterprise," it inevitably fell to "officers of conservative conviction [to] initiate active and realistic anti-Communist educational programs." And if those officers—the very men who would actually fight "the next brushfire or full-scale war"—believed that a clear understanding of communism and a little "old-fashioned patriotism" was as essential for their troops as training in how to handle a M2 machine gun, then surely such instruction should be given.[45] (The historian Jonathan Schoenwald reports that William Buckley, the magazine's founder and editor in chief, also contacted Walker directly to tell him that *National Review* was prepared to go even further in its support if the general would divulge all the details of the Pro-Blue program to the magazine, but that the offer was not taken up.)[46]

For Robert Welch and the Birch Society, both the Walker affair and the Fulbright memo were matters of considerable if initially rather confusing concern. In the May 1961 issue of the *Bulletin*, for example, Welch revealed that Walker had been a subscriber to *American Opinion* for three years and that the Society had supplied material "on two or three occasions" for the special projects office of his command, including *The Life of John Birch*, although no orders had been received during the past year. (Rather mischievously, he also said that he hoped that the orders for other books used in the program, such as J. Edgar Hoover's *Masters of Deceit*, had been in "considerably larger quantities" than his own had been.) By June 1, however, the Founder was reporting that it was "well established that the officer who, acting on orders . . . from Walker, [to] set up the 'Pro-Blue Program' . . . had never even heard of the John Birch Society until months after [it] was underway," and that the effort to tie the program to the Society was something that had been seized upon by the *Overseas Weekly* because of the "campaign of adverse publicity" that was being directed toward Birchism at that time. Such a piece of opportunism notwithstanding, however, Welch believed that Kennedy's decision to "summarily remove" Walker from his command reinforced the Society's broader contention that "these are times when the unbelievable and the 'impossible' happen while you wait."[47]

After seeming to downplay the importance of the issues, come September— after the Fulbright memorandum had become a national cause célèbre—Welch was telling Birch Society members in no uncertain terms that supporting Senator Thurmond's demand for an investigation of the "military gag rules" was the "most IMPORTANT item" in that month's agenda. The intervening months had evidently allowed Welch to see more clearly what was really going on. "It is almost certain now that the smear campaign against us was designed not only to put a stop to, or handicap, our own very extensive showings of *Operation Abolition* and *Communism On The Map*," he wrote, "but as a vital part in a program to stop the military from its widespread showings of the same films, and from other effective patriotic activities and purposes." After all: "One of the most vital and necessary steps to the Communists in their take-over of any country is the suppression or elimination of patriotic officers, with a resulting demoralization of the total armed forces of that country." Launching a massive letter-writing campaign in support of Thurmond's Senate Resolution 191, to be called Operation FIB (aka the "Fulbright Intimidation Binge"), Welch explained that there had "seldom been as much reason for the Society to stir up a storm of protest," and he encouraged every Bircher to do their duty.[48]

The Senate Armed Services Committee's subsequent decision to authorize a hearing was "probably the most important . . . specific victory" achieved by the Birch Society since its formation, Welch informed readers of the October issue of the *Bulletin*.[49] Noting that the committee had received 150,000 letters and telegrams as it made its deliberations, Welch congratulated all the many different patriotic groups that had cooperated together in "one drive with great effectiveness," but he understandably singled out his own members for the "perfectly wonderful job" they had done of "speaking up in unison on behalf of the men who are fighting for the right to fight our enemies." The battle was not over yet, however. Echoing Goldwater, Welch feared that "the Liberals" would try and convert the investigation into "a namby-pamby whitewash" of Fulbright, McNamara, and all the others who were attempting to muzzle the nation's armed forces, and that it would take a "continuing, and Herculean effort to prevent them from accomplishing their purpose." Accordingly, Birchers were implored to redouble their efforts in preparation for the Preparedness Subcommittee hearings, and in particular to offer support to the only two "aggressive" communist-fighters on the subcommittee, Thurmond and Bridges. Indeed, as far as Welch was concerned, the hearings were now a "major battleground" comparable with the movement to impeach Earl Warren—the only difference being that the latter had been an offensive initiated by the Birch Society, whereas the fight over the removal of Walker and the Fulbright program had been thrust upon the Society from the outside, requiring it to adjust its efforts "to the timing and the actions of the Liberals."[50]

On November 2, 1961, General Walker resigned from the U.S. Army—in part so that he would be able to speak unencumbered by his position at the forthcoming subcommittee hearings. A statement of his reasons for doing so, addressed to the Senate Armed Services Committee, was released through Thurmond's Senate office, which although an unusual move was one that reflected the senator's role as Walker's apparent personal champion in the affair.[51] His career had been "destroyed in its usefulness" to the United States, the now former general explained, and he wanted to be "free from the power of little men, who, in the name of my country, punish loyal service to it."[52] Emphasizing his experience and expertise as a commander of front-line troops in the Cold War—the Twenty-Fourth Infantry Division had been stationed in Augsburg because it was one of the places where any Soviet invasion of Europe was expected to begin—Walker's job, he said, had been to instill in his troops an "effective realism," and his Pro-Blue program had merely implemented the 1958 directive from the National Security Council to achieve those ends, but it was the "expressed decision of higher echelons that I may not provide my fellow-soldiers with the degree of information that I consider imperative to their morale and their capacity to survive."[53]

Walker drew on the views of General Douglas MacArthur—whom he quoted directly elsewhere in the statement, along with Generals Mark Clark and John R. Deane—to recall how in Korea he had seen "stalemate become a substitute for victory," and reminded the committee that the nation was at war, a war the United States was "losing . . . every day."[54] What was more—and here the general's affinity with the views of the Birch Society was revealed most starkly—these defeats were taking place within the country itself. Communism and communists had infiltrated almost every aspect of American life, Walker explained:

> We employ its agents in the teaching professions, allowing them to work on the fertile minds of youth seeking a champion to pit against a scapegoat. They infest our entertainment media. They long ago have infiltrated our government so that a scheme of subversion can be traced through three decades.
>
> Even our free press is exploited by Communist propagandists. Communist collaborators find rabid and militant defense among certain groups of our citizens, some of whom are sincerely confused and misguided.[55]

It was with a "heavy heart" that he was taking leave of his military duty, Walker admitted, but he was resigning rather than accepting retirement—with all its "emoluments and benefits"—because he was unwilling to compromise his principles, and he hoped to "find other means of serving my country in the time of her great need, in order to pursue the dedication of a lifetime."[56]

After all the agitation and anticipation the hearings themselves were something of a letdown. Chaired by John Stennis (D-MS) but dominated by the relentless interventions, questioning, and grandstanding of Thurmond, they were long, slow, and largely inconclusive, with 67 witnesses appearing over 36 days, producing 3,347 pages of testimony.[57] It was certainly no repeat of the fabled Army-McCarthy hearings of 1954.

Walker in particular proved to be much less impressive in person than he had appeared on paper or in the press. Appearing before the subcommittee on April 4 and April 5, he covered all the aspects of the Pro-Blue controversy but added very little to what was already known, denying that it was based on any program of the John Birch Society, that he had tried to influence the votes of the troops under his command, or that he was in any way threatening the principle of civilian control of the armed forces. He also condemned the "subversive" activities of the *Overseas Weekly* in making the original allegations against him. The problem was that despite Thurmond's considerable efforts to present him in the best possible light, the general's performance made him easy to categorize—and essentially dismiss—as conspiratorial, paranoid, and extremist. He told Senator Henry "Scoop" Jackson (D-WA), for example, that there could be no middle ground in the ongoing struggle against the Soviet Union. "When you are fighting communism and there is a cold war on, there are only two sides of a line," he explained, although actually seeming to present three. "You are either assisting or helping, or you are neutral and not helping, or you are opposing."[58] He also emphasized the internal threat facing the nation and linked it to the recent "big propaganda front . . . by the ultra-liberal press against the Birch Society," informing Senator Bob Bartlett (D-AK) that the communists hadn't dared attack the armed forces directly so they had assailed the Birch Society "while they infiltrate and do all the other things they possibly can in the one greatest obstacle [*sic*] in their road: the military services." Such was the nature of the international conspiracy of "debauchery and atheistic treachery" known as the Cold War, he said.[59]

The Special Preparedness Subcommittee's findings were submitted to Richard Russell (D-GA), chairman of the full Armed Services Committee, in October. The majority report, endorsed by Stennis, Symington, Jackson, Saltonstall, and Smith, ran to forty-six pages. Bartlett departed from it slightly in a two-page individual comment but was otherwise in "solid agreement" with its findings. Thurmond rejected it completely and submitted an enormous 157-page minority report in dissent. Among the majority report's findings and recommendations was that the traditional principle of military subordination to civil authority be given "unwavering adherence and that it not be weakened in any particular"; that the executive branch had "the inherent power to require that military officers submit public statements for policy review prior to delivery"; that the armed services had a responsibility to "furnish training and teaching which will instill and develop in military personnel firm belief in, and appreciation for, the American principles of democracy and freedom and an awareness of the threat of communism to this country and the free world"; and that the Department of Defense should provide better guidance and clearer direction so that every commander "will be better able to select intelligently the specific troop information material which is best suited to the needs of his command."[60]

As anodyne as they might have appeared, the publication of the subcommittee's findings was greeted with cries of "whitewash" by the nation's anticommunist activists. Worse, Welch explained in the January 1963 issue of *American Opinion*, the findings meant that the campaign against Walker had succeeded. His case would now "serve as an example and warning to other patriotic officers, so as to put an end to all such activities on the part of the military everywhere." Welch also detected a "deeper significance" to the affair, something "beyond the direct scope of Senator Thurmond's investigation." In an echo of Walker's testimony—which was itself a ventriloquization of Welch's views—it was that the whole "muzzling the military" campaign had been part of an "international Communist program" that had been at work for twenty years around the world. "The demoralization and destruction of the military forces of each nation, which the Communists are moving to take over, has been a 'must' on their schedule since long before they applied this formula to the United States," Welch wrote. Despite his best efforts, Thurmond had not even scratched the surface of the execution of this "blueprint design" for America.[61]

Other significances could also be found in the Walker affair, however. Concerns about military-civilian relations and fears about the possibility of military dictatorship in the United States could be traced back as far as George Washington, of course, but they were given a much-renewed emphasis by the frustrations and anxieties of the early Cold War—and such fears were never more keenly felt and expressed than in the years 1961 and 1962.[62] After all, manifestations of "public uneasiness and . . . rumblings of discontent" about these matters, combined with overseas examples—in France, Argentina, Peru, and the Communist bloc—of the "difficulties which arise when the military attains or threatens to attain a dominant position" were what prompted the Senate Preparedness Subcommittee to "restate and reaffirm" the principle of civilian supremacy over the military in the United States in its final report.[63] More particularly, though, as the Fulbright memorandum had more than demonstrated, it was the rise of right-wing groups like the John Birch Society and their apparent close association with the military that made these concerns especially acute.

Indeed, appearing in the midst of the lion's den—that is, for the opening session of the National War College and the Industrial College of the Armed Forces on August 21, 1961—at the invitation of Robert McNamara, Fulbright maintained his basic contention that military personnel who lent their support "to any groups or organizations which espouse policies that run counter to those of the Commander in Chief and which have the effect of generating distrust and suspicion among the people" were doing a disservice both to the American people and to the armed forces themselves. Radical extremism, whether of the left or the right, was the true enemy of a democratic society, he explained. Such "disloyal opposition" had destroyed the Weimar Republic in Germany and now plagued postwar Italy and France, and he argued that if the United States was "to meet the challenges of our times, we must reject the false and simple solutions of irresponsible extremists who cannot, or will not, accept the world as it is." Such were the "imperatives of military responsibility."[64]

Eisenhower had famously expressed his concerns about the potential influence of the "military-industrial complex" in the United States during his January 1961 farewell address.[65] His successor reiterated them two months later in a much less heralded speech on the defense budget. Speaking on March 22, the new president declared: "Neither our strategy, nor our psychology as a nation—and certainly not our economy—must become dependent upon the permanent maintenance of a large military establishment." "Our arms must be subject to civilian control at all times," he added.[66] As we have seen, MacArthur's "insubordination" of President Truman during the Korean War was never far from the surface of discussions concerning these issues, and Kennedy experienced his own struggles to "control the generals" during the Bay of Pigs invasion of Cuba and the subsequent missile crisis.[67] But at root it was the new administration's ostensibly more flexible, less overtly belligerent approach to the Cold War—one emphasizing economic development, humanitarian assistance, and increased educational opportunities as means of combating the appeal of communism in the so-called Third World, for example—that was so disconcerting to more hard-line anticommunists both within the armed forces and without.

As Richard Gid Powers has written, as the Walker affair unfolded, ardent anticommunists were "staggered to learn that the patriotic anticommunism that had become almost a civic religion was now being criticized as political opinion, and extremist politics at that."[68] To be sure, the Kennedy White House and even its harshest critics were in broad agreement about the threat atheistic communism represented for the world and its inhabitants, but they differed sharply about the best way to deal with the dangers and especially over the extent to which it posed an *internal* threat to the United States. Indeed, it was precisely the gaps that were opening up in the Cold War anticommunist consensus that were fueling the increasingly ill-tempered contest between conservatives and liberals in the country. As an unnamed Pentagon official had commented to Cabell Phillips about Walker's Pro-Blue program, although his point had much wider application: "There is a big gray area here where the difference between right and wrong—between saying too much and not saying too much—is terribly hard to distinguish."[69]

Fascism Rising?

The idea that the John Birch Society was a fascist political organization—especially its Nazi variant—was one that was expressed frequently following the Society's sudden emergence into the public realm at the beginning of 1960. As we saw in the previous chapter, characterizations of Welch as the Birchers' "Führer" and *The Blue Book* as his *Mein Kampf* were relatively commonplace. "What the society is up to sounds ominously like what the Nazis once were up to in Germany," declared the Wisconsin Democrat Henry Reuss on the floor of the House on April 12, for example, while the Rabbinical Council of America referred to the "serious dangers" posed to the country by the "narrow Fascist-like and bigoted Birch Society," and FDR's youngest son, the Republican John Aspinwall Roosevelt, denounced it as a "vicious, scurrilous and thoroughly un-American organization with incipient Hitler-like tendencies" around the same time.[70] But these fears were magnified considerably—and the rhetorical denunciations amplified accordingly—by the Walker affair and the revelations of the Fulbright memorandum and all its attendant controversy. The notion that dissident generals with the American military were not only members of the Society but apparently actively promoting its ideas was doubly combustible.

Milton Young's castigations of the Birch Society as a fascist group certainly reached new heights. Speaking in the Senate on July 14, 1961, the Republican from North Dakota declared the "organizers" of the Society in particular to be as serious a threat to the nation's security and way of life as the communist menace itself. "Only the lack so far, of M-1 rifles and a military organization separates the John Birch Society and its duce Mussolini, Robert Welch, from fascism and Nazism," the senator stated. "His doctrine is fascism and his goal is power. He is aping Adolf Hitler and using the tactics Hitler used on his road to power."[71]

The fear that the rise of the Birchers heralded a military-cum-fascist takeover of the country was one especially expressed by radical left-wing groups in the United States, including the Communist Party USA, the Socialist Party–Social Democratic Federation, and the Socialist Labor Party. Welch and Thurmond were not inventing things when they claimed that the *Worker* or the *People's World* were out to "get them" (although, as we have seen, this did not mean that such publications were the driving force behind some Moscow-directed conspiracy either). After all, the Birchers' program of "less government, more responsibility and a better world" was hardly one that was going to be warmly embraced by the communist or socialist-inspired Left in the United States; the direct exposure of such groups in Europe to the bitter, violent, and ultimately genocidal realities of fascism was always going to make their American counter-parts especially sensitive to the possibility of its emergence in the New World.[72]

Mike Newberry's forty-seven-page pamphlet *The Fascist Revival: The Inside Story of the John Birch Society* was published in June 1961. Emphasizing the prominent role of big businessmen (including past NAM presidents Cola G. Parker, F. Gano Chance, and William J. Grede) and retired military officers (such as Colonel Laurence E. Bunker and Lieutenant General Charles B. Stone) on the Birch Society National Council, Newberry argued that the organization was firmly in the grip of men "playing with fascism."[73] Indeed, as far as the *Worker* columnist was concerned, there were enough military men in its leader-ship "to form their own General Staff." Referring to Welch as the "Führer" throughout, Newberry attempted to explicate the rational political basis for the Birch Society's seeming hysterical anticommunism. Hitler had originated the anticommunist or anti-Comintern axis, he explained, and fascists always used this as their main propaganda weapon. "By blacklisting, persecuting, and jailing 'Communists,' the legal precedent and political foundation is established for the destruction of the liberties and rights of the whole people and the path to fascism is cleared of its first obstacle—democracy." Given the Birch Society's well-documented hostility to the "perennial fraud" of democracy, the implication was clear. Defending the "rights of the Communists" must be the "first line of defense of democracy," Newberry declared. The "fascist revival" would not be defeated otherwise.[74]

The general secretary of the American Communist Party, Gus Hall, incorporated the Walker affair, as well as the revelation of the existence of the secret 1958 NSC directive, into Newberry's analysis in an article in the *Worker* in July. (Although published in June, Newberry's pamphlet was clearly written prior to the news about General Walker's activities being made public.) It was the opinion of the Communist Party that "there can be no question but that the threat from the extreme right is serious," Hall wrote. Attributing the situation to changing international circumstances in which the United States, faced with wars of national liberation and the forces of socialism, could no longer have its way in the world unchallenged, Hall argued that the rise of the ultraright was a much more serious development and represented a much "greater threat than the movement led by the late Senator Joe McCarthy." Unlike previous "fascist currents," the present one being "spearheaded" by the Birch Society was not only taking the form of "a membership organization, in conspiratorial action groups, including secret military formation," it was also spreading its influence "among the higher military personnel." For Hall, though, the Walker case was merely "the symptom of a much deeper affliction." The effect of the 1958 NSC directive, in combination with "CIA and similar training in subversive and putschist activities, cannot help but create our own 'French generals,' who feel at home in Fascist circles, and are ready to lend themselves to their objectives." It was all an outgrowth of "20 years of militarization, of the close cooperation between the Armed Forces and monopoly in handling a $40 billion budget annually, and of a desperation born out of a bankrupt foreign policy."[75]

A Socialist Party-Social Democratic Federation (SP-SDF) pamphlet, *The American Ultras: The Extreme Right and the Military Industrial Complex*, appeared in 1962. Written by the organization's national secretary, Irwin Suall, it opened with an introduction by Norman Thomas, in which the six-time presidential candidate warned about the dangers facing the country from the John Birch Society and other "irrational groups" that were attempting to revive the politics of the "witchhunt" at home while making the "terrible war of the nuclear age" more likely abroad.[76] (Fear of a revival of the "dark times" of the McCarthy years was also a prominent theme in the Socialist Labor Party's pamphlet *"Rightism" Is American Fascism!* produced about the same time.)[77] Although its overall argument was the same as Newberry's and Hall's, Suall's pamphlet was much more detailed, wide-ranging, and nuanced in its analysis than that of his ostensible colleagues in the struggle. It also explicitly drew on the fallout from the Fulbright memorandum to bolster its assessment of the threat being posed by the Birch Society and its allies.[78]

"The American Ultras have strong connections with the leaders of powerful corporations; their activists are high in the military; and they can summon up community support across the nation from every know-nothing, bigoted and anti-democratic tendency in the land," Suall argued. However, not "every General [or] every corporate executive" could be said to belong to the movement. Rather, what the SP-SDF had uncovered in its investigation of the Birchers, Schwarz's Christian Anti-Communism Crusade, Hargis's Christian Crusade, Benson's Harding College, et al., was "a significant, and most dangerous, tendency for an important section of the military-industrial complex to put its enormous power behind right-wing extremism" in the United States. Like Hall, Suall attributed the rise of the "ultras" to the Cold War international crisis of the time. But he did not see them as "carbon copies" of the "classic" fascist movements of Mussolini's Italy, Franco's Spain, or Hitler's Germany. "There is no domestic unrest in American society capable of serving as a base for militant mass movements of the right," he argued. Nor did he see them as being on the brink of national power, or as standing ready to launch an imminent coup d'état, regarding such views as "hysterical."[79]

To Suall's mind, the threat was more insidious. "A good part of their power is organized on conspiratorial lines," he wrote. "Another part derives from the 'informal' workings of military and corporate elites, most of them out of sight. As a result, the extent of ultra strength is less visible than that of classic Fascism. And in so much as they succeed in imposing their doctrine upon the nation, they create the conditions for the advance of Communism and the further growth of Ultra sentiment." Yet despite the warnings, there was also a begrudging admiration for the energy and achievements of these activists of the ultraright. It was time the "Democratic Left got radical," Suall contended; it was time for it to "match the militancy and dedication of the resurgent right," and "gain a sense of history and purpose equal to that of the bosses and the brass." The civil rights movement had already demonstrated that working men and women had "the passion to fight for justice, to risk and to struggle," he said, and he urged all of "the liberal community . . . from the center on left" to unite in a common struggle. "The American Ultras are not a fascist menace right now," the pamphlet's final sentences proclaimed, "but they are a sign of the gravity of the crisis, of the conflicts to come. We will ignore this evidence at our peril."[80]

The most imaginative publication on the fascist nature of the radical Right in the United States at this time was a small book entitled *Birch Putsch Plans for 1964*.[81] Published in 1963, it claimed to be the story of "John Smith," the supposed pseudonym of a former associate of Robert Welch, whose position was so strongly against Welch's that he felt "his views should be public, but his name should not," as told to Stanhope T. McReady. (The book draws considerably on both Suall's *American Ultras* and Newberry's *Fascist Revival* for its content. Its style, though, hints strongly that Newberry might well have been its real author.) As its title suggests, the book purports to reveal secret plans that were afoot through the Birch Society to capture the White House in the 1964 presidential election in order to turn America into a totalitarian, fascist state. Welch himself was not the actual mastermind of this dramatic plot, however. Smith's "shocking" revelation was that Welch and his Society were merely acting as fronts on behalf of the real, malign power behind the scenes—a deeply mysterious and unidentified figure who, Smith said, "never speaks and never writes in public."[82] A profoundly conspiratorial text purporting to reveal the existence of an extraordinary conspiracy against democracy in the United States, the book concludes:

> The present-day radical right movement in the United States is not the handiwork of mentally-retarded persons, though such persons may be found among the millions of right radicals. It has been created by [an] intelligent and cunning group of conspirators, whose aim it is to change the system of government in the United States. Psychopaths are needed by the conspirators only to remove all those who are resisting the conspiracy, or who may do so in the future.
>
> Such is the ominous nature of the conspiracy being hatched by right-wing radicalism, by American fascism, which is out to seize power in our country.[83]

Enter the Minutemen

For those like Milton Young, who believed that the only thing standing between the Birchers and fascism was a military organization—as opposed to those like Hall, who believed they already had one—news that a paramilitary group led by a Birch Society member was preparing to "fight in the streets" as the country's "last line of defense" against communism was frightening in the extreme.[84] The group called itself the Minutemen and was led by Robert DePugh. (In October 1961, for example, police raided a meeting of nineteen Minutemen, including one woman and a boy, in Shiloh, Illinois, and recovered a large cache of weapons that included two Browning automatic rifles, a Browning machine gun, a M-14 rifle, and mortars.)[85] Speaking at a fund-raising dinner for the Democratic Party at the Hollywood Palladium on November 18, President Kennedy criticized both the Minutemen and the Birch Society in his most outspoken attack yet on the "discordant voices of extremism" at work in the nation. "There have always been those fringes of our society who have sought to escape their own responsibility by finding a simple solution, an appealing slogan, or a convenient scapegoat," he declared. "They look suspiciously at their neighbors and their leaders. They call for 'a man on horseback' because they do not trust the people. . . . They equate the Democratic party with the welfare state, the welfare state with socialism and socialism with communism. They object quite rightly to politics' intruding on the military—but they are anxious for the military to engage in politics." Warning against the dangers posed by "armed bands of civilian guerrillas" in particular, the president urged his fellow countrymen not to listen to such "counsels of fear and suspicion"—"to concentrate more on keeping enemy bombers and missiles away from our shores and . . . less on keeping neighbors away from our shelters."[86]

Appearing on NBC's *Meet the Press* the day after the president's speech, Barry Goldwater tried to find some room for maneuvering within these "discordant voices." The Minutemen were certainly a danger, he conceded, but not the Birch

Society, and in a foretaste of the partisan politics that would dominate the 1964 presidential election, he attacked the "extremists of the left" who surrounded Kennedy.[87] The apparent association between the Birch Society and forces of violence only increased in February 1962, however, when the homes of two clergymen were bombed as they were taking part in a panel discussion entitled "The Extreme Right—A Threat to Democracy?" sponsored by the Los Angeles Business and Professional chapter of the American Jewish Congress. The moderate California Republican senator Thomas Kuchel, who was soon to take over Milton Young's mantle as the most prominent critic of the Birch Society in Congress, responded to the bombings by denouncing the paranoia of the Minutemen and other "degenerate" extremists in the United States who, he said, were doing the work of the communist Left so well that Khrushchev himself would be "glad to be underwrite their expenses."[88]

Although DePugh was a Bircher—he would not be expelled from the Society until 1964—the Minutemen were not under Welch's control, and by no means did they operate as the Society's military wing. As John George and Laird Wilcox have noted, the organization, formed in 1960, was essentially "an extension of . . . DePugh's personality," a "one-man show" with only two hundred "genuine, active, committed" members and another four hundred on the periphery, contributing money or receiving its literature.[89] But it was also the case that DePugh and his small band of followers shared many of the same views as the Birch Society, especially concerning the threat of internal subversion in the United States—at least initially; DePugh's politics became increasingly erratic during the 1970s. Indeed, it was the fact that DePugh was trying to recruit members from the ranks of the Birchers that eventually led to his removal from the Society.[90] And certainly the association between the two groups was strong enough to enhance the claims of those who saw fascism on the march and, as a result, regarded the Birchers as "the most dangerous organization in America."[91]

Not surprisingly, the attempt to portray the Birch Society as fascists masquerading as "conservatives" or "patriots" was greatly resented and widely disputed both by Birchers themselves and by members of the wider anticommunist network in the United States. Appearing before Senate Subcommittee on Internal Security for its hearings into "The New Drive against the Anti-Communist Program" on July 11, 1961, Edward Hunter, one of America's leading experts on communist "brainwashing"—as well as one of the authorities relied upon in General Walker's Pro-Blue program—memorably contended, for example, that not "since the most virulent days of Goebbels' 'hate' propaganda" had anything appeared in the United States comparable to Mike Newberry's *The Fascist Revival*. The booklet's publication and its "vituperative" tone were evidence that the Communist Party would like to "create a new, Pavlovian trigger word for this period in its psychological warfare, and believes 'Birchite' might be put into the language this way, replacing 'McCarthyite,'" Hunter explained. This new "scare word" would "evoke a conditioned response in a background of fear, founded on the specter of a Fascist plot inside the United States, which would attack all minorities, and spread terror to everyone." It was classic "psywar" and evidence that the CPUSA was working hand in hand with the "Red network headquartered in Moscow."[92]

A. J. MacDonald of the Los Angeles-based Political Research Bureau in his 1963 pamphlet *Kangaroo Court versus The John Birch Society* advanced a similar argument in defense of the Society. Although not a Bircher himself, he was "deeply disturbed" by the attempt to smear the Society as "fascist-" and "Nazi minded." The campaign bore all the hallmarks of the "international Communist conspiracy," he said; radicals, pseudoliberals, and "prostituted intellectuals" had joined forces in the "most gigantic witch-hunt of modern times."[93] The sympathetically inclined California Senate's Un-American Activities Sub-committee also defended the Society, eventually reporting in 1963 that it had found no evidence that the Society was "a secret, fascist, subversive, un-American, anti-Semitic organization."[94]

One does not have to embrace the hyperbolic, conspiratorial reasoning of Hunter and MacDonald, or embroil oneself too deeply in the fiercely contested realm of fascism studies, to suggest that attempts to characterize the Birch Society as a fascist political organization are somewhat problematic. Even if one could agree on a definition of what fascism is, or was—and no one can—there is the added complication, to which both Hunter and MacDonald allude, that the term itself has become, to a considerable extent, a very widely deployed and effective term of political abuse (as the Birch Society's opponents knew only too well). Nonetheless, we can argue that the Birch Society failed to manifest enough of what might be called the generally agreed upon characteristics of fascism to warrant the classification.[95] The contentions of his critics notwithstanding, Welch displayed none of the traits of the fascist charismatic leader, and he did not evoke any of the typical responses in his "followers." Nor did he—or the Society as a whole—regard capitalism as fundamentally deficient or socially divisive; on the contrary, both Welch and the Birchers extolled its virtues as the very engine of American progress and prosperity. Indeed, Mussolini's and Hitler's attempts to "harness the economy to a centrally conceived national goal without resorting to socialism or communism" (as described by the historian Alan Brinkley) would have been anathema to Birchers.[96] Anti-Semitism is also not a trait that can be convincingly attributed to the John Birch Society, as the California Senate's Un-American Activities Subcommittee noted correctly.[97] More philosophically, Welch had an entirely traditional view of the basic constraints of human nature and its eternal "truths" in contrast to the fascists' belief in the mutability and perfectibility of man. Finally, no ringing declarations of the transcendent power or extraordinary destiny of the *Volk* are to be found embedded in the Society's literature.

To be sure, the Birch Society was virulently anticommunist and extremely suspicious about the merits of democracy—other commonly agreed-upon fascist traits—but the former view was shared by the overwhelming majority of American society at the time, and the latter had led Welch to embrace not fascism but an older, republican-based model of American politics. This is not to say that there weren't fascistically inclined or anti-Semitic individuals within the Birch Society—Mike Newberry's description of National Council member and arch–conspiracy theorist Professor Revilo P. Oliver as a "philosopher of American fascism" is certainly not too far wide of the mark.[98] It is also not to ignore the fact that many of the most important figures of the postwar American extreme Right (including Willis Carto, George Lincoln Rockwell, Ben Klassen, Tom Metzger, and Robert Jay Matthews) passed through or were associated with the Society at some period in their lives. But the crucial point is that they passed *through* the Society; they left, or were expelled from the organization, because it failed to meet their political needs.[99] What's more, to focus only on the "extremists" who once belonged the Society is to ignore the many more mainstream conservatives and thousands of ordinary Americans who also joined or were equally associated with the Society at one point or another. (Hillary Clinton was a "Goldwater Girl," after all.)[100]

Before leaving the subject, however, it is also important to acknowledge the entirely understandable reasons why worries about a potential fascist uprising in the United States were so pronounced at this particular point in time. The horrors of the Second World War had occurred only sixteen years earlier, after all; and if anyone needed any extra reminder of those horrors, the trial of Adolf Eichmann, which began on April 11, 1961—almost contemporaneously with the Walker affair—no doubt provided it.[101] During those sixteen years, moreover, the melding of communism and fascism into a combined totalitarian "Red Fascist" threat was another widely embraced notion, one the "authoritarian" Birch Society could readily be subsumed within.[102]

The Reuther Memorandum

In the changed context of the Walker case, the Fulbright memo, and the emergence of the Minutemen, Robert Kennedy moved away from his earlier expressed position, which had been that perhaps the best way of dealing with the radical Right was not to pay it a great deal of attention. In the fall of 1961, he asked the leaders of the United Automobile Workers union and close confidants of the Kennedys, Walter P. Reuther and Victor G. Reuther, together with the civil rights lawyer Joseph L. Rauh Jr., to prepare a memorandum on the situation. (Walter Reuther in particular had had a great deal of first-hand experience in dealing with the radical Right as a consequence of his own political and union activities.)[103] Details of the group's recommendations were leaked to the press shortly after the memorandum was sent to the attorney general on December 19, 1961. When combined with the also supposedly "secret" recommendations of Senator Fulbright, the news—hardly surprisingly—merely increased the agitation of the groups whose activities it was intended to curtail.

Focused on the familiar suspects of the Birch Society, Schwarz's Christian Anti-Communism Crusade, Hargis's Christian Crusade, and Benson's Harding College, along with the more recently formed Minutemen, the Reuther memorandum warned that the radical Right was stronger and "almost certainly better organized than at any time in recent history. More significant yet, they are growing in strength and there is no reason to expect a turning of the tide in this regard during the foreseeable Cold War period ahead. And, possibly most significant of all, their relationship to and infiltration of the Armed Services adds a new dimension to the seriousness with which they must be viewed."[104] The "infiltration" of the military by the forces of the radical Right was clearly the cause of the greatest concern for the Reuther brothers and Rauh. Citing, like Fulbright, the French military's revolt against de Gaulle's Algerian policy as evidence of the potential dangers facing the country, the memorandum urged the administration to "get off the defensive" in the Walker case in particular (the memorandum was written before the Senate Preparedness Subcommittee hearings, it should be noted).[105] The "degree of tolerance" for radical right-wing views within the armed forces was shocking, the memorandum argued, and having given the appropriate warnings Secretary of Defense McNamara should start dismissing those generals and admirals who had "lost confidence in democracy and who feel that the danger to our country is treason at home rather than the strength of the international Communist movement abroad."[106]

Indeed, the memo's stress throughout was on the need for *action* on the part of the Kennedy administration. There should be "deliberate Administration policies and programs to contain the radical right from further expansion and in the long run to reduce it to its historic role of the impotent lunatic fringe," it said.[107] The attorney general's "subversive list" should be expanded to include right-wing extremists. The FBI should begin infiltrating such groups, their tax-exempt status investigated by the IRS, and the radio and television licenses of stations broadcasting their programs revoked. As for the Minutemen, immediate steps needed to be taken for their disbandment. "There is no warrant for permitting groups to organize into military cadres for the purpose of taking the law into their own hands," the memo declared.[108]

More broadly—and most revealingly of all perhaps—the Reuther memorandum recommended a substantial toning down of anticommunist rhetoric in the United States. The radical Right fed on charges of "treason, traitors and treachery," it explained. Its roots were in the "very real sense" among the American people that "domestic Communism has succeeded in betraying America and threatens its very survival." Putting the domestic communist threat "in proper perspective" was therefore likely to alleviate much of the problem. Every administration since the end of World War II had "maximized the Communist problem," the memo declared, but there was no longer any need to "dramatize the domestic Communist issue." Reflecting back the Kennedy administration's own preference for a more flexible approach to the Cold War, its authors argued that the need now was "to rein in those who have created the unreasoned fear of the domestic Communist movement in the minds of the American people and slowly to develop a more rational attitude toward the strength of this movement." Fifteen years of "overstating a problem" could hardly be reversed overnight, and it was admittedly somewhat "late in the day" to begin dealing with the all the problems of "radical right Generals and Admirals and Minutemen," the Reuthers and Rauh admitted, but, they said, it would also "never get earlier."[109]

As Phillip Finch has written, the Reuther memorandum is not necessarily one of the "nobler legacies" of the Kennedy years, encouraging as it does the use of presidential power and influence to destroy troublesome political opponents.[110] (It also seems to prefigure the notorious "enemies list" of the Nixon White House, as well as the more recent controversy over the "targeting" of Tea Party and other conservative groups by the IRS during the Obama administration.)[111] But the extent to which any of the memo's recommendations were actually implemented and against whom is not entirely clear. Robert Goldstein, in his 1978 study of political repression in the United States from 1870 to 1976, argues that with the exception of the American Nazi Party, for example, one of the striking features of the Kennedy administration was the "immunity" of extreme right-wing groups like the John Birch Society from "official harassment, even though their influence was far greater than that exerted by the CP [Communist Party] or other left-wing remnants" at the time.[112] More recent research by John A. Andrew shows that the IRS was indeed deployed against the Birch Society and Hargis's Christian Crusade, among other right-wing organizations, in just the way the Reuther memorandum recommended, but the question of whether such activities should be understood as an example of "political repression" as opposed, say, to simply enforcing a nation's already-existent laws is an open one.[113] What is more certain, however, is that the memo was swiftly pounced upon by the radical Right as further evidence—as if any more was needed— of the Kennedy regime's perfidious nature, as well as its "softness" toward the whole communist problem.[114] It also provided a ready-made explanation for any subsequent difficulties or travails such groups might face in the future.[115]

Takeover

Fears about the military seizing power in the United States and about the extent to which groups like the John Birch Society had infiltrated the armed forces were not to be found just in the political realm during the early 1960s; they were a common feature of the period's cultural landscape. One of the top ten bestselling books of 1962, for instance, was Fletcher Knebel and Charles W. Bailey II's *Seven Days in May*. Written in the fall of 1961—in the aftermath of the Bay of Pigs invasion and in direct response to the Walker affair and the issues it raised about civilian control of the armed services—the novel is set in a slightly futuristic 1974. It concerns an attempted coup d'état organized by the chairman of the Joint Chiefs of Staff, four-star air force general James Mattoon Scott, and his allies in the U.S. military and elsewhere—including what is referred to throughout as the right-wing "lunatic fringe" of American politics—against the presidency of Jordan Lyman, an Ohio Democrat, who has just signed a nuclear disarmament treaty with the Soviet Union. The plot is uncovered by the director of the Joint Staff, Marine colonel Martin "Jiggs" Casey, who reveals it to the president and thus sets in motion a race against time—the seven days of the book's title—to prevent the coup from taking place.[116]

Knebel and Bailey were both Washington correspondents and the book is filled with pointed real-life references to General Walker, the Birch Society,

Joe McCarthy, and Douglas MacArthur. It is even prefaced with a quotation from Eisenhower's farewell address warning about the dangers of the nation's military-industrial complex. This mixing of the real and the fictional is well illustrated in the following expository disquisition by President Lyman to his advisers on the problems facing the (real) United States in the nuclear age and the reason for General Scott's appeal in the (fictional) nation:

> In a monolithic state—and that's what Russia has been for centuries, under czars and commissars both—people never get used to influencing their government, and they don't miss it. But a democracy is different. Each of us has got to feel that we can influence events, no matter how slight the influence. When people start believing they can't they get frustrated, and angry. They feel helpless and they start going to extremes. Look at the history—Joe McCarthy, then the Birch Society, now the popularity of this fanatic MacPherson.

> . . . People have seriously started looking for a superman. . . . Wise men . . . know that there aren't any supermen. . . . The trouble is that democracy works only when a good majority of citizens are willing to give thought and time and effort to their government. The nuclear age, by killing man's faith in his ability to influence what happens, could destroy the United States even if no bombs were ever dropped. That's why I decided I had to bring off that treaty if it was the only thing I ever did.

> . . . I don't know if it's enough, though. Maybe it's coming too late. The climate for democracy is the worst it's ever been. Maybe General Scott thinks he holds salvation in his hands. If he does, he's pitifully mistaken, and I feel sorry for him.[117]

The reference to MacPherson is to one of Scott's non-military accomplices, Harold MacPherson, a radio and television personality, who is the character most clearly associated with the Birch Society in the novel, and, along with the "fascistic" Colonel Broderick, one of its most dislikable.[118] Lyman reports at one point, for example, that the FBI "has quite a file" on him, and that he belongs to "several of those far-right-wing groups. A couple of them [with] a lot of retired military men in their memberships."[119]

The novel was turned into a film by director John Frankenheimer and screenwriter Rod Serling (of *Twilight Zone* renown) in 1963, with Burt Lancaster as Scott, Kirk Douglas as Casey, Fredric March as Lyman, and Hugh Marlowe as McPherson.[120] Made with the encouragement and cooperation of JFK, who had apparently read and enjoyed the novel—the president even moved out of the White House for a few days so that filming could take place there—the film is a reasonably faithful depiction of the novel's story and themes; the most notable addition is a *cinéma vérité*-style opening depicting a demonstration against the ratification of Lyman's treaty with the Soviets which ends in a riot (a quick and effective illustration of the tensions both in the film and in the real United States of the time). The film was not released until 1964, after Kennedy's death and also after the ratification of the Nuclear Test Ban Treaty of 1963. The eighteen senators who voted against the treaty, including Strom Thurmond, Margaret Chase Smith, and Barry Goldwater, were all reserve officers in either the U.S. Army or Air Force.[121]

Frankenheimer had already made a significant contribution to the Cold War thriller genre with his 1962 film *The Manchurian Candidate*, based on Richard Condon's 1959 novel. Both film and book address a dizzying array of contemporary issues surrounding communist subversion, mind control, right-wing extremism, propaganda, media spectacle, familial and sexual anxiety, and political paranoia in the United States.[122] The plot revolves around Sergeant Raymond Shaw (Lawrence Harvey in the film) who, along with other members of his unit, including Major Ben Marco (Frank Sinatra), is captured and "brainwashed" by Sino-Soviet forces during the Korean War. Programmed to kill, Shaw is returned to the United States and the dubious and sinister care of his Soviet agent mother (wonderfully played by Angela Lansbury), as part of a plan to assassinate the presidential nominee and install Shaw's stepfather, the buffoonish, McCarthyesque senator Johnny Iselin (James Gregory) in his place as a Moscow stooge. Major Marco foils the plot at the last minute after his own brainwashing has unraveled.

J. Hoberman has suggested that Condon's novel functions as a "comic version" of Robert Welch's *The Politician*. Both the book and the film's depiction of Shaw and Marco's brainwashing as taking place—from their "altered" perspective—during a ladies garden club meeting certainly, if perhaps not intentionally, calls to mind Mosk's description of Birchers as "little old ladies in tennis shoes." But overall *The Manchurian Candidate*'s engagement with the politics of the "ultras" is much less overt than in *Seven Days in May*.[123] The brainwashing theme, though, was one that had a great deal of resonance both for Birchers and within the wider culture of the time.

The term itself was the coinage of Edward Hunter in his 1951 book, *Brainwashing in Red China*; he believed it to be the literal translation of the Chinese *hsi-nao*. But it did not come into widespread use—with Hunter as its most effective popularizer—until the Korean War. ("Menticide," the term employed by Hunter's great rival Joost Meerloo, did not catch on in quite the same way.)[124] It was the apparent vulnerability of large numbers of American POWs to the mind control techniques of their communist captors in Korea, combined with their more generally lamentable performance in captivity (which the journalist Eugene Kinkead famously characterized as "give-up-itis" in a 1957 *New Yorker* article)—not to mention the war's frustrating stalemate—that Condon and Frankenheimer were drawing on in their work.[125] They were the same issues that had motivated the adoption of the 1958 NSC directive on the need for better and more coordinated efforts by the United States to fight the Cold War. They were a particular motivation for Walker's Pro-Blue program; and they also occupied a great deal of time during the Senate Preparedness Subcommittee hearings into the military's education and speech review policies.[126]

Discussing the failings of American troops in Korea and the differences

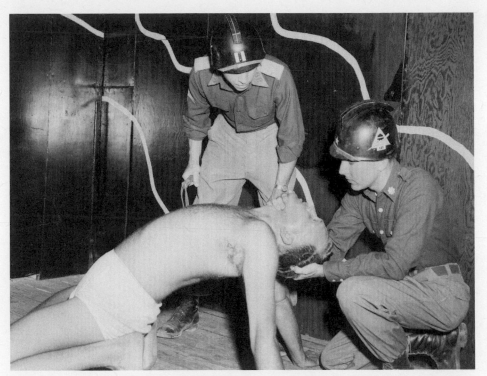

Figure 3.1. A U.S. airman takes part in antibrainwashing training at Stead Air Force Base in Nevada, September 1955. In defending the seventeen-day course, the Air Force argued that it did not "degrade or break down" those who took part in it. © Bettmann/CORBIS

between them and those who had fought in World War II during the Senate subcommittee hearings, Lieutenant Colonel William E. Mayer of the U.S. Army Medical Corps lamented, for example, that those in Korea were generally "more dependent people, psychologically, upon outside authority," showed "less initiative," and had "less inclination to initiate action than was characteristic of our soldiers 15 years ago." It was these "striking" differences, Mayer explained, that had made American soldiers especially vulnerable to communist brainwashing techniques. Connecting the problem with the wider Cold War struggle, he said that the communists had devised such an effective system of "controlling people" because "they have not only taken over roughly 40 percent of the human race, but they are successfully controlling this quantity of the human race in a tyranny which is increasingly oppressive, which has grown rapidly, which is remarkably intrusive, and because they have never been threatened by anything which could be termed a revolution."[127]

In this, Mayer was echoing the views of Edward Hunter, among many others, about the intentions behind the whole communist experiment. "The war against men's minds has for its primary objective the creation of what is euphemistically called [the] 'new Soviet man,'" Hunter wrote in his 1956 book, *Brainwashing: From Pavlov to Powers*:

The intent is to change a mind radically so that its owner becomes a living puppet—a human robot—without the atrocity being visible from the outside. The aim is to create a mechanism in flesh and blood, with new beliefs and new thought processes inserted into a captive body. What that amounts to is the search for a slave race that, unlike the slaves of olden times, can be trusted never to revolt, always to be amenable to orders, like an insect to its instincts. The intent is to atomize humanity.[128]

Fortunately, Mayer and Hunter were both of the view that such efforts could be resisted. The communists might have created a "tyranny exceeding in effectiveness any previous tyranny," Mayer said, but they had not "devised anything that ordinary, properly informed, healthy young Americans cannot beat" if they were properly trained and prepared.[129]

Indeed, one of the few things General Walker's supporters and opponents could agree upon—with the notable exception of Senator Fulbright—was what one of Walker's early detractors, William Proxmire, said was the need for American troops to be "*indoctrinated* in freedom."[130] No contradiction was to be found in such a seemingly Orwellian desire—one expressed by many involved throughout the Walker affair, including Senators Thurmond, Mundt, and Goldwater. It merely reflected the widely expressed sentiment of the time, which held that the United States was suffering under what historian Susan Carruthers has called an "ideology gap": the belief that without considerable help—and a great propagandizing effort—the rather ill-defined American "way of life" would be no match for the "concrete, all-encompassing political philosophy" that was being relentlessly drummed into the unfortunate, zombified communist inhabitants of "Totalitaria."[131]

The Birch Society articulated these concerns as forcefully as any other group in American society during this period. In fact, they were an almost constant feature of its rhetorical architecture. In the February 1960 issue of the *Bulletin*, for example, Welch argued that one of the main things the Society was trying to prevent was the "conversion of our civilization into a collection of standardized robots." And on January 1, 1961, he warned that unless the Birchers were successful, the nation's children—and their children after them—would live "as pitiful robots in the misery, and under the terrorism, of a world-wide police state" just as Nikita Khrushchev himself had "prophesized."[132] Such arguments spoke to wider understandings about the difference between "free" and "captive" nations and peoples during the Cold War. But the tropes and imagery of brainwashing were used in other ways too. Welch considered the American people themselves as having been "so brainwashed and befuddled" by pro-communist propaganda that they could no longer recognize "idiocy or treason" in their own government. He denounced the "institutions of higher brainwashing" for preventing conservative scholars from making their way in the academy. And he argued that the Birch Society should focus its recruitment efforts on the "more literate and more intelligent" section of the American public who had "not yet been completely brainwashed," and who could see "how far and how completely Communists and Communist influences" had crept into their communities.[133]

Yet perhaps the most interesting example of a Birch Society member's use of the motif is to be found in crime novelist Elizabeth Linington's 1965 recruitment tome, *Come to Think of It—*. In the book, Linington—who wrote prolifically under the pseudonyms Dell Shannon, Lesley Egan, Egan O'Neill, and Anne Blaisdell—describes her own personal "awakening" after new neighbors move into the house next door, and the husband, whom she identifies only as Mr. John Doe, turns out to be a member of the John Birch Society. ("I knew this man was definitely not anti-Semitic personally, nor was he a 'racist'; he had an extremely tolerant and broadminded attitude toward Negroes," she writes; and he "was about the last man I could imagine being a fanatic of any kind.")[134] As a result of these initial conversations, Linington begins a "little investigating" of her own that leads to her eventual recognition that the Birch Society is the only organization that can do something about the dangers facing the nation. "It's an odd and frightening feeling," she says, when others can't see for themselves that "it is happening here"—that the "enemy [is] in the process of secretly preparing to take over." This sense of frustration leads to the following extraordinary passage, one that recalls nothing so much as the justly famous final scene of the very urtext of Cold War anxiety, subversion, and "alien" infiltration, the 1956 film *Invasion of the Body Snatchers*. "All these unaware people walking the streets, shopping, planning bridge-club meetings, talking about where to go on vacation next summer," Linington writes: "You want to scream at them— because you know. It's happening, the Enemy is here and now, we're far, far down the road to enslavement—listen to me! Stop and listen—none of these little things could matter less, because if you *don't* listen, and find out, and *do* something about it, by next year or the year after or the year after that . . . you and your bridge club will be sharing quarters in a concentration camp, and no more vacations ever again. *Listen—*"[135]

Walker, Oswald, Extremism, and the Cold War

On February 2, 1962, the now Mr. Edwin A. Walker announced that he would be running as a Democratic candidate for governor of Texas.[136] His performance during the campaign showed that his less than inspiring appearance before the Senate Preparedness Subcommittee had been no one-off. Walker was a poor public speaker and a lackluster candidate for high political office. As the historian Clive Webb has observed, like many other former military men entering the political arena, Walker "lacked the populist touch and assumed that leadership was something he deserved rather than needed to earn."[137] The former general finished dead last in a field of six in the Democratic primary, receiving only 134,000 of the 1,400,000 votes cast. It was only during the campaign that Walker finally admitted he was a member of the John Birch Society, telling reporters that he had joined in 1959—although he claimed never to have attended another meeting thereafter.[138]

In October 1962, Walker was charged with "inciting rebellion or insurrection" and detained for psychiatric testing following his involvement in a riot in Oxford, Mississippi, over the admission of James Meredith as the first African American student to the University of Mississippi. The charges were subsequently dropped (see Chapter 4).[139] Then, on the evening of April 10, 1963, Walker was the subject of an assassination attempt by Lee Harvey Oswald, who fired at him—and only narrowly missed—using the same high-powered rifle Oswald would employ to kill President Kennedy seven months later, while Walker was working quietly on his income tax return in the dining room of his Dallas, Texas, home. (Walker died of natural causes in 1993, aged eighty-three.)[140]

The attempt against Walker's life was uncovered only when the Warren Commission investigated Kennedy's death. Depending on which Kennedy assassination theory one adheres to, it was a consequence of Oswald needing to demonstrate to his KGB case officer that he was capable of pulling off the president's killing; a hatred of the former general's "fascist" right-wing politics; Oswald's desire to make a name for himself; or simply psychosis.[141] The Warren Commission, relying on the testimony of Oswald's widow, Marina, contended that it was because Oswald was concerned about "his place in history," and because he believed Walker to be comparable to Adolf Hitler and that "if someone had killed Hitler in time it would have saved many lives."[142]

There is also the tantalizing suggestion—in an admittedly macabre example of life-imitating-art-imitating-life—that Oswald may have been "inspired" to kill both Walker and Kennedy by his viewing of Frankenheimer's *The Manchurian Candidate*. Whether or not this was the case—and even advocates of the argument admit that it cannot be proved conclusively that Oswald ever watched the film, although it was certainly playing in and around Dallas, where Oswald was living at the time, in late 1962—it is certainly true that Frank Sinatra withdrew the film from circulation for twenty-four years, shortly after the president's murder (although whether this was out of grief or guilt about Kennedy's death, or because of a dispute with its distributor United Artists over money, is itself a matter of dispute).[143] In any event, one of the most significant effects of Kennedy's assassination, as will be discussed further in the following chapter, was to illustrate in the most graphic way imaginable the dangers of extremist politics in the United States, especially right-wing politics. (This was a little ironic given Oswald's Marxist leanings, not to mention his attempt to kill Walker, but it was based, in part, on Dallas's well-earned reputation as a veritable bastion of right-wing extremism in the country.) Kennedy's death also fostered an explosive growth in America's conspiracy culture, of course.

The frustrations and anxieties of the Cold War were already doing a great deal of work in this area. Exemplified by the Walker affair—which was itself crucially magnified in its perceived importance and political impact by the general's apparent association with the Birch Society and other like-minded activists—

we have seen in this chapter how various groups and individuals, conservative and liberal, anticommunist and antifascist, were tightly bound together in a conspiratorial dance of suspicion and fear, whether about a potential military takeover of the country or the totalitarian possibilities of brainwashing.[144] This sense of mutual dependency was also much evidence in the 1964 presidential election campaign, which we now turn to examine.

Chapter 3

Extremism

As the campaign season formally got under way at the end of August 1964, the *New York Times* reporter Anthony Lewis predicted that whether the contenders liked it or not, there would be three key themes in the fast-approaching presidential election: civil rights, the nation's nuclear policy, and extremism.[1] In reality the three issues were closely intertwined. For example, the Democratic Party nominee, Lyndon Johnson, was seen in many quarters as an extremist for having successfully achieved the passage of the Civil Rights Act of 1964, while his Republican counterpart, Senator Barry Goldwater, was regarded as an extremist for having voted against it (on the basis of states' rights rather than any racist grounds, the Arizonan attested).[2] The Democrats also worked especially hard—and very effectively—to suggest that Goldwater was too unstable and too dangerous to be given the opportunity to put his finger on the nation's nuclear button. This was exemplified by probably the most famous campaign advertisement in American politics, the "Daisy ad," which managed to damn Goldwater without even mentioning his name by depicting a sweet little girl innocently picking flower petals in a meadow as an ominous male voice counted down to the explosion of a nuclear device.[3]

This approach by the Democrats was made all the more plausible by Goldwater's acceptance speech at the Republican national convention in San Francisco on July 15, with its especially damaging declaration that "extremism in the defense of liberty is no vice" and "moderation in the pursuit of justice is no virtue."[4] Indeed, in Lewis's view the question of political extremism had not really been an election issue until Goldwater made his speech. This, though, is to ignore the extent to which the "extremist" label had dogged Goldwater—and conservatism more generally—for a considerable time prior to the events at the Cow Palace. Goldwater may have played into the Democratic Party's hands with his "defense" of extremism, but the issue was already sitting squarely on the table, as the governor of New York, Nelson Rockefeller, had more than demonstrated during the Republican primaries, and the Democrats were always going to use it against him.

The John Birch Society played a crucial role in the various debates taking place about extremism in American society during this time, not only with respect to the Goldwater campaign, but also in terms of broader discussions about the "legitimacy" of conservatism as a political philosophy and its effectiveness in achieving practical political power. This chapter examines these debates and contestations, including the fallout from the assassination of President Kennedy and fears that Birchers were secretly maneuvering to achieve a takeover of the Republican Party (as California attorney general Mosk had warned about back in 1961). Throughout, as we shall see, the participants in them often struggled to arrive at a clear understanding of what "extremism" actually was—other than a highly partisan, polemical label that could be deployed to discredit the positions of your opponents while adding luster to your own.

Who Speaks for American Conservatism?
William F. Buckley Jr., *National Review*,
and the Question of Robert Welch

Conservatism in the United States was at a very low ebb at the end of the Second World War because of the combined achievements, electoral as well as practical, of Franklin D. Roosevelt's New Deal coalition and the new warfare state, both of which transformed American political culture in the years between 1933 and 1945.[5] By the late 1950s and early 1960s, however, owing to the intellectual efforts of a diverse group of thinkers (including Friedrich A. Hayek, Whittaker Chambers, Richard Weaver, James Burnham, Peter Viereck, and Russell Kirk), changing domestic and international circumstances (not the least of which was the onset of the Cold War), and the considerable energies of the movement's activists and popularizers, the situation was beginning to be turned around. As the grand chronicler of this oft-told story, George H. Nash, points out, the period from the mid-1950s to the mid-1960s were important years of "self-definition" and "preparation" for the conservative movement in the United States—the years when the American Right made "its first significant forays out of the wilderness."[6]

Although the John Birch Society, along with other members of the radical Right, is usually pushed to the margins of this story as conservatism's "lunatic fringe," it actually played a crucial role in conservatism's revival in at least two senses.[7] First, it provided a considerable amount of direction, energy, guidance, inspiration, and resources, within a well-organized institutional framework, for would-be conservative activists at a point when they needed it most. Robert Welch was not exaggerating when he claimed—as he did frequently, during the Society's early years—that there was "a new force" upon the conservative scene.[8] The rapid growth of the Birch Society and its almost uncanny ability, as we have already seen, to draw attention to itself and its causes and activities demonstrated as much. (The Society claimed to have eighty thousand members by 1961, although outsider observers put the figure closer to sixty thousand. It also had twenty-eight staff working in its Belmont, Massachusetts, headquarters, thirty full-time traveling coordinators, one hundred partially paid or volunteer coordinators, and an annual revenue of $1.6 million.)[9]

The second and perhaps even more important way in which the Society contributed to the conservatives' errand out of the "wilderness" was by providing something for more "respectable" conservatives to define themselves *against* and differentiate themselves *from*. This became particularly important as the amount of negative publicity about the Birchers grew, and the more widely they became viewed as the paradigmatic example of right-wing extremism in the United States. The crucial dynamic in this respect was the one between William F. Buckley Jr., creator and editor in chief of the movement's premier publication, *National Review*, and Welch, as the Birch Society's leader and founder. The relationship was so important because by the early 1960s, Buckley was beginning to function as a kind of gatekeeper for the conservative movement as a whole—in the process of self-definition going on within conservative ranks, more often than not it fell to Buckley and his *National Review* colleagues to decide who was to be counted in, and who was to be left out.[10]

The movement's enfant terrible, and later its patron saint, Buckley possessed credentials that were certainly impressive.[11] Born in 1925 to wealthy Roman Catholic parents, he published his first book at the age of twenty-six, in 1951: *God and Man at Yale* was an impassioned attack on his alma mater for its abandonment of both Christianity and free enterprise economics. His second, *McCarthy and His Enemies*, a muscular defense of the Wisconsin senator that turned on the distinction between McCarthy the man and the–*ism* that bore his name, appeared in 1954. (Buckley wrote it with his brother-in-law, L. Brent Bozell Jr., who would go on to ghostwrite Goldwater's *The Conscience of a Conservative* in 1960.) In 1955, with the aid of Willi Schlamm, Buckley founded *National Review*, a new weekly conservative news magazine, and began staffing it with some of the brightest stars in the burgeoning conservative universe, including James Burnham, Russell Kirk, Whittaker Chambers, Frank Chodorov, Willmoore Kendall, and the novelist John Dos Passos. William Rusher became the magazine's publisher in 1957, and by 1961 it had a circulation of fifty-four thousand (in 1964, the figure was ninety thousand).[12]

National Review was the forum in which the three strands of American conservatism—libertarianism, traditionalism, and anticommunism—struggled for intellectual dominance and eventually became "fused" together.[13] But it was also one of the movement's key institutional organizers—helping to create the conservative student organization Young Americans for Freedom in 1960, and the New York Conservative Party in 1961, for instance—and spreader of the word.[14] And initially, at least, Buckley and Welch were on the same page when it came to the revival and strengthening of conservatism in the United States. They shared all the key tenets of the conservative faith, including a reverence for Senator McCarthy, and both were committed to—and skilled in—the arts of political activism and publicity generation. Certainly, Welch could have been speaking for them both when he wrote in *The Blue Book* that the "greatest enemy of man is, and always has been, government. And the larger, the more extensive that government, the greater the enemy." In contrast to the collectivist, the "true *americanist*"—Welch used "Americanist" (usually capitalized), "conservative," and "anticommunist" as virtual synonyms—"believes that the individual should retain the freedom to make his own bargain with life, and the responsibility for the results of that bargain; and that means are as important as ends in the civilized social order which he desires."[15] Buckley and Welch also both rejected the "Modern Republicanism" of Dwight Eisenhower, wanting it to be replaced by "real" conservatism. Not that Buckley and Welch were alone in such a view. According to William Rusher, for instance, "modern American conservatism largely organized itself during, and in explicit opposition to, the Eisenhower Administration."[16]

Welch was also one of the original investors in *National Review*, buying $1,000 of Buckley's privately issued stock to help get the magazine off the ground in 1955, and another $1,000 in 1957.[17] In a letter thanking him for the first contribution, Buckley referred to Welch as "the author of two of the finest pamphlets this country has read in a decade [*May God Forgive Us* (1952) and *The Life of John Birch* (1954)]," and promised him that the new publication would "synchronize" the currently "desperately isolated voices" of conservatism in the United States and "make the country at last listen to a growing unisono."[18] Yet there were also tensions between the two men—tensions that centered, not surprisingly, on the conspiracism so often at the root of Welch's politics.

In November 1958, for example, Buckley wrote to Welch to ask for a copy of *The Politician*, which had been privately doing the rounds of prominent conservatives. As did almost every other response to the manuscript, inside and outside the conservative movement, Buckley's reaction to the letter, once he had read it, focused on Welch's claims about Eisenhower. "I for one disavow your hypotheses. I do not even find them plausible. I find them—curiously— almost pathetically optimistic," he wrote. "If Eisenhower were what you think he is, then the elimination of Eisenhower would be a critical step in setting things aright. In my view things will not get better but very possibly worse when Eisenhower leaves the White House. And the reason for this is that virtually the entire nation is diseased as a result of the collapse of our faith. We suffer, as Richard Weaver so persuasively concludes, from anomie, from which we are not likely to emerge with our whole skins, barring a miracle."[19] Buckley was just as hostile to communism—and collectivism—as Welch, of course, but he rejected the reductive explanation that communism and communist conspiracies were responsible for all the nation's ills, seeing them as a product of a much wider decline in religious, moral, and political standards. Just like later liberal critics— the Kennedy brothers, William Fulbright, Walter Reuther et al.—Buckley and his *National Review* colleagues were in basic agreement with Welch about the external threat posed to the United States by the USSR, but they completely rejected his assessment of the *internal* threat communism posed. (Or, as Russell Kirk more memorably and more pithily put it a couple of years later: "Eisenhower's not a Communist—he's a golfer.")[20]

Buckley was also disturbed to discover, following the formation of the Birch Society in December 1958 (of which Welch informed him in an "off the record" letter in January), that a number of people connected with *National Review*, including Spruille Braden, Clarence Manion, and Revilo P. Oliver, had become members of its National Council, and that Willi Schlamm—who had resigned from the magazine in 1957—and *National Review* writer Medford Evans were on *American Opinion*'s editorial board. In addition, *National Review*'s most important financial backer, the textile magnate Roger Milliken, had also become a member of the Society.[21] Determined to criticize the Birch Society's views—although whether this was for intellectual reasons or because he wanted to fire a shot across the bow of a potential rival in the conservative movement is not entirely clear—Buckley authorized the publication, in April 1959, of an article by the former communist Eugene Lyons that took Welch to task for arguing that Boris Pasternak's novel *Doctor Zhivago* had been "censored" by the Soviet authorities in order to trick the West into accepting what was really an anticapitalist work.[22] The generally negative response to Lyons's article as an attack on "fellow conservatives" was such, however, that Buckley was forced to back off. Medford Evans, for example, told Buckley that in his view, "*National Review* should refrain from making any criticism of other conservative periodicals except in the one case when we earnestly feel that a spokesman for conservatism has made a grievous error."[23]

In their exchange of correspondence at the end of 1959, Welch had told Buckley that "at least ninety-five percent" of those who had read the manuscript of *The Politician* "completely *agree* with one or the other of my two conclusions, and invariably state that it makes no difference, so far as the tragic results are concerned, as to which is right."[24] A truce had been easier to maintain while the contents of *The Politician* remained confined to inner conservative circles, but became much less so once they became public knowledge (following Jack Mabley's article in the *Chicago Daily News* in July 1960) and the Birch Society found itself the subject of widely expressed fears concerning its "extremist" and even "fascist" nature. Buckley was well aware, of course, that some of these attacks were also motivated—as Welch himself constantly maintained—by a desire to discredit the broader conservative movement by targeting it at one of its most vulnerable points.[25] But this was precisely the problem: as far as Buckley and many other conservative leaders were concerned, the Birchers were a clear liability to the movement as a whole.

In January 1962 a number of key conservative figures, including Buckley, Russell Kirk, director of the American Enterprise Institute William Brody, and public relations consultant Jay Hall, who had represented General Motors in Washington, met at the Breakers Hotel in Palm Beach, Florida, to sound out Barry Goldwater on the 1964 presidential election.[26] Discussion inevitably turned to the issue of the Birch Society. Buckley and Kirk wanted Goldwater to take a stand, but the senator was reluctant to attack the Society publicly. He believed it contained many good people alongside the "kooks" and "fanatics"— indeed, in his 1979 memoir, Goldwater still maintained that most Birchers were "patriotic, concerned, law-abiding, hard-working, and productive."[27] He also knew that they were among some of his most ardent and active supporters. Goldwater's problem was not with Birch Society members, but with its leader-ship and Welch in particular—and this was the case even though Welch conducted himself as if he were the senator's number one booster: Welch contributed financially to Goldwater's 1958 reelection campaign; spoke at an "unauthorized rally" in support of Goldwater's nomination for the presidency in

Chicago, in 1960; promoted Goldwater's book *The Conscience of a Conservative* in the pages of the *Bulletin*; and generally characterized the Arizonan as the greatest of American *Americanists*.[28] Goldwater had also read the manuscript/ letter version of *The Politician*. In fact, Welch had hand-delivered a copy to the senator at his Arizona home. Goldwater's response was less than enthusiastic, however; he telephoned Welch the next day to advise him to burn every copy he had. "I want no part of this," Goldwater told him. "I won't even have it around."[29]

Goldwater left the Breakers Hotel meeting without committing himself either way, but after a little reflection he wrote Buckley and Kirk to tell them that he would like to see Welch resign, or the Society disband.[30] Two very public attacks on Welch, but significantly not on the Birch Society as a whole, followed; apparently the Birch Society's members were valued even if the organization's leader wasn't. Writing in the Catholic weekly *America* on February 17, 1962, Kirk charged that Welch had "done more to injure the cause of respectable conservatism than to act effectively against communism." Many decent people belonged to the Society, but "the lunatic fringe" controlled it, he said.[31] The other assault appeared in *National Review*, the flagship journal of conservatism, on February 13. It was entitled "The Question of Robert Welch" and Buckley was its author.

Buckley began by noting that in the preceding weeks a "number of conservative spokesmen whose credentials and sincerity are unassailable," including Kirk, Congressman Walter Judd (R-MN), the conservative radio broadcaster Fulton Lewis Jr., and Goldwater, had begun calling into question Welch's "qualifications to lead a national, anti-Communist and anti-statist movement." The basic dilemma these leaders faced—although it was one obviously shared by "conservatives throughout America," Buckley included— was easily stated, he said. It was: "How can the John Birch Society be an effective political instrument while it is led by a man whose views on current affairs are, at so many critical points, so critically different from their own, and, for that matter, so far removed from common sense?" Clearly, Welch was damaging the cause of anticommunism in the United States.[32] Why? "Because," Buckley wrote, "he persists in distorting reality and in refusing to make the crucial moral and political distinction . . . between 1) *an active pro-Communist*, and 2) *an ineffectually anti-Communist liberal*." Taking Welch to task for his fundamentalist and unrepentantly conspiratorial view of politics, as expressed in *The Politician* and elsewhere, Buckley argued that Welch brooked "no disagreement on his central thesis" that the American government was itself "under [the] operational control of the Communist Party." "Woe unto the man who disagrees with Mr. Welch," the article warned. "He is 1) an idiot, or 2) a Comsymp, or 3) an outright Communist."[33]

Buckley acknowledged that the Birch Society contained "some of the most morally energetic, self-sacrificing, and dedicated anti-Communists" in the country, but he argued that Welch himself was promoting a "split in the conservative movement." The "extravagance of his remarks" repelled rather than attracted new followers to the cause, and for all his "good intentions," Welch threatened "to divert militant conservative action to irrelevance and ineffectuality." Buckley concluded: "There are, as we say, great things that need doing, the winning of a national election, the re-education of the governing class. John Birch chapters can do much to forward those aims, but only as they dissipate the fog of confusion that issues from Mr. Welch's smoking typewriter. Mr. Welch has revived in many men the spirit of patriotism, and that same spirit calls now for rejecting, out of a love of truth and country, his false counsels."[34] It was a devastating critique, but the response it generated, while positive in some quarters, also indicated that the Birch Society still had plenty of supporters and sympathizers. Certainly, Welch did not rush to act on Buckley's implicit suggestion that he resign as the Society's leader, nor did its members rise up to oust him (which is not to say that there weren't rumblings of discontent within the organization over Welch's leadership, and especially his more outré statements; there were.)[35]

Admiral Arthur Radford, a former chairman of the Joint Chiefs of Staff, was among those who wrote National Review to express support for Buckley's article.[36] Another was Senator Goldwater, who repeated his assertion that the best thing Welch could do to serve the cause of anticommunism in the United States was resign. It was a difficult thing to suggest given Welch's dedication to the cause, but "we cannot allow the emblem of irresponsibility to be attached to the conservative banner," Goldwater said.[37] The former actor turned aspiring politician Ronald Reagan commended Buckley for giving "a voice to the conscience of conservatism," and the Texan Republican senator John Tower also wrote to congratulate Buckley and to associate himself with the article's conclusions (he had already entered the article into the Congressional Record as a "detailed and documented . . . airtight case" against Welch on February 6).[38]

There were other correspondents, however. Those like Mrs. Kenneth L. Myers of Wichita, Kansas, who objected to Buckley's "unwarranted attack" on another conservative spokesman; Mrs. Paul H. Dolan, of Saratoga, California, who wanted Buckley to "LAY OFF!" and mind his own business when it came to the Birchers; and Mrs. M. N. Fuller of Midland, Texas, who argued it was better to work on Welch's assumptions rather than "wake up one day soon to find our freedoms are gone . . . or [with] a bullet in the back of the head as a reward for our 'it's not as bad as Mr. Welch thinks' brand of patriotism."[39] In total, the magazine received 350 letters on the "question" of Robert Welch, the overwhelming majority of which were critical of Buckley's stance; it also lost about seventy subscribers, and twenty $100-plus donors withdrew their financial support, as a result of the affair.[40]

Away from the pages of National Review, other conservatives joined in the chorus of disapproval being directed Buckley's way. Fulton Lewis, for example, used his syndicated "Top of the News" column to deny that he ever made the remarks Buckley had attributed to him (at a Human Events conference in Washington, DC). The radio host and ardent anticommunist disagreed with "some of the things" both the Society and Welch stood for, just as he disagreed with his wife and family on some matters, he explained, but it was "a fabrication without the slightest foundation" that he had "criticized Robert Welch's direction of the society," and it was "quite beyond" him how Buckley "could have gotten any such idea."[41]

The conservative activists—and John Birch Society members—Phoebe and Kent Courtney weighed in with two articles in the March 1962 issue of the *Independent American*, of which they were, respectively, editor and publisher. "Where did you and Senator Goldwater ever get the naïve idea that by getting rid of Robert Welch as the head of the John Birch Society, the members of that nationwide organization would over night become docile precinct workers for the 'Modern Republican' party in the next election?" asked Phoebe Courtney in an open letter to Buckley. Both he and Goldwater should have known, she said, that "Welch and the members of the autonomous John Birch Society could never be 'manipulated' to suit the purposes of any political party which espoused and supported positions not in keeping with a strong anti-Communist posture." In his "Defense of Robert Welch," Kent Courtney contended that until recently both Welch and Buckley had "served their respective causes with great distinction," and while Welch continued to do so, this was not the case for "young Buckley, author of 'God and Man at Yale.'" Mr. Courtney recommended that Buckley, having "decided to break his Quixotic lance [*sic*]" on Welch and the Birchers, return "for another semester at Yale, where he can get re-acquainted with God, and possibly obtain some grace, because there was certainly no grace and no wit" in his February 13 article.[42]

In the March issue of the *Bulletin*, Welch and the Birch Society attempted to take the high road with "A Fable for Conservatives," a cautionary piece about "Senator A and Publisher B and Broadcaster C and Organizer D" who had begun "to pull a few of the props out from under the Liberal Establishment" before becoming embroiled in an unseemly squabble over allegations of extremism and questions about who conducted themselves with "reasonable propriety" and who didn't—all of which ultimately served "Communist purposes."[43] Although Welch couldn't stop himself from responding to three of his detractors personally later in the issue, he did at least try to rein in some of his barbed comments for the greater good of "peace in the conservative family."[44]

Thus, because it was a "political year," Welch was willing to make "due allowances" for Goldwater, even if the senator was definitely "off base" in trying to run the Birch Society from the outside. Similarly, while it was clearly the case that Russell Kirk had got "lost" when leaving his ivory tower to wander in the "rough terrain marked CONSPIRATORIA," Welch urged Birchers to "keep right on buying, distributing, and recommending" his books "in the field of political philosophy which he knows so well." Nor was he going to stop recommending *National Review* (even though, he hastened to point out, Buckley had attacked Welch once before, with Eugene Lyons's article back in 1959), as the magazine continued to have "an appeal to the academic world," which was of "tremendous value to the Conservative cause."[45]

Welch acknowledged some "basic and completely honest disagreement between some of our critics and ourselves, as to what might be called this whole conspiratorial theory and explanation of the Communist advance," but when looked at objectively, he said, history simply had the habit of proving the Birch Society version of events to be the correct one. Everywhere he spoke, he noted, refugees from the Communist bloc would seek him out with "tears in their eyes" to tell him: "Thank God there is somebody in America who really understands the way the Communists work, and is trying to wake up others. Don't let *anybody* discourage you from the job you are doing."[46]

One of the things Buckley and Welch's very public contretemps revealed— or more precisely the reaction it produced, perhaps—was that the conservative house contained many rooms, and that for now, at least, the Birchers were sitting relatively comfortably in one of them (their eviction, as we shall see, only came later, in the aftermath of the Goldwater campaign). This reflected not just the long-established imprecision of conservatism as a political philosophy, but more particularly the still ongoing struggle to define exactly what this new version of American conservatism would look like. Indeed, as Jonathan Schoenwald has argued, the "lack of a single definition" of conservatism was one of the main reasons for the "rampant factionalism" that existed in the movement in the first half of the 1960s.[47]

Another thing the dispute evidenced was that the Birch Society and "extremism" were increasingly becoming major issues in the partisan poli- tics of the period. The 1962 political season Welch wanted his readers to take into account when assessing Goldwater's criticism of the Society in March demonstrated this clearly enough, most notably in the gubernatorial contests in California between Edmund "Pat" Brown and Richard Nixon, and in Michigan between George Romney and John Swainson.[48] (So extensive was Romney's attack on what he called the "purveyors of hate" in Michigan—by which everyone knew he meant the Birch Society—that, in September, Welch felt compelled to issue an open letter to him declaring that the "open season" on the Birchers was now closed. Nixon's denunciation of the Society was no less vociferous, but Welch had long since given up on him; he was an opportunist, not a real conservative, Welch believed, describing him in *The Blue Book*—not entirely unfairly—as "one of the ablest, shrewdest, most disingenuous, and slipperiest politicians that ever showed up on the American scene," and as someone who wasn't "committed to anything other than the career of Richard Nixon.")[49]

Perhaps the best illustration of the extent to which the Birchers were becoming a partisan issue, however, was the televised debate between the respective chairs of the Democratic and Republican parties, John M. Bailey (Connecticut) and William E. Miller (New York), as part of NBC's *The Campaign and the Candidates* on the evening of September 3, 1962. As if participating in some poorly constructed vaudevillian comedy routine, each man denied their party had a problem with members of the Society in their own ranks while furiously denouncing their opponent for refusing to disavow the Birchers operating in theirs.[50]

All of this foreshadowed the 1964 presidential election to come, but before we examine that, we first need to turn to the events of November 22, 1963. This is because not only did Kennedy's death provide one of the crucial backdrops against which the contest between Goldwater and Johnson had to play out, but both the president's murder and the Birch Society's poorly judged response to it considerably amplified the debates going on in American society about the nature and dangers of political extremism to the country.

Did Communism Kill Kennedy?

The assassination of President Kennedy in Dallas, Texas, on November 22, 1963, profoundly altered the political context the Birch Society (along with everyone else) was operating in—at least in the short term. As a result, in the "interests of good taste," the Society halted the distribution of the December issue of its monthly magazine *American Opinion*—originally due to be mailed out to subscribers that fateful November day—because it contained two articles highly critical of the Kennedy administration. On the evening of the president's death, Welch sent a telegram to Mrs. Kennedy expressing the Society's "deep sorrow" both for the nation's and her own loss. And a rally and a dinner to have been held in Boston over the weekend of November 23–24 to celebrate the fifth anniversary of the Birch Society were cancelled.[51]

Yet the public statement the Society released in response to Kennedy's death also indicated that such gestures, however genuine they might have been, could not be taken as a sign of any fundamental change in either the organization's worldview or its practical political approach. In fact, in the words of the statement, the "terrible tragedy" merely served to confirm "everything which the John Birch Society has feared for our country and to which we have been so bitterly opposed." During the past several years "Communist pressures have increasingly made the assassination of heads of state a weapon of political action," the statement explained. To support the argument, it pointed to the killing of the Dominican Republic's dictator General Rafael Trujillo in 1961, the execution—following a military coup—of Iraqi prime minister General Abd al-Karim Qasim in February 1963, and the just-weeks-old death of South Vietnam's president Ngo Dinh Diem. The Society was "both horrified and saddened," it said, "to see that weapon now used in our own country."[52]

The deaths of Trujillo, Qasim, and Diem *were* all related in one way or another to fears of communist takeovers in their respective nations, and so the statement's reference to "Communist *pressures*" leading to each leader's death was technically accurate. Trujillo was killed in a roadside ambush on May 30, 1961. The CIA had been working with President Romulo Betancourt of Venezuela, whom Trujillo had tried to murder in 1960, to remove the Dominican dictator, amid concerns about a communist takeover of the country in the wake of the failed Bay of Pigs invasion of Cuba, but the Kennedy administration played no direct role in his assassination, it seems. Disgruntled members of the Baath Party overthrew Qasim's regime with alleged assistance from the CIA, on February 8, 1963. The principal motivating factors of the plotters were potential communist influence in Iraq and control of the nation's oil resources. Diem was killed by a group of South Vietnamese military officers led by Major

General Duong Van Minh on November 2, 1963. By this stage the Kennedy administration was convinced that Diem could not win the Vietnam War and it gave at least tacit encouragement for the coup, if not for Diem's assassination.[53] Of course, a less carefully attentive reading of the Birch Society's statement might lead one to conclude that the communists themselves had carried out the killings—which was no doubt what the author (presumably Welch) intended. A similar ambiguity is evident in the press release's subsequent reference to "the weapon" of assassination now being used in the United States. It was clearly the case that Kennedy had been assassinated, so the release was simply describing what had happened. But when combined with the suggestion that communists might have been the assassins behind the deaths of Trujillo, Qasim, and Diem, a darker implication quickly rose into view: that the communists had now also killed the president of the United States.

By the following month the seemingly carefully crafted *implication* that communism was to blame for Kennedy's death had been jettisoned for a much more straightforward explanation. "We believe that the president of the United States has been murdered by a Communist within the United States," the Society declared in a full-page advertisement that ran in newspapers around the country from December 15 to 18, including in the *New York Times*, the *New York Daily News*, the *Washington Post*, the *Los Angeles Times*, the *Chicago Tribune*, the *Salt Lake Tribune*, and the *St. Louis Globe-Democrat*.[54] "Communism killed Kennedy," stated the Society's new range of stickers, which it began offering for sale in the December issue of the *Bulletin*.[55] It is not entirely clear what prompted this change in strategy—perhaps Welch and his colleagues had simply felt it inappropriate to make such an explicit contention so soon after the president's death. Whatever the reason, the new campaign generated for the Society an enormous amount of controversy, criticism, and—it must be said—publicity.

Entitled "The Time Has Come," the ad began with the view of former Democratic Texas congressman, inaugural chairman of the House Committee on Un-American Activities, and frequent *American Opinion* contributor Martin Dies that when a communist like Lee Harvey Oswald commits a murder he is always "acting under orders." It then quoted from an October 18, 1960, speech by the nation's foremost authority on the communist menace, J. Edgar Hoover, in which the director of the FBI had declared: "We are at war with the Communists, and the sooner each red-blooded American realizes that the better and safer we shall be." From this impressive and apparently authoritative opening salvo, the ad moved on to predict that the communists would not rest on their success in killing Kennedy, but would use the shock, grief, and confusion of the American people to push forward even faster with their plans for taking control of the United States. "For five years The John Birch Society has said that, regardless of the external threat, Communism was a serious internal menace in the United States. And we were right. We believe that this has now been proved, tragically but conclusively," the ad proclaimed. It then turned to the more prosaic but still important matters of recruitment and fundraising; it was a paid advertisement, after all—one that cost the Society somewhere in the region of $35,000 to place in the nation's media.[56] "The time has come for . . . good Americans to join us in this fight against the powerfully organized 'masters of deceit,'" it said (employing a passing reference to Hoover's 1959 book), before encouraging readers to contact the Executive Committee of the Society—composed of William Grede, A. G. Heinsohn, Fred C. Koch, Clarence Manion, and R.W. Stoddard—with either a financial contribution or a request for more information on the organization and its activities.

The ad was essentially a distillation of the views of Welch, Dies, and Revilo Oliver that had been expressed, or would be expressed subsequently, in much greater detail in a series of articles published in the *Bulletin* and *American Opinion* about the nature of the communist conspiracy in the United States and its role in Kennedy's death. And there was some dispute within the Society over this. Welch, for example, argued that the assassination had not been planned by the "top command of the international Communist conspiracy" based in Moscow—which he thought had been taken by surprise by Oswald's actions—but had instead been "carefully plotted by one or more Communists very high up in their hierarchy" within the United States.[57] Dies, employing all his experience in detecting the "'fine hand' of the Communist conspiracy," in contrast believed—although it was a "tentative conclusion," he said—that Oswald "was acting under instructions which had their original source in Moscow," and that these instructions had probably been relayed to Oswald "through Castro."[58] Oliver, a professor of classics at the University of Illinois in Urbana-Champaign, straddled these two positions, referring more opaquely to the success (of the always capitalized) "Communist Conspiracy" in killing the president—although he was of no doubt that the "the *International* Communist Conspiracy" would always be the nation's ultimate enemy.[59]

The three men were in complete agreement, however, that one of the principal objectives of the conspiracy—although this was not something referred to in the "The Time Has Come" ad—had been to attack and discredit, if not destroy, anticommunist and other conservative forces within the United States, including the Birch Society. As Welch put it in the December 12, 1963, issue of the *Bulletin*,

> the assassination of the President was not only to have been blamed in a general way on the spirit of hatred supposedly created by the so-called "right-wing extremists." But it was to be proclaimed loudly and emphatically that the actual assassin was a member of some right-wing group which was directly responsible for the crime. Thus the mind of America was to be converted temporarily into an unreasoning mob mind, boiling over with misunderstanding, anger, and excitement. And with that springboard from which to jump, the wholesale arrests of anti-Communists was to have been carried out just as rapidly as possible.[60]

Once captured, Oswald would "spread the lie of a Right-wing conspiracy . . . much like the plot in a recent motion picture entitled *The Manchurian Candidate*," explained the anonymous writer of *American Opinion*'s newspaper "corrections" page in January 1964. The problem—and here again Dies,

Oliver, and Welch were in agreement—was that Oswald had botched this plan when he shot Dallas police officer J. D. Tippit while trying to make his escape. As a result, Oswald had been arrested sooner than had been expected and his communist affiliations made public before the right-wing cover story could be fixed securely into place. Indeed, in Oliver's view, both Oswald's arrest and the fact there were enough "honest American newsmen, in the United States and abroad, to make it impossible to conceal the Conspiracy's connection with the bungled assassination" were encouraging signs that the conspiracy's control over the country was not yet totally complete.[61]

But if the aim had been to destroy the American right wing which, in the view of the Birch Society at least, was demonstrating its ability to "attract a mass following by offering Goldwater as an alternative to Kennedy," and thereby threatening the conspiracy's control over both the American people and the American government, why not simply assassinate Goldwater, since he was the focal point of this rising conservative movement? The self-serving answer provided by the January 1964 issue of *American Opinion* was that such an action "would only have made it more possible for a Robert Welch to run for President."[62]

Welch's belief that only people who had been "brainwashed" or "beguiled for years" by the incessant flood of communist propaganda could fail to recognize the "truth" behind the Kennedy assassination notwithstanding, it is easy to see why the Birch Society's views on the matter would be controversially received.[63] Oliver, though, raised the degree of contention to a whole new level with his ill-advised reflections on how the slain president should be remembered, as part of his "Marxmanship in Dallas" article in the February 1964 issue of *American Opinion*.

Keen, as always, to display his erudition—and presumed superiority—Professor Oliver argued that the maxim *de mortuis nil nisi bonum* ("Of the dead, nothing but good," or as it is more usually and colloquially phrased, "Speak no ill of the dead") was a taboo for "barbarians, who indulge in tribal howling and gashing of cheeks and breast whenever a big chief dies or an eclipse portends the end of the world." No one paid such regard for Adolf Hitler and he was "certainly as defunct as Jack and therefore presumably as much entitled to post-mortem consideration," Oliver observed. "Rational men will understand that, far from sobbing over the deceased or lying to placate his vengeful ghost, it behooves us to speak of him with complete candor and historical objectivity. Jack was not sanctified by a bullet," he continued, before laying bare just what kind of historical assessment he believed such candor and objectivity should produce in great detail:

> The departed Kennedy is the John F. Kennedy who procured his election by peddling boob-bait to the suckers, including a cynical pledge to destroy the Communist base in Cuba. He is the John F. Kennedy with whose blessing and support the Central Intelligence Agency staged a fake "invasion" of Cuba designed to strengthen our mortal enemies there and to disgrace us—disgrace us not merely by ignominious failure, but by the inhuman crime of having

lured brave men into a trap and sent them to suffering and death. He is the John F. Kennedy who collaborated with Khrushchev, to stage the phoney "embargo" that was improvised both to befuddle the suckers on election day in 1962 and to provide for several months a cover for the steady and rapid transfer of Soviet troops and Soviet weapons to Cuba for eventual use against us. He is the John F. Kennedy who installed and maintained in power the unspeakable Yarmolinsky-McNamara gang in the Pentagon [Professor Adam Yarmolinsky was one of McNamara's special assistants in the Defense Department] to demoralize and subvert our armed forces and to sabotage our military installations and equipment. He is the John F. Kennedy who, by shameless intimidation, bribery, and blackmail, induced weaklings in Congress to approve treasonable acts designed to disarm us and to make us the helpless prey of the affiliated criminals and savages of the "United Nations."

. . . So long as there are Americans, his memory will be cherished with distaste. If the United States is saved by the desperate exertions of patriots, we may have a future of true greatness and glory—but we shall never forget how near we were to total destruction in the year 1963. And if the international vermin succeed in completing their occupation of our country, Americans will remember Kennedy while they live, and will curse him as they face the firing squads or toil in a brutish degradation that leaves no hope for anything but a speedy death.[64]

The *New York Times* justified its decision to be the first newspaper to run the Birchers' ad on First Amendment grounds. It was part of the responsibility and freedom of the press to publish such material no matter how strongly the paper itself might disapprove of the views being expressed, or "despise" the goals of the political movement such advertising was promoting, the paper explained.[65] (Not all the nation's newspapers felt this way; both the *Wall Street Journal* and the *Dallas Morning News* refused to run the ad, for example.) Many of the *Times'* letter writers who responded to the ad accepted these arguments, and like Donald A. Field of Oradell, New Jersey, made the further case that it was a sign of a healthy democracy that organizations like the Birch Society were able to express their views in this way.

Many others, though, found both the ad and the *Times'* decision to publish it to be in bad taste, to be disrespectful to the memory of the late president, and as simply adding to the nation's climate of hate and intolerance. Herman F. Reissig, the international relations secretary for the Council for Christian Social Action, described the ad as "a new low" for the Birch Society, while New Yorker A. Aitchess thought it only appropriate that the line "The time has come" was one spoken by the Walrus in Lewis Carroll's fantastical story *Through the Looking Glass*. Robert H. Hamill of Boston, Massachusetts, and Jesse S. Moore of Scarsdale, New York, both objected to the ad's inference that communists had "ordered" Kennedy's assassination or that Oswald was "employed in some way by the Soviet Government," when there was no evidence to support either proposition—uncovering such evidence, if any existed, was why the Warren

Commission had been established, Moore added.[66] The *Times*' letter-writers were not the only people offended by the Birch Society advertisement, either. The American Communist Party, if for fairly obvious reasons, was particularly upset by what an editorial in the *Worker* called the ad's "scurrilous diatribe of unmitigated lies and hate mongering against the Communists . . . and all democratic thought."[67]

The critical reaction to the ad was nothing compared to the hostility that greeted the February publication of Oliver's "Marxmanship in Dallas" article, however. On February 13, for instance, members of the Arizona state legislature condemned Oliver's "character assassination" of Kennedy, and two days later student demonstrators spent nine hours picketing the Phoenix branch of the American Opinion Library, carrying signs that read "Hate Killed J.F.K" and "Students Protest John Birch Society." An editorial in the March 1 issue of the *Milwaukee Journal* condemned the "twisted" and "bizarre" world of the Birch Society and of Oliver, who, the paper said, stood "revealed and condemned by his own words."[68]

The trustees of the University of Illinois met in Urbana-Champaign on March 18 to consider a report of the Faculty Senate's Academic Freedom Committee, which had been asked to decide if Oliver was, in the words of one newspaper headline writer, "a jerk or a genius?"—or, more politely, whether any disciplinary measures should (or could) be taken against him.[69] Although critical of Oliver's lack of good taste, in an 8 to 1 vote the trustees accepted the committee's recommendation against imposing any formal punishment on him, on the basis of academic freedom. "That Mr. Oliver's views are not shared by this academic community is certain," explained the university's president, Dr. David Henry, but as "unsupported . . . unreasoned and vitriolic" as his attack on the character and patriotism of President Kennedy had been, the professor would not be losing his job over the affair.[70]

Despite having described Oliver's article as "superb commentary" when it was first published in February, the flood of negative publicity it generated was such that by May the Founder was clearly beginning to think it might be prudent to backtrack a little. He was not in complete agreement with what Oliver had written, Welch said at a news conference in St. Louis on May 13. "I definitely did not agree with some of his premises and some of his conclusions," Welch explained, although without getting into "a song and dance about academic freedom," he still felt the article had been "worth publishing."[71] Nor was Welch the only one attempting some fancy footwork. In an episode bizarre even by Birch Society standards, Cardinal Richard Cushing, the Roman Catholic archbishop of Boston, had announced in April that he was retracting his endorsement of the Society—which he had first given in 1960—because of Oliver's article, only to retract his retraction four days later because he said he had been the victim of a hoax, which had led him to his "unjustified" condemnation of the organization.[72]

Overall, the fallout from both the Kennedy assassination and the Birch Society's reaction to it was damaging for the Society, seeming to provide not just further confirmation of the extremist nature of the organization, but also the most potent illustration imaginable of the dangers such extremist politics posed to the nation. Professor Donald T. Rowlingson of Boston University wrote in the context of the debate over the merits of the "The Time Has Come" advertisement, for example, that "by emphasizing the Communist affiliations of the assassin the Birchers are blind to the basic fact that it was an *extremist* who did the job. Having watched Hitler grasp power in Germany in 1932–33 on the pretext of protecting the nation from the 'menace' of Communism, I am less than convinced that right-wing extremism is any less dangerous here than left-wing extremism."[73] It was a lesson expressed widely in the aftermath of Kennedy's death.

Delivering his eulogy before the late president's coffin as it lay in the Capitol Rotunda on November 25, 1963, Chief Justice Earl Warren reflected that while the motives of the "misguided wretch" who had carried out "this horrible deed may never be known to us . . . we do know that such acts are commonly stimulated by forces of hatred and malevolence, such as today are eating their way into the blood stream of American life." He lamented, "What a price to pay for this fanaticism!"[74] Speaking before a joint session of Congress on November 27, Lyndon Johnson sought to bring the mourning nation together by calling on Americans "of all races and creeds and political beliefs to understand and to respect one another." The newly installed president declared from the rostrum of the House, "Let us put an end to the teaching and the preaching of hate and evil and violence. Let us turn away from the fanatics of the far left and the far right, from the apostles of bitterness and bigotry, from those defiant of law, and those who pour venom into our Nation's bloodstream."[75]

Senator Fulbright made a similar argument during the Rockefeller Public Service Awards luncheon in Washington, DC, two weeks after the assassination. A "prevailing atmosphere of suspicion and hate" had "spawned" the murder of the president, the senator proclaimed. His wide-ranging analysis of America's "tendencies toward violence and crusading self-righteousness" encompassed the nation's Puritan and frontier past as well as the contemporary problems of urban crime, extremist political movements, and frequent acts of violence against the civil rights movement, such as the bombing of the 16th Street Baptist Church in Birmingham, Alabama, in September 1963, in which four young African American girls had lost their lives. Fulbright hoped that some kind of redemption would result from Kennedy's death. "That redemption could issue from a national revulsion against extremism and violence," he said, "and from a calling forth of the basic decency and humanity of America to heal the wounds of divisiveness and hate."[76]

Intended to help bring about national reconciliation and a more tolerant political atmosphere, such declarations nonetheless also contributed to the widespread sense that right-wing groups like the Birch Society were at least partly to blame for the president's death and should take their share of the responsibility for it. After all, it was these groups, along with the perpetrators of racially inspired violence like the Ku Klux Klan, that were most closely identified with the forces of "fanaticism" and "extremism" being denounced so vociferously. Indeed, although he didn't express it publicly, Warren, as one of his biographers has noted, "personally blamed the radical right and Texas's extremely conservative oil millionaires" for Kennedy's murder.[77] Fulbright's credentials as an implacable foe of right-wing extremism were more than well established, as we saw in the previous chapter.

The fact that the assassination had taken place in Dallas—home to General Edwin Walker, Dan Smoot, Texas oilman H. L. Hunt (one of the millionaires who so concerned the chief justice), and a host of right-wing groups, including the Defenders of American Liberties and the Birch Society—only compounded the association.[78] Indeed, the president's advisers had had serious doubts about the wisdom of Kennedy visiting the city on November 22. Just four weeks earlier, during a trip there to celebrate United Nations Day, Adlai Stevenson, Kennedy's chief delegate at the UN, had been jostled, booed, spit upon, and hit with a picket sign by what the president of the Dallas United Nations Association described as a "concerted action by members of Edwin Walker's followers and the John Birchers."[79] On November 4, Texas Democratic national committeeman Byron Skelton had sent Robert Kennedy a newspaper report about Walker, who had publicly called his brother "a liability to the free world." "A man who would make that kind of statement is capable of doing harm to the President," Skelton had advised the attorney general.[80] And on November 22 itself, Kennedy had been shown a Birch Society ad published in the *Dallas Morning News* that very morning that accused the president of being soft on communism, and of allowing his brother to prosecute any patriotic American who had the temerity to criticize the administration. "We're heading into nut country today," Kennedy told his wife. "But . . . if somebody wants to shoot me from a window with a rifle, nobody can stop it, so why worry about it?"[81]

In these circumstances, it is easy to see why many people believed that members of the Birch Society, and those like them, might have been behind Kennedy's murder. (After learning of the assassination, Richard Nixon called J. Edgar Hoover; his first question was, "What happened, was it one of the right-wing nuts?")[82] Some people, though, went further than others in blaming the organization. On November 22, for example, Thomas Lloyd Thompson, a thirty-three-year-old freelance writer from Phoenix, fired two shots from his .357 magnum revolver through the windows of the Birch Society offices in the city, because, he said, the Birchers had "killed my man." (Convicted of malicious mischief and various traffic offenses, Thompson was sentenced to ten days in jail for the incident.)[83] The Los Angeles office of the Society was also forced to close for the day in the face of protests against it, and a brick was thrown through the window of Welch's office in the Society's headquarters in Belmont, Massachusetts, which was also on the receiving end, as Welch recounted in the December issue of the *Bulletin*, of numerous threatening phone calls, as well as "insults and cat-calls" from cars of "shouting college-age youngsters" who were circling the building.[84]

The Birch Society's high-profile contention that the communists had killed Kennedy, by adding fuel to an already volatile situation, only served to increase the opprobrium directed toward it. After all, avoiding such a conclusion, and thereby averting the possibility of the next world war, was one of Lyndon Johnson's primary motivations in creating the Warren Commission to investigate the president's death.[85] It was also the principal reason why, despite its many flaws—the failure of key witnesses to discuss the Kennedy administration's plots to kill Fidel Castro, the close involvement of the CIA and the mob in those plots, and so on—the commission's conclusion, published in September 1964, that Oswald had acted alone when he shot Kennedy, was so warmly embraced by the nation's political establishment (if not its conspiracy theorists).[86]

The FBI's investigation into the assassination also concluded that Oswald acted alone. But the bureau had its own powerful incentives for reaching such a finding. This was because of what Hoover himself called the agency's "gross incompetence" in failing to keep a careful watch over Oswald in the weeks leading up to the president's visit to Dallas: the Dallas office of the FBI had known not only that Oswald was a prominent and possibly deranged communist agitator, but also that he worked in a building, the Texas School Book Depository, that overlooked the route of the president's motorcade.[87] However, with the aid of a secret informant on the commission—congressman and future president Gerald Ford (R-MI)—the extent of the FBI's failings in this regard were also kept from the Warren Commission investigators. Given all this—and also because Oswald was "silenced" by Jack Ruby—it is little wonder that both the Kennedy assassination and the Warren Report contributed enormously to the explosive growth in America's conspiratorial culture in the years that followed.

It was in the midst of this maelstrom of violence, uncertainty, extremism, and anxiety that, on January 3, 1964, Barry Goldwater formally launched his bid to become the next president of the United States. And it is to this campaign, and to the John Birch Society's involvement in it, that we now turn.

Barry Goldwater and the Birch Takeover of the GOP

Born in Phoenix, Arizona, in 1909 to a Jewish father and an Episcopalian mother, Barry Morris Goldwater is an interesting and complex figure.[88] Heir to a department store business started by his grandfather, he chose instead to go into politics, winning his first election to become a member of the Phoenix City Council, in 1950, aged forty. Two years later he was elected to the U.S. Senate, the unlikely victor, on Eisenhower's coattails, over Democratic majority leader Ernest W. McFarland. A relatively undistinguished Republican loyalist during his first few years in Washington, Goldwater really began to come into his own— and thereby become regarded as one of the leading conservative politicians in the nation—after 1957, when he began attacking the "irresponsible" spending of the Eisenhower administration and its "tendencies to bow to the siren song of socialism," just as ferociously as he had always attacked "power-hungry labor bosses" like Walter Reuther.[89]

In January 1960 John Birch Society National Council member Clarence Manion suggested to Goldwater that he write a book outlining his conservative beliefs. Manion hired Brent Bozell to "ghost" it, and by 1964 the result, *The Conscience of a Conservative*, had sold 3.5 million copies. His second book, *Why Not Victory?*, with its warning that the United States was fast losing the struggle against the "international conspiracy" of communism, was published in 1962. It too was a best seller. Clearly Goldwater was becoming a national political figure—his "How Do You Stand, Sir?" newspaper column, also largely ghosted by Bozell, ran in 140 papers—while his status within the conservative faction of the GOP was enhanced considerably by his role as chairman of the Senate Republican campaign committee, a position that required countless hours of traveling around the country, fund-raising, and promoting the Republican cause. Goldwater was an impressive standard bearer for conservatism: he was dedicated, photogenic, and loyal to his friends and colleagues (he refused to vote for the censure of his friend Joe McCarthy in 1954, for example), as well as a former fighter pilot and an officer in the air force reserve who was not afraid to speak his mind. Yet he was also unpredictable, prone to public misspeaking, and, as someone who "cheerfully broke all the basic rules of politics," not an especially effective political campaigner.[90] In addition, he was a somewhat reluctant presidential aspirant, and this reluctance only increased following the assassination of Kennedy, with whom he'd had a friendship since their days together in the Senate. Indeed, it was only Goldwater's sense of obligation to those who had worked so hard on his behalf that kept him in the race.[91]

Another major problem facing Goldwater was that he was strongly identified with both the radical Right in general and the John Birch Society in particular. (Indeed, the identification was so strong that Radio Moscow somehow managed to drag it into the Sino-Soviet split in April 1964, arguing that the "reckless character" of the Chinese leadership had "much in common with the attitude of rabid anti-Communists [such as] Sen. Goldwater and members of the John Birch Society.")[92] In a rare degree of historical unanimity, most observers agree with the Arizonan's own view that "the bullet that killed John Kennedy also destroyed whatever possibility there ever was for a Goldwater presidency."[93] It is also the case, however, that Goldwater's chances for winning the presidency, however slim they might have been, would have been enhanced—or at least the margin of defeat might have been reduced—had the senator made a clear statement repudiating the Society.[94] He certainly had every opportunity to do so. On the day he announced he was running for the White House, for example, a reporter asked Goldwater where he stood with regard to the Birchers. His reply was that he would take a stand against any organization that "wants to overthrow our government by violence or treason," but that he could see "no reason to take a stand against any organization just because they're using their constitutional prerogatives, even though I disagree with most of them."[95]

If it would have been to Goldwater's political advantage to repudiate the Society, why did he not do so? There are a number of reasons. First, he knew many prominent Birchers personally and liked them—people like Manion, and fellow Arizonans Frank Cullen Brophy and Denison Kitchel, who were key members of his inner circle of advisers.[96] Second, he had a great deal of respect for the ordinary members of the Society and their dedication to the conservative cause;

they were, he told reporters, the "finest people" in his community. Whatever Welch's conspiratorial excesses, Goldwater regarded the Birchers as fellow conservatives—as people who had essentially the same political views as he did. This in turn points to a third reason why he was reluctant to repudiate the Society's members, which is that he needed their energy, their enthusiasm, and their dedication to round up the votes he was pursuing. Birchers and other right-wing grassroots activists played the "decisive role" in Goldwater's crucial California primary victory against Governor Rockefeller, for example.[97] As Donald Critchlow points out, however, they did so somewhat surreptitiously, Goldwater's advisers having adopted a strategy of "don't ask, don't tell" when it came to the use of Birch Society members in the campaign. (The Goldwater campaign adopted this strategy, Critchlow says, because while it was worried about being perceived as being too closely associated with an "extremist organization," it had also seen the damage Nixon's denunciation of the Society had done to his gubernatorial campaign in 1962, and it didn't want to run the risk of "alienating" the Birchers in the same way.)[98]

The slipperiness of the term "extremism," and its protean and obviously partisan characteristics, combined with a certain political naïveté on the part of many conservatives at the time, provides a fourth reason why Goldwater failed to publicly repudiate the Birch Society. Goldwater and his advisers were as aware as Buckley and Welch that the "extremist" label was often employed simply as a term of political abuse, but they don't seem to have fully realized just how damaging its effective—and almost continuous—deployment could be. Convinced of the righteousness of their own cause—as Welch was, and for much the same reasons—they believed all they had to do was get their message out to the American people, and the votes would come pouring in. If they did not regard themselves or their ideas as extremist—and obviously they didn't— then so too, they reasoned, would the electorate be able see through the political games being played against them to the "truths" that lay beyond.

Such political naïveté was no doubt reinforced by the inexperience of those running Goldwater's campaign—the much-maligned "Arizona mafia"— but it was also exacerbated, as Mary Brennan points out, by the widespread (and genuinely held) belief of many conservatives that "the only dangerous extremism existed on the left."[99] Goldwater was himself a prime example of the tendency.

For example, in November 1961, during an address in Atlanta, Georgia, to Republican leaders from twelve southern states, Goldwater had taken aim at the Kennedy administration because of the influence within it of the liberal pressure group Americans for Democratic Action (ADA). (Formed in 1947 by such luminaries of the Left as Eleanor Roosevelt, Hubert Humphrey, Walter Reuther, and John Kenneth Galbraith, and despite its consistently anticommunist stance, the ADA had long been a favorite target for American conservatives.) "President Kennedy talks of extremists," Goldwater explained. "Well, all he has to do is turn around in his rocking chair and the White House is full of them. The first forty wagons in the New Frontier are driven by the Americans for Democratic Action"—Kennedy's appropriation of imagery that rightly belonged to real Westerners such as himself was a clearly a constant source of irritation for Goldwater. "These are the people we should be worried about. These people are not Democrats. The nicest thing we can say about them is that they're socialists."[100] Three years later, in the midst of the presidential campaign, he made the same case. "This extremist thing is not worthy of the discussion at any reasonable level, unless it's the left-wing extremists who are in government," the senator told journalists in Sacramento on March 17, 1964.[101]

This isn't to say that Goldwater wasn't above getting involved in the delicately nuanced game of partisan political linguistics when he considered it necessary to do so. His attacks on the Kennedy administration were certainly evidence of this. And he was also willing to play the game against members of his own party. During the California primary, in the face of constant barbs from the "moderate" Rockefeller campaign that a victory for Goldwater would be a victory for the Birch Society and that Goldwater was "out of the mainstream" of the Republican Party, he responded by claiming that it was he who represented "true Republicanism" and that Rockefeller and his supporters were the "Republican extremists."[102] Above all, though, Goldwater seemed to regard all the questions about extremism as a distraction from the more substantive and serious issues of the day—a "phantom issue," as he described it.[103] It was an apt choice of words, but not for the reason Goldwater thought. The issue was real enough, and his failure to exorcise it at the outset of his campaign, if not earlier, meant it was one that would haunt him all the way to polling day.

Significantly, Goldwater's unwillingness or inability to repudiate the Birchers only served to reinforce fears that the Society was intent on "taking over" the Republican Party as a vehicle to pursue its own interests. As the Mosk Report illustrated, such fears had existed for some time, but they were given renewed emphasis by the events of 1963 and 1964, especially after Bircher Robert Gaston, a thirty-two-year-old Los Angeles attorney, defeated Kenneth Davis, a thirty-year-old Pasadena stockbroker, to become the new president of the Young Republicans of California in February 1963. Gaston had won—in a 189 to 170 vote—despite warnings from the outgoing president, Harry Keaton, that the organization was facing a "power grab by the leadership of the John Birch Society." It was a "shabby spectacle," Keaton said, "to see these fine young men and women used by the professional Birch staff to further the unannounced objective of capturing control of the Young Republicans," and he predicted that a such a "takeover . . . would be disastrous" for the entire Republican Party.[104] The following week, after a bad-tempered, noisy, and extremely bitter contest, the moderate William Nelligan, a fifty-four-year-old officer of the Communications Workers of America, narrowly defeated the Birch Society–backed Harry Wardell, a retired naval officer, to become president of the California Republican Assembly. At the outset of the convention, the outgoing president, former Kansas governor Fred Hall, had warned the delegates that the Birch Society was trying to gain control of the assembly as a staging post to allow it to take over the Republican State Central Committee, which would then enable it to elect an "ultra conservative" delegation to the 1964 national convention. It was not possible to be a Bircher and a Republican, Hall contended. The Society's

"totalitarian philosophy" was "repugnant to the Constitution and every democratic institution that we have."[105]

Surveying these events, one of the leaders of the progressive Republican
faction in Congress, California senator Thomas Kuchel, urged his fellow party
members to "stand up and fight" against what he said was "an attempted coup
d'état by right-wing extremists."[106] Kuchel's intervention marked the beginning
of his ascension to supplanting Milton Young as the most outspoken opponent
of the Birchers in Congress. Kuchel even coined a catchy new phrase to describe
them. They were "the fright peddlers," he told his Senate colleagues on May
2, and he had "nothing but seething contempt" for the "ludicrous leaders of
the Birch Society" and "any and all of the several hundred similar self-styled
patriotic groups" who were "doing a devil's work" in politics.[107] In July, the
Democratic National Committee issued an eight-page compilation of newspaper stories with the arresting title "FAR RIGHT GRABS FOR GOP."[108]

It was in this context that Rockefeller sought to offer himself as the
moderate alternative to Goldwater's extreme conservatism. On July 14, the
New York governor issued a two-thousand-word public statement attacking the
"vociferous and well-drilled extremist elements boring within the [Republican]
party" that utterly rejected the "fundamental principles of our heritage," and the
"purveyors of hate and distrust" who were every bit as dangerous to America as
the radical Left. And at a news conference a few days later, he urged Goldwater
to disown supporters on the radical Right lest the Arizonan become "captive" to
the extremist elements that were seeking to gain control of the party.[109]

There was certainly a well-organized attempt going on to capture the
Republican Party for conservatism, but Robert Welch and the Birch Society
were not directing it. This is not to say that Welch and his colleagues would
not have liked to have been a greater influence within the GOP—they obviously
would—but there is little evidence to support the contention that there were
actively trying to "take it over." The same cannot be said for members of the
so-called Syndicate. Led by *National Review* publisher William Rusher and
political strategist F. Clifton White, the Syndicate—which was also known as
"the Hard Core" or "the Old Friends"—had not only secretly taken control
of the Young Republicans (YR), but, as Geoffrey Kabaservice has written, by
1961 its members "had clandestinely resolved to use their control of the YRs,
their network of contacts, and the Young Americans for Freedom to secure
the 1964 GOP presidential nomination for Barry Goldwater."[110] This was not
an entirely fanciful enterprise. As Kabaservice says, the truth was that in the
early 1960s the Republican Party was "ripe" for a takeover of this kind, with four
distinct factions—the moderates, the progressives, the stalwarts or Taftites (the
supporters of Welch's great hero, Robert Taft), and the conservatives—duking it
out, with varying degrees of effectiveness, for supremacy.[111]

The conservatives may have been the smallest of the four factions in 1960,
but they were better organized, more energetic, more disciplined, and more
ideologically coherent than their rivals in the GOP. They also had the fiery zeal
typical of new converts to help drive them forward. This was especially true of
those in the vanguard of the conservative movement, including the Syndicate

and the Birch Society. Indeed, despite—or perhaps because of—their ardent anticommunism, Welch, Rusher, and White all sought to emulate the successful secret, manipulative, disciplined, last-man-standing-at-the-end-of-the-day-wins tactics employed by the American Communist Party during its heyday in the 1930s and 1940s.[112] The Syndicate's mastery of these methods was amply demonstrated during the 1963 Young Republican national convention in San Francisco, when endless roll calls, arcane points of parliamentary procedure, raised voices, protests, fistfights, and some straightforward intimidation were deployed to ensure that conservative candidates won the day. The press blamed Birchers for the chaos, but it was Syndicate forces that inflicted the damage.[113]

White and Rusher, along with Congressman John Ashbrook of Ohio, had also been the driving forces behind the formal, if initially secret, Draft Goldwater campaign, which began in June 1961—Goldwater didn't find out about it until November.[114] But all this political maneuvering put Welch and the Birch Society in a difficult position because—as Welch and his lieutenants such as John Rousselot never tired of pointing out—the Society was supposed to be an *educational* organization, not a partisan political one. After all, as Welch had explained in one of his rather more gnomic pronouncements in *The Blue Book*, the country was at the stage "where the only sure political victories are achieved by non-political organization."[115] Yet at the same time Welch had not been shy in personally endorsing and supporting candidates he favored, or encouraging Birch Society members to work as hard as possible to get conservatives—of both parties—elected to public office. Such encouragement was always accompanied with the caveat, however, that "the Society takes no direct part in partisan politics, nor does it presume to tell our members how to vote with regard to specific candidates" (as Welch put it before the party conventions of 1960).[116] Thus could Welch maintain in July 1964, to the incredulity of most outside observers, that the Society was taking "no position" in the forthcoming November election.[117]

Changed circumstances often lead to changed plans and altered strategies, of course. The sudden and enormous amount of attention directed the Society's way in 1960 and 1961 meant it could no longer operate behind the scenes, quietly building up support within the conservative community, as it would have preferred. A similar situation occurred between 1963 and 1964. Simply put, the rise of Goldwater was just too good either to ignore or to downplay. When Welch wrote *The Blue Book* in 1959, he was expecting many years to pass before a viable conservative candidate would be ready to lead the Republican Party on a national basis. Someone like Goldwater or Senator Bill Knowland (R-CA) might be able to provide effective conservative leadership in their own states, Welch had thought, but nothing could "come out of the present shattered Republican Party" country-wide for the "foreseeable future." This was why Welch had established a "non-political organization"; along with other conservative groups, it would provide "help and backing . . . outside of the straight political organization" to help push the GOP in a more conservative direction.[118]

But the foreseeable future had come sooner than expected. Because of the considerable efforts of the various elements of the conservative movement (the

Birch Society included), because of the factionalized nature of the Republican Party, because of the liberal advances of Kennedy's New Frontier, because of the rise of the civil rights movement, and because of the seeming gains of the international communist conspiracy on the world stage—all these developments had combined to create an opportunity for a "real" conservative candidate like Barry Goldwater to take his shot at the presidency. The time was now. "The crucial years are on us," Welch wrote in December 1963. "We have about one more year . . . in which we shall be able to carry on the fight [against communism] under approximately the same conditions that prevail today; and then, if we have gained enough during that period—but only if we have gained enough—approximately four more years, or until the end of 1968, when we can still fight an educational (and thus indirectly but effectively a political) form of warfare, but under far greater handicaps and harassment than we face today."[119] The Society could not entirely abandon its nonpartisan, educational stance—it had repeated it too often and too loudly, and no one likes a hypocritical flip-flopper—but its members didn't have to be highly skilled in the art of cryptography to be able to read between the Founder's lines, which is why so many Birchers readily went to work for the Goldwater campaign.

In the end the Republican Party nomination came down to a straight fight in California between Rockefeller and Goldwater, as other potential nominees—U.S. ambassador Henry Cabot Lodge, Governors George Romney of Michigan and William Scranton of Pennsylvania, New York City–bound Richard Nixon—either remained on the sidelines, entered too late, or fell by the wayside. When

Figure 4.1. Barry Goldwater, the 1964 Republican nominee for the presidency, addresses a Young Republicans rally in San Francisco, California, June 29, 1963. © Ted Streshinsky/ CORBIS

Goldwater won the California primary, one would have expected the party to pull together in a forceful display of unity for the upcoming general election. The opposite happened, and as a result the nominating convention at San Francisco's Cow Palace was a disaster both for Goldwater's candidacy and the GOP. The factionalism of the party was laid bare for all to see.[120]

Scranton and his supporters insisted, for example, that the Republican platform explicitly repudiate extremist groups such as the John Birch Society, and also affirm the constitutionality of the Civil Rights Act of 1964, which Goldwater had voted against.[121] In his July 13 keynote address, Oregon governor Mark O. Hatfield attacked the "bigots in this nation who spew forth their venom of hate." Such groups "parade under hundreds of labels," Hatfield declared, but they included the Klan, the Communist Party, and the Birch Society, and they "must be overcome."[122] Rockefeller tried to speak in favor of the plank on extremism on the convention floor the following day, but his words were continuously drowned out in a chorus of boos, catcalls, and chants of "We Want Barry!" Neither convention chair Senator Thurston Morton of Kentucky nor master political operative Clif White could restore order to the proceedings. (White had control of his own troops, it should be said. It wasn't the official convention delegates—a hundred of whom were Birchers—who were the problem. Most of the vitriol pouring down on the governor was actually coming from the spectator galleries.) Amid the chaos and with the television cameras rolling, Rockefeller sought to remind his audience that America was "still a free country." "Some of you don't like to hear it, ladies and gentlemen," he went on, providing a compelling image of the seemingly brutish nature of the extremism that had overtaken the party, "but it is the truth."[123]

Goldwater's supporters easily voted down the civil rights and antiextremism planks, and conventional political wisdom, not to mention common sense, seemed to require Goldwater to do something to try and reconcile the warring factions—for his own sake, if not the party's. Yet he made no attempt to do so. Instead, he went out of his way during his acceptance speech on July 15 to welcome anyone "who joins us in all sincerity," while "those who do not care for our cause we do not expect to enter our ranks in any case." He then uttered the two sentences that had been double-underscored in the press copies of the speech as well as his own reading copy—the two sentences with which he would forever be associated: "I would remind you that extremism in the defense of liberty is no vice! And let me remind you also that moderation in the pursuit of justice is no virtue!" As Nixon commented, Goldwater had not only failed to heal the party's wounds, he had "opened new wounds and then rubbed salt in them."[124]

Goldwater may have believed that Eisenhower had been an "extremist for liberty" when he sent thousands to their deaths in order to defeat the Nazis during the Second World War, as he told the former president in a hastily arranged meeting to explain his remarks following the speech, or that what he had said was really no different from JFK's inaugural promise to "pay any price" or "bear any burden" to assure "the success of liberty." He may have taken comfort in the assurances of his speechwriter, Harry Jaffa, a Claremont College history professor, that the statement was inspired by the works of Cicero, or he may just have run out of patience at the "unfairness" of all the attacks against him during the previous months and simply wanted to strike back. But whatever his motivation, either he or his advisers should have also known that in the context of the times—the Kennedy assassination, the violent opposition being faced down by the civil rights movement on an almost daily basis, the widely expressed fears about a Birch takeover of the GOP, and so on—that speaking in defense of "extremism" was akin to signing his political suicide note.[125]

The response was as swift as it was predictable. Rockefeller immediately issued a statement describing Goldwater's extolling of extremism as "dangerous, irresponsible and frightening." Any sanctioning of lawlessness, vigilantism, and the "unruly mob" was to be deplored, he said; and trying to justify oneself by claiming to be acting in the "defense of liberty" was what Communists, Klansmen, Birchers, and tyrants always did. "The stench of fascism is in the air," declared California governor Pat Brown. There were "dangerous signs of Hitlerism in the Goldwater campaign," echoed Rev. Martin Luther King Jr. "When, in all our history, has anyone so bizarre, so archaic, so self-confounding, so remote from the basic American consensus, ever gone so far?" the eminent historian Richard Hofstadter enquired. Even the Chad Mitchell Trio reentered the fray, following-up their John Birch Society satire with a song entitled "Barry's Boys," in which Goldwater was "The Fascist gun in the West."[126]

Needless to say, Goldwater had also handed the Democrats one of its major campaign issues on a silver platter. Johnson made sure that his platform contained the plank denouncing extremism that the Republicans had rejected—indeed, it was almost identical to the one Scranton had proposed. "We condemn extremism, whether from the right or left, including the extreme tactics of such organizations as the Communist Party, the Ku Klux Klan and the John Birch Society. We know what violence and hate can do. We have seen the tragic consequences of misguided zeal and twisted logic," it read.[127] Johnson's running mate, Hubert Humphrey, took on the traditional vice-presidential role of election attack dog with glee, denouncing extremism and Goldwater's "flirtation" with the Birch Society, at every opportunity.[128] (Here too Goldwater and his team had erred. Instead of using the vice-presidential position as a means of broadening the ticket, they had selected the equally conservative—and equally inept campaigner—Republican National Committee chairman and congressman William Miller of New York to be their candidate. Examining his three months of work at the end of October 1964, the New York Times contended that Miller's "distortions and wild charges" had only served to confirm his reputation as a "political hatchetman," with few qualifications for the position.)[129] Johnson himself predicted that only an election victory for him would bring an end to extremist groups like the Klan and the Birch Society that had "infected" the country.[130]

Winning the presidency was always going to be a difficult task for Goldwater, of course. Kennedy's death and Johnson's presentation of the Civil Rights Act as something that needed to be passed in honor of his memory had seen to that. Goldwater also had to contend with his opponent's considerable political acumen, his ambitious plans for a Great Society, and his indisputable status as a son of the South. Certainly the factionalism of the GOP and the inexperience of Goldwater's advisers didn't help. Nor did the candidate's own gaffes, such as recommending the use of low-yield atomic weapons to defoliate the forests of Vietnam, arguing for the removal of Castro by rearming Cuban exiles in the United States, telling an audience in Texas that an aerospace contract it had just received should have gone to a company in Seattle, and speculating about making Social Security voluntary or dismissing it as "free retirement."[131] Then there was the unrelenting hostility and ridicule of the press. The "most one-sided and unfair press coverage ever deployed in a presidential campaign," according to a venerable British observer of the American political scene, Godfrey Hodgson.[132] William Buckley simply described it as "vile."[133] (Only three major papers—the *Los Angeles Times*, the *Chicago Tribune*, and the *Cincinnati Enquirer*—endorsed the Arizonan.)[134] Above all of this, though, tying it all together, was the issue of extremism. It was Goldwater's reputation as an extremist that the press played on mercilessly, that Johnson and the Democrats exploited so effectively, and that allowed Goldwater to be convincingly characterized as a nuclear nightmare just waiting to happen. As Mary Brennan has written, the damage the issue caused to Goldwater's campaign was "incalculable."[135]

Except in terms of votes cast, of course. And on election day, the results were close to apocalyptic. Johnson won a record 61 percent of the popular vote (43 million to Goldwater's 27 million) and 90 percent of the Electoral College (486 to 52). The Democrats also added thirty-eight new congressmen and two new senators, so they now had a two-thirds majority in both houses of Congress. Many feared that Goldwater had killed the Republican Party.

Aftermath

Appearances can be deceptive, however, and it gradually became clear that, for the conservative wing of the Republican Party at least, Goldwater's campaign had not been the unmitigated catastrophe it seemed at the time. As has been widely discussed, conservatives were now in control of the machinery of the party at all levels, the campaign had provided a vital "training ground" for a generation of activists in developing the skills they would put to more successful use in subsequent electoral contests, and in Ronald Reagan—who had expertly delivered a televised paean to conservatism entitled "A Time for Choosing" (more usually referred to simply as "The Speech") in support of Goldwater's presidential aspirations—conservatives had unearthed the candidate who would lead them, eventually, to the promised land.[136]

Conservatives also discovered that they could raise large sums of money through the use of direct-mail solicitation techniques. Pioneered by Richard Viguerie, the former executive director of Young Americans for Freedom, these methods were crucial to the development of the New Right in the United States.[137] Significantly, this method of fund-raising also helped to further marginalize the voices of the radical Rightists. As Allan Lichtman has noted, organizations like the Birch Society, Christian Crusade, and the Christian Anti-Communism Crusade had so much influence in the conservative movement during the early 1960s not just because they could call upon the most energetic activists, but also because they were the richest groups on the scene.[138] Conservatives could also take comfort in the extraordinary popularity of pro-Goldwater publications like Phyllis Schlafly's *A Choice Not an Echo*, John A. Stormer's *None Dare Call It Treason*, and J. Evetts Haley's *A Texan Looks at Lyndon: A Study in Illegitimate Power*, which among them sold sixteen million copies. Clearly there was a considerable conservative constituency in the country—as the post-election rallying cry of "27 million can't be wrong" tried to build on. (Interestingly, the arguments and analysis put forth by Schlafly, Stormer, and Haley were in many respects very close to, if not indistinguishable from, those of the Birch Society.)[139]

Overall, then, as Jonathan Schoenwald has written, the 1964 election was "a milestone in the growth and development of post-World War II conservatism."[140] It was also a disaster for the Birch Society. Reflecting on the election in the December 1964 issue of *American Opinion*, Welch tried to put a brave face on the results. The fault lay with the "Republican leadership," not with Goldwater himself, Welch believed. The senator had "displayed plenty of lion-like courage," and in Welch's view much of the criticism being directed his way "overlook[ed], or the critics fail[ed] to understand, the incredible array of hidden forces that were organized against him." Presented with the "first really practicable opportunity in thirty years to undeceive [the American people], there were very few campaigners, even among the Conservatives, who took the trouble and had the courage to tell the people even a fraction of the truth." Although Republican leaders had been "willing to state their positions on many controversial issues, or in general to stand behind positions already taken," they had not explained and expounded on "the correctness and reasonableness" of their positions on topics such as the "'Civil Rights' slogan and drive," which Welch insisted "was a most important and integral part of the longrange Communist plans for the gradual takeover of the United States," or the Social Security system, which was "nothing more than one of the insidious but gigantic steps whereby a central government is gradually establishing itself as the Communist 'Big Brother' of George Orwell's *1984*."[141]

There were some "twenty-six million Americans [the final tally had not yet been made available] who had somehow found out enough of the truth for themselves, in one way or another over recent years, to make them Conservatives," Welch argued. "But they had precious little help, towards informing and converting others, from any of the politicians in the late lamented campaign." Things might have been different, Welch mused, if only the "Republican leadership, from the very hour Goldwater was nominated . . . had come out fighting unequivocally and unceasingly" for real conservative principles and policies, if they had devoted "every dollar" and "every hour" to the cause, and if every campaign speech had been "of the same kind and calibre as the one speech delivered by Ronald Reagan, and the last-minute contribution by John Wayne." The Goldwater-Miller ticket may still not have won, Welch conceded, but it "would certainly have come closer."[142]

It was not an analysis likely to persuade Welch's numerous critics. On the contrary, moderate and conservative Republicans alike agreed that one of the principal things that needed to happen in the aftermath of the 1964 election was the ostracization and marginalization of the Birch Society. Welch's demurrals and Goldwater's distinctions notwithstanding, the close association between Goldwaterism, extremism, and Birchism was widely seen as one of the main explanations for the enormity of Goldwater's loss.

At a conference of Republican leaders held at Columbia University in December 1964, for example, William Scranton argued that Birch Society members needed to be ousted from the party in order to "erase the stigmas" left by Goldwater's defeat. "A political party is not a narrow political society," the governor explained. "Anyone seeking a ready-made, fully developed dogma ought to join the John Birch Society or the Americans for Democratic Action, depending on his point of view."[143] That same month saw the creation of the American Conservative Union (ACU). Republican congressmen Donald C. Bruce (Indiana) and John Ashbrook became, respectively, its chairman and vice-chairman, with *National Review*'s Frank Meyer as treasurer and William Rusher its political action director, while William Buckley and Brent Bozell both became members of its board. Birchers could become members of the ACU, but they were forbidden from becoming officers, directors, or advisers of the organization.[144]

In June the following year, Goldwater announced the creation of the Freedom Society Association (FSA), for which he would serve as the honorary chairman; Denison Kitchel would be its president. It was an educational organization, Goldwater explained, and its aim was to "channel conservative voters and political action into a more moderate and acceptable force than the John Birch Society or other right-wing groups." Indeed, active Birchers and Klansmen were specifically excluded from the FSA's membership, which reached thirty-eight thousand. (The aim had been to recruit 150,000 members.)[145] On September 30, 1965, the joint Republican congressional leadership called a news conference. The Birch Society was its subject and the statements made at it were emphatic. "The John Birch Society is not a part of the Republican party," declared Everett McKinley Dirksen of Illinois, the Senate minority leader. "There just isn't any room in our party for an organization that operates in secrecy to achieve its goals." "There's just no place for that organization in the Republican party," concurred Gerald Ford, the Republican leader in the House.[146]

The excommunication of the Birch Society from the Republican Party was almost complete, but it fell to the editors of *National Review* to read the society out of the conservative movement entirely. This they endeavored to do in a twelve-page special feature in the magazine on October 19, 1965. The attempt to walk the tightrope between Welch and his followers had not been a success—both would now have to go. Having reviewed *National Review*'s coverage of the Society over the previous three years, including Buckley's "The Question of Robert Welch" article from 1962, the editors concluded that "three things have become clear." The first was that Welch's views "have not changed, on the contrary they have become . . . more virulent." (The official publication of *The Politician* during this time, albeit absent the direct claim that Eisenhower was a "dedicated, conscious agent" of the communist conspiracy from its manuscript/letter iteration, had not helped the Founder much in this regard.) The second thing was that there was "no effective movement from within the Society to contain Mr. Welch's utterances, or to remove him as the Society's leader." And the third was Welch's success in continuing to "influence his membership to believe those surrealisms which he first ventilated in *The Politician*," because "as the membership comes to believe the Welch analysis, it ceases to be effectively anti-Communist."[147]

An article by James Burnham—"the country's leading anti-Communist strategist," the editors pointedly noted—tried to demolish Welch's thinking on American foreign policy, but it was Frank Meyer who delivered the coup de grâce. He wrote:

> The false analysis and conspiratorial mania of the John Birch Society has moved beyond diversion and waste of the devotion of its members to the mobilization of that devotion in ways directly anti-conservative and dangerous to the interests of the United States. It is no longer possible to consider the Society merely as moving towards legitimate objectives in a misguided way. However worthy the original motivations of those who have joined it and who apologize for it, it is time for them to recognize that the John Birch Society is rapidly losing whatever it had in common with patriotism or conservatism—and to do so before their own minds become warped by adherence to its unrolling psychosis of conspiracy.[148]

National Review's understanding of the Birch Society was given the imprimatur of the academy with the publication of Richard Hofstadter's extraordinarily influential essay "The Paranoid Style in American Politics" in *Harper's Magazine* the following month (and its republication in book form the year after). Exponents of the paranoid style, Hofstadter argued—the Birch Society and Goldwater both being prime examples (not surprisingly, given that they clearly provided the principal motivation for the essay in the first place)—did not see "conspiracies or plots here and there in history." Rather, they regarded a "'vast' or 'gigantic' conspiracy as *the motive force* in historical events." To people like the Birchers, history itself was a conspiracy and what was needed to defeat it was "not the usual methods of political give-and-take, but an all-out crusade." These paranoid spokesmen, Hofstadter continued, were always "manning the barricades of civilization" and were constantly living "at a turning point." For them, time was "forever just running out." They were double sufferers from history, Hofstadter said, since they were "afflicted not only by the real world, with the rest of us," but by their "fantasies" as well.[149] Similar academic and quasi-academic assessments soon followed.[150] Birch Society members had not just been pushed to the margins of the conservative movement; they had become poster boys for a political syndrome, and exemplars of a very particular strain of American political extremism.

Reagan, Nixon, and the Shape of Things to Come

One of the ironies of this assessment of the Birch Society was that it came after the organization had begun a campaign to improve its public image—the official publication of *The Politician* was one part of it. On June 1, 1963, for example, five members of the National Council—Clarence Manion, Revilo Oliver, businessman Robert D. Love, the editor and publisher of *Farm and Ranch* magazine Thomas J. Anderson, and the writer Slobodan M. Draskovich—spoke and answered questions about the Society in a day-long public meeting in downtown Manhattan. The event was part of a series of regional meetings (there were nine in all) intended to combat the assertions of the Society's critics that it was secretive and just as monolithic as the Communist Party it opposed.[151] Don Vondra, the Society's Colorado coordinator, even ventured into the hostile environs of a meeting of the International Brotherhood of Electrical Workers in Pueblo, Colorado, to press the Birch case.[152] John Rousselot, who had lost his congressional seat in the 1962 elections and had become the Society's full-time Western district governor, was appointed as its first national director of public relations in July 1964.[153]

It was all to no avail, however. The Society's identification with the forces of extremism was too strong to be overcome—and, as we have seen, it had itself done (and said) much to justify the application of the label. The Society did not cease its political activities or its attempts to gain access to the Republican Party in the aftermath of Goldwater's devastating loss, but it would never again come close to the potential level of influence—and notoriety—it had in the years 1963 and 1964. Once the official and more "responsible" faces of American conservatism turned away from Birchism, they never looked back. In October 1965 even Goldwater himself admitted that the Republican national convention should have adopted a resolution condemning extremism in 1964—although, as the *New York Times* reported, "he was still not sure" how to define the term.[154]

Ronald Reagan, for one, clearly demonstrated that he understood the lessons of the Goldwater campaign on his way to becoming the governor of California. Reagan knew just as many Birchers as Goldwater, and like Goldwater his politics and theirs were hardly worlds apart. (He certainly seemed to be channeling Robert Welch when he told the press in 1952, for example, that "lots of people in our community [the Hollywood film industry] don't realize that their thinking is dictated, in that it was implanted by the Communists a few years ago. Their minds need reconditioning.")[155] Yet he handled the Birch accusations leveled against him deftly in 1966, telling reporters that "if anyone chooses to vote for me they are buying my views, I am not buying theirs," and suggesting that a congressional investigation might be appropriate to "clear the air" as to whether the organization was subversive or not.[156] Certainly the Birch issue never dogged Reagan the way it had dogged Goldwater. Indeed, it was barely an issue at all. (Other conservative gubernatorial candidates who were successful in 1966 included Claude Kirk in Florida, Paul Laxalt in Nevada, and John Williams in Arizona.)[157]

The thousands of Birchers who went to work for George Wallace's presidential campaign in 1968—they "dominated the Wallace movement in nearly a dozen states from Maine to California," observes Dan Carter—in contrast demonstrated that they had not understood the lessons of 1964 quite so well.[158] Their involvement with Wallace's American Independent Party only succeeded in further identifying the Society with the forces of racism and extremism—albeit one capable of winning 13.5 percent of the popular vote.[159]

Nixon's narrow victory in 1968 (with 43.4 percent of the popular vote to Hubert Humphrey's 42.7 percent) may not have led to the White House being occupied by a conservative of the hue all the movement's activists could embrace warmly. It did show, however, that it was possible for a conservative Republican to become president of the United States—in part thanks to the pioneering "southern strategy" of the Goldwater campaign, of course—thus paving the way for the more universally welcomed success of Reagan twelve years later.[160]

There is an understandable tendency to marginalize the role played by organizations like the John Birch Society whenever this tale of eventual conservative triumph is recounted. But, as we have seen, it is a mistake to do so. The Society had an important part to play in the story, both positively, in the sense of showing a way forward for conservatives in terms of the energy, excitement, discipline, and focus that could be directed to the cause, and negatively, by providing something for a more moderate—and electorally viable—conservatism to position itself against. Indeed, to a considerable extent, the Birch Society functioned as bridge between the older conservatism of the 1950s and the modern version of conservatism that now seems to dominate the Republican Party.

PART II

Chapter 4

Rights

In September 1956, two years before the formation of the John Birch Society, Robert Welch published "A Letter to the South: On Segregation" in *One Man's Opinion*, the precursor to *American Opinion*. Speaking in the first person plural, Welch argued that "we had come to believe it to be inevitable, and desirable, that *formal* segregation would eventually be abandoned everywhere in the South," leaving only "a voluntary and incomplete segregation in purely social activities, resulting from the rights of any man, white or colored, to have friends of his own choosing, and from the tendency of those with like interests and friends in common to associate together." Welch knew that such a situation would not be to the liking of many of his readers, but it was, he thought, what "enlightened opinion" would eventually produce. Considerable improvements had already been made in the Jim Crow South, he said. Admittedly, the conditions of "our Negro population" were still "far-from-equal," as the Fourteenth Amendment to the Constitution required, but "the gap between the positions of colored man and white man has been getting perceptibly narrower," and were there "any satisfactory statistics on the subject," they would surely show "the material standard of living of the average American Negro" to be higher than that of the "average Englishman."[1]

The whole situation had been changed, though—and progress toward "voluntary desegregation" put back a generation—by the Supreme Court's 1954 decision in *Brown v. Board of Education*.[2] The "ordinary colored people of the South" should not be blamed for these developments, he said, because they were "easily . . . misled by clever agitators, as you would be if you were in their position." In most cases, the native North Carolinian went on, wrapping his paternalism up with religious sentiment, "they know not what they do; and if there was ever a time and place when patience and charity and a huge reservoir of deep good will were needed, it is in the South today." As far as Welch was concerned, the blame rested "squarely on the shoulders of the Communists." The "rising racial bitterness" the *Brown* decision had produced was "the finest grist the Communists have yet been able to obtain for their American mill," he contended. It was "exactly the same kind of raw material out of which they have so successfully manufactured violent strife in one country after another." And it was all part of their "larger and longer plans."[3]

Welch took no real position as to "how far and how fast" those living in the South should legally attempt to comply with the Supreme Court's ruling on desegregation—"we have neither the knowledge nor the presumption out of which to offer any advice," he said—but he was very worried about those who were advocating "direct resistance": "Our friends in the South write us that they will not be *forced*; that nothing will *force* them to immediate desegregation, short of civil war. And what we are trying to tell you, what this whole letter is really about, is the very real danger of this extreme result; of a civil war that would engulf the South and spread through race riots and other Communistic-fomented disorders into a chaotic terror over our whole nation." Civil war was what the communists wanted, the future Founder made clear. After all, "Communist-initiated civil wars, whether in China or Vietnam or Spain or Yugoslavia, never start as full-fledged warfare." Instead, "they always begin as localized clashes, over some such principle as 'agrarian reform' or 'abolition of tyranny,' that has no easily apparent connection with plans for Communist conquest." And in the present instance, he believed, "the phrase is 'civil rights.'"[4]

It wasn't possible any longer to keep saying "it can't happen here," Welch argued. "*It is happening here*, right now. In Mississippi and South Carolina, and all over a fourth of our country the Communists have already entered—incipiently, insidiously, patiently, farsightedly, deceptively—onto the last stage, the physical-fighting stage, of their three-pronged strategy for making the U.S. a group of provinces ruled by Moscow." And there was only "one thing" the communist plotters feared, and that was "the truth about their methods and their plans."[5]

The rise of the civil rights movement and the increasing militancy and effectiveness of the "freedom struggle" in the aftermath of the *Brown* decision was perhaps the most significant political development in the United States during the second half of the twentieth century. The 1960s was one of the pivotal decades in this story, as evidenced by the successful passage of the Civil Rights Act in 1964 and the Voting Rights Act in 1965. This chapter examines the Birch Society's struggle to come to terms with the civil rights movement, as well as the emergence of black power and black nationalist groups during the 1960s, and documents the increasingly rightward shift of the Society during this time. As we shall see—and as Welch's "Letter to the South" presaged—the Birch Society understood the civil rights movement not as an attempt by fellow citizens to obtain their legal rights, or to improve their position in a deeply racist society, but as part of an already-existent plot to further the communist conspiracy in the United States. It was a response that provides a telling illustration of how ideological rigidity can too easily blind people to the actualities of the world they live in.

A resistance to the perceived dangers of excessive government power and a constitutionally based defense of states' rights were the two other reasons why the Birch Society opposed the civil rights movement. Such arguments usually functioned as little more than a convenient fig leaf for the defenders of racism and white privilege in the South, of course, so it is particularly interesting that this does not seem to have been the case for the Birch Society, despite repeated attempts to depict the organization as fundamentally racist (Birchers were just "Ku Kluxers out of nightshirts," in the view of former president Harry Truman, for example).[6] Indeed, as Alan Westin discovered in his investigation of the Society for *Commentary* in 1961, "anti-Negro" sentiment formed no explicit part of its program, and although few in number, African Americans were welcome in the Society, both in the South—where chapters were segregated—and in the North, where they were integrated.[7]

There were certainly Birchers who were racist, and the Society as a whole moved increasingly to the right on racial issues as the decade wore on, with thinly disguised racist sentiments increasingly slipping into its discourse, but during the early 1960s at least, Welch made strenuous efforts to keep overt racists (and anti-Semites) out of the organization. Importantly, and unlike the Citizens' Councils, for example, the Birch Society was not formed in opposition to the desegregation process. Its driving motivations came from its anticommunist, antiliberal conservatism, and its understanding of the civil rights movement was, until the mid-1960s, largely contained by and subsumed within this foundational framework.

Recognizing the ambiguities to be found in the Birch Society's approach to the civil rights of African Americans, Seymour Martin Lipset and Earl Raab nonetheless argued that "while the emergent nativism directed against Negroes [during the 1960s] may have been reflected by many people drawn to the Birch Society, and by many of the articles and publications disseminated by the Birch Society, the Society itself did not consciously attempt to build a mass appeal around the issues." Similarly, in her book *Roads to Dominion*, Sara Diamond concludes that unlike other radical Right groups such as Willis Carto's Liberty Lobby, "the John Birch Society did not officially peddle theories of racial biological determinism" as part of its opposition to the activities of the civil rights movement.[8]

Before exploring these matters further, however, it is first necessary to examine the Birch Society's considerable efforts to impeach the judge who presided over the *Brown* decision—as well as many other decisions that were just as antithetical to those desired by conservatives of the time—the chief justice of the Supreme Court, Earl Warren.

The Movement to Impeach Earl Warren

Despite the views expressed in Welch's "Letter to the South," in truth the issue of civil rights was not a major concern of the Birch Society during the first couple of years of its existence. *The Blue Book*, the Society's foundational text, contains only the briefest mention of the issue, in a discussion of the three methods available to the communists for taking over the United States, and essentially repeats Welch's take on the matter from 1956, when he said that Moscow was attempting to foment civil war in the country by using the slogan of "civil rights" in the same way that "agrarian reform" had been used to foment trouble in China. This was also the extent of the issue's discussion in *The Politician*, the Society's more troublesome shadow text.[9]

It was something of a surprise, then, when Welch used the January 1961 issue of the *Bulletin* to announce a major new campaign for a "solemn, responsible, and deliberate effort" to impeach Earl Warren (an indication of the campaign's significance was that it was the only item on the month's agenda).[10] In part, this was simply a case of the Birch Society reacting to the pressure of events; the civil rights movement had increased in importance and impact during the 1950s and early 1960s, so the organization was forced to respond. In part, it was a consequence of needing to give the Society's members something substantive to do; after all, a great deal of the Society's appeal rested upon its reputation as an *activist* organization, and its last major campaign had been the Committee Against Summit Entanglements, protesting—and attempting to prevent—Soviet premier Nikita Khrushchev's official visit to the United States to meet with President Eisenhower in September 1959, more than a year previously.[11] And, as crucial as Warren's involvement in the *Brown* decision was, the movement to impeach him was also motivated by considerations beyond the battle over integration and the civil and political rights of African Americans in the United States.

Indeed, as far as Welch was concerned, it was more directly related to the Society's broader concerns about the ongoing attempt to make the United States into a democracy rather than the republic the nation's founding fathers had originally intended it to be. Such a move—from a country "governed by laws" into one "governed by men unchecked by law and precedent"—was "the most comprehensive and necessary part of the whole program of the Communists to bring us into their imperial system," Welch explained, and while the process may have begun under the presidency of Franklin D. Roosevelt, it was Warren who was doing the most to bring it to fruition. "He [Warren] epitomizes the newborn theory that our Constitution means absolutely nothing against the changing sociological views of the Supreme Court Justices of any given decade or generation; that both our Constitution and our laws are simply whatever the Supreme Court says they are," Welch wrote, as he officially launched the campaign to unseat the chief justice.[12]

The "most important *specific* result of Warrenism" was clearly the "storm over integration," Welch acknowledged, but this had to be understood as part of a wider plot to expand the powers of the federal government and destroy "all remaining vestiges of States' Rights" in the United States. "It is that residual hard core of local government and regional rights, that ready framework for resistance to a monolithic dictatorship in Washington, that the Communists *must* destroy," Welch argued, and it was with this aim in mind that beginning in the 1920s communist agents had "counted on using racial strife as the one great means and excuse by which they would ultimately reduce our state lines to no more significance within the nation than our county lines now have within the states." Because of this, for Welch, Warren's impeachment was about much more than simply expressing opposition to the Supreme Court's decision in

Brown. It would "dramatize and crystallize the whole basic question of whether the United States remains the United States, or becomes gradually transformed into a province of the world-wide Soviet system," and it would also "'put the fear of God' in the whole pro-Communist hierarchy that already controls our government—but which does not yet control our people except by deception and manipulation."[13]

Welch and the other Birch Society leaders were under no illusion that removing the chief justice would be easy. The process was difficult—requiring a majority vote on each article of impeachment in the House of Representatives and a two-thirds vote in favor of conviction in the Senate, which acts as both judge and jury in such circumstances—and obviously fraught with complex political calculations (and ramifications), all the more so when the pressure to initiate proceedings was coming from outside of the political establishment itself. Warren, like any other American, was entitled to a "completely fair trial," Welch noted, and there could no guarantee of his conviction—this would be "for the Senate to decide entirely on the basis of the evidence and the arguments brought forth" at the trial—but the Society was "demanding" his impeachment because it was "convinced that the evidence of his abuse of his high office is amply sufficient to warrant his arraignment."[14]

Although there were "several different approaches" that might be taken against him, Welch argued that the best ground to secure Warren's indictment was to be found in his failure to hold his office "during good Behaviour" as set out in Article III, Section 1 of the Constitution. (The phrase has been interpreted by the courts to mean behavior of the same level of seriousness denoted by "Treason, Bribery, or other high Crimes and Misdemeanors," which are the grounds for impeachment for the president, vice president and other "civil Officers of the United States" in Article II, Section 4 of the Constitution.) To support this assessment, Welch pointed not just to *Brown*, although he described it as "the most brazen and flagrant usurpation of power that has been seen in three hundred years, in any major court in the whole Anglo-American system of jurisprudence," but also to Warren's involvement in a series of other decisions—*Pennsylvania v. Nelson* (1956), *Konigsberg v. State Bar* (1957), *Watkins v. United States* (1957), *Sweezy v. New Hampshire* (1957)—that to Welch, as to many other conservative and anticommunist activists, not only trampled further on the principle of states' rights, but also protected and extended the rights of communists and other leftists, thus making the nation even more vulnerable to internal subversion.[15] It was the totality of Warren's involvement in these areas—his overall record as chief justice of the United States—that, the Birch Society believed, warranted his impeachment.[16]

Pennsylvania v. Nelson concerned Steve Nelson, a member of the American Communist Party who in 1952 had been convicted of violating the Pennsylvania Sedition Act for advocating the overthrow of the U.S. government by force or violence. The Pennsylvania Supreme Court had reversed the conviction on the basis that the federal Smith Act of 1940, which outlawed the same conduct, superseded the state law, a decision the Warren Court upheld in a six to three vote. In *Konigsberg v. State Bar* the court voted five to three to allow Raphael

Konigsberg to be admitted to the California Bar Association despite his refusal to answer questions about his membership in the Communist Party or about his political beliefs in general.

The decisions in *Watkins v. United States* and *Sweezy v. New Hampshire*—both handed down on June 17, 1957, a date known to anticommunists in particular as "Red Monday"—addressed the extent to which legislative institutions were permitted to inquire into the political affiliations and associations of those before them. John T. Watkins was an organizer for the United Automobile Workers who had been convicted of contempt of Congress for his refusal to answer questions about other people he knew who may have been members of the Communist Party when he appeared before the House Un-American Activities Committee (he *had* answered questions about his own participation in communist activities). Paul Sweezy was a professor at the University of New Hampshire convicted of contempt for failing to answer questions by New Hampshire attorney general Louis C. Wyman about his involvement in the Progressive Party—as well as the content of his lectures and writings—during a state legislative investigation. Both Watkins's and Sweezy's convictions were overturned by the Supreme Court, the former in a six to one vote and the latter by the margin of six to two.

In *Watkins*, the chief justice had stated that there was no "congressional power to expose for the sake of exposure," and in *Sweezy* he declared that the American form of government was "built on the premise that every citizen shall have the right to engage in political expression and association."[17] In making these decisions, the Supreme Court was clearly turning away from the perceived excesses and hysteria of the Second Red Scare years. Although curiously absent from Welch's discussion of the "abuses" of the Warren Court in the January 1961 issue of the *Bulletin*, another decision handed down on Red Monday reinforced the point. It was *Yates v. United States*, and it reversed the Smith Act convictions of fourteen leaders of the CPUSA.[18]

Widely celebrated by liberals, the Supreme Court's shifting position in this area caused just as much consternation among the country's conservatives and anticommunists as the *Brown* decision had. Certainly, Welch and the Birch Society were far from alone in their condemnations of Warren and his cohorts. Reflecting on the *Nelson* decision, for example, Senator Joe McCarthy (R-WI) declared the Senate had "made a mistake in confirming as Chief Justice a man [Warren] who had no judicial experience and very little legal experience," while James O. Eastland (D-MS)—the powerful chairman of both the Senate Judiciary Committee and the Senate Internal Security Subcommittee, as well as a committed segregationist—denounced the Supreme Court as a whole for being composed of "politicians instead of lawyers."[19] Numerous conservative publications, including the *Chicago Tribune*, the *New York Daily Mirror*, and William Buckley's *National Review* joined in the chorus of disapproval—"The boys in the Kremlin may wonder why they need a 5th column in the United States so long as the Supreme Court is determined to be so helpful," was the *Tribune's* editorial response to Red Monday, for example—while conservatives, anticommunists, and segregationists in Congress introduced over a hundred anti-Supreme Court measures and resolutions between January and August 1957. After the Red Monday decisions, President Eisenhower reportedly came to view his appointment of Warren as chief justice as the "biggest damn fool thing I ever did."[20]

The Birch Society was not even alone in calling for Warren's impeachment. Four months before Red Monday, on February 22, 1957, Georgia's General Assembly had overwhelmingly passed a resolution calling for Warren and his "liberal" colleagues to be removed from office for "undertaking by judicial decrees to carry out communist policies" and for "high crimes and misdemeanors too numerous too mention." Senator Strom Thurmond (D-SC) made the same call at the same time.[21] It was also the first solution to the "crisis" represented by the Warren Court in Rosalie M. Gordon's widely circulated and highly influential book, *Nine Men against America: The Supreme Court and Its Attack on American Liberties*, originally published in 1958. In Gordon's view, although the Supreme Court's "attack" on American civil liberties and the whole constitutional system—its "tendency to usurp the powers of the Congress and the states, to tailor its decisions in favor of the communist conspirators, to further entrench the labor-union monopoly, [and] to treat the Constitution as though it did not exist," as she put it in the book's preface—had begun under in the 1930s, the situation had become immeasurably worse since Warren's appointment as chief justice in 1953. Her solutions, in addition to impeachment, for thwarting Warren's "judicial tyranny" and preventing the country's "headlong plunge into authoritarian government," included: term limits; the periodic reconfirmation of justices; a requirement that "at least one of each two successive nominees to the Court should have had ten years of judicial experience"; and the removal of the president's power to appoint federal judges, with this role given to the Senate instead.[22]

Nine Men against America was a particular source of inspiration for Welch and the Birch Society. It was reprinted by the organization and sent to all chapter leaders—as well as to individual subscribers to *American Opinion*—in March 1961, and in July Welch argued that if only "we could get one million Americans to read [the book] . . . Warren's impeachment . . . would follow as surely and swiftly as children dash for an open box of candy."[23] Such an attitude again reflected the wider belief of the Society that it had access to particular "truths" and that its main job was simply to convey those "truths" to an ignorant or skeptical American public. It also revealed a touching faith in the power of words and persuasion to change people's minds and opinions. "Very few people can read even the first few pages of the book and not see immediately that there is more to this uproar about the Warren Court and its assaults on our Constitution than they had suspected," Welch contended, and he called on Birchers to become "bibliographical philanthropists," buying up and passing on as many copies of Gordon's work as possible.[24]

The same attitude was evident in the mechanics of the campaign itself. The actions the Society urged its members to engage in to realize this "huge undertaking" included writing letters—"in restrained language," with "sound reasons" and as "convincingly" as possible—to the nation's congressmen, asking them to do their part to bring about Warren's impeachment, as well as to newspapers in the hope of soliciting editorial support. They were encouraged to form "Impeach Warren Committees" in their local towns and areas, and to have any other organizations to which they belonged pass resolutions urging Congress to vote for impeachment and to transmit those resolutions directly to the Speaker of the House and to as "many individual members of the House" as they could manage. Birchers were to study the subject as thoroughly as possible "so as to be better prepared" to state their case, and to enlist the support of as many of their friends and acquaintances as they could reach. Petitions were to be circulated— the initial target (announced in the July 1961 issue of the *Bulletin*) being to obtain ten million signatures by December 31, with the aim of having articles of impeachment successfully introduced in the House in January 1962—billboards erected, stickers posted, and impassioned and informative speeches made.[25]

Overall, then, the "Movement to Impeach Earl Warren" seemed to bear all the hallmarks of a highly organized and coordinated pressure group campaign, one premised on the power of persuasion to make its case. Quixotic, perhaps, but a legitimate activity on the part of concerned citizens in a democratic society. This, though, was not how it was generally received or understood. On the contrary, along with Welch's conspiratorial accusations in *The Politician*, the Society's campaign against Warren was one of the primary pieces of evidence used to illustrate its irrational, extremist, and dangerous nature during those crucial first months of public exposure in 1961 and 1962.

It was a "contemptible and vicious thing to suggest the impeachment of one of the great men of our time," complained California Republican senator Thomas Kuchel at a press conference in March 1961 (although, as Warren had been one of the senator's principal sponsors in politics, Kuchel did have something of a personal stake in the matter).[26] "That anyone should propose impeachment of this great American or imply in any way that he is disloyal, is ridiculous and outrageous," echoed Kuchel's North Dakotan senatorial colleague and fellow long-running Birch Society opponent Milton Young, seeing the Society's campaign as an attempt to undermine the American people's confidence in its leaders.[27] "The outrageous campaign of slander [the Birch Society] has launched against Chief Justice Warren is indicative of the woeful inappropriateness of their self-assumed anti-Communist label," contended Democratic congressman John Shelley. Warren had "consistently championed principles of civil rights and civil liberties which are the bulwark of individual freedom," the Californian explained, freedoms that marked "the root distinction between a democratic society and a totalitarian one." And while no one could quarrel with anybody raising questions about the "wisdom of any government's policy or action," Shelley wanted to draw the line at "pressure campaigns aimed at disrupting the normal concept of government," or which misled and manipulated public opinion. Such "dangerous practices" needed to be exposed, he insisted.[28]

Much of the congressional reaction to the campaign in particular suggested that what many of the nation's legislators really found objectionable about the Birch Society was its sheer effrontery in getting involved in a matter that was more properly left in the hands of the professional politicians of Washington. The fact that the Birch Society was even attempting to direct a letter-writing campaign in favor of Warren's impeachment was too much for the Wisconsin Democrat Henry Reuss, for example. "Recently my office has been flooded with letters from throughout the country suggesting that Chief Justice Warren is a traitor and demanding his impeachment," he wrote Francis Walter (D-PA), the chairman of HUAC, urging Walter to undertake an investigation of the Society. "Many of the letters are mimeographed, are similarly worded or bear other evidence of an organized campaign," Reuss complained—even though it is difficult to conceive of any effort to lobby Congress that could be remotely effective unless it was "organized" in some way or another.[29] Similarly, rather than thinking of the letters being sent to Congress as evidence of a genuine—if narrow—expression of discontent with some of the recent decisions of the Supreme Court, Senator Young believed they only revealed the extent to which Welch's followers had been "duped by this demagog."[30] An editorial in the *Chicago Sun-Times* took essentially the same position. The coordinated nature of the Birch Society's campaign and the fact that so many of the letters the newspaper received from Birch members had the "same theme" running through them made the Society's efforts comparable to the "brainwashing" methods employed by communists to "impress their views on communities," the paper argued.[31]

As for the chief justice himself, he maintained a dignified public silence throughout the attempt to have him impeached. He was never disturbed by the campaign, he said in his memoirs, because he never believed it had any chance of success, because it sapped the "energy and resources" of the Birch Society, and because he "recognized it for what it was—an expression of dislike on the part of vested interest groups who were offended by the [Supreme] Court's interpretation in various cases that came before us."[32]

The Birch Society did have its defenders, of course, even within Congress. They included the South Carolina Democrat Mendel Rivers, who took the view that the "death knell . . . for the Constitution" had sounded on the "fateful day" *Brown v. Board of Education* had been decided, and Senator Barry Goldwater (R-AZ), who, although not agreeing with the "assumptions" behind the Birch campaign—just as he didn't agree with "a lot of Warren's decisions"—nonetheless believed that "every man has a right to say Warren should be impeached."[33] But overall the reaction to the Society's campaign was extremely hostile. Indeed, despite the fact that when launching the Movement Welch had insisted that "sheer noise-making" formed no part of the Society's aims, and that it would not be seeking publicity simply for the sake of publicity, this hostility may well have persuaded the organization's leadership that it had little to lose when, in August 1961, it announced a new feature of the campaign designed, it seemed, just to direct more attention the Birchers' way: *viz.*, an essay contest open to the nation's undergraduate students on the subject of the best grounds for Warren's impeachment, with $2,500 in prize money.[34]

Welch told the *New York Times* that the aim of the contest was to "stir up a great deal of interest among conservatives on the campuses on the dangers that face this country," but the controversy it produced spread far beyond the nation's universities and colleges. Whitney North Seymour, the president of the American Bar Association, for example, decried the contest's "personal vilification of one of the chief officers of our Government." The Birch Society was not offering "legitimate criticism of [Supreme Court] decisions," Seymour informed the 4,500 members of the association gathered in St. Louis for its annual convention; rather it was showing "disrespect for our institutions" that maintain "liberty under law."[35] The nationally syndicated columnist Roscoe Drummond took the Society to task for its "extreme, radical, and reckless methods," which, he said, were doing more to hurt the anticommunist cause than help it, while Thomas M. Storke, editor and publisher of the *Santa Barbara News-Press*, as well as a long-standing friend of the chief justice, offered $1,500 in prize money for a counter-essay contest on "The Problem of Character Assassination: (1) Legal Redress, (2) Psychiatric Remedy."[36] (Informed of the Birch contest, Warren joked that perhaps his wife should enter, as she knew more about his faults than anyone else.)[37]

The winner of the Birch Society's contest, unveiled at a rally in Los Angeles on February 5, 1962, was a twenty-three-year-old called Eddie Rose who, *Time* magazine delighted in recounting, had "flunked out" of the UCLA engineering school, attended Los Angeles City College for a year, and was "now taking extension courses in engineering at U.C.L.A." (Rose was not a member of the Society himself; he only shared "about 98 percent of their views," he said.) Somewhat perversely, the Society decided to keep the text of the prize-winning essay a secret, although the competition had apparently been such a success that a new one was shortly to follow. This time the nation's college students would be rewarded for writing the best review of Gordon's *Nine Men against America*.[38]

The Society's original intention had been for the results of its contest to be announced during the first week of January, presumably to coincide with what it was anticipating to be the successful introduction of articles of impeachment against the chief justice that month (the date Welch had targeted in the May 1961 *Bulletin*). January 1962 arrived, however, and no bill of impeachment had been passed in the House. In that month's issue of the *Bulletin*, Welch admitted that he simply didn't know when such a bill would now be introduced—his estimate was that at present only "about one-third" of House members would vote for Warren's impeachment if "offered the opportunity to do so." He still believed, however, that the campaign was a crucial one. "I personally do not think we can save our country unless we can ultimately impeach Warren," the Founder informed his readers, but his use of the adverb *ultimately* signaled a significant change in the status of the Movement within the Society's overall plans and strategies.[39]

Launching the campaign against Warren the previous year, Welch had said there was "no limit" to the effort each member of the Society could put into it, and that it should engage the "fullest extent of the time and energy" every member could spare. By June 1962, however, the project was being described as simply part of the "long-range" educational activities of the organization.[40] The goal of having Warren impeached never disappeared completely from the Society's agenda: Pictures of anti-Warren billboards erected by the Society's members (by roadsides, driven behind cars, and even on boats) appeared periodically in the *Bulletin* in the years that followed.[41] Birchers picketed and heckled the chief justice during his public appearances.[42] In November 1963, Father Francis E. Fenton, a Roman Catholic priest and member of the Birch Society National Council, was censured by his diocese in Bridgeport, Connecticut, for petitioning his parishioners to support Warren's impeachment during his Sunday sermons, and so on.[43] But, after all the intense activity of 1961, it was never again the organization's principal focus.

This was understandable enough. Indeed, it probably represented a realistic shift of emphasis, given that impeaching Warren seemed a prospect far from likely to be achieved in 1962, or at any other time in the near future. Moreover, although the chief justice was still in office—Warren would not retire from the court until 1969—from a certain perspective the Society's campaign against him could still be considered to be a successful one. Not only did it energize the Birch Society internally, it also helped to thrust the organization to the forefront of the conservative and anticommunist movement of the time. The publicity the Movement to Impeach Warren generated for Birchers was not wasted in this respect. Nonetheless, the level of activity and commitment the campaign demanded of Birchers could hardly be sustained indefinitely, and there were other events pressing for the Society's attention going on at the same time, events that were difficult to ignore or downplay. Many of these were connected with the growing strength of the civil rights movement, and one of the first, to which we now turn to examine, involved James Meredith and the further misadventures of General Edwin A. Walker.

The Riot at Ole Miss and the Return of General Walker

With the aid of the National Association for the Advancement of Colored People (NAACP) and the backing of several decisions in the federal courts, James Meredith, a twenty-eight-year-old veteran of the U.S. Air Force, had been trying since January 1961 to become the first black student to enroll at the University of Mississippi—known as Ole Miss—in Oxford, Mississippi. He was opposed in his efforts by numerous Mississippians, including most of the state's congressional delegation; almost the whole of the state legislature; the state's governor, Ross Barnett ("No university will be integrated in Mississippi while I am your governor," Barnett had promised); and the university itself. Matters came to a confrontational head in September 1962, following an order of the Fifth Circuit Court of Appeals that the university end its "callous campaign of delay, harassment, and masterly inactivity," and register him.[44]

Determined to avoid a violent standoff, the Kennedy administration negotiated secretly with Barnett, most often through Attorney General Robert Kennedy. The agreement they eventually reached to enable Meredith to complete his enrollment on October 1—after numerous previous attempts had been unsuccessful—saw the governor promising to maintain order on the campus, with the federal presence on the scene being limited to about five hundred U.S. marshals, and units of the U.S Army remaining on standby in

Figure 5.1. Former major general Edwin Walker is led away at bayonet point by U.S. troops after refusing to move from the courthouse in downtown Oxford, Mississippi, during the attempt to prevent James Meredith from registering at the University of Mississippi, October 1, 1962. © Bettmann/CORBIS

Memphis, Tennessee, sixty-five miles away. (The president federalized parts of the Mississippi National Guard in the early hours of September 30.) On the night of September 30, however, as an angry crowd of between two thousand and three thousand people began pelting the marshals with a fusillade of bricks, bottles, stones, and Molotov cocktails, Barnett reneged on the deal, withdrawing the state's highway patrol officers and leaving the federal marshals hopelessly outnumbered and outmatched. By the time the National Guard arrived from Memphis, a full-scale riot was in progress. Two people died and 375 were injured, including 160 marshals, before order was restored—and Meredith admitted to the university.

Prominent amidst the rioting—indeed, according to the Justice Department, one of its principal instigators—was the recently retired Major General Edwin A. Walker. Walker was arrested on charges of sedition and insurrection on October 1. Unable to raise $100,000 in bail, he was flown in a border patrol plane to the U.S. Medical Center for Federal Prisoners in Springfield, Missouri, and placed under psychiatric evaluation pending his trial.[45] ("Imagine that son of a bitch having been a commander of a division up till last year. And the Army promoting him," reflected President Kennedy on discovering Walker's involvement in the rioting.)[46]

Walker had believed that communists were stirring up trouble with the civil rights movement back in 1957 when, in an ironic quirk of history, he had been the commander of the 101st Airborne Division charged by President

Eisenhower with desegregating Central High School in Little Rock, Arkansas, but at the time his sense of military obligation and discipline had outweighed the pull of his own political beliefs. ("We are all subject to all the laws, whether we approve of them or not," Walker told the white students of the Little Rock high school. "If it were otherwise, we would not be a strong nation, but a mere unruly mob.")[47] No such constraints existed after he had resigned from the army, of course, and Walker increasingly involved himself in the desegregation struggle.

Walker was drawn to the state of Mississippi and to Meredith's attempt to enroll at Ole Miss in particular as one of the frontlines in the fight. In the Mississippi state capital on December 29, 1961, with Governor Barnett and other leading segregationists in attendance, the former general stated:

> I have been asked why I came to Jackson. I came here to bring the Texas State Flag and to place it beside your Mississippi State Flag. I came here to meet the Communists on their battlefield right here in Mississippi. . . . I was determined to meet their challenge on the hottest battlefield I can find. It is *here*, where I stand in Jackson, Mississippi. . . . We are at war. You are infiltrated and your cause starts in every home, church, school, street corner, and public gathering. Man your weapons and attack![48]

The martial metaphors were also in evidence in Shreveport, Louisiana, on September 26, when Walker appeared on the radio station KWKH, just before heading off to Oxford. "We have listened and we have been pushed around by the anti-Christ Supreme Court," he stated. "It's time to rise. . . . Ten thousand strong from every state in the nation." Asked afterward by reporters whether he was attempting to mobilize an armed militia, Walker replied that white citizens had to do "whatever is necessary" to resist federal tyranny.[49]

News of Walker's arrest and the federal government's so-called invasion of Mississippi sent shockwaves through the segregationist and ultraconservative sections of the United States, the Birch Society included. The organization had been "flooded" with telegrams and long-distance telephone calls from both members and non-members demanding action, Welch reported in a hastily appended postscript to the September issue of the *Bulletin*, written on the morning of October 2, 1962. The problem for the Society, though, was in determining exactly what action (or actions) it was supposed to undertake. Welch characterized a typical exchange on the subject as follows:

> Caller: "Do something!"
> We: "O.K. But what? You tell us."
> Caller: "I don't know *what*, but do something anyway!"[50]

The Society would not be rushed into a precipitous or foolhardy response, Welch explained. "The more hectic the excitement and confusion, the more clever the provocations of the Left to tempt us to rashness, the more need there is for us to remain resolute but calm." Accordingly—and because "crises" of the kind represented by the events at Oxford were "almost certain to start coming faster now with every passing month"—instead of offering an immediate plan of action, Welch set out some general principles that were intended to guide Birchers both in the present situation and in future confrontations.

Chief among these was the Founder's belief that Birchers "must not go off 'half cocked.'" "Despite any inner fire of angry resentment, and the visible injustices and urgencies in a rapidly developing crisis," he wrote, "we must have patience . . . the patience to make all that we do as effective as we can." The Society was in it for the long haul, after all. Its aim was to "win a total war, not to destroy ourselves by heroic but foolhardy suicide in a particular battle"—and especially not on a battlefield chosen by the enemy (the martial metaphors were contagious, it seemed).

The situation in Mississippi was a "veritable trap" for "Conservative and Constitutionalist Americans," Welch explained, one Walker had fallen into. Despite this, however, Welch still believed that it was important to be "loyal to our friends . . . even when we think they have made mistakes." This was particularly so because the Birch leader regarded Walker's imprisonment as "a fantastic persecution, obviously intended as a precedent for the incarceration, without trial, of other enemies of the Left." Hence, in what was to be the only specific action the Society indicated it would be taking to aid the errant general—and even this was somewhat tepid—Welch declared that "we shall do all that we can to see that [Walker] is represented by adequate and able legal counsel, and given the full protection of whatever laws we have remaining in this country."[51]

John Rousselot, the Birch Society member and California Republican congressman, reinforced what seemed to be Welch's attempt to distance the Society from Walker. If it was established that the general had incited insurrection at Ole Miss, his membership of the Society should be revoked, Rousselot asserted.[52] In part, this was a reflection of just how far Walker's star had fallen since the initial, heady days of the Pro-Blue scandal the previous year, thanks to his lackluster appearance before the Special Preparedness Subcommittee and his disastrous performance in the Texas gubernatorial primary campaign. In part, it was a reflection of the fact that the Society was desperately trying to fend off accusations that it was an extremist or fascist organization, and Walker was widely seen as a poster boy for both. Above all, though, it was a reflection of Walker's increasing association with segregationism and the forces of massive resistance in the American South, an association the Birch Society had no desire to be linked with itself.

Welch made this abundantly clear in the following month's *Bulletin*. "We take absolutely no position on the desirability, propriety, or wisdom, on the part of the University of Mississippi, of admitting a colored student to enroll, or of refusing admission," he wrote. "For the Society as a whole would certainly be badly divided on the issue." Reflecting the extent to which the civil rights of African Americans were still seen largely as a "southern issue" in 1962—they would not really become a "national" one until the following year—Welch pointed out that "most of [the Society's] members in Wisconsin would take an opposite view of the question from the one held by most of our members in Alabama." And this, he continued, "was the basic reason why the people of Wisconsin and those of Alabama, and preferably even smaller groups of our people, should be allowed to decide such matters for themselves."[53] Consistent with the position the Society had mapped out in the Movement to Impeach Warren, as well as with Welch's views in his 1956 "Letter to the South: On Segregation," the issue at hand for Welch was not segregation or desegregation— it was what he considered to be the overweening (and unconstitutional) power of the federal government and its attempts to "*force* Mississippi to admit [Meredith to the University]." "We still do not believe that the Federal Government should have anything to do with the matter," he asserted.[54]

In keeping with the Society's general modus operandi, members were encouraged to lodge their protests against the sending of federal troops to Mississippi through letters, telegrams, and telephone calls to Congress, the attorney general, or the White House. One particular form this protest might take, Welch suggested, was through the slogan "Cuba, Si—Mississippi, No!" There was a more "flagrant demand" for the swift dispatch of the United States' armed forces to Cuba, where the "vicious Communist" Fidel Castro had "robbed and tortured and imprisoned and murdered American citizens who were entitled to the protection of their government," than in the actions of Governor Barnett telling "one American citizen that he cannot go to a college where he isn't wanted," Welch believed.[55]

Ironically, it was actually Kennedy's preoccupation with events in the Caribbean and the Cold War more generally, coupled with a lack of direct personal investment in the issue, and the power of the southern wing of the Democratic Party in Congress that, to a considerable extent, explained the administration's muted response on the question of civil rights in Mississippi and elsewhere throughout 1961 and 1962 (including its willingness to engage in secret negotiations with obstructionist governors like Barnett about the observance and enforcement of the nation's laws).[56] Indeed, although one might have expected Meredith's enrollment at Ole Miss—made possible, in the end, only through the dispatch of the nation's armed forces—to have been widely celebrated by civil rights activists around the country as evidence of Kennedy's commitment to the cause, this was far from the case. Instead, in the words of the historian Harvard Sitkoff, "knowing the hundreds of unlawful acts by white supremacists that the Kennedy Administration did nothing about," civil rights leaders saw the president as "a temporizer and a manipulator, devoid of any true sense of moral urgency concerning the race issue. He would act when it suited his needs, not the movement's. He would act the hero in the victory at Ole Miss but remain on the sidelines during the really fundamental attempt at racial change in Albany, Georgia."[57] The secret negotiations between the Kennedys and Barnett over Meredith's admission to the University of Mississippi "made Negroes feel like pawns in a white man's political game," lamented Martin Luther King Jr. privately (in public, he praised the president's handling of the affair), and this experience, along with the failure of Albany, helped convince him of the need to launch the massive—and ultimately successful—campaign to desegregate Birmingham, Alabama, in 1963.[58]

Bob Dylan managed to encapsulate the events of Ole Miss in one minute and forty-five seconds in "Oxford Town," a deceptively simple protest song that appeared on his album *The Freewheelin' Bob Dylan* in 1963. Written for a competition in the folk magazine *Broadside* to find a "good lasting song" to mark Meredith's enrollment at the university, which the magazine called "one of the most important events" of 1962, Dylan powerfully evoked both the violent realities of the American South at this time and the seeming indifference to those realities in much of the rest of the nation in six short verses. Oxford, Mississippi, Dylan sang, was a place where everybody had their "heads bowed down."[59]

As for General Walker, the psychiatrists who examined him determined that he was not suffering from "paranoid mental disorders," as had first been suspected. Fit therefore to stand trial, Judge Claude Clayton reduced his bail to $50,000, and Walker was released from hospital on November 6, 1962. A federal grand jury refused to indict, however, and the Justice Department dropped the charges against him.[60] Walker emerged from his experience a hero to the segregationist Right in the United States. The Mississippi State House of Representatives gave him a standing ovation when he visited the institution in December 1962, and the following year he was invited to address the leadership conference of the Citizens' Council of America held in Jackson, Mississippi.[61] As the historian Clive Webb recounts, he was now acting as a link between the disparate groups of the far Right, associating both with "extremist" groups such the American Loyal Rangers, Americans for Preservation of the White Race, and the National States' Rights Party, and more "moderate" organizations, including Fred Schwarz's Christian Anti-Communism Crusade and Billy James Hargis's Christian Crusade. (For example, Hargis and Walker undertook a cross-country speaking tour together in 1963 as would-be latter-day Paul Reveres warning about the continuing perils of international communism. The tour was called Operation Midnight Right.)[62]

With respect to the Birch Society, distancing itself from Walker did not mean abandoning the broader lessons and dangerous tendencies it believed had been demonstrated by the events at Ole Miss. Or that it wouldn't try to capitalize on them. In 1963, the Society published and heavily promoted Earl Lively Jr.'s book, *The Invasion of Mississippi*, and a year later it did the same thing with the official report by the General Legislative Investigating Committee of the State of Mississippi into "The Occupation of the Campus of the University of Mississippi, September 30, 1962, by the Department of Justice of the United States."[63] As one might expect, both publications traded heavily on what was regarded as the shocking and unaccountable abuses of federal power required to bring about Meredith's enrollment at the university. The members of the General Legislative Investigating Committee warned, for example, that "what has happened in Mississippi is an illustration of what may happen to any individual in the United States or any State when the desire of the Attorney General of the United States or the President of the United States may be opposed to a State or an individual."[64] This, of course, had been Welch's position all along. As he had argued back in 1956, not only *could* it happen here, in his view it already *had*.

The Civil Rights Movement and the John Birch Society

The success of the campaign by the Southern Christian Leadership Conference (SCLC) against segregation in Birmingham, Alabama, helped to transform both the civil rights movement and the Kennedy administration's attitude toward it. Birmingham was the most segregated city in the South and one of the most violent—indeed, with eighteen racially motivated bombings between 1957 and 1963 alone, many of its black residents knew it better as "Bombingham."[65] Led by Martin Luther King Jr. and Fred L. Shuttlesworth—the founder and leader of the Alabama Christian Movement for Human Rights—and in the face of a brutal response by public safety commissioner Eugene T. "Bull" Connor, civil rights workers and committed local citizens undertook wave after wave of boycotts, sit-ins, marches, and mass meetings between April 3 and May 8, 1963, before securing a written agreement from the city's business leaders to desegregate its lunch counters, restrooms, fitting rooms, and drinking fountains; hire more black workers; and create a biracial committee to address future issues in the city.[66]

The hard-fought—if limited—victory in Birmingham led to a new surge of militancy within the civil rights movement. More than 100,000 people in 115 communities took part in demonstrations across the South in the months that followed, with close to 20,000 being arrested. (After all, if segregation could be overturned in Birmingham, it seemed reasonable to assume that it could be overturned anywhere.) Significantly, poor, working-class, and unemployed blacks were now being drawn into the freedom struggle, especially as it spread out of the South and into the North. Such people often had much less sympathy with, or patience for, the nonviolent philosophy of the SCLC. Indeed, the approach had barely held in Birmingham, and many activists in other civil rights groups, such as the Congress of Racial Equality (CORE) and the Student Non-Violent Coordinating Committee (SNCC), were increasingly willing to leave the strategy behind.[67] It was these developments, coupled with the seemingly widespread appeal of fiery black-nationalist leaders like Malcolm X, that King had in mind when he warned in his "Letter from Birmingham Jail" that he was convinced that "if our white brothers dismiss as 'rabble rousers' and 'outside agitators' those of us who employ nonviolent direct action, and if they refuse to support our nonviolent efforts, millions of Negroes will, out of frustration and despair, seek solace and security in black nationalist ideologies—a development that would inevitably lead to a frightening racial nightmare."[68]

Worried about the possibility of more widespread violence, personally sickened by the brutality on display at Birmingham—the arrests, the beatings, the snarling dogs, the fire hoses trained on children, all of which could be witnessed live on the nation's television sets—and concerned about what all of this was doing to the country's reputation overseas, Kennedy took to the airwaves on June 11 to announce his support for a civil rights bill he was putting before Congress. Among other things, the bill included provisions for desegregating public accommodations such as hotels, restaurants, and retail establishments; empowered the attorney general to initiate school-desegregation suits; expanded funds for job training for African Americans; and created a Federal Community Relations Service to work for improved race relations. Amendments to the original bill by congressional liberals added provisions for a permanent Full Employment Practices Commission and for federal officials to be able to register black voters.[69]

Hoping to strengthen the bill further—its voting rights section covered only federal elections, for example—as well as to ensure its successful passage in Congress, civil rights activists led by A. Philip Randolph and Bayard Rustin organized a massive March on Washington for Jobs and Freedom for August 28 in Washington, DC. Attended by an estimated 250,000 people, including about 50,000 whites, and remembered most often for King's powerful "I have a dream" speech, the march was the largest political assembly in the United States up to that time.[70]

The John Birch Society's response to these developments was both to considerably increase the amount of time and attention it devoted to the question of black civil rights and to frame the issue within the organization's broader conspiratorial understanding of communism's determination to take over the United States. Alan Stang's article "The New Plantation," which appeared in the June 1963 issue of *American Opinion*—and which became part of his book-length study, *It's Very Simple: The True Story of Civil Rights*, published in 1965—in many ways typified the organization's newfound focus on and understanding of the issue of civil rights in America.[71] It begins with a discussion of the writer James Baldwin's account of his violent feelings after being refused a cup of coffee at a diner. As a result of his book *The Fire Next Time* and its stark warning about the violent future that was awaiting the country if the demands of the civil rights movement weren't met, Baldwin, along with Malcolm X, was widely seen as the "face" of the new "black threat" facing the United States.[72] How was the "current Negro revolt" supposed to deliver "Mr. Baldwin's desire for a cup of coffee," Stang wanted to know?[73]

Answering this question required a fuller understanding of the nature of rights, the profound failings of liberalism, and the absolute centrality of capitalism to the construction of a just society, Stang contended. "A right," he explained, "is the absolute and inviolable power to dispose of a specific property—of one's own property," and he defined property as "a specific, identifiable entity, a material extension of one's consciousness," the protection of which was the "only legitimate function of government." The word for an individual who does not have the "absolute and inviolable right to dispose of his own property," or who "must produce on someone else's command, at someone else's whim" is "a slave," Stang believed.[74]

The problem for those like Baldwin, the SCLC, the NAACP, and the Kennedy administration, with their demands for their "'right' to jobs, to housing, to education, to medical treatment . . . [or] to eat where they choose," Stang asserted, was that all these things needed to be "produced" and "paid for," and that this was a task that by necessity fell to the capitalist: "If a man wishes a home, another man, the capitalist, must provide that home—and in a desirable neighborhood. If a man wishes recreation, another man, the capitalist, must provide that recreation. If a man wishes a job, the capitalist must provide that job. He must—by right. The right of him who entertains a wish." But if the capitalist was "forced" to produce these things by the government, he could no longer be said to be free, or to be exercising his own rights. On the contrary, Stang wrote, he would himself become a "slave" (hence the article's title).[75]

Not content with this particular piece of rhetorical and philosophical ingenuity, Stang contended further that every man—including Mr. Baldwin— was "by nature irrevocably a property owner"—the property in question being his own life—and that every man was also therefore "irrevocably a capitalist." A principle once established and acknowledged must be "rigorously applied to all the events it governs," with no exceptions, Stang continued. To wit:

> If . . . a Negro properly has the right to vote, to own a house and decide who will set foot in it, or to apply for a job, the owner of the job properly has the right to deny that job—because the applicant has blue eyes or a peculiar accent, went to Purdue instead of Princeton, is a Democrat or a Republican, a man or a woman—or because he is a Negro. The "son of a bitch" who creates the job does not take it away from the man who applies for it. Before the appearance of this "son of a bitch" the job simply did not exist.[76]

To think otherwise was to embrace the credo of Soviet Russia, a place where the real meaning of "rights" had vanished into the ether. ("Suppose one man has four suits, and the next man has two. Is the next man not entitled to one of the first's?—entitled by right?" or "Suppose one man has two tickets to *My Fair Lady*, and the next man has only a deck of cards. Is the next man not entitled to see the show?—entitled by right—his right to 'adequate recreation'?" Stang asked, by way, he thought, of illustrating the absurdity of it all.)[77]

Like Welch in his 1956 "Letter to the South," Stang did not blame African Americans themselves, or even the NAACP, which he said was "probably not a Communist organization, nor even a Communist front." They had been "gulled" by the Communist conspiracy, he explained, which was trying to "capture" the U.S. government through a "process of internal corruption and dissolution . . . [and] total moral and philosophical confusion." Stang did not believe that one had to specifically identify the means by which the conspiracy was influencing or controlling the activities of the civil rights movement, however; one only had to pay attention to the *consequence* of its actions.[78] In the case of the NAACP, its "impeccable legalism" in pursuit of a Fair Employment Practices Commission, socialized medicine, federal aid to education, housing codes, and so on, served only to "introduce the Federal government, in the name of 'human rights,' to yet another previously inaccessible sphere of American life," Stang argued. And in so doing, it was producing "the very thing it claims to oppose, not freedom for the Negro, but slavery for all." The NAACP, James Meredith, and the hundreds of children sent into the streets of Birmingham by the SCLC, Stang pronounced, had all been "turned with promises of the coming freedom into agents of the festering moral and epistemological chaos which is the real enemy of our civilization."[79]

In article after article, speech after speech, public declaration after public declaration, the Society's leaders, spokesmen, and sympathizers hammered away at their central contention that communists and communism were really behind the civil rights movement in the United States. Communists had "betrayed a good cause," declared former congressman Rousselot in speeches around the country. The International Communist Conspiracy was using the civil rights movement "as part of a world revolution against what they have elected to call 'colonialism'" in order to establish a "beachhead ready for exploitation in the final struggle," contended Medford Evans. "Instead of the abolitionist of yesterday, we now have the Socialist conspirator carrying on his own game, stirring up strife in the entire nation," wrote Governor Barnett in an article entitled "The Rape of Our Constitution and Civil Rights" published by the Society in September 1963. "Communist control of the 'Civil-Rights' movement is no longer a matter of conjecture. It is a matter of fact," announced former chairman of the House Committee on Un-American Activities Martin Dies (D-TX) in May 1965. Undercover Birch journalists infiltrated civil rights meetings to find the movement's "hypnotic" anthem "We Shall Overcome" sung relentlessly until its lyrics were changed to "We Shall *Overthrow*," and the unfortunate Birchers almost found themselves beguiled into joining in.[80]

Often the charges of communist control and influence were much more specific than they had been in Stang's more philosophical analysis of the ills of the "new plantation." Time and again, for example, the Society published a photograph of Martin Luther King at the 1957 convention of Tennessee's Highlander Folk School (see Figure 7.1) in the belief that it provided incontrovertible evidence of King's indoctrination at a communist training school, or they highlighted his association with such "known" communists as Stanley D. Levison, Jack O'Dell, and Bayard Rustin.[81]

Welch himself set out the Society's case plainly enough in his open letter to Nelson Rockefeller in the midst of the battle to secure the Republican Party presidential nomination and the Birch Society's contentious involvement in it during August 1963. "For approximately forty years," Welch informed the governor, "the Communists have been telling their agents and their followers . . . and hence all the rest of us who were willing to listen . . . exactly what uses they planned to make of the racial problem in America." Referring to the prominent American communist John Pepper's 1928 pamphlet *American Negro Problems* to illustrate his point, Welch noted that it contained every "major argument, method, and objective being used today to stir up racial riots and to advance the Communist cause through racial agitation." He then quoted (accurately)

Pepper's views that the "'black belt' of the South . . . *constitutes virtually a colony within the body of the United States of America*," that the CPUSA needed to recognize the "right of national self-determination for the Negroes," and that "*Negro* Communists should emphasize in their propaganda *the establishment of a Negro Soviet Republic*." "How do you feel about this Soviet Negro Republic, Governor?" Welch asked. "With Atlanta, perhaps, as its capital? And Martin Luther King as its 'President'? And all of the cruelty and horror that would be imposed both on the white people and the colored people of the South—who were living together so peacefully, with such steadily improving relations, until May, 17, 1954." In keeping with the organization's faith in the persuasive power of all things textual, the Birch Society reprinted Pepper's pamphlet, along with James W. Ford and James S. Allen's *The Negroes in a Soviet America* (1935), in furtherance of its case.[82]

The Birch Society was far from alone in regarding the civil rights movement as being secretly beholden to, if not entirely controlled by, subversive communist forces, of course. Such beliefs were almost an article of faith for segregationist opponents of the freedom struggle in the South, and they had also found a home in the highest political office in the land, thanks in large measure to the tireless, obsessive, and often illegal efforts of FBI director J. Edgar Hoover. Convinced that communism had been behind the civil rights movement from its inception, Hoover bombarded the Kennedy administration with documentation on the subject, especially with regard to Martin Luther King's role in the supposed conspiracy. Indeed, the Kennedys' suspicions about the extent of communist influence over King and the civil rights movement is another reason why the administration was reluctant to engage with the issue more fully before 1963.[83]

It is certainly true that the Communist Party had a long-standing interest in the question of black civil rights. As the historian Adam Fairclough points out, during the late 1920s and early 1930s the CPUSA was the only political party in the United States to take racial equality seriously, and it attracted black and white recruits to its ranks precisely because of this.[84] (For example, when William Z. Foster put himself forward as the Communist Party candidate for president in 1932, his running mate was the black Alabaman—and subsequent coauthor of *The Negroes in Soviet America*—James W. Ford.)[85] It is also the case that the party regarded black Americans as a potentially rich pool of recruits for the broader communist cause. But this did not mean that communists—much as they may have liked to—were secretly directing the civil rights movement from behind the scenes, especially not the eviscerated American Communist Party of the late 1950s and 1960s.[86] Indeed, for all the considerable resources at its disposal—and despite the desperate desires of its director—the FBI, tellingly, was never able to uncover any direct evidence to prove the assertion.[87]

Yet for all this, it is important to understand why a belief in communist control of the civil rights movement could seem plausible to many people, and why its rhetorical and propaganda value was often too good for opponents of the movement, including the Birch Society, to resist. The Highlander Folk School may not have been a communist training school, for instance—it was founded in 1932 as an interracial workshop, promoting the Social Gospel and "citizenship training"—but it had a definite "leftist" feel to it, and Martin Luther King may have been there only once, but he *had* been there and an actual communist—Abner Berry, a reporter for the *Daily Worker*—*was* sitting with him in the photograph that was taken of his attendance.[88] (Not surprisingly, when Governor Ross Barnett appeared in the Senate alongside his Alabama colleague George Wallace to testify against the civil rights bill, one of the props they came armed with was a poster-sized blowup of the image.)[89] Similarly, close political associates of King like Bayard Rustin, Stanley Levison, and Jack O'Dell *did* have communist connections: Rustin had resigned from the party in 1941; Levison was probably a member of the communist underground, whose work with the party may have continued up to as late as 1957; O'Dell was involved with the party throughout the 1950s and was fired from the SCLC by King in June 1963 following pressure from the Kennedy administration (via the FBI) over his communist associations.[90]

The Birch Society's use of John Pepper's pamphlet *American Negro Problems* is particularly revealing in this respect. As previously noted, Welch was not inventing things or misquoting from the document when he talked about Pepper's advocacy of "Negro self-determination" or a "Soviet Negro republic," but this was only part of the story, and it would have taken a very determined effort on the part of a Birch member or anyone else to uncover the tortuous and convoluted nature of the whole tale.

Pepper had arrived in the United States from the Soviet Union as Joseph Pogany in 1922. He became a prominent if contentious figure in the American communist movement, presenting himself as some kind of official spokesman for the Comintern (which he wasn't) and a self-appointed "authority on the American Negro question."[91] His 1928 pamphlet had arisen from a resolution he had submitted to the Sixth World Congress of the Communist International held in Moscow that year. It was published alongside three other articles on the subject of American Negro rights in the Comintern's theoretical organ, the *Communist International*, and then, owing to Pepper's influence within the American Communist Party, republished as a pamphlet in its own right in the United States. It was because of this subsequent and separate publication, Theodore Draper notes, that *American Negro Problems* acquired "an importance . . . the Comintern never intended." It was simply a discussion paper, nothing more; and certainly not official Communist International policy. "In actuality," Draper writes, "Pepper was already *persona non grata* in the Comintern, and [the] article further contributed to his undoing by going far beyond anything the Comintern contemplated."[92] Indeed, Pepper's view of the Black Belt as a "virtual colony" of the United States and his slogan of a "Negro Soviet Republic" were both determined to be "incorrect" by the Comintern in 1930, before being buried again in 1958, when the whole notion of Negro self-determination was definitively rejected by Moscow.[93]

Along with placing an unsustainable amount of weight on supposedly "official" communist texts like *American Negro Problems*, the Birch Society also endeavored to persuade doubters that its position on racial issues was the correct one by promoting the views of black conservatives such as Manning Johnson and George Schuyler.[94] As a repentant ex-communist, Johnson was an especially attractive figure. Explaining to Governor Rockefeller why he was being sent a copy of Johnson's "moving and powerful" book *Color, Communism and Common Sense*, which the Society had recently republished, Welch described Johnson as "one of the truly great men that America has produced" and someone who had been "lured" into the Communist Party by his youthful idealism but who had seen the truth—"*who knew*" firsthand about the "tremendous harm" the communists had planned for the United States.[95] It was not a strategy without risks, however, as the organization discovered on June 3, 1965, when the African American congressman Charles C. Diggs Jr. (D-MI) revealed on the floor of the House that Rev. J. L. Ward, a black minister purportedly from Memphis, Tennessee, whom the Birch Society had been using in its promotional literature, was actually "an itinerant preacher" with "no stature in the [local] community, let alone on any national level." Diggs resented the attempt by the Birch Society "to clean up its image by falsely representing to the public that any responsible Negro leader has endorsed its organization and the undemocratic principles for which it stands," he said.[96]

The Birch Society unleashed its usual panoply of would-be persuasive techniques to try to prevent the passage of the civil rights bill—letters, petitions, public statements, newspaper advertisements, and the like—but, having been seemingly bogged down interminably in Congress before Kennedy's assassination, the bill was signed into law by President Lyndon Johnson on July 2, 1964.[97] Defeat had to be accepted, Welch acknowledged in that month's *Bulletin*, but the contest over the bill had been "a serious skirmish" and the Society's enemies would be making a big mistake if they believed it "discouraged" by what had happened. "We have hardly even begun to fight," he declared.[98] Its next battle, along with other opponents of the civil rights movement, would be over the voting rights of black Americans.

If the events at Birmingham had been the crucial turning point leading to the passage of the Civil Rights Act, those that took place in Selma, Alabama, provided the decisive spur that produced its successor, the Voting Rights Act of 1965. Selma had 15,000 blacks of voting age within its total population of 29,000, but only 355 registered black voters, and as such it was well chosen by King and the SCLC as the place to illustrate the extraordinary extent of black disenfranchisement in the South. But Selma was also selected for another reason, which was that in Sheriff Jim Clark it had a public official who could be expected to react violently to the marches and protests of civil rights activists, thereby providing the movement with a graphic dramatization of still existent white oppression that would hopefully force the federal government to act. Backed by Alabama governor George Wallace and the local political establishment, Clark and his officers did not disappoint, clubbing, beating, and assaulting demonstrators with electric cattle prods. The scenes of violence culminated on March 7, 1965, with "Bloody Sunday" on Selma's Edmund Pettus Bridge, when six hundred demonstrators were met with a barrage of tear gas, rebel yells, and beatings with bullwhips and rubber tubing wrapped in barbed wire by local and state police, including some on horseback. On March 15, Lyndon Johnson formally proposed a new voting rights bill before a joint session of Congress. Despite extensive filibustering in the Senate, the bill, which outlawed discriminatory devices such as literacy and constitutional interpretation tests and authorized federal officials to register qualified voters, was signed into law on August 6.[99]

For many the crowning achievement of the civil rights movement, to the Birch Society these events were simply a continuation of the developments it had been decrying for the past several years. The "assault on Selma" had not been about voting rights at all, wrote Scott Stanley, the managing editor of *American Opinion* and one of the founding members of Young Americans for Freedom, in May 1965. King and his team of outside agitators had descended on the "lovely tree-lined" community of Selma "to deliberately create disorder and chaos" in the name of "Communist Revolution."[100] If a society's structure is determined by "individual choice and cultural patterns, no one's rights are violated," contended Jim Lucier, an aide to Strom Thurmond and a frequent contributor to *American Opinion*. "But to remake the pattern of society by governmental action is an act of despotism" since a government that is "efficient enough to enforce equality is efficient enough to enslave everyone equally." Lucier averred, "Not everyone should vote, if voting is to be an intelligent act and a worthy responsibility of citizenship."[101] Medford Evans objected to what he called the "sociocircus" that had taken place at Selma. It was "an era of images," he said, "when the media mould men's minds through mendacity," and he offered a robust defense of Jim Clark, who like other local sheriffs around the country Evans saw as a vital impediment to the imposition of totalitarianism on the United States.[102]

Law, Disorder, and the Challenge of Black Power

On August 11, 1965, just five days after the signing of the Voting Rights Act, a massive riot broke out in Watts, a predominantly black and run-down area of southeast Los Angeles, following a dispute between a twenty-one-year-old unemployed African American called Marquette Fry and officers from the Los Angeles police during a routine traffic stop. Five days later, after the dispatch of almost fourteen thousand National Guardsmen, order was restored. Thirty-four people died, 1,072 were injured, and 4,000 arrested in the mayhem of those five days. Nine hundred seventy-seven buildings were also destroyed, at an estimated value of $200 million. As one historian has put it, when the smoke cleared, Watts and the other areas of LA affected by the riot resembled nothing so much as a "war zone."[103] But Watts proved only to be the beginning. In the three years that followed, major disturbances broke out in scores of American cities, including New York, Philadelphia, Newark, Cleveland, Detroit, Chicago, Baltimore, and Washington, DC.[104]

There were many competing explanations for the Watts riot, just as there would be for those that came after it. Many blamed police brutality.[105] Others said it was a result of the poverty, poor housing, and the unyielding structural inequalities that life in America's northern ghettos was mired in. Chief William Parker, the head of the Los Angeles Police Department, said it was the fault of the civil rights movement for teaching people that they didn't have to obey laws they considered unjust.[106] Ronald Reagan, running to replace Pat Brown as the governor of California, blamed liberals and their "philosophy that in any situation the public should turn to government for the answer."[107] The official McCone Commission report—named after its chair, the former CIA director John McCone—adopted what became known as the "riffraff" theory, essentially explaining away the riot as a "senseless" explosion of violence by a tiny minority of alienated blacks.[108] Militant black and white radical groups, on the other hand, took it be the opening salvo of "The Revolution."[109]

Not surprisingly, the John Birch Society understood Watts, as well as the later riots that rocked the country, within the narrative framework it had already established, but they also led the Society—and other conservatives— to place an increasing emphasis on the importance of "law and order" issues. The Society's correspondents on the scene, Gary Allen and Bill Richardson, provided a purportedly "first-hand" account of the "hell" that had engulfed the City of Angels in the September 1965 issue of *American Opinion*. Replete with photographs of the devastation, the article rejected completely any notion that poverty or inequality might provide an explanation for the rioting. "If the Welfare State is the land of milk and honey, as 'Liberals' maintain," the authors wrote, with withering if unconvincing sarcasm, "then California is Paradise and Watts its crowning glory," a place where "California's politicians, dispensing a free living to the non-productive at the expense of the productive, have constructed a beacon-light attraction to the shiftless . . . from all over the country." Having softened up the American people through "sit-ins, shop-ins, lie-ins, mass parades, and the like," and then by acts of "overt physical violence," the riots were the "third phase" in the communists' five-phase program for taking over the United States, Allen and Richardson maintained, with leaders in groups like SNCC and CORE who were "not directly identified with the [Communist] Party" having been secretly trained to lead the "insurrection."[110]

When Allen returned to the significance of Watts in the May 1967 issue of *American Opinion*, he still believed it had been intended as a "rehearsal for a nationwide revolution," but his attention was more firmly focused on black nationalist and black power groups than the "so-called 'Civil Right's' organizations" he had denounced so vociferously two years earlier. Watts had "been made into a symbol for the Communists' revolutionary Black Nationalists," he wrote. "It packs the same emotional wallop for the forces of Black Power that Pearl Harbor did to Americans during World War II."[111] It was a shift of emphasis that reflected the fracturing of the civil rights movement that had occurred in the aftermath of the Voting Rights Act, Watts, and the failure of Martin Luther King's 1966 campaign in Chicago, as well as the rise to prominence of such spokesmen of "black power" as Stokely Carmichael, H. "Rap" Brown, and Huey P. Newton.[112] It was a situation that many in the Birch Society struggled to come terms with. The violent assertiveness and street-smart rhetorical bombast of the advocates of black power, with their incendiary talk of "smash[ing] everything Western civilization has created," seemed a whole different category of communist-inspired menace than the proponents of integration had been.[113] It was also clear that barely disguised racist sentiments were increasingly slipping into some of the Society's discourse, as Allen's and Richardson's references to the "shiftless," "welfare-dependent" residents of Watts illustrated.

Gary Allen dismissed the attendees at a three-day black power conference in Berkeley at the beginning of 1967 as "racists, fanatics, psychotics, and schizoids," but other prominent Birch writers still hoped to persuade black Americans of the folly of these new ways, often seeking refuge in a highly romanticized past in order to do so.[114] For example, E. Merrill Root, *American Opinion* editor, poet, and bestselling author of *Collectivism on the Campus* (1955) and *Brainwashing in the High Schools* (1958), went back to the "tragic War Between the States" to make his case that the "Negro soul at its best . . . has been a center of truth, of loyalty, of good returned for evil, of kindness and love." During the Civil War, "the Negroes of the South did not cry: 'Burn, Baby, Burn!'" as rioters and onlookers had done during Watts, he said. Rather, with "most of the men of the South away at war, the Negroes kept the plantations, and protected wives and children, and did not riot and murder and burn to gain their freedom."[115] The "Barnum-black revolutionaries" of the black power movement "never mention that there are problems within the community which politics alone can never solve, but which can be resolved only by individual effort resulting from intelligent and dedicated leadership; problems with which Booker T. Washington would have known how to deal," George Schuyler argued in March 1967. "Negroes who claim to represent 'the masses,'" he continued, "should be ashamed that during the past decade they have not ended illiteracy in their communities, have not carried out campaigns to increase the number of commercial and manufacturing assets of their people, and have not used their eloquence to spur Negroes to end by self-improvement the social evils surrounding them which they irresponsibly blame on 'Whitey.'"[116]

In 1967, Robert Welch issued a public declaration addressed "To the Negroes of America." It provides an instructive comparison with his more-than-decade-old "Letter to the South." There was the same emphasis on the dangers of the communist conspiracy, and the same intermingling of Christian piety and paternalism, but the overall tone was much different, the confidence of 1956 replaced by something closer to exasperation—if not desperation—that black Americans were still falling for the "stupidities" and "vicious lies" of those intent on misleading them. "We, the good white people of America, do not want our cities to be burned, our country torn to pieces, and the ruins taken over by the Communists," Welch wrote:

We know that you, the Negro citizens of America, do not want this either. But you are being deceived and inflamed today by Communist lies in the hope that you will actually help the Communist-led agitators to achieve those results. Wake up, my friends. Stop listening to the voices of Satan, which preach the Communist theme of *hatred* as the very core of their strategy. Go to work to make all other good people of your race understand how they are being used as fools, and snared by Communist bait.

Wherever doubt exists, remember just one rule. . . . It is a very simple rule: *Not hatred but love is the Christian and the American way of life*. And goodwill towards all men of all races is as much a part of the greatness of America as are its prosperity and freedom.[117]

Despite this, though, the Society still sought to capitalize on the chaos and menace of the "black power years," releasing and promoting filmstrips such as Bill Richardson's *Civil Riots/USA*—"From Los Angeles the cries of 'Kill Whitey,' and 'Burn, Baby, Burn' echoed across the Nation, shocking Americans as never before. For a time the cliché 'It can't happen here' was muted," ran an advert for the film—and its own *Anarchy–U.S.A.*[118] It also launched new ad hoc committees—committees affiliated with the Society, and which promoted its objectives, but which were composed primarily of nonmembers—such as TACT (Truth About Civil Turmoil), which ascribed the urban riots to communist machinations, and pushed harder on older ones such as the Support Your Local Police committees.[119] The latter had begun in the context of the "disturbances" in Birmingham and Oxford, where, as Welch put it in the July 1963 issue of the *Bulletin*, the police had been "doing a superb job of maintaining law and order" until the interference of the federal government. Intended to lend support for those opposing the establishment of civilian police review boards, they were given a new lease of life by the even greater disturbances of 1965 to 1968.[120] In the aftermath of the riots in Newark and Detroit in July 1967, for example, Welch reported that he had a "whole folder full of material on the new drive of the federal government to undermine local police forces, and subject them to neutralizing controls and handicaps."[121]

Just as the advocacy of states' rights could function as both a genuine desire for more localized government and disguised racism, so too could the demand for "law and order" reflect a real concern about crime and public civility and coded racial fears and anxiety. This was especially so after the passage of the Civil Rights and Voting Rights Acts, when overt racism became, nominally at least, less publicly and politically acceptable. In the context of the "white backlash" against the success of the civil rights movement, the urban disorders of the mid-1960s, and the widespread resistance to federal pressures to integrate housing and schools in the North, both George Wallace and Richard Nixon proved adept at mastering the language of "law and order" during the 1968 presidential campaign, for example, and the same slippages were also at work in the Birch Society's crusades to aid the police and drive the "Communist Revolution" off America's streets.[122]

The Birch Society's support for the police also raised another issue, however, one illustrating that in a rights-based society like the United States there would always be competing claims about whether some rights were more important than others. Between 1964 and 1966—the years of what might be called the great "Birch police scare"—from Santa Ana on the West Coast to Philadelphia on the East, the question was raised as to whether police officers had the "right" to be members of the John Birch Society.[123] Matters came to a head in New York City in 1966 after Police Commissioner Howard R. Leary stated that he would allow his officers to belong to the Society, provided their membership did not "impair their efficiency."[124] Contention swiftly followed.

The mayor of New York, John Lindsay, believing the Society to be "hostile to everything I think is decent," ordered Leary to prepare a further report on the extent of the Birchers' penetration of the city's police.[125] Roy Wilkins, executive director of the NAACP, said that the civil rights organization did not believe that somebody could be "a 100 per cent John Birch member and a 100 per cent . . . policeman at one and the same time."[126] "A police officer is sworn to treat all people equally. He cannot function with the type of mental attitude that comes with being a member of the John Birch Society," concurred CORE's national director Floyd McKissick, while William Booth, the head of New York's Commission on Human Rights, argued that under no circumstances should Birch policemen be assigned to police civil rights demonstrations.[127] In a letter to the *New York Times*, Alan Miller, a local rabbi, asked whether a Jew in prewar Germany would have felt "reassured had he been informed that membership on the part of German policemen in the Nazi party was not objectionable, as long as 'they were not taking a position contrary to the policies and practices of the Berlin Police Department,' and as long as their membership did not 'impair their efficiency.'" To permit public officials in "so critical an area" to be members of an avowedly "anti-democratic organization" was not freedom, it was anarchy, Miller argued, and he urged the city authorities not to "tax the patience of our Negro and liberty-loving citizens too far."[128]

According to Birch spokesman John Rousselot, there were about 500 Birch Society members in the city's 27,000-strong police force.[129] At least one of them, patrolman John Donahue, was happy with his decision to be a member of the Society. He had joined, he said, out of fear about his son's future as a result of all the urban unrest that was taking place—all the "bloodshed and violence." "I think some of these demonstrations in the streets start out good, but the Communists come down and cash in on them," the officer explained to a news reporter.[130] The Society had external defenders too—even if most of them were motivated by the wider principles seemingly at stake rather than any particularly warm embrace of the Birch philosophy. For example, the *New York Times*, the New York Civil Liberties Union, and the Birchers' old foe William Buckley all argued that policemen had civil rights too.[131] "The police are the guardians of civil rights, and they would be sent out on the streets of New York with a dubious standard to uphold if they were first deprived of their own rights to hold an opinion," as one of the *Times*' editorials on the subject put it.[132]

The dispute was resolved at the end of May 1966, following the determination of Corporation Counsel J. Lee Rankin that Birch Society was not a political organization within the meaning of New York's state penal code or the city's charter. Policemen, Rankin concluded, had a constitutional right to be members of the John Birch Society.[133]

1968 and the Coming Apart of America

On April 4, 1968, Martin Luther King was shot and killed as he was standing on a balcony of the Lorraine Motel, in Memphis, Tennessee, by a single bullet fired by James Earl Ray. King was in the city to show his support for striking sanitation workers who were trying to form a union. His death set off another wave of rioting across the United States, including in Washington, DC, where federal troops had to be dispatched to guard both the White House and the Capitol building. Forty-six people died across the country in the week of violence that followed King's murder and twenty thousand were arrested. Two months later, on June 5, Robert Kennedy, who was running to be the Democratic Party's nominee in the forthcoming presidential election, was assassinated in a hallway of the Ambassador Hotel in Los Angeles by a twenty-four-year-old Arab nationalist called Sirhan Sirhan.[134] As the 1968 election approached, there was a widespread sense that the United States was a country tearing itself apart.

This was certainly a view shared by the John Birch Society. Responding to King's assassination and the riots that accompanied it, Susan Huck, the analysis editor of the Society's *Review of the News* magazine, worried that unless the mass of America's law-abiding citizenry woke up soon, the United States might become "the first nation ever to sleep through a civil war."[135] Gary Allen, introducing the Society's annual "scoreboard" of communist influence around the world in the July-August 1968 issue of *American Opinion*, described 1968 as "the year of crisis." When the scoreboard had been launched in 1958, the amount of communist influence in the United States had been 20 percent to 40 percent. In 1968, it was 60 percent to 80 percent. The figure was so high, Allen explained, as a result of the "vast welfare spending" of Lyndon Johnson's Great Society programs, and because of "Communist-led student revolts, Communist-led Black Nationalist riots, and international Communist aggression," and in particular because the "Communists' Black Power assault" on the United States had shifted its "street revolution into high gear."[136]

Characteristically, both Huck and Allen understood King's assassination in conspiratorial terms. It was a "set up," Huck declared: the "Communists and their Black Power fanatics [had] been working to create just a situation for years." Echoing the Birch Society's response to the assassination of President Kennedy five years earlier, Allen pointed out that no movement "has ever used assassination so effectively and frequently as the International Communist Conspiracy."[137] It was hardly a surprising assessment. As the Birch Society struggled to come to terms with the rise of the civil rights and the black power movements, and the challenge they posed to the nature and extent of Americans' "rights" during the 1960s, the one thing that remained constant was a belief in the Communist Conspiracy. From the Supreme Court's decision in *Brown v. Board of Education*, through the riot at Ole Miss, to the massive civil disobedience at Birmingham and Selma, and on to the urban unrest and political assassinations of 1968, this was what provided the Birch Society with its ideological bedrock. It was why the organization had been formed and it was the reason why it fought on.

There were many other apparent indicators of societal breakdown and dysfunction for those inclined to look for them as the 1960s drew to a close, of course, including widespread drug use, pornography, promiscuity, campus radicalism, and antiwar protests. Although this chapter has focused primarily on racial matters, it is important to note that the Birch Society, along with other conservatives and many others in American society, was concerned about them all.[138] The war in Vietnam was a particular cause of concern, to say the least, and it is this, along with the Birch Society's understanding of the international communist threat more generally, to which we now turn to examine.

Chapter 5

War

"In summary, Gentlemen, we are losing, rapidly losing, a cold war in which our freedom, our country, and our very existence are at stake. And while *we* don't seem to know we are losing this war, you can be sure the Communists do." So did Robert Welch inform the eleven men who gathered in Indianapolis to help him establish the John Birch Society in December 1958.[1] In truth, it was a common enough concern. The world of the mid- to late 1950s was hardly one that could be said to be conforming to American interests and expectations. There had been no victory in Korea. Ho Chi Minh had triumphed over the French at the battle of Dien Bien Phu. The Hungarian uprising of 1956 had been ruthlessly crushed under the wheels of Soviet tanks. And the space age marvels of *Sputnik I* and *II*, coupled with the embarrassing failure of the United States to get its own *Vanguard* satellite off the launch pad, all combined to give seeming weight to Soviet premier Nikita Khrushchev's promise to "bury" Western capitalism beneath communism's historically predetermined advance.

Nor did the 1960s seem to offer much prospect for improvement. Within just a few weeks of the Birch Society's formation, after four years of struggle, Fidel Castro's guerrilla army finally ousted America's longtime ally Fulgencio Batista from Cuba, while during the 1960 presidential election, the Democratic Party's candidate, John F. Kennedy, campaigned ominously—if erroneously—on the back of the "missile gap" he claimed existed between the United States and the USSR. Kennedy was determined to reverse this sorry situation. "We will mould our strength and become first again," he declared in his stump speeches. "Not first if. Not first but. Not first when. But first period. I want the world to wonder not what Mr. Khrushchev is doing. I want them to wonder what the United States is doing."[2] Kennedy, Castro, and Khrushchev would bring the world to the brink of nuclear annihilation in October 1962, of course, and it was also Kennedy who laid much of the groundwork for the United States' war in Vietnam, arguably the greatest disaster of twentieth-century American foreign policy.

The John Birch Society's writers and spokesmen in general examined, interpreted, and assessed all these events in great detail, but this was especially true of its founder, Robert Welch. Unlike his engagement with the civil rights movement, which largely seemed reactive—something forced upon him by the pressure of events—Welch's interest in American foreign policy and the progress of the Cold War was deep and long-standing. It was an area he considered to be his realm of special expertise. Two of the books he had written before *The Blue Book, May God Forgive Us* (1952) and *The Life of John Birch* (1954), were both largely concerned with matters of U.S. foreign policy—Mao's defeat of Chiang Kai-shek and the "loss" of China to communism most of all—and the same was true of much of *The Politician*.[3]

Endeavoring to make it clear why he considered his expertise to be greater than that of other prominent anticommunists in the field, Welch flaunted his "credentials" in *The Blue Book*. He had been to Formosa and talked personally with Chiang Kai-shek, he said, and he had also been to West Germany to meet with Chancellor Konrad Adenauer (the meetings had taken place during the mid-1950s while Welch was on the board of directors of the National Association of Manufacturers).[4] He knew or was conducting a "voluminous" correspondence with leading anticommunists both in the United States and around the world; he was a diligent reader of both "anti-Communist books and objective histories"—the potentially damning distinction presumably being no more than a slip of the pen—which revealed "piecemeal the horrifying truth of the past two decades"; and above all, he was completely versed in the litera-ture—international as well as domestic—of communism itself: its periodicals, monthlies, and key texts. This was particularly important, Welch argued, because "it is to the presentation by the Communists themselves . . . that *the serious student of the conspiracy* goes to learn of their progress and plans."[5] Less tangibly, but no less importantly, Welch also claimed to possess a "fairly sensitive and accurate nose" in the area—something, he said, which J. B. Matthews (the long-anointed dean of the anticommunist Right in the United States, as well as the short-lived staff director of Senator McCarthy's Investigations Subcommittee on Government Operations) and his (infamous) files would be able to confirm.[6]

This chapter examines Welch and the Birch Society's claim to expertise in the realm of foreign affairs and the Cold War, with particular respect to two of the most dramatic and consequential overseas crises of the 1960s in Cuba and Vietnam. In order to fully understand the Birch Society's reaction to these events, however, it is first necessary to trace Welch's views about the origins and early years of the Cold War more broadly, as well as to consider his and the Society's criticisms of the Eisenhower administration's handling of world affairs during the 1950s—what Joseph McCarthy along with many other conservatives and anticommunists of the time, including Welch, considered to be America's "retreat from victory" following the end of the Second World War.[7]

Robert Welch, Cold War Analyst

The Cold War—"a fatal struggle for freedom against slavery, for existence against destruction"—had begun in 1917, with the Russian Revolution, Robert Welch explained in *The Blue Book*. Lenin had been intent on world domination from the outset, Welch believed, and in the thirty-five years following Lenin's death (in 1924) his acolytes and successors had been patiently and determinedly implementing the "brilliant, farseeing, realistic, and majestically simple" strategy he had laid out for them. It was a strategy that "has been paraphrased and summarized as follows," Welch said: "'First, we will take eastern Europe. Next, the masses of Asia. Then we shall encircle the last bastion of capitalism, the United States of America. We shall not have to attack; it will fall like overripe fruit into our hands.'" It could also be restated as, "For the Communists, the road to Paris led through Peking and Calcutta."[8]

In *The Strange Tactics of Extremism* (1964), Harry and Bonaro Overstreet, two of the Birch Society's most vociferous contemporary critics, reported that despite having read through Lenin's *Selected Works* and consulted with research scholars at Stanford and the curator of the Slavic Room of the Library of Congress who had read *The Complete Works*—in Russian—they could find no evidence that Lenin had uttered the words Welch attributed to him, or any "record whatever" of his having laid down such a strategy for worldwide conquest.[9] But although Lenin's "words" appeared in quotation marks, Welch had, typically, been careful in how he introduced them: they were Lenin's words "paraphrased and summarized," and Welch had simply neglected to identify who had done the paraphrasing and summarizing. More broadly, however, the idea that the Soviet Union was an expansionist nation, hell-bent on world conquest, was hardly a novel assessment to make in 1958. It was closer to being an article of faith, both within American policy-making circles and outside them, and distinguishing what was commonplace—part of the wider anticommunist consensus of the time—from what was distinctive or unusual about Welch and the Birch Society's understanding of the Cold War is important for coming to terms with their appeal, as well as the criticism and condemnation they attracted. Admittedly this is not a straightforward process, complicated as it is by the tendency of Welch and other Birch thinkers to move effortlessly from the conventional to the absurd, the insightful to the fantastic, and the justified to the unsustainable in much of their analyses. But it is a necessary one.

Welch's *Blue Book* reconstruction of the origins of the Cold War continued with a discussion of the "first great break for the Communist conspiracy," Franklin D. Roosevelt's formal recognition of the USSR in 1933, which, Welch contended, had saved the Soviet Union from financial collapse. The "second break" came with World War II, the war having been "largely brought on through the world-wide diplomatic conniving of Stalin's agents, for the advantage of making Russia a wartime ally of the Western nations." (The carefully placed "largely" again provided Welch with some much-needed room for maneuver should anyone try to lay the blame for the conflagration more firmly on Hitler's shoulders than Stalin's.) With the war underway, Stalin brutally "swallowed up" Poland, Estonia, Latvia, and Lithuania, the Founder recounted, with these conquests being acquiesced to by Roosevelt and Winston Churchill at the Teheran Conference of 1943 and Yalta in 1945. And once the war was over, the Soviet Union was allowed to conquer the rest of Eastern Europe, including Hungary, Yugoslavia, Romania, Bulgaria, Czechoslovakia, and East Germany, placing them all "behind the Iron Curtain," and so completing the first of Lenin's three steps for world domination.[10]

The Teheran Conference was the most important of the Big Three wartime conferences, but it is Yalta that has come to symbolize, for conservatives in the United States especially, the weakness, secrecy, betrayals, callous indifference, and immorality believed to have birthed the Cold War, just as "appeasement" functioned as shorthand for all the follies that aided fascism's rise. It was at Yalta, as Welch saw it, that "Roosevelt and Churchill gave Stalin many countries which were not theirs to give, without even a word with or to the peoples of those countries who had fought as our allies in the war."[11] The West's "betrayal" of Poland was a particular source of consternation for Welch as it was for many others (the Birch Society was still promoting former U.S. ambassador to Poland Arthur Bliss Lane's first-hand account of it during the 1960s).[12] But, again it is well to remember that "the myth of Yalta" was very much a live political issue in early Cold War America, one frequently played for clear partisan advantage.[13] It was certainly a matter of recurring and grave concern for Welch's great political heroes, Senators McCarthy and Robert Taft, but it also animated the Republican Party as a whole.[14] The party's official platform of 1952 promised, for example, to "repudiate all commitments contained in secret understandings, such as those of Yalta, which aid Communist enslavements." "Teheran, Yalta and Potsdam were the scenes of . . . tragic blunders with others to follow," the party maintained throughout the election campaign.[15]

With Eastern Europe secured for communism, next came Asia. Welch believed the Soviets to be "three-fourths" of the way toward completing the second step of their three-part program in 1958. They had occupied all of Sakhalin and the Kuril Islands and established a People's Republic in Mongolia in 1945. They had set up "their government" in North Korea and taken over Manchuria in 1948. Stalinist agents had completed their conquest of mainland China by 1950, invaded Tibet in 1951, "imposed a truce so shameful" in Korea in 1953 "as to be incredible in the light of past American history," and conquered "the better half of Indochina" during the summer of 1954 thanks to the efforts of Ho Chi Minh, Zhou Enlai (the Chinese premier and foreign minister), and "other tools of the Kremlin."[16]

It was a litany of failure. But the greatest failure had been the "loss" of China to communism in 1949. Indeed, it was this event more than any other that had driven Welch's pre-Birch Society political career. It was the subject of his first two political books. And it provided the touchstone for his understanding of the entire Cold War. Crucially, a belief in the centrality of *American* power, *American* will, and *American* politics lay at the heart of Welch's analysis of Mao's defeat of Chiang Kai-shek and his Nationalist forces. China had been the United States' "only really effective ally" in the Second World War, Welch wrote in *May God Forgive Us*, and it was "utterly unconceivable" that Mao should be able to conquer the country within five years of its end, except through a combination of "trickery, chicanery and treason." "At every step Mao could have been stopped by *our* government," Welch believed, but instead "*we* deliberately turned over rule of China's four hundred million people to Stalin's stooge."[17]

Like other members of the so-called China Lobby, of which he himself was a part—the "China Lobby" was a pejorative term used by opponents to describe the close-knit mix of businessmen, politicians, church groups, and journalists who were the Nationalists' most ardent supporters in the United States—Welch rejected completely the Truman administration's official explanation for the "loss" of China.[18] This was made in a white paper released by Secretary of State Dean Acheson in 1949. It argued that the result of the Chinese civil war "was beyond the control" of the U.S. government, and that it "was the product of internal Chinese forces, forces which this country tried to influence but could not."[19] Unprepared to recognize or acknowledge the corruption, weakness, and ineffectiveness of Chiang's regime, or the strengths and powerful appeal of Mao's promise of reform to China's impoverished peasantry, as well as its sophisticated elites, Welch instead blamed America's actions and inactions for the perceived catastrophe.[20] It was the United States that had "allowed" Stalin to make his gains in the Far East at Yalta, pulled its forces out of China, and refused to send arms to Chiang. Time after time, Welch argued, it was the United States that had failed to take the "firm" stand that would have stopped Mao dead "in his tracks."[21]

What this reflected, of course, was a fervent belief in the awesome capabilities of American power, and the ability—if not the right—of the United States to direct the world's affairs. In this formulation—one widely shared at the dawn of the Cold War, as it still is in some quarters—other nations, if not whole continents, were the United States' to "win" or to "lose," and the critical factor determining the outcome of any particular event would always be what America did or did not do. Grounded in deeply rooted notions of American exceptionalism and a militant national chauvinism, it is a belief as evident in Ronald Reagan's Tom Paine–derived claim that it was within the power of the United States "to begin the world again" as in George W. Bush's hopes for "transforming" the Middle East in the wake of the terrorist attacks of 9/11.[22] Yet in the late 1940s and early 1950s it also reflected a profound sense of anxiety about America's place in the world in the aftermath of the Second World War, a world in which for all its economic and military dominance—and despite its hard-won victory—America and American interests seemed strangely vulnerable to the "alien" virus of communism and its Red Army carriers.[23]

This sense of anxiety and vulnerability was heightened considerably by another great shock of 1949, the explosion of the Soviet Union's own atomic bomb. Revelations that Soviet spies like Julius Rosenberg, Theodore Hall, Klaus Fuchs, and David Greenglass had been operating in the United States and may well have helped accelerate the Soviets' development of "the bomb" only compounded the issue, giving an additional shot in the arm to the fast-growing Second Red Scare, and providing the essential element of plausibility to the Republican Party's "communists-in-government" assault on the Truman administration. No great leap of imagination was required to move from Soviet spy rings stealing the secrets of the A-bomb at Los Alamos to traitorous "China hands" in the State Department selling out the Generalissimo.[24]

The key figure in all this was Alger Hiss. Convicted of perjury—at the second attempt and because the statute of limitations for an espionage charge had expired—in January 1950 for lying under oath about having passed State Department documents to Whittaker Chambers, an ex-communist turned repentant professional anticommunist, during the 1930s, Hiss was the symbol nonpareil of treason in high places for McCarthyites, Birchers, and many others throughout the 1950s and long beyond.[25] Hiss had been a political adviser in the State Department's Far Eastern Division from 1933 to 1944, but his presence at Yalta—where, according to Welch, he was to be found "whispering advice" into the ailing Roosevelt's ear—together with his involvement in the Dumbarton Oaks conference that led to the establishment of the United Nations, as well as its first meeting at San Francisco in 1945, allowed the "web of subversion" to be cast ever wider.[26]

Throughout the 1960s, the Society ran a campaign against the organization centered on the slogan "Get US Out!"[27] Welch and the Birch Society's hostility to the United Nations is traceable, in part, to suspicions about Hiss's involvement in its formation, as well as to broader concerns about Moscow's presumed desire for a "world government" that would enable it to more efficiently create a tyrannical "international police state." But at a deeper level, it was really about the fear that by joining such "international monstrosities" as the UN, the World Health Organization, UNESCO, and NATO, the United States was willingly circumscribing its ability to project its enormous power onto the world stage for its own motives and in furtherance of its own interests—that it was yet another step further away from the deserved spoils of victory.[28]

In this respect, the claims of the Republican and McCarthyite Right of the early to mid-1950s and—the much less well-received—Birchite Right of the late 1950s and the 1960s were very similar: they insisted that a great deal of America's external difficulties were attributable to disloyalty, betrayal, and sabotage *within* the United States. (Could there be a more convincing explanation for the failure of a great power like the United States to impose its will on the world? the advocates of this position asked.) This, in essence, was the point Welch was clumsily trying to make in *The Politician*. It was simply "not possible to lose so much ground, so rapidly, to an enemy so inferior, by chance or by stupidity," he wrote in the letter/book's introduction in August 1958. Explaining all of the U.S. losses in the Cold War up to that point called "for a very sinister and hated word, but one which is by no means new in the history of governments or of nations," Welch said, and that word was "treason."[29] Seven years earlier on the floor of the Senate, McCarthy had made precisely the same case when he asked: "How can we account for our present situation unless we believe that men high in this Government are concerting to deliver us to disaster?" It must be the product of a conspiracy, McCarthy famously went on, "a conspiracy on a scale so immense as to dwarf any previous such venture in the history of man."[30]

One of the major problems for the Birch Society in its attempts to revive the conspiratorial logic of the Second Red Scare in this way, however, was that people had already lived through it once and there was a distinct lack of enthusiasm among wide swaths of the population—and more particularly among the nation's political elites—for its return. Anticommunism remained the essential element of the United States' foreign policy consensus, of course. But 1958 was not 1948, and while there had always been varieties of anticommunism at play within this consensual framework (liberal, conservative, religious, internationalist, militantly nationalistic, and even isolationist) one of the main effects of McCarthyism had been to severely weaken—if not entirely discredit—the counter-subversive tradition that was so clearly the wellspring of Welch's worldview.

The geopolitical landscape had also altered. Stalin had died in 1953 and his eventual successor, Nikita Khrushchev, had both denounced the monstrous crimes of his predecessor and moved the Soviet Union away from the position that war with the capitalist, imperialist West was inevitable. As he set the USSR on a course of economic modernization, "peaceful coexistence" became the new watchword.[31] This didn't mean that Moscow wouldn't try to exploit any perceived American weakness, or that it wasn't willing to flex its muscles when the occasion seemed to warrant it—Khrushchev's November 1958 ultimatum to the occupying powers of West Berlin to leave the city within six months demonstrated that clearly enough. It did mean, though, that there was a significantly new Cold War context facing the Birch Society when it came into existence at the end of 1958.

Khrushchev, *Sputnik*, and the Committee Against Summit Entanglements

Robert Welch regarded peaceful coexistence as just as much of a sham as containment, and he castigated the Eisenhower administration for having "abandoned any thought of 'liberation'" for the "enslaved peoples" of Eastern Europe.[32] It was true that Eisenhower and his future secretary of state, John Foster Dulles, had found it politically expedient to talk about "liberation" and the "rollback" of the Soviet Union's gains in Europe during the 1952 election campaign, but they never seriously considered putting it into practice once they were in office. Instead, along with a healthy dose of skullduggery and subversion on the "periphery" of the Cold War in places like Iran and Guatemala, their "New Look" foreign policy relied on massive nuclear retaliation as a means of deterring Soviet aggression.[33] James Burnham, the conservative thinker—and former Trotskyist—most closely identified with the strategy of "liberation," had also shown himself to be flexible in the face of changing circumstances. (Burnham caused a major rift within the offices of *National Review*, when he wrote about the Hungarian uprising of 1956 in his column, "The Third World War," arguing that America should negotiate with the USSR to secure Hungary's neutrality rather than intervening militarily.)[34] Such flexibility was not for Welch, though, as he made clear in a remarkable open letter to Premier Khrushchev on March 3, 1958. (It was published in the April issue of *American Opinion* and a gift subscription to the magazine was supposedly included with Khrushchev's personal copy of the letter).

Prompted in large part by widespread American anxiety over the successful launch of the world's first man-made satellite, *Sputnik Zemlya* (Companion of Earth), on October 4, 1957, followed a month later by *Sputnik II* and the world's first canine cosmonaut, Laika, what was particularly striking about Welch's letter was its utter dismissal of the claims of economic and technical advancement coming out of the Soviet Union.[35] Sent into orbit by a huge R-7 intercontinental ballistic missile, *Sputnik* was a profound shock to Americans, because it seemed to indicate that the Soviet Union was ahead in both the scientific and nuclear arms races. As the Defense Department and the CIA raced to decode the satellite's mysterious and strangely hypnotic beeping—which in actuality contained no meaning at all—Senate Majority Leader Lyndon Johnson (D-TX) warned that the Soviet Union would soon "be dropping bombs on us from space like kids dropping rocks onto cars from freeway overpasses."[36] In November, the *Washington Post*'s leaked account of the Gaither Report—the report of an independent committee commissioned by Eisenhower to investigate America's strategic vulnerability in the light of *Sputnik*'s success—contained the terrifying news that the United States was "in the gravest danger in its history," a nation "moving in a frightening course to the status of a second-class power" and "exposed to an almost immediate threat from the missile-bristling Soviet Union."[37]

Welch did not see it this way, though. "From the past actions of yourself and your associates," Welch informed the premier, "it seems likely that your beeping moonlet was a glittering sample, contrived at all-out cost for the display window, with nothing in stock behind it but an exhausted shop. Otherwise, why would you go to such extreme lengths, through every pipe in your propaganda organ, to convince us of the opposite." *Sputnik*'s launch reminded Welch of the Potemkin villages that had supposedly been used to fool Catherine the Great during her visit to the Crimea in 1787, he said:

> With one missile weighing . . . 165 pounds, and another one much more vaguely presented for our imaginations to endow with some frightening statistics, you would have us visualize behind them a flotilla of space ships ready to head for Mars. And we are to take for granted that, just as a by-product of building your Sputniks, or vice versa, you have or will soon have a battery of intercontinental missiles ready to pinpoint Times Square, the Boston State House, and Capitol Hill as targets from five thousand miles away. Pfui! We don't claim your grapes are sour, Comrade Khrushchev. Knowing what an inveterate liar you are, we don't believe they even exist.[38]

Although undoubtedly based on his innate ideological sense of American superiority and communism's fundamental weaknesses, rather than any access to classified information—an approach that calls to mind Ronald Reagan's similar sense about the state of the Soviet Union's capabilities in the mid-1980s—Welch's assessment was actually very close to the truth.[39] As a result of the high-altitude flights of U-2 spy planes and other intelligence sources, Eisenhower knew—although he could not disclose the information publicly for fear of jeopardizing those sources—that the Soviet Union was well behind the United States in terms of its missile technology, nuclear stockpile, and general military capability. Indeed, it would not be until July 1959 that the R-7 missile would be capable of carrying a nuclear warhead, and as late as February 1960, there were only four operational R-7s in the entire Soviet Union.[40] Given this, there is a double irony in the fact that Eisenhower both acquiesced to the Gaither Report's recommendations for an increase in military spending (although admittedly not to the full extent the report suggested) and handed the Democrats one of the key issues—the purported "missile gap"—that would be used to win back the White House in 1960.[41]

A further factor informing Welch's analysis was his basic belief in the tension between surface appearance and underlying realities, together with an unwavering confidence in his own ability to move from one to the other. It was this confidence that presumably motivated Welch to begin the letter with his conviction that Khrushchev was not even the USSR's "real" head of state, but rather the "front man" for Georgi Malenkov or some other figure operating "behind the scenes." Admittedly, even the most seasoned of Kremlinologists had difficulty penetrating the inner workings of the Soviet Union in the 1950s and 1960s, but it was another example of Welch's tendency to wrap more or less cogent analysis up with the fantastical and the conspiratorial.[42] Similarly, although not discounting the strength of the USSR's conventional army— "massive enough and brutal enough to overrun all of Europe at will"—Welch clung to the notion that the greatest threat to the United States was to be found not in "your military strength or ours," but in "our internal security against treason." Just as the Soviet Union had stolen the secrets of the atom bomb from the United States, so he speculated that the Soviets' success in launching the *Sputniks* (they had flown, after all) may have been down to two factors: "(1) the theft of the know-how from various agencies of our Defense Department; and (2) the deliberate holding back of such a launching by ourselves through the influence of treason at work in our government."[43]

"We know, Comrade Khrushchev, how deep, how far, and *how high* your infiltration has gone," Welch went on:

> Not too many miles from where we are writing these lines, there is a president of one institution of higher learning (not Harvard, incidentally), the president of one sizable bank, the dean of one law school, the editor of one newspaper, and the judge of one court whom we believe to be Communists; not merely ideological sympathizers with a communism which they foolishly mistake for humanitarianism, but active agents of an international conspiracy, subtly working for Communist conquest of the world.

Welch lamented the fact that so many Americans were unaware of how much hidden pressure the "unseen tentacles" of the Communist Conspiracy were exerting on the United States because of the highly effective control its agents had gained over the "media of mass communication," a process he characterized, McCarthy-like, as "probably the most gigantic accomplishment of its kind in human history." "You have created a blanket of twisted information, misleading slants, subtle propaganda, and brazen falsehoods between the American people and any clear view of your activities," Welch told Khrushchev.[44]

Yet Welch believed that there was still "one, all-powerful weapon" that anticommunist patriots had at their disposal, and that weapon was "the truth." Having the American people realize the truth was the "only thing in all the world today that you and your cohorts fear," Welch maintained, and he urged Khrushchev to call off the conspiracy and concentrate all his "energy and cleverness into raising the mental and physical living standards of the Russian people" so that he would "become a man who really changed the course of history in a happier direction, instead of merely a nasty blot on one of its gloomiest pages." If not, Welch advised, then there were thousands of "truth-seeking" Americans like himself who were prepared to take the fight to the conspiracy directly—to "rip your whole blanket of lies and subtle censorship into shreds—something you fear infinitely more than all of our hydrogen bombs and NATO alliances."[45]

It was a bravura performance, and when it was announced, in August 1959, that President Eisenhower had invited Khrushchev to become the first Soviet leader to visit the United States, Birch members got the chance to translate Welch's stirring words into action, albeit not through the offices of the Birch Society itself but rather through a front group called the Committee Against Summit Entanglements (CASE). CASE had begun life in April 1959, when just a few chapters of the Birch Society had been formed, in anticipation of a summit meeting between the United States, France, Great Britain, and the USSR to discuss the continuing "abnormal situation" of Berlin—the "bone" in Khrushchev's "throat," as he referred to it—that was expected to take place in July.[46] (Discussions about a nuclear test ban treaty and a more general reduction in Cold War tensions were also going on among the Great Powers at the same time.) Front groups were seen by Welch as one of the best means to beat the communists at their own game, but the fact that the Society was in its infancy no doubt contributed to the decision to oppose the summit through the means of a "committee" of this kind.

The 1940s and 1950s were the golden age of the activist political committee in the United States. Two notable examples are the Committee to Defend America by Aiding the Allies, created in 1940 to lend support to Roosevelt's increasingly interventionist foreign policy during the Second World War, and the Committee for the First Amendment, established in 1947 in support of the Hollywood Ten filmmakers investigated by HUAC. But the most likely source of inspiration for CASE was the Committee for One Million Against the Admission of Communist China to the United Nations—more usually known as the Committee of One Million—formed in 1953. Certainly it was one of the China Lobby's most prominent figures—and Welch's close personal friend—the wealthy businessman Alfred Kohlberg, who came up with CASE's catchphrase, "Please, Mr. President, Don't Go!," which adorned the petitions the committee began circulating in the hope of persuading Eisenhower not to attend the proposed meeting with his Soviet counterpart.[47]

CASE's aim was to get ten million people to sign its petitions, each of which provided ten specific reasons why the summit needed to be opposed, including that it would serve only to further increase Soviet prestige; that it would "weaken the position of the firm anti-Communist statesmen, in all the governmental circles of the remaining free world"; and that Eisenhower would be at a distinct disadvantage in negotiating with an absolute dictator like Khrushchev. Overall, "to negotiate is to surrender," the petitions maintained.[48] Each petition had space for twenty signatures, and seventy thousand of them had been printed and distributed when, on August 3, President Eisenhower announced that before any summit would take place, there would first be an exchange of visits between himself and Khrushchev, with the Soviet premier due to arrive for a two-week tour of the United States on September 15, after which the president would go to Russia.[49]

CASE shifted its emphasis accordingly, and armed with a slightly revised slogan of "Please, President Eisenhower, Don't!" quickly became one of the leading organizations opposed to the impending appearance of the "Butcher of Budapest" on American soil. The committee also drew up a new petition which argued, inter alia, that because of Khrushchev's "utter lack of conscience" and "unrivalled blood-letting" it would be "a crime against humanity" for the Soviet leader to be received as "an honored guest" of the U.S. government; that the visit would be a "propaganda triumph" for the USSR; and that past experience had more than demonstrated "that any agreement or understanding" that might be reached "would be ignored or broken as soon as it suited the convenience of Khrushchev or his successors." Written in the form of an open letter to Eisenhower, each petition ended with the following summation and plea:

> This is a war to the death; and none the less because the Soviet Union chooses to fight that war in its own fashion, with its own weapons of trickery, terror and treason. The recognized head of the Soviet Union is Nikita Khrushchev. There is no possible question but that the royal reception planned for him by our government will, at this stage of the struggle, give immense aid and comfort to the most vicious and most dangerous enemies our country has ever faced. . . .
>
> We respectfully urge you, Mr. President, with all of the earnestness we can convey, to reconsider your decision; and to insist that the Soviet Premier postpone his visit to our country until he has shown, by his treatment of the captive nations and their enslaved peoples, that he is no longer the enemy of freedom and of ourselves.[50]

In order to increase the pressure on the administration, the petition was also made into a full-page advertisement and published in almost one hundred newspapers around the country, including the *New York Times*, the *Chicago Tribune*, the *Detroit Free Press*, the *Santa Ana Register*, the *Arizona Republic*, the *Oakland Tribune*, the *Houston Chronicle*, the *Washington Star*, and the *Wall Street Journal*.[51]

Welch was the chairman of CASE, and its Executive Committee and National Board were both largely made up of such formative Birch figures as Fred C. Koch, Revilo P. Oliver, Cola G. Parker, Clarence Manion, and Thomas J. Anderson. As befitting a front organization, however, not all of CASE's members were fully paid up members of the Society. Among the more prominent of these fellow travelers were General Albert C. Wedemeyer, the commander of American

forces in China during the Second World War; the libertarian Austrian econo-
mist Ludwig von Mises; and most interestingly of all, given subsequent events,
the Arizonan Republican senator Barry Goldwater and the *National Review*
editor William Buckley Jr.

During the 1964 presidential election campaign, Goldwater denied that he
joined CASE knowing that it was a Birch front group. He also denied that Welch
had personally asked him to serve on the organization's Executive Committee,
even though Welch had written publicly about his invitation to Goldwater in
the June 1961 issue of the *Bulletin*.[52] As for Buckley, despite his later attempts
to excommunicate the Birch Society from the conservative movement, such
evasionary tactics were not available to him. He himself had initiated the contact
with Welch (through Revilo Oliver, who also wrote for *National Review*) to
find out why he had not been asked to participate in CASE's original campaign
against the summit, as well as to try and mend some fences between himself
and Welch over *National Review*'s publication of a critical article on the Society
by Eugene Lyons—and it was as a result of their correspondence that Buckley
became a member of CASE's National Board.[53]

Goldwater and Buckley's involvement with CASE showed the extent to
which the burgeoning conservative movement in general was concerned
about the implications of the proposed exchange of visits. *National Review* ran
its own extensive campaign against them, selling "Khrushchev Not Welcome
Here" stickers and publishing numerous articles on the subject.[54] In conjunction
with Crusade for America, a right-wing organization devoted to exposing
communists and "Communist fronters," it also organized a protest rally at
Carnegie Hall for September 17, when the Soviet leader was due to be in New
York for an address to the United Nations. At a press conference to announce the
rally, Buckley threatened to dye the Hudson River red so that Khrushchev would
enter the city to a "river of blood," while attendees at the event itself—there were
2,500 in total—wore black armbands to show their grief for communism's many
victims.[55] Featured among the speakers were Birch National Council member
Clarence Manion; the editor of *Christian Herald*, the Reverend Daniel Poling;
Senator McCarthy's widow; J. B. Matthews; and *National Review*'s own L. Brent
Bozell. But the star of the show was Buckley; indeed, in the view of one of his
biographers, it was Buckley's coruscating denunciation of Khrushchev's visit
at Carnegie Hall that evening that turned the thirty-three-year-old into "*the*
leading conservative in the nation."[56]

Other groups to oppose the visit included the Committee for Freedom of
All Peoples, formed by Senators Styles Bridges (R-NH), Thomas Dodd (D-
CT), and Paul Douglas (D-IL), along with Congressman Walter Judd (R-MN),
which called for an extended period of national mourning, and the liberal
antitotalitarian organization Freedom House, which suggested that perhaps the
best way to greet the Soviet leader's American tour would be with a broad-based
and persistent "civil silence." Numerous local and individual protests were also
organized, including hunger strikes, upside-down flag flying—the international
symbol of distress—and one by a woman on a Los Angeles street corner about

Figure 6.1. President Dwight D. Eisenhower receives a gift from Soviet premier Nikita Khrushchev during his 1959 visit to the United States, as Vice President Richard Nixon watches. © Jerry Cooke/CORBIS

which the Soviet delegation officially complained because of her prominently displayed "DEATH TO KHRUSHCHEV, THE BUTCHER OF HUNGARY" sign.[57]

Overall, though, at least from the perspective of the Eisenhower administration, the visit was a successful one. The Soviet leader had been impressed with the scale and extent of American affluence, as had been intended, and once he had gotten over his fear that Camp David might be an internment camp, the discussions between Khrushchev and Eisenhower there had been cordial.[58] No major agreement was reached, but Khrushchev rescinded his ultimatum on Berlin and the two leaders concurred that disarmament was the really crucial issue between them. A summit of the four occupying powers intended to solve the matter of Berlin once and for all was planned for Paris the following May.[59]

Having failed to prevent Khrushchev's visit—although Welch believed that all the effort had been worthwhile, because it had prevented the tour from being turned into a "triumphal procession" and "brought home to millions of Americans" the "real nature" of the Soviet Premier—CASE now had another issue to pursue. The slogan changed once again—first to "Stay Away—USA! The Summit Leads to Disaster!" and then to "If You Go, Don't Come Back!"—but the tactics and hyperbolic rhetoric remained essentially the same.[60] "The Summit is a precipice at which the appeasement-minded leaders of the remaining free world will be pushed over the edge. Beyond that precipice there can be only a cataclysmic tumbling into the abyss of a one-world socialist government," warned Welch in December 1959, as he urged Birchers to do all they could to prevent it taking place.[61]

In the end, the summit was derailed not by CASE's petitions, postcards, or newspaper advertisements, but by the shooting down of a U-2 spy plane, the unlikely survival of its pilot, Francis Gary Powers, and by President Eisenhower's (eventual) refusal to deny that he had been responsible for its flight. The plane was shot down by the Soviets on May 1, 1960, two weeks before the Paris summit was due to begin. Believing that Powers would commit suicide rather than be captured alive—each U-2 pilot carried a poisoned needle for just this purpose—the president initially stuck to the agreed-upon CIA cover story, which held that the recovered wreckage was nothing more than an American "weather plane" that had accidently strayed into Soviet airspace. On May 7, Khrushchev revealed publicly that Powers was alive and demanded an equally public apology from Eisenhower; privately, he urged the American president to say that the mission had been unauthorized so that the summit could still proceed. Eisenhower refused. He had approved the flight personally, was unwilling to pass the blame on to someone else, and was worried that doing so would give the impression that he wasn't in control of his own government. The summit collapsed and Khrushchev's invitation to Eisenhower to make his return visit to the Soviet Union in June was withdrawn.[62]

If the outcome was just what CASE had been agitating for, the circumstances of the summit's cancellation—although officially it had only been "postponed"—were less than ideal, as Welch observed in the June issue of the *Bulletin*. On the one hand, all the "patriotic Americans" who had campaigned against the summit had good reason to "rejoice," he said, and members of the Birch Society in particular could take "much pride and satisfaction" in the part they had played. About six hundred thousand anti-summit postcards had gone into the mail, letters and telegrams had "flooded the White House," and the Society's "Stay Away—USA!" message had appeared in newspapers with a circulation of three million around the country. Yet there was no denying the fact that it had been the U-2 incident that had caused the summit to be abandoned. As Welch saw it, the "loss of prestige by the United States, and the buildup of Soviet prestige, through the 'humiliated' Eisenhower's reactions to the bullying Khrushchev's bluster, were important gains for the Kremlin," not least because it now seemed that any future summit meeting was dependent on "the willingness of Khrushchev and the Soviets to participate, rather than on the consent of Eisenhower as in the past." And as "prestige and emotional attitudes" were both "far more important weapons to the Communists than either bombs or butter" in what he now called the "Lukewarm War," Welch believed the failure of the summit to be a "considerable attainment by the agents of the Kremlin."[63]

Attempting to salvage something from the situation, Welch returned once again to the issue of internal subversion, which he believed to be the real cause of the majority of American woes around the world. It was "almost certain," he said, that Powers's U-2 plane had been "deliberately flown into Russian territory at [that] particular time" so that Moscow could shoot it down. Faced with the groundswell of opposition to the summit within the United States by CASE and its allies, "Communists in Washington as well as Moscow" had decided that they "did not dare go through with their plans as to what the 'Summit' was to accomplish," and so had cast around for "some way to seize the initiative, twist appearances, save face, and make it seem that the conference had been postponed *for their reasons*."[64] Ironically, the thinking in Washington and Moscow was along much the same lines. The day after the summit's collapse, in a letter to Alberto Lleras Camargo, the president of Colombia, Eisenhower contended that Khrushchev had "embarked on a calculated campaign, even before it began, to insure the failure of the conference and to see to it that the onus for such failure would fall on the West, particularly the United States." For his part, Khrushchev was convinced that hard-liners in Washington—especially Allen Dulles, the director of the CIA—had secretly ordered the U-2 mission with the aim of sabotaging the summit, and with it the possibility of improved relations between the United States and the USSR.[65]

The collapse of the Paris summit ended any prospect of disarmament or détente during the Eisenhower years. The president made no attempt to deal with Khrushchev or the Soviet Union during his remaining eight months in office, leaving the issue (along with secret plans for the invasion of Cuba) to be dealt with by his successor. As for Welch and the Birch Society, they could look back on the Committee Against Summit Entanglements with a considerable amount of satisfaction. The use of fronts had been shown to work. CASE had attracted a great deal of attention and support in three successive campaigns, including from leading figures in the wider anticommunist and conservative movements. The Society had demonstrated its ability to mobilize people, to raise funds—all those petitions, postcards, and newspaper advertisements had to be paid for, after all—and to generate slogans and strategies suitable to the image politics of the dawning media age. No less importantly, as a result of its use of petitions, the Society had also collected the names and addresses of tens of thousands of potential new recruits.[66] CASE may not have actually prevented any of the summits it opposed from taking place, but it was an important stepping-stone for the Birch Society as it endeavored to turn itself into a major "new force" on the American political scene.[67]

Cuba, Si! Castro—and Kennedy—No!

As 1958 turned into 1959, one of the key questions raised by Fidel Castro and his July 26 Movement's guerrilla campaign to overthrow the corrupt and reactionary regime of Fulgencio Batista in Cuba was whether or not Castro was a communist. Realizing that Batista's time in power was probably coming to an end, the Eisenhower administration had refused to offer him any support during the final stages of the conflict; there *had* been a great deal of support before this. However, as the administration was also uncertain about Castro's ultimate intentions—would he lean toward the United States or the Soviet Union?—and concerned about the extent to which communists might be influencing or even directing the revolution, neither was the White House willing to back Castro (even though there was a great deal of sympathy for the revolution in many quarters of the United States at the time).[68]

The issue continued to plague the administration during 1959, following Castro's triumphant entry into Havana on New Year's Day. During his high-profile tour of the United States in April that year, for example, Castro repeatedly denied that he was a communist, even convincing Vice President Richard Nixon, who, after a private meeting with him in Washington, described Castro's associations with the Cuban Communist Party, the Partido Socialista Popular (PSP), as being the result of nothing more than political naïveté. The CIA likewise advised Eisenhower that there was still a possibility of the United States developing "a constructive relationship" with the Castro government, thereby keeping the country out of the Soviet camp.[69] (The Soviets had played no part in the Cuban Revolution, but once it was won, they made moves of their own to improve relations with the nation, aided in no small measure by their contacts with Castro's brother Raúl, who was a member of the PSP.) Through 1960, however, as a consequence of the implementation of his promised land reform, the nationalization of American-owned property, and his increasingly bellicose talk of spreading revolution across Latin America, the U.S. government came to the decision that the Cuban leader would have to be removed. An economic embargo of the island was imposed, assassination attempts authorized, diplomatic relations broken off, and by January 1961, when President Kennedy assumed office, an invasion plan to overthrow the Castro regime was in place.

Kennedy had made Cuba one of his campaign issues. For example, speaking in Cincinnati on October 6, 1960, he had vilified the Eisenhower administration for allowing a "Communist satellite" to be established just ninety miles from the United States, "eight minutes by jet." Castro was "not just another Latin American dictator," the presidential hopeful declared; his ambitions went "far beyond his own shores," and he now had "a base from which to carry Communist infiltration and subversion throughout the Americas."[70] Although not without some reservations about their viability, once in the White House Kennedy put the invasion plans into effect. Predicated on the ill-advised assumption that dis-content with the Castro regime was so extensive that the landing of a small band of CIA-trained Cuban exiles would trigger a national uprising on the island, the Bay of Pigs invasion—which began on April 17 and was over by April 19—was a humiliating disaster for the new president. One hundred and forty members of the 1,453-strong invasion force were killed and 1,189 were captured in the debacle, and Kennedy was forced to send Castro various agricultural supplies in order to get them back.[71]

Robert Welch and the Birch Society never entertained the slightest doubt about what Castro was, of course. "Castro is a Communist. Period," and the Society had been saying so since the previous August, Welch wrote in the December 1959 issue of *American Opinion*. The Cuban prime minister had "been a conscious and dedicated agent of the Kremlin ever since his student days. His whole 'revolution' followed the Communist pattern, used Communist techniques, and was supported and managed by Moscow."[72]

Although Castro's demise was exactly what the Birch Society hoped for, Welch, like many others, was quick to condemn the "insurrectionary fiasco" of the Bay of Pigs, and especially the added indignity of the proposed exchange of "500 giant tractors" for "Castro's prisoners of war."[73] "The venality of our government in cooperating with, condoning, or even permitting any such humiliation of the American nation and people is almost beyond belief, even in these days when the unbelievable occurs every hour on the hour," Welch informed readers of the June 1961 issue of the *Bulletin*, before suggesting a new letter-writing campaign to ridicule both the scheme and its perpetrators. Birchers should send short letters to the nation's newspapers, he advised, asking such (supposedly humorous) questions as: "Since Communist agents will unquestionably be substituted by Castro for the anti-Communist prisoners, before actual delivery is made to this country, would it be all right for us to substitute peanut-vending machines for the tractors just after the final inspection of the shipment?"[74]

More substantively, Welch believed that a familiar pattern was to be detected in the wreckage of the affair. "When all the smoke has cleared away," three things will have happened, he predicted:

(1) The anti-Communist Cuban patriots, both in this country and in Cuba, who are most dangerous to the Castro regime, will have been tricked into exposing themselves and then killed or captured, with all potential resistance in the future thus largely destroyed.
(2) The United States will have suffered further terrific losses in prestige, especially in Latin America, among the very people it is supposed to be supporting and leading in their opposition to the Communists.
(3) Fidel Castro will have emerged far stronger than ever, not only having put down a revolt, but as the Communist David who had defeated the great capitalist Goliath.

It was the U-2 summit episode all over again. All three developments had been "'planned that way' by Fidel Castro and his pro-Communist allies within our government," Welch believed.[75]

The official publication of *The Politician* in March 1963 provided the Birch Society's leader with the opportunity to set out a more detailed version of the argument through an epilogue, which updated the manuscript to include an analysis of key events that had occurred since 1958 (the year the "book" had previously ended). This was important because it allowed Welch to make the case that the internal subversion he had identified as the primary cause of the United States' Cold War woes had continued on into the new administration—that there had been "no change in the course or purpose of our Government as a whole" and that the government remained, "as it became under Eisenhower, the most powerful force promoting the world-wide Communist advance."[76]

Cuba was exhibit number one in the indictment. "The delivery of Cuba into Communist hands, and eventual conversion . . . into the Communist spearhead for subjugating all the Americas" had begun when the Eisenhower administration had stopped sending weapons to the Batista regime, while allowing Castro, "by transparent subterfuge, to get all the arms from this country that he needed," Welch said. Although it had been on a "telescoped scale as to both time and area," it was essentially a repeat of the situation with Chiang Kai-shek and Mao, when China had been "delivered" into communist hands "a dozen years before," he argued. The subterfuge had continued with Castro's 1959 American tour and his meetings with various U.S. government officials and representatives, which had the aim—the "program was obvious," Welch said—of "using American support, American prestige, American money, and American good will to build up Castro, and get him solidly established."[77] Meanwhile, Castro had been working behind the scenes to establish his "subservience to Moscow and actual enmity for the United States, so as to lay the groundwork for the next stage in this Communist advance." This had come with the severing of diplomatic relations with Cuba on January 3, 1961: one of the last "official acts of the Eisenhower Administration," it was particularly significant, Welch explained, because it had "enabled the Kennedy Administration to inherit Castro as a clear-cut enemy."[78]

"Having leaned on Washington to make himself strong enough to be a conspicuous Communist enemy, Castro's game now was to raise himself higher, to an entirely new level of prestige and power, by repeated defeats of the United States, diplomatically and even militarily," with the Cuban leader "able to count on the full cooperation of Washington at every turn," Welch went on. This was the real significance of the apparently botched Bay of Pigs invasion. It had been "*planned to happen* . . . from the very inception of the whole scheme," Welch alleged, as a means of making Castro stronger and cutting off the potential for any future insurrection against him (the "same formula used in Poland and in Hungary in the fall of 1956"); to decrease American prestige on the world stage (the "same formula used in Vietnam in 1954, in Lebanon in 1958, and more recently in Laos"); and to increase Castro's (just as the Suez crisis had been used to enhance the prestige of Egyptian president Gamal Abdel Nasser).[79]

It was an idiosyncratic interpretation of events, to say the least, but Welch did show that he had learned something from the fallout over his original version of *The Politician*, with its claim that President Eisenhower was "a dedicated, conscious agent of the Communist conspiracy" in the United States. No such accusation was made against his successor. The conspirators at work inside the Kennedy White House were kept vague and general. It was "still too early" to identify the specific individuals who were exercising a "controlling influence" in the administration, Welch argued, although he did point out that key architects of the Cuban fiasco such as CIA director Allen Dulles and deputy director for plans Richard Bissell provided a suspicious element of "continuity" between the Eisenhower and Kennedy presidencies.[80] (Both Dulles and Bissell were fired by Kennedy in the aftermath of the Bay of Pigs, but with their roles in the conspiracy complete, this was presumably no great loss to the communist cause.)

In a press conference about the Cuban invasion on April 21, 1961, Kennedy dismissed the Birch Society's claims of internal U.S. subversion as failing to wrestle "with the real problems which are created by the Communist advance around the world." He made the same case in January 1962, when he argued that one of the primary reasons for the growth of right-wing groups like the Birchers was their misdirected desire "for solutions and safety in a complicated and dangerous world." It was regrettable, he said, that so many members of the Society were devoting their time and energies to the search for the enemy within, rather than dealing with all the external problems the country continued to face.[81]

This was also the theme of New Jersey Republican senator Clifford Case's address to the annual meeting of the Anti-Defamation League in New York's Savoy Hilton on January 13. It was understandable, he said, that developments since the end of the Second World War—the "growing menace of Communist power" and the possibility of nuclear destruction, in particular—would feed "a yearning for all-embracing solutions of the sort that the extremists purport to offer." But the "patent absurdity" of the Birch Society's insistence that the real danger was to be found "from communism here at home" needed to be resisted. If not, the senator warned, the "constant reiteration of the extremists' theme that the [external] struggle is not necessary—even that it is irrelevant—may by slow degrees erode, at first our understanding of the problems which we face, and then our will to meet them in rational ways." And the result "could be disastrous for America and for mankind."[82]

Welch's sarcastic response to the growing chorus of this kind of criticism came in the April 1962 issue of *American Opinion*.[83] "Of course we realize that the International Communist Conspiracy does not exist, and that there is no such thing as internal subversion," he said, before recounting a story of a farmer fascinated with a giraffe, who having studied the creature long and hard, feeding it lettuce and getting two fingers bitten off, patting its hunches only to be kicked in return, finally walks away, "bloody but superior," to inform the "stupid yokels who were not as sophisticated as he was: 'I still say that there ain't no such animal.'"[84] Others may think the Communist conspiracy to be "entirely imaginary," Welch explained, but the Birch Society was going to continue to keep telling the world all "about the animal; about its teeth, its hooves, and the kind of food on which it thrives. As well as about the victims— not at all imaginary—whom it has already trampled to death." This was the role of the magazine's writers, Welch said, people like Slobodan Draskovich, E. Merrill Root, Edward Hunter, and Revilo P. Oliver, who as "some of America's foremost experts on the mythical beast do a superb job of following its tracks, explaining its cunning methods, anticipating its rampages, and encouraging those who would destroy it."[85]

True to his word, in a speech before 1,200 people in Garden City, Long Island—right in Senator Case's own backyard—on June 18, Welch denounced the Kennedy administration for continuing the practices of the Eisenhower years. "There is a Moscow-Washington program of degrading the United States in the eyes of the world," he declared. "We've delivered Cuba into Communist hands . . . and eventually all of Central and South America, and Europe except West Germany, will be Communist."[86]

One of the principal consequences of the Bay of Pigs invasion was to push Cuba and the Soviet Union closer together. This, together with the Kennedy administration's ongoing "obsession" with removing Castro from power, Khrushchev's adventurism and concerns about the still unresolved situation in Berlin and the Soviet Union's continuing nuclear inferiority, as well as Castro's own recklessness combined with legitimate fears about another American invasion, were the factors that led to the Cuban missile crisis of October 1962, the closest the world has come to a full-scale nuclear war. U-2 spy planes again played a key role, providing definitive photographic evidence of the construction of intermediate- and medium-range ballistic missile sites on the Caribbean island. When operational—which, based on photographs taken on October 14, the CIA estimated to be in a matter of weeks—missiles launched from these sites would have the capacity to strike deep within the United States, with possible casualties of up to eight million Americans.[87]

In the nearly catastrophic thirteen days that followed the discovery of the missile sites, the Soviet Union and the United States went "eyeball to eyeball" (as Secretary of State Dean Rusk famously expressed it). The United States threatened massive nuclear retaliation against the USSR if any missiles were launched from Cuba against targets in the Western Hemisphere, a naval blockade was imposed to prevent any further Soviet vessels reaching the island, and various negotiating stratagems—both public and private—were employed before a means to resolve the crisis was found. The deal finally struck was that the Soviet Union would remove the missiles from Cuba in return for a noninvasion pledge from the United States. Unbeknownst to the public at the time, as a result of some back-channel diplomacy involving Robert Kennedy and the Soviet ambassador, Anatoly Dobrynin, the United States had also agreed—at some point in the near future, once the immediate crisis had passed, so that there would appear to be no "linkage" between them—to remove Jupiter missiles in Turkey that were aimed at the Soviet Union, even though they were technically under the control of NATO. Castro, to his considerable irritation, was a virtual bystander in the negotiations between the two superpowers.

Although presumably grateful not to have been destroyed in a nuclear conflagration, the Birch Society's response to what it called the "second Cuba fiasco" was hardly congratulatory. Writing in the December *Bulletin*, Welch described the crisis as a "grandstand play, carefully timed . . . to help elect favorites of the Administration and to defeat Conservatives of both parties" in the November 1962 elections.[88] (This was also Richard Nixon's explanation for his failure to become the governor of California. The "Cuban thing" had prevented him "from getting our message through," he said.)[89] In a comparison that critics might reasonably complain betrayed a serious underestimation of what had been at stake in the Caribbean, Welch also contended that one of its "obvious purposes" had been to "take the minds of the American people off the invasion of Mississippi"—the September 1962 riot at Ole Miss, following James Meredith's attempt to enroll there, discussed in the previous chapter—and to "bring about a situation in which the prestige and power of the United Nations could be enhanced." However, the "*major purposes* of the whole maneuver" did not really become clear until after the elections, Welch said, when—following weeks of continued negotiations on the practicalities of how the agreement to resolve the crisis was to be actually implemented—Kennedy announced the formal ending of the U.S. quarantine, the final removal of the missiles, and his noninvasion pledge.[90]

All roads inevitably leading back to China, Welch complained that Kennedy's "guarantee" not to invade Castro's Cuba, given in exchange for Khrushchev's "worthless promise" to remove his missiles, was a betrayal of anticommunist Cubans comparable with Eisenhower's betrayal of Chiang Kai-shek's Nationalist forces during the Formosa/Taiwan Strait crises of 1954 and 1958.[91] And what made the situation worse, he argued—in a textbook example of Senator Case's chief complaint about the Society—was that Kennedy's guarantee had been given "as if we were in craven fear of a *military attack* from Soviet Russia . . . when for a quarter of a century the only weapon the Soviets themselves have ever used to conquer *any* country has been internal subversion." The resolution of the Cuban missile crisis had "turned out to be an even greater victory for Castro and Khrushchev" than the Bay of Pigs crisis had been, Welch said.[92]

Recognizing the limited ability of even the John Birch Society to influence geopolitical events of this nature, Welch admitted it was difficult to say what the organization's members should do to try to remedy the situation. ("Don't jump on [us] just because we do not have all of the answers, at least until you find somebody that does," he scolded complaining readers.) But he did recommend Birchers to buy and begin distributing a new postcard containing the message: "Don't Worry—They Are Still Ninety Miles Away!"[93]

The turn of the year brought with it some renewed energy. *American Opinion*'s resident Cold War specialist, Dr. Slobodan Draskovich, sought to dismantle the conventional wisdom that getting the Soviet Union's missiles out of Cuba had been a victory for the Kennedy administration in an article entitled "The Ventriloquist and the Dummy" for his monthly column "On the Cold War Front" in the magazine's January 1963 issue—Castro being the dummy in question and Khrushchev his ventriloquist operator. A member of the Birch Society's National Council, Draskovich was an interesting figure. A leader of the Yugoslavian émigré community in Chicago, where he edited the weekly Serbian newspaper *Srpska Borba* (The Serbian struggle), and the author of *Tito: Moscow's Trojan Horse*, he had immigrated to the United States in 1947, having been a prisoner of war in Italy and Germany during World War II, and a professor of economics at the University of Belgrade before that. His argument was that ordinary Americans had been "brainwashed" into believing that Kennedy's "toughness" had brought about the ending of the crisis in Cuba, and that this represented a possible turning point in the broader Cold War struggle. Although it was the "Pavlovian Century," the unconditioned mind knew, he said, that if "Nikita Khrushchev is dismantling Soviet missiles, and withdrawing his bombers from Cuba, it is only *because they have accomplished their mission*." The events of October 1962 had done nothing to make the United States stronger in the world, Draskovich argued; instead, Americans had "paid a fantastic price" for the missiles' removal: the "consolidation of Communism in Cuba," a ticking "time bomb . . . within ninety miles of our shores."[94]

"Cuba Free—In '63" briefly became the Birchers' new rallying cry—one suggested by the members of the Society themselves, as Welch was careful to note—and the Society threw its support behind other anti-Castro organizations such as the Committee for the Monroe Doctrine.[95] It also tried to prevent the passage of the Limited Test Ban Treaty, which prohibited nuclear tests in the atmosphere, the oceans, and outer space, and was one of the more positive and substantive results of the crisis—the other being the establishment of a "hotline" to provide a direct telegraphic link between Moscow and Washington to aid in the management of any future crises.[96] But it was evident that the Birch leader's heart was not really in these efforts. "We are sorry to say that we see no chance of accomplishing this objective [of Cuba Free—In '63], and we have no specific action to recommend for this purpose at the present time," he confessed in the September issue of the *Bulletin*. Cuban freedom would not be won until the communist influence had been routed from Washington, he explained, and with Kennedy still in the White House, that still seemed a distant prospect.[97] It was also the case, though, that there was another major foreign policy issue pressing for the Society's attention in 1963, and that, of course, was the war in Vietnam. If the communist advance had not been stopped in the Caribbean, perhaps it could yet be turned around in Southeast Asia.

Waist Deep in the Big Muddy: The Vietnam War and the John Birch Society

As with many other Cold War issues, Welch's interest in the situation in Vietnam predated the formation of the Birch Society. In the original manuscript version of *The Politician*, for example, he had criticized the division of the country at the seventeenth parallel as a result of the Geneva Accords of July 1954, as handing "the better half" of Vietnam to Ho Chi Minh and "making unwilling slaves out of thirteen million Vietnamese" people.[98] (In Welch's view—one he was still expressing in 1965—anticolonialism was one of the crucial elements of the communists' "Big Lie" strategy, and the world would be a much better place if former colonial powers like Great Britain and France were still implementing their "benign and peaceful" rule in nations like Ghana and North Vietnam.)[99] Similarly, in February 1958—ten months before the Indianapolis meeting out of which the Birch Society would emerge and long before most ordinary Americans were thinking about the country—he published an informative and highly prescient article by Hilaire du Berrier entitled "About South Vietnam."[100] In the same way that Slobodan Draskovich functioned as one of the organization's primary Cold War analysts, du Berrier became the Birch Society's in-house expert on the war in Vietnam, writing regularly about the subject in the years to come, and even sending back first-hand dispatches from the war zone in his *American Opinion* column "From Saigon."[101]

If anything, du Berrier's background was even more interesting than

Draskovich's.[102] Born in Flasher, North Dakota, in 1906, du Berrier spent his early years as a member of a flying circus before offering his aeronautic skills to the Ethiopian leader Haile Selassie to help rebuff the invading army of Mussolini in 1936. A committed monarchist, he next involved himself in the Spanish Civil War, acting as a spy for Franco's forces in the mistaken belief that this would lead to the restoration of King Alfonso XIII to the Spanish throne. From Spain, he moved on to China, running a Nationalist spy-ring in Japanese-occupied Shanghai in support of the Chiang regime. (Du Berrier seems to have shared Welch's view that Franco and Chiang were the only two men to have "beaten the Communists at their own game.")[103] Interned—and apparently tortured—by his Japanese captors, du Berrier was rescued by an advance team of the Office of Strategic Services, which recruited him as a specialist in Indochina affairs. The appointment only lasted a few months, however, as du Berrier believed—amazingly—that the organization led by William "Wild Bill" Donovan and the forerunner to the CIA was too left-wing in its "direction of purpose and teamwork."[104] As a result, the adventurer-cum-spy turned his hand to journalism, becoming the (short-lived) head of *Newsweek*'s Far East desk, and publishing, with the aid of a wealthy Los Angeles-based backer, his own "private intelligence letter" on the rapidly deteriorating situation in the region, *H du B Reports*.

Du Berrier's 1958 article for *American Opinion* accurately cataloged the nepotism, political corruption, economic mismanagement, and repressive policies of the United States' "man" in South Vietnam, Ngo Dinh Diem. (A devout, French-educated Catholic in a predominantly Buddhist nation, Diem became the president of the Republic of South Vietnam when he ousted the French puppet emperor Bao Dai in a rigged referendum in 1955. Although he was an elitist autocrat who often failed to follow American advice, Diem's nationalist and anticommunist credentials convinced the Eisenhower administration to throw its support behind him, including when he refused to implement the 1956 nationwide elections intended to bring about Vietnam's reunification under the Geneva Accords—as all parties realized, such elections would have led to reunification under Ho Chi Minh's rule, not Diem's.)[105] "A paid propaganda campaign could convince American public opinion that Diem is indispensable in far away Southeast Asia—and may keep him in power," du Berrier wrote. "But your Vietnamese, there on the ground, knows the truth from fiction. He sums it up, '*Unless we can get Diem out and install a broad government with popular support, the Reds will come in.*'"[106]

Du Berrier had put his finger on the fundamental problem that would plague successive U.S. administrations for the next seventeen years until the "Reds" did finally "come in" in 1975. He returned to what he called "The Diem Myth" in October 1963, just a few weeks before the South Vietnamese leader was overthrown and brutally murdered in an American-supported coup d'état led by General Duong Van Minh and other dissident South Vietnamese military officers on November 1, 1963. Du Berrier updated his analysis to detail the persecution and imprisonment of Buddhist protestors against the regime— "the monks, nuns, old women, and children clubbed into insensibility within the confines of Diem's barbed wire," as he put it—as well as the continuing cost to the

American taxpayer (which he estimated at close to a million dollars per day) of keeping the "most corrupt government in Southeast Asia" going.[107] (Since taking over the presidency in 1961, the Kennedy administration had steadily increased American involvement in the war, with the result that by 1963 there were over sixteen thousand military "advisers" in the country, some fighting alongside the Army of the Republic of Vietnam, which was itself largely equipped by the United States, in its struggle against North Vietnam and the National Liberation Front's—Vietcong—guerrilla insurgency in the South.)[108]

Du Berrier's view of the coup was set out most clearly in his 1965 Birch Society–published book, *Background to Betrayal: The Tragedy of Vietnam*. In it, he took issue with other "good conservatives" who were claiming that communists and communist agitators must have been behind the coup, because it was "they" who had benefited most from Diem's removal. His own deep knowledge of the realities of Diem's regime allowed him to get beyond such "surface thinking," he explained. "If the police state of Diem and [his brother] Nhu and the stupidity or intent of the small group of Americans supporting it created a climate ideal for Communist agitation," he wrote, "they—not the Communists—should be blamed when the Communists exploit it." The real crime, du Berrier argued, had been in choosing the Diem family to rule South Vietnam "in the first place, putting it in power, refusing to let the Vietnamese topple our protégés while change was yet possible and then permitting our team to wash their hands of responsibility when the coming explosion threatened to compromise them."[109]

Unimpressed by the succession of leaders that had followed Diem, General Minh and Nguyen Khanh included, du Berrier argued that "anarchy" and "pandemonium" had been the ultimate result of the coup, and his book concluded with his attempt to answer the question, "How did we ever get involved in South Vietnam?" It was one being asked by an increasingly clamorous public, du Berrier said (although, in truth, apathy and disinterest would only finally give way in response to the large numbers of American soldiers returning to the United States dead or injured, following Lyndon Johnson's fatal escalation of the conflict in early 1965).[110] Returning to the origins of the Cold War—and seconding the views of Welch—the answer du Berrier offered was that the "senseless, stupid crusade against colonialism, agreed upon by Roosevelt and Stalin at Teheran, led us up to our waists in the quagmire of Indochina. Determination to replace the allies we were ousting drew us in the rest of the way."[111] It was a reasonable enough analysis—as indeed was the book as a whole—but it concluded with some wishful thinking and a dash of conspiracism. In du Berrier's view,

> a one-hour, carrier-based airstrike could have destroyed Ho chi Minh's deci-
> mated army in March 1954, saved the beleaguered garrison at Dien Bien Phu
> and changed the course of history. But there was a virus in the bloodstream of
> America that desired a Vietminh triumph. The story of Indochina is the story
> of the decline of the West. Only an informed public, such as America did not
> have on November 3, 1964 [the date of LBJ's presidential victory], will bring
> the victory at the polls which alone will eradicate the virus and prevent many
> more Indochinas to come. All of the force of America's massed left, from the

White House down, was regimented to silence those who would tell America the truth.[112]

While Kennedy and his "whiz kids," led by Secretary of Defense Robert McNamara, had been in charge of the war, the Birch Society's writers and critics had derided their "no win" strategy.[113] A. F. Canwell made hay with McNamara's middle name—which was Strange—for example, and even the Society's film critic, Jack Moffitt, got in on the act during a review of Marlon Brando's *The Ugly American*, based on the best-selling novel of the same name.[114] The critique, which was common in conservative circles at the time—and has remained so ever since—continued with the Johnson administration.[115] (Driven by a combination of factors, including a sense of commitment to the policies of his predecessors, a belief in the "domino theory," and fear about a revival of McCarthyism if another Asian nation was "lost" to communism, Johnson's escalation of what he came to call "that bitch of a war" included authorizing the persistent aerial bombing of targets in North Vietnam—operation Rolling Thunder—and the deployment of U.S. ground troops. In 1965 there were over 180,000 American soldiers in Vietnam, and by 1968, the figure was 500,000, with thousands dying each month.)[116]

Earl Lively Jr., the author of *The Invasion of Mississippi* and a former U.S. Air Force pilot, analyzed "the curious doctrine" of limited warfare in the October 1964 issue of *American Opinion*. His article provides a good example of the Birch Society's critique of the prosecution of the war under President Johnson. It was a doctrine first applied during the Korean War, Lively explained, when U.S. forces led by General MacArthur were denied the possibility of attacking the communists in their "privileged sanctuary" beyond the Yalu River—the border separating North Korea from China—but it had become much more entrenched under both the Kennedy and Johnson administrations because of the "dictates of civilian planners" veering further and further away from sound military strategy. (Truman and the joint chiefs had forbidden attacks across the Chinese border during the conflict in Korea for fear of instigating a third world war. Lively obviously did not think this qualified as a sound strategy.) Instead of employing the overwhelming power of America's military and technological capabilities in Vietnam, "the 'whiz kids' have made counter-insurgency the focal point of [U.S.] military activity, and the chief export item of our military aid," Lively said. But this emphasis on guerrilla warfare and the battle for "hearts and minds" was simply playing to the communists' strengths. It was "like arguing that the best way to protect yourself from a savage is to throw away your pistol and pick up a club—because that's what he uses."[117]

Lively was careful not to criticize America's fighting forces themselves. "Make no mistake about it, these troops are highly-trained, dedicated, capable men; the tragedy lies in their being wasted in a 'no-win' situation," he said. "Once the politicians permit our boys to win, victory can *surely* be gained against North Vietnam with the same forces capable of defeating the Soviet Union!"[118] The solution was obvious, Lively believed: "Ho chi Minh is the enemy. His sanctuary is not in Red China; it is in North Vietnam. Until we bring our power to bear in that sanctuary, we cannot expect to win." While it would have been better not to have been "lured" into the conflict in the first place, now that the United States was fully engaged it was vital, he argued, that military commanders "be given freedom of option." This included not just the application of American airpower, but also the use—"if needed"—of tactical nuclear weapons. Seemingly unconcerned about the prospect of this leading to a broader conflagration, Lively argued that "it is preposterous to believe that Red China, without atomic weapons, a navy, or [an] intercontinental air force, already tottering on the brink of collapse, and saved once from U.S. military destruction by the armistice in Korea, would go to war against us over an attack on North Vietnam. And it is even more ridiculous to think that the USSR would resort to open war against us in such an instance—and invite nuclear destruction from SAC [Strategic Air Command] and our missile complex."[119]

As the war in Vietnam heated up, so too did the protests against it at home. Dr. Martin Luther King Jr. called the United States the "greatest purveyor of violence in the world today." The Arkansas senator and chairman of the Senate Foreign Relations Committee J. William Fulbright denounced the nation's "arrogance of power." Draft cards were burned, thousands of people took to the streets, and the president was taunted with chants of "Hey, hey, LBJ / How many kids did you kill today?" and "Ho, Ho, Ho Chi Minh / The NLF is gonna win."[120]

Although they were always a minority of a minority, it was the student radicals of the New Left who particularly attracted the Birch Society's attention as well as its considerable ire.[121] Reporter Bill Richardson and photographer Ken Granger traveled to the University of California at Berkeley to cover what Richardson called the "pro-Vietcong demonstrations" going on there on October 15 and November 20, 1965, for example. The protests had been "a Communist operation from start to finish," Richardson recounted in the January 1966 issue of *American Opinion.* "Fifteen thousand Communist-led demonstrators marched to support a Communist enemy which, as their marching feet pounded the California pavement, was killing American soldiers in the stinking jungles and rice paddies of Vietnam." Having covered the parades, listened to the speeches, and interviewed some of the participants, the Birchers found themselves in "a snake pit," Richardson said, a place where "the real became unreal" and where "treason was the norm," but what was worse was that because of the failings of the press, ordinary Americans were not getting "all of the facts." There were no headlines such as "Communist Demonstrations Attempt to Destroy American Fighting Morale" in the wake of the Berkeley protests, he complained. The "uninformed journeymen" TV and news reporters who had been dispatched to cover them simply did not have the necessary skills and training to reflect what had really taken place. They had merely reported "the obvious. And the obvious is all that the Communists want reported."[122]

The following month, Jere Real, a doctoral student in literature at the University of Virginia and a former air force officer, reported on the antiwar efforts of Students for a Democratic Society (SDS), the most prominent New Left group of the time. He was particularly concerned by the "fact-finding" trip one of its leaders, Tom Hayden, had recently made to Hanoi in the company of the communist historian Herbert Aptheker and the pacifist Yale professor Staughton Lynd. (There were a number of such visits to North Vietnam during the war, the most notorious being actress Jane Fonda's in July 1972.)[123] As far as Real was concerned, SDS's "outlandish" views on Vietnam included that it was a "civil war in which the United States has no part," that it was "immoral," and that the United States was the "aggressor" (all of which were the standard antiwar arguments of the time.) "It seems absurd that students could accept such inversions of the truth concerning blatant Communist aggression in Southeast Asia," he said, "but it accept it they do!" And he regarded the organization overall as "revolutionary": as seeking to "topple virtually every edifice of American society and replace it with a collectivized society where every man's life is subject to the social needs of the community in which he is little more than a conforming piece of machinery."[124]

One of the largest and most dramatic demonstrations of 1967 was the October 21 March on the Pentagon, the culmination of a week of protests against the war organized by the National Mobilization Committee to End the War in Vietnam. A crowd of almost one hundred thousand had gathered to hear speeches and protest songs at the Lincoln Memorial in Washington DC, before close to thirty-five thousand moved on to the Pentagon, the very symbol of American military power, and attempted to encircle, or maybe even levitate it (which was the particular aim of arch-prankster Abbie Hoffman). Protestors who remained into the evening were violently dispersed by club-wielding federal marshals and tear gas.[125]

The Birch Society's chief news analyst, Susan Huck, dissected the events in the January 1968 issue of *American Opinion*. It was "yet another carefully planned and staged propaganda assault on the American people," the Birch Society's *Review of the News* editor concluded. But it was also "a microscopic example" of the United States' "plight in Vietnam itself," where "we spend any amount of money to deploy overwhelming military power—and then carefully refrain from using it"—a reference to what Huck saw as the regrettable nonengagement of the troops President Johnson had carefully stationed around the capital during the protests. (Fearful of a siege, Johnson had deployed troops to protect the Pentagon, the Capitol, and the White House during the protests, as well as secretly stationing some in the basement of the Commerce Department.)[126] "Our government seems to have gotten us into a *lovely* box—a 'heads they win, tails we lose' situation," Huck went on. "Since 'victory' is officially renounced as an American policy, we are left with the choice of surrendering to the Communists or bleeding indefinitely . . . and if the United States can be further ripped apart by dissension . . . well, just wonderful!" The mobilization of October 21–22 had taught thirty-five thousand "American youngsters . . . that *there is no penalty* for treason, for sedition, for assault, for public indecency, for taking dope right under the noses of the 'forces of law and order,' for destroying property and mobbing opponents and attacking U.S. soldiers," she lamented. And then there was the impact the "spectacle" would have overseas: demoralizing "our boys in Vietnam," emboldening the Eastern bloc, and leading "not-yet Communist ruled" nations to "have serious doubts about the health and sanity of the American body politic."[127]

The Birch Society's chief complaints about the activities of the antiwar movement—that they were making "victory" in Vietnam more difficult, and that they were aiding, if not being secretly directed or controlled by, the nation's external enemies—were shared by some of the most senior members of the American political establishment, including President Johnson, Secretary of State Dean Rusk, and FBI director J. Edgar Hoover. (Many of the movement's leaders had "close Communist associations *but they do not appear to be under Communist direction. . . . Covert or overt connections between these US activists and foreign governments are limited. . . .* On the basis of what we now know, we see no significant evidence that would prove Communist control or direction of the US peace movement or its leaders," the director of the CIA, Richard Helms, reported back to a still-disbelieving Johnson after the March on the Pentagon protests, based on NSA, CIA, FBI, and military sources.)[128] The extent to which the antiwar movement contributed to the ending of the war, or instead lengthened it by encouraging Hanoi to keep fighting, has also been hotly debated. The historian George Herring argues that its impact was more limited and subtler than is commonly believed. "It [the antiwar movement] forced Vietnam into the public consciousness and challenged the rationale of the war and indeed of a generation of Cold War foreign policies," he argues. "It exposed error and self-deception in the government's claims, encouraging distrust of political authority. It limited Johnson's military options . . . [and it] caused fatigue and anxiety among the policy makers and the public, thus eventually encouraging efforts to find a way out of the war."[129] It is worth remembering, however, that in its distaste for, and opposition to, the antiwar movement, the Birch Society was clearly on the side of the majority in the United States—what Nixon would come to call the "silent majority." As Herring also notes, public opinion polls at the time consistently revealed the protestors to be even more unpopular than the war itself.[130]

Despite this, the Society still found itself at the center of controversy. In June 1967, the Anti-Defamation League (ADL) accused it of exploiting "American anguish over Vietnam" through its nationwide campaign to convince the American public that the war effort was under "Communist control." Launching its new report on the Society, authored by Benjamin Epstein and Arnold Forster, the ADL's national director Dore Schary argued that the Birch Society was increasingly shifting its resources away from the fight against the civil rights movement and toward the war in Vietnam as a means of attracting new recruits.[131] (There had been a slight decline in the number of Birch chapters in operation between 1966 and 1967, Epstein and Forster noted in their report, from five thousand to four thousand, but they still estimated the number of members to be in the range of seventy-five thousand to eighty-five thousand.)[132]

The particular source of contention was the Society's recently issued pamphlet, *The Truth about Vietnam* (which was followed within a few months by *More Truth about Vietnam*). Written by Welch, the twenty-page pamphlet was essentially a distillation of all the Society's thinking on both the Cold War and the war in Vietnam over the previous nine years. It was true, as the ADL charged, that the pamphlet claimed that U.S. actions in Vietnam "were being conducted exactly according to Communist plans and wishes," but this was hardly a revelation; Welch and his colleagues had seldom strayed from this core belief since the Society's founding—as anyone who had read any Birch literature, attended a chapter meeting, or heard Welch speak could surely testify.[133] In fact, one of the few things that was really new about *The Truth in Vietnam* was the Society's latest slogan, the vaguely Orwellian "Victory, Then Peace!"[134]

Nonetheless, Welch still felt the need to defend himself. Writing in the *Bulletin* in July, he noted that the ADL had made "no attempt to refute any of the facts assembled" in his pamphlet, but he was particularly concerned about the charge that he was exploiting American "anguish" over the war. Nothing could be further from the truth, Welch said; he was merely urging the administration to do all it could to actually bring about victory in Vietnam—"as so many of our ablest military men say could be done if there were only the will to win"—and once this was achieved, Birch members would be "loudest in our praise [of the government's] patriotism and good sense."[135]

As always, ordinary Birch members were encouraged to write letters—as many as five a week—to the nation's "opinion molders," to circulate petitions, and to generally agitate for a victorious conclusion to the war. They were also encouraged to visit veterans' hospitals in the hope of providing comfort and encouragement to wounded soldiers returning from the war zone. An ad hoc committee, TRAIN—To Restore American Independence Now—was also organized.[136] But, of course, "victory" remained elusive. And in the *Bulletin* for December 1967, there were signs that the daily carnage of the Vietnam War was perhaps starting to get to the Birch Society's founder and principal spokesman. "Almost all men, always and everywhere, want peace," Welch noted—the "almost" being a typical Welchian touch. "It is governments that make war, not people," he went on. "War is the sport of kings, the suicide of republics, and the idiot's delight of democracies." But lest his members start to think their leader was going soft on them, he was quick to add that "in all ages its primary purpose—*and result*—has been to increase the dominions or the powers of government." From the bombing of Pearl Harbor, through the Korean War, and on to the killing fields of Vietnam, the lesson to be drawn—at least as far as Welch was concerned—remained the same. It was that "bigger governments make bigger wars; and bigger wars, in turn, make still bigger governments." He had pointed all this out back in 1958 in *The Blue Book*, he said.[137]

A World Gone Crazy

Between 1958 and 1968, Robert Welch and the Birch Society's other foreign policy analysts offered the organization's members guidance during confusing and dangerous times—in a "world gone crazy," as Welch put it in the autumn of 1960.[138] Playing on their claims of expertise, they sought to interpret this world for Birchers—and anyone else willing to listen—and tried to suggest practical ways in which the United States' apparent "retreat from victory" at the end of the Second World War could be reversed. As we have seen, their solutions often involved simply unleashing the awesome might of America's military machine:

what was needed to "win," they believed, was simply the *will*; the nation more than already possessed the *means*.

This emphasis on the internal causes of America's external problems brought the Society into conflict with the nation's political elites, because it provided an unwelcome reminder of the damaging excesses of the Second Red Scare years, when the notion that "politics stops at the water's edge" had been brutally exposed for the convenient fiction it was (and remains).[139] Proponents of the new Cold War consensus had no desire for a repeat of that particular scenario. Yet a fear that McCarthyism was undergoing a revival in the 1960s, with the Birch Society as its spearhead, still managed to influence the decision making of those charged with directing the nation's foreign policy at this time, contributing substantially to the United States' problems in both Cuba and Vietnam. "I knew Harry Truman and Dean Acheson had lost their effectiveness from the day that the Communists took over in China. I believed that the loss of China had played a large role in the rise of Joe McCarthy. And I knew that all these problems, taken together, were chickenshit compared with what might happen if we lost Vietnam," explained Lyndon Johnson, for example, although arguably drawing exactly the wrong lesson from Truman and Acheson's travails with the Wisconsin senator.[140]

Dwight Eisenhower had had his own encounters with the Birch Society, of course, and one can also make the case that Welch and his highly active and voluble colleagues in the Committee Against Summit Entanglements had a significant part to play in the failure of détente between United States and the Soviet Union at the end of the 1950s, by constantly challenging the White House's dealings with the "butcher of Budapest." With the benefit of hindsight, it is now possible to see the crushing of the uprising in Hungary in 1956 (as much as that in Czechoslovakia in 1968) not as a sign of Soviet strength and unlimited global ambition, but as an indicator of its weakness and vulnerability.[141] But this was not how it was generally understood at the time, and it is important to acknowledge the extent to which many of the Birch Society's views about the Soviet Union—and indeed about the Cold War in general—were the utterly conventional pieties of the day. Nor was the Birchers' desire for "victory" especially out of the ordinary, speaking as it did to a deep-seated belief in the divinely sanctioned and historically inevitable—and previously self-evident—story of American success, as well as to the nation's innate righteousness and "goodness." "Trying to live in 'peaceful coexistence' with the Communists is only a lingering and painful form of suicide," Welch believed, and making concessions to the Soviets—any concessions—was "like playing poker honestly against a known card shark with a marked deck, who is using chips that he didn't buy and does not intend to redeem."[142] In this sense, even the Birchers' unrelenting emphasis on the machinations of the "enemy within" could be a source of comfort and reassurance, since once the internal cancer had been removed there would be nothing to prevent the United States from resuming its rightful place at the pinnacle of world history. This was supposed to be the "American Century," after all.[143]

Chapter 6

Conspiracy

Conspiracies and conspiracy theories saturated the thinking and political activity of the John Birch Society between 1958 and 1968. Events big and small, from the Cold War and the rise of the civil rights movement to the "smear" campaign against the Society itself, were seen more clearly through a conspiratorial lens, Birchers believed. Conspiracies "explained" the admonishment of General Walker, the assassination of John F. Kennedy, the Watts riots, and the inability of the United States to secure victory in the jungles of Vietnam. They made comprehensible otherwise inexplicable reversals of fortune such as the Bay of Pigs debacle or Barry Goldwater's disastrous election campaign of 1964. They accounted for—and connected together—such seemingly unrelated events as efforts to fluoridate the water supply, gun control legislation, and President Johnson's "war on poverty" (all examples of dangerous and malignant collectivism, in Birchers' eyes).[1]

A particularly striking, if tragic, illustration of the depth of the Birch Society's conspiratorial inclinations occurred in March 1962, when Newton Armstrong Jr., a nineteen-year-old San Diego college student and editor of a conservative campus magazine called *Evolve*, was found dead, hanging from a rope attached to a ceiling beam, in his parents' bedroom. Both his father—an active member of the Birch Society (he was running for the county Republican Central Committee at the time)—and the organization as a whole immediately shifted into conspiratorial mode. It wasn't possible for his son to have bound himself with the rope that killed him, Armstrong Sr. believed, contending instead that his death was a "ritualistic murder" committed by "Communists or other subversives."[2] In the May 1962 *Bulletin*, Robert Welch reported that he had been asked by Armstrong to put aside "any questions of 'good taste' that might be involved" and to use "any and all publicity" about the murder of his son "to help to wake up other patriots as to what is already starting to happen in this country."[3]

Welch had agreed to the request, he said, because although the young man's death was the "first murder for political reasons . . . of which a member of the JBS family has been the victim," it was also indicative of the broader "actions" and "pressures" that members—and "even prospective members"—of the Society were being made to bear, and unless something was done, "many patriotic citizens like ourselves" would soon be "disappearing into concentration camps."

Armstrong Jr.'s murder, Welch argued, was comparable with that of John Birch himself, both men having given their lives "to the task of discovering and of making others realize the nature, methods, and purposes of the Conspiracy that seeks to enslave us." As a result, in addition to establishing a Newton Armstrong Memorial Fund, Welch encouraged all Birch Society members to write their local newspapers demanding that the case be given "the publicity and attention which would certainly be normal and expected for an unsolved murder with such overtones of national significance and interest."[4]

The coroner's initial verdict of suicide was upheld in June 1962, following a six-week investigation by District Attorney Don Keller; the DA explained the strange positioning of Armstrong's hands, which had prompted his father's initial suspicions, as being the result of the youth trying to abort the suicide by relieving the pressure of the rope around his neck, but instead getting them entangled in it. Keller's decision, though, only produced a renewed barrage of publicity by the Birch Society, including a nation-wide postcard campaign centered on the question: "Dear Comrades—Did your Communist friends murder Newton Armstrong Jr.?" Despite describing the campaign as the "most pressure" he had ever experienced in any investigation he had been involved in, Keller refused to reopen the case.[5]

Critics, opponents, and observers of the Society, both at the time and ever since, have generally regarded the organization's embrace of the conspiratorial as a sign of its irrationality and extremism. Contemporary responses to the Birchers from various sectors of American society constantly emphasized its conspiracism and used it as a means of marginalizing and delegitimating the Society and its activities. This is not especially surprising, of course. Along with an advocacy of violence, conspiracy thinking has long marked one of the dividing lines between the acceptable and the unacceptable in mainstream political discourse. "They believe the unbelievable," declared the Democratic Wisconsin senator Gale McGee. They were "fright peddlers," concurred his California Republican colleague Thomas Kuchel—people who saw plots everywhere and who defiled "the honorable philosophy of conservatism" just as much as communists defiled that of liberalism. Other senators saw them as heirs to the Know Nothing Party of the mid-nineteenth century (the view of North Dakota's Milton Young), or as purveyors of "muddleheaded nonsense" in the manner of Lewis Carroll's *Alice in Wonderland* stories (per Senator George McGovern of South Dakota).[6]

Outside of Congress, critics of the Society as diametrically opposed politically as California attorney general Stanley Mosk and National Secretary of the Socialist Party-Social Democratic Federation Irwin Suall could at least agree on the centrality of conspiratorial reasoning to the Birch Society, even if they differed as to its potential ramifications. Mosk, for example, seemed to regard the Birchers as essentially absurd, caught up in a swirling "vortex of fanaticism and despair." "For the paranoid, life is a nightmare," he wrote in his 1961 report on the Society to Governor Brown: "Only he can see The Enemy. Only he understands the nature of the Peril. The more he acts upon his systematized delusions, the more he is cast out by his fellow man for his oddness. This only serves to feed and confirm his dark suspicions and moves him to ever more bizarre beliefs. As these beliefs become ever more bizarre, he is ever more the outcast."[7] In contrast, Suall was at pains to warn about the dangers the (potentially fascist) "Ultras" posed to the very democratic structure of the United States. "The focus of the Ultra," he wrote in March 1962, "is the conspirator, the spy, the traitor, the infiltrator. . . . The method of the Ultra is the anti-conspiracy conspiracy as well as the mass movement. The vision of the Ultras is not an insurrectionary seizure of power but the counter-infiltration of the 'already Communist-infiltrated' institutions of American society. . . . The immediate problem is to contain Ultra power within existing institutions, and to push it back."[8]

Contemporary academic and journalistic observers of the Society also participated fully in the conspiratorial denunciation of the Birchers, setting a pattern that would be followed with varying degrees of emphasis and sophistication in the years to come. Most influentially, in an essay on "pseudo-conservatism" for Daniel Bell's 1963 edited collection, *The Radical Right*, Columbia University history professor Richard Hofstadter characterized the conspiratorial believers of the Birch Society as being "in our world but not exactly of it."[9] In his subsequent essay on the paranoid style in American politics, Hofstadter stated that they projected into the political arena "utterly irrelevant fantasies and disorders of a purely personal kind."[10] This critique was echoed in Seymour Martin Lipset and Earl Raab's study of the persistence of right-wing extremism in American life, *The Politics of Unreason* (1970) and in scores of other works that have examined the Birch Society.[11]

Such criticisms of the Birch Society's conspiracism are neither without merit nor insight, but they are limiting in a number of significant and consequential respects. First, as Jack Bratich has argued, the dominant approaches of Hofstadter, or Lipset and Raab—and indeed their political and journalistic advocates and followers—tend to intertwine "a form of thought (irrational conspiracy theories) with a form of political activity (extremism)." The result, Bratich says—which he regards as a form of "conspiracy panic"—is that certain forms of knowledge or understanding "are presented as inherently dangerous, certain styles of dissent are disqualified, and new forms of consent are forged." Put another way, what Bratich is arguing is that the application of the—intentionally delegitimizing—conspiracy label is itself often a purely political maneuver, one used as a means of shoring up support for those applying the designation against those to whom it is applied.[12]

This was certainly evident in many of the contemporary responses to the emergence of the Birch Society, which, as we have seen, demonstrated a great deal of anxiety among the nation's political and cultural elites about both a revival of the dark days of the Second Red Scare and the potential unraveling of the current Cold War consensus. A *New York Times* editorial from April 22, 1961, entitled "John Birch Fantasies," illustrates the point clearly, stating: "The latest publicized addition to the lunatic fringe of American life is the John Birch Society. Lost in a world of fantasy, the John Birchers are busily looking for Communists in the White House, the Supreme Court, the classrooms, and, presumably, under the bed. In the process they lose sight of the real Communists and of the real problems communism poses before us in Laos, Vietnam, Cuba and elsewhere." Not coincidentally, this echoed precisely the views of President Kennedy (which he had made clear in a press conference the previous day, as discussed in Chapter 5).[13]

Another example of the perceived threat Birchers posed to the consensus politics of the period is provided by one of Hofstadter's colleagues at Columbia University, Alan Westin. Addressing the 1961 meeting of the National Community Relations Advisory Council, the coordinating body of various Jewish groups in the United States, he denounced the Birch Society as "the least useful organization to appear on the American political scene in the last hundred years," and argued that its "prescription of cancelling out the twentieth century would rip apart the social structure and community consensus of the nation and would lead us into a quicksand of reaction."[14] Father John Cronin, the Catholic Church's preeminent anticommunist expert, made essentially the same case in his 1962 book, *Communism: Threat to Freedom*. Birchers and other prominent anticommunists of the 1960s were "vigorously fighting problems that were mostly solved by 1950," Cronin contended. They were "exploiters of unrest" who, with their belief in an imminent communist takeover and in their attempts to link the "Communist menace with unpopular social philosophies or movements," were presenting "an inaccurate and distorted view of the Communist threat."[15]

In addition to recognizing the political and ideological interests at work in the application of the conspiratorial label, it is also vitally important to examine the political, rhetorical, and intellectual functions that conspiracy theories have for the people that employ them.[16] After all, Robert Welch and his fellow Birch-theorists and writers were hardly reluctant or apologetic advocates of a conspiratorial approach to the world. On the contrary, they embraced and loudly trumpeted their conspiracy theories and their conspiratorial assessments. The crucial question (one which all too often goes unasked) is: Why? What did this provide for the Birch Society's leaders and for their followers? And, what did they find so useful or persuasive in this way of seeing and thinking?

"Conspiracism is, first and foremost, an explanation of politics," Michael Barkun has written. "It purports to locate and identify the true loci of power and thereby illuminate previously hidden decision making."[17] Given this, it is important to understand that revealing the "truth" behind the surface of things can be empowering. A profound sense of superiority comes with the unraveling of secrets (as well as an accompanying disquiet that there are still other secrets waiting to be brought out into the light). This was especially so in Cold War America, where the "torments of secrecy" were particularly heightened.[18] There is also a considerable degree of comfort to be had in the gaining of special knowledge, of being privy to the previously undisclosed workings of the world, of becoming aware of what is "really going on." And this is true as much for those who uncover that knowledge as it is for those to whom it is passed on.

Figure 7.1. A billboard claiming to identify Dr. Martin Luther King Jr. at a communist training school stands on the route from Selma to Montgomery, Alabama, March 1965. © Bettmann/CORBIS

The establishment and conveyance of this "expertise" offers guidance in navigating the world as it currently is, but also, crucially, points the way forward, indicating how the world (or the United States, to be more specific) can be changed for the better. Exposing the conspirators is, after all, the first step toward liberation and ultimate freedom. In this sense, then, although it may seem paradoxical given their almost unrelenting emphasis on the fiendishly complex machinations and awe-inspiring power of the conspiracy's originators, a belief in conspiracism as the driving force of political activity offers its adherents control and an enhanced sense of agency. It restores intentionality and morality to history, placing the blame for all of the "bad things" that happen in the world to (ultimately) identifiable individuals or groups, and holding out the hope that by thwarting the activities of these individuals or groups ("the International Communist Conspiracy") order can restored and the world set right.[19]

All of these processes were at work for the Birch Society as it sought to bring about a world of "less government and more responsibility" and vanquish the twin evils of collectivism and communism within the United States.[20] Yet the Birchers were hardly unique in their conspiracism, and we need to see the Society as belonging to, rather than separate from, the wider political and cultural landscape of the 1950s and 1960s, a landscape in which conspiratorial impulses and rhetoric were deeply embedded. The differences between the "extremist" Birch Society and more "mainstream" political actors of the time with regard to the communist threat in particular were often a matter of degree and emphasis rather than basic understanding, and this is yet another of the limitations of Hofstadter et al.'s more psychologically oriented approach.

Finally, as historians such as Bernard Bailyn, Gordon Wood, and David Brion Davis have made clear, we need to acknowledge the extent to which conspiracy theories and conspiratorial thinking have been part of American political life and American identity since the very foundation of the country, leading to a long-established and thoroughly ingrained "counter-subversive tradition," one that has recurred throughout American history, in which the search for the "enemy within" plays a crucial role.[21]

These, then, are some of the central issues explored in the remainder of this chapter. It also considers the contribution that television, advertising, and the age of "the Image" made to the Birchers' conspiracism, as well as the extent to which their use of conspiracy theories might be understood more metaphorically than literally, before concluding with an examination of the negative impact Welch and his colleagues' shift to a broader conspiratorial mythology involving the Bavarian Illuminati and the "Insiders" had on the Society toward the end of the 1960s.

Cold War Ideology and the Politics of Conspiracy

The dominant theme of the Cold War—its "controlling metaphor," in the view of Daniel Rodgers—was the epic struggle between "freedom and slavery."[22] Every nation in the world would have to choose between two radically different ways of life, President Truman declared in March 1947, announcing the famous doctrine that would come to bear his name. "One way of life is based upon the will of the majority, and is distinguished by free institutions, representative government, free elections, guarantees of individual liberty, freedom of speech and religion, and freedom from political oppression," he said. "The second . . . is based upon the will of a minority forcibly imposed upon the majority. It relies upon terror and oppression, a controlled press and radio, fixed elections, and the suppression of personal freedoms."[23] Significantly, the foundational texts of American strategy in this Manichean struggle—George Kennan's "long telegram," with its nightmarish specter of the Soviet government as "a conspiracy within a conspiracy," and National Security Directive (NSC) 68, with its characterization of the Soviet Union as a "slave state" intent on the "implacable" imposition of its will on the world—were steeped in the language of conspiracy: of plots, secrecy, dark deeds, and sinister subversive desires. NSC 68 stated, for example, that

> it is quite clear from Soviet theory and practice that the Kremlin seeks to bring the free world under its dominion by the methods of the cold war. The preferred technique is to subvert by infiltration and intimidation. Every institution of our society is an instrument which it is sought to stultify and turn against our purposes [*sic*]. Those that touch most closely our material and

moral strength are obviously the prime targets, labor unions, civic enterprises, schools, churches, and all media for influencing opinion.[24]

As Arnold Offner points out, by acting on such ideas the Truman administration created "a powerful and long-enduring national security ideology" that was "made to order for Senator Joseph McCarthy of Wisconsin, and others who railed against alleged communists and conspiracies at home and abroad."[25]

More than this, though, in its conspiratorial fusion of radical Protestantism with classical republican and liberal thought, it was a national security ideology that also drew on a "deep and extended tradition" in American life—"a specifically 'American' language of politics, unthinkable anywhere else"—one that could be traced back to Thomas Jefferson's talk of George III's "deliberate, systematical plan of reducing us to slavery" in the Declaration of Independence, and was more recently evident in Franklin D. Roosevelt's determination to resist the evil "designs" of Nazi Germany during the Second World War.[26] Welch and his fellow Birchers drew upon both this specifically Cold War language and its deeper heritage in their own conspiracy-driven concerns.

Indeed, with only slight modifications it would have been very easy to substitute some of Welch's pronouncements on the nature of the communist threat with those of the United States' political and strategic leaders noted above. "This is a *world-wide* battle, the first in history, between light and darkness; between freedom and slavery; between the spirit of Christianity and the spirit of anti-Christ for the souls and bodies of men," Welch wrote in *The Blue Book*, for example, although it could just have easily come from the Truman Doctrine speech.[27] "Communist influences are now in almost complete control of our Federal Government. These same influences are very powerful in the top echelons of our educational system, our labor-union organizations, many of our religious organizations, and of almost every important segment of our national life," Welch warned in the February 1961 *Bulletin*, presenting as actuality what Paul Nitze and the other drafters of NSC 68 had only predicted might happen if the Soviet Union and its agents weren't thwarted. The imagery may have been different but the sentiment was the same. "Insidiously but rapidly the Communists are now reaching the tentacles of their conspiracy downward through the whole social, economic, and political pyramid," Welch wrote.[28]

Of course, it wasn't just the nation's foreign policy and political elites who helped spread the conspiratorial word. "Thanks to Hollywood movies and other cultural clues, Americans already knew that Communists didn't play fair, that Red Subversives favored the same methods as the criminal underworld," notes Susan Carruthers, discussing the popular notion of "communist gangsterdom" during the early Cold War period.[29] This too was something Welch and his followers were keen to emphasize. "We are fighting against the most cruel, amoral, cunning, ambitious, extensive, powerful, and successfully organized gang of completely merciless criminals the world has ever seen, and we know it," Welch informed Birchers in August 1961, in a fairly typical example of the formulation.[30]

The Birch Society's notion of "reversal" held that through their use of slogans and catchphrases, the Soviets had mastered the art of transforming the very appearance of things (or events) so that they might be presented in almost exactly the opposite way to what they actually were; carried to its logical conclusion, it would mean that all Birchers were really communists operating in disguise, noted the journalist and researcher George Thayer.[31] While much derided, even this had its official analog in the practices of the most well-respected and widely cited anticommunist "expert" of them all, J. Edgar Hoover: his idea of "Aesopian language" was used to devastating effect in the Smith Act convictions of the Communist Party leadership in 1949 (which were upheld by the Supreme Court in 1951).[32]

But that was the 1940s and 1950s, when such formulations and assessments were much more acceptable. As Earl Haynes concludes in his study of communism and anticommunism in the Cold War era, "For all its sporadic ugliness, excesses, and silliness, the anticommunism of the 1940s and 1950s was an understandable and rational response to a real danger to American democracy." The beliefs of the Birch Society in the 1960s, in which "paranoia and conspiracy were not simply part of the . . . message but its all consuming core," Haynes, like many others, consigned to the "lunatic fringe of politics."[33] To do so, though, is to ignore the extent to which Cold War thinking and Cold War logic—including its conspiratorial underpinnings—had penetrated the very fiber of the American body politic during the conflict's foundational years. Certainly, the traumas of McCarthyism had severely damaged the most fervent iteration of anticommunist politics in the United States—the one to which the Birchers were the true heirs. But this did not mean that the ideas, beliefs, and impulses that had animated America's initial response to the Cold War—of which McCarthyism was a part—had somehow disappeared when the 1950s ended and the 1960s began, especially given just how badly the Cold War seemed to be going in that new decade.[34]

This, for example, is the liberal Massachusian John F. Kennedy running for the presidency in 1960: "The enemy is the Communist system itself—implacable, insatiable, unceasing in its drive for world domination. This is not a struggle for supremacy of arms alone. It is also a struggle for supremacy between two conflicting ideologies; freedom under God versus ruthless, godless tyranny."[35] And this is Kennedy in office a year later, a month after the Bay of Pigs invasion:

> The great battleground for the defense and expansion of freedom today is Asia, Africa and the Middle East, the lands of the rising peoples. The adversaries of freedom did not create the revolution, but they are seeking to ride the crest of its wave, to capture it for themselves. Yet their aggression is more often concealed than open. They have fired no missiles, and their troops are seldom seen. They send arms, agitators, aid, technicians and propaganda to every troubled area. But where fighting is required, it is usually done by others, by guerrillas striking at night, by assassins striking alone—assassins who have taken the lives of 4,000 civil officers in the last twelve months in Vietnam

alone—by subversives and saboteurs and insurrectionists, who in some cases control whole areas inside independent nations.[36]

This is just rhetoric, one might object, the linguistic currency *du jour*, and Kennedy is talking about the external threat facing the United States, not the internal one as the Birch Society constantly did. This is true, of course, but it is also the case that the characterization of the Soviet Union as an implacable, ruthless, cunning, and subversive adversary was by this time simply second nature to aspirant and established politicians of both major political parties— part of the price of doing political business in the United States. Kennedy may well have been less bellicose in his beliefs in private, but the American people were not privy to his private thoughts, and in public he "hewed carefully to the ideological line his predecessors laid down," as did his successor Lyndon Johnson.[37] In these circumstances, it was asking a great deal of ordinary Americans—including those who joined the Birch Society—to parse the difference between the internal and external menace posed by communism.

The influential Michigan Republican senator Arthur Vandenberg had advised Truman to "scare hell out of the American people" if the president wanted to generate support for his doctrine.[38] Truman had done his best, and successive waves of politicians, journalists, military officers, and cultural producers of all kinds had done the same. Every administration since the end of the Second World War had "maximized the Communist problem," but there was no longer any need to "dramatize the domestic Communist issue," the Reuther memorandum had advised President Kennedy in the autumn of 1961.[39] But it was too late for that genie to be fully returned to the bottle from which it had sprung. Maximization and dramatization had already had their effects. This is not to argue that Welch and his cohorts had a legitimate case to make in their wild charges of internal communist subversion in the years following the Birch Society's formation. They did not. But it is to suggest that their conspiracism does not to have to be seen as the product of some psychological defect or personalized fantasy; that there is a more public, more rational, and more comprehensible explanation.[40]

If an anticommunist conspiracism was one of the essential ingredients of the Cold War consensus, this was particularly the case for those of a more conservative disposition. Ardent anticommunism was the "glue" that held the emerging conservative movement together, after all, and its more conspiratorial components were especially prominent among the forces of the New Right, which were shortly destined to become the predominant force on the American Right as a whole. Ronald Reagan was clearly citing Robert Welch when he stated—in 1960—that "one of the foremost authorities on communism in the world today has said, we have ten years. Not ten years to make up our minds, but ten years to win or lose—by 1970 the world will be all slave or all free."[41] (Indeed, despite his later successful attempts to keep the Society at a distance, Reagan was initially not averse to associating with Birchers, including speaking at a fund-raising dinner for John Rousselot in 1963, for example.)[42] In his chapter

"The Soviet Menace" in *The Conscience of a Conservative*, Barry Goldwater had similarly tried to warn the American people that

> we are confronted by a revolutionary world movement that possesses not only the will to dominate absolutely every square mile of the globe, but increasingly the capacity to do so: a military power that rivals our own, political warfare and propaganda skills that are superior to ours, *an international fifth column that operates conspiratorially in the heart of our defenses*, an ideology that imbues its adherents with a sense of historical mission; and all of these resources controlled by a ruthless despotism that brooks no deviation from the revolutionary course.[43]

Phyllis Schlafly's best-selling *A Choice Not an Echo* was also firmly rooted in the conspiratorial.[44] Jerome Himmelstein has commented with respect to the New Right of the mid-1960s that whether "they identified it as a conspiracy or a culture, all conservatives had the same enemy—the liberal establishment."[45] Corey Robin goes so far as to suggest that conservatives in general "thrive on a world filled with mysterious evil and unfathomable hatreds, where good is always on the defensive and time is a precious commodity in the cosmic race against corruption and decline."[46]

Whether or not this is the case, for Robert Welch there was also a very specific and more concrete reason for his conspiratorial inclinations, which was his belief that both his great political heroes, Robert Taft and Joseph McCarthy, had been "betrayed" at crucial points in their careers by the Republican political establishment. Taft, the venerable Republican senator from Ohio—"Mr. Republican," as he was known—had been the leading voice of conservatism within the GOP since the 1930s.[47] A steadfast opponent of Franklin D. Roosevelt's New Deal and a prominent isolationist turned reluctant internationalist, Taft was widely expected to be the Republican Party candidate in the 1952 presidential election (having narrowly lost out to Thomas Dewey in 1948). Desperate to avoid yet another defeat in the election, however (the Republicans had not held the presidency since Herbert Hoover), and believing, in the words of a series of *New York Times* editorials, that "Taft Can't Win"—a view supported by contemporary public opinion polls—the powerful eastern wing of the party had other ideas.[48] Led by Dewey and Henry Cabot Lodge in particular, this more moderate and liberal "Eastern Establishment" successfully persuaded the retired general Dwight D. Eisenhower to make his entrance in the political arena to take on Taft. At the national convention in Chicago, Eisenhower—a member of the Republican Party of only several months' standing at that point—won the nomination on the first ballot, and as Donald Critchlow writes, Taft's loss "took on mythic proportions for many on the Right who believed that the nomination had been stolen, once again, by the eastern wing of the party."[49]

A number of factors explained Taft's defeat in 1952, including the usual convention chicanery, organizational and tactical mistakes by the Taft campaign, the negative impact of the senator's isolationist history, the potency of the "Taft Can't Win" argument, and the genuine and widespread appeal of

Eisenhower, the great hero of World War II. Taft himself blamed the media. The most important reason for his defeat, he explained in a post-convention memorandum, was that "control of the press enabled the Eisenhower people to do many things which otherwise could not have been done."[50] This was certainly part of the lesson Robert Welch, who ran as a Taft-pledged candidate for the convention in the Fifth Congressional District of Massachusetts, took from the experience. But it was not the only one. Taft's failure to win the nomination in 1952 was "the dirtiest deal in American political history," he wrote in *The Blue Book*, one Richard Nixon had "participated in if not actually engineered . . . in order to make himself vice-president (and to put [Earl] Warren on the Supreme Court)."[51] Indeed, as well as providing one of the principal launching pads for his career in conspiracism, for Welch, Taft's loss was *the* great missed opportunity of postwar conservatism, the pivot on which all-recent American history turned. Had Taft been nominated in 1952, it was "almost certain" that he would "have been elected president by a far greater plurality than was Eisenhower, that a grand rout of the Communists in our government and in our midst would have been started," and even that Senator McCarthy would still be alive, Welch asserted.[52]

It was the communists who had determined that Taft had to be defeated, and who "behind the scenes pulled out all [the] stops and combined many powerful chords of planning, propaganda, and pressure" to bring about that end, Welch declaimed in his "Through All the Days to Be" speech of 1961. A prime example of the "reversal principle" in operation, it was the communists who had come up with the catchphrase "I like Taft, but he can't win," Welch said. Recognizing Taft as a fundamental threat to their interests, someone who would "set the Communists back a whole generation in their plans for global conquest," they had taken their greatest weakness—"the overwhelming certainty that Taft, if nominated, would win over any opponent by a huge margin"—and "by daring and bluff" converted it into their "greatest item of strength in the particular circumstances." It had hurt the communists "to have so many millions saying, 'I like Taft,'" Welch argued, but that was the "price to pay . . . for having the same millions mouth, with the assurance of sad but superior knowledge," the second part of the slogan, "but he can't win."[53]

The strategy had worked so well, Welch believed, that it was deployed again against Joe McCarthy in 1954, at a time when "the most important thing in the world" was to destroy the Wisconsin senator and the broader anticommunist cause for which he stood. On this occasion the slogan the communists devised and implemented was "I like what McCarthy is trying to do, but I can't stand his methods." It may have been less catchy than the anti-Taft one, but supported by "an unmeasurable campaign of lies and distortions" it had had the desired effect, Welch contended.[54]

Other than the underlying communist conspiracy, the common factor in the downfalls of both Taft and McCarthy was Dwight Eisenhower. It was he who had "stolen" the Republican nomination from Taft and he, as Welch put it in *The Politician*, who had "frantically determined, in whatever way and at whatever cost, not only to liquidate McCarthy's investigations and McCarthy's influence, but to humiliate McCarthy personally in such vicious fashion as utterly to discourage any other patriot who might be attempted to take up the same torch."[55] Indeed, perhaps the best way to understand *The Politician* is to see it as Welch's attempt to exact revenge from both Eisenhower and the American political system in general for what he believed had been done to Taft, McCarthy, and other conservatives in the United States under the misguided influence of "Modern Republicanism." As the Founder explained to the press in the midst of the initial outpouring of controversy over what at that stage was still the "letter" version of the manuscript, he had written it, he said, because "the Eisenhower Administration visibly double-crossed, and thus helped eliminate from public life, some very staunch and loyal members of the Republican party who had been leaders among conservatives in both houses of Congress."[56]

Taft's defeat in 1952 in particular functioned as a kind of "original wound" for Welch, something he returned to obsessively to explain what was going wrong for him, the John Birch Society, or the United States as a whole, whether that was Richard Nixon rather than Barry Goldwater likely becoming the Republican Party's presidential candidate in 1960 (the immediate issue at hand in the extract from *The Blue Book* quoted above), or the "smear" taking place against the Birch Society in 1961 (one of the key themes of the "Through All the Days to Be" address). Seemingly unable to come to terms with the senator's death, in July 1953 Welch even raised the possibility that he might have been murdered. "We don't know whether the peculiar cancer of which Bob Taft died was induced by a radium tube planted in the upholstery of his Senate seat, as has been so widely rumored," he wrote in the November 1959 issue of the *Bulletin* with a dash of his characteristic circumspection.[57]

The Hidden Persuaders and Other Metaphors

The Republican national convention of 1952 was the first to be televised, and its winner, Dwight Eisenhower, became, in the words of Thomas Doherty, America's "first true television president." He was the first president "to permit his press conferences to be recorded and televised . . . the first president to telecast a live cabinet meeting, the first president to telecast special ceremonies such as the signing of bills and the lighting of Christmas trees, and the first president to inform and rally the nation through the systematic deployment of direct address."[58] In 1952, "Ike" also had the distinction of becoming the first American national leader to be "sold as a product."[59] The age of the "the Image" had arrived and with it a deep anxiety about what all this stress on the visual—on appearance, persona, telegeniety, and performance—meant for the American political system. Meshing with broader cultural and specifically Cold War induced anxieties about consumerism, soulless modernity, anomie, brainwashing, totalitarianism, and the manipulative possibilities of advertising and propaganda, it was a climate more than supportive of conspiracism and conspiratorial interpretations.

Vance Packard introduced *The Hidden Persuaders* (1957), his best-selling exposé of the dangerous potential of new market research techniques and advertising in both the economic and political realms, by describing the "large-scale efforts" that were being made by corporations, political consultants, and psychology professors to "channel our unthinking habits, our purchasing decisions, and our thought processes by the use of insights gleaned from psychiatry and the social sciences." These were "subterranean operations," Packard explained; efforts that typically took place "beneath our level of awareness; so that the appeals which move us are often, in a sense, 'hidden.' The result is that many of us are being influenced and manipulated, far more than we realize, in the patterns of our everyday lives."[60] In his highly prescient *The Image* (1961), Daniel Boorstin similarly sought to penetrate "the thicket of unreality which stands between us and the facts of life," as well as the "illusions" that passed for actuality in a stage-managed culture obsessed with (non-) news events and celebrities. Connecting the United States' foreign policy concern with "prestige"—what would later come to be called "credibility"—with a domestic political emphasis on "a competition for . . . or between images," Boorstin contended that Americans were suffering "more every day from the blurriness and the rigidity of our image-thinking."[61]

Other substantive contributions to, and analyses of, this culture of anxiety were made by David Riesman's *The Lonely Crowd* (1950), Theodore White's *The Making of the President, 1960* (1961), and the Canadian academic Marshall McLuhan's idea, introduced into wide circulation in 1964, that "the medium is the message," but perhaps its best dramatization—and certainly the most entertaining—can be found in Elia Kazan's 1957 film *A Face in the Crowd*.[62] Representing what the critic J. Hoberman has termed the "new totality"—the merging of "politics, advertising, and show business"—the film depicts, and issues a non-too-subtle warning about, the media-propelled transformation of a vulgar, guitar-picking vagrant called Larry "Lonesome" Rhodes (Andy Griffith) into a populist and demagogic threat to American democracy.[63] "Politics has entered a new stage, the television stage," one of the characters in the film declares. "Instead of long-winded public debates, the people want capsule slogans: 'Time for a change!' 'The mess in Washington!' 'More bang for a buck!' Punch lines and glamour." Rhodes, backed by shady political figures operating behind the scenes, is the "force" that knows how to exploit this new media environment better than anyone else.

Back in the increasingly mediated and suspect "real" world, beginning in April 1953 the CIA undertook a decade-long, billion-dollar program to "probe two key aspects of human consciousness—the mechanisms of mass persuasion and the effects of coercion on individual consciousness." This extraordinary "mind-control" project, known as MKUltra, led by Dr. Sidney Gottlieb, the head of the agency's Technical Services Division, had two principal goals: "improved psychological warfare to influence whole societies and better interrogation techniques for targeted individuals."[64] As Alfred W. McCoy has recounted, many of the experiments the CIA carried out—often on unknowing subjects, including North Korean prisoners of war and children attending a summer camp, and with occasionally fatal results—involved the use of LSD. Fed by widespread fears of communist advances in "brainwashing" techniques—"the impetus for going into the LSD project specifically rested in a report, never verified . . . that the Russians had bought the world supply," Gottlieb later said— the mind, as discussed in Chapter 2, had become just another battleground in the Cold War struggle.[65]

Underpinning many of these concerns and anxieties was the popular and broad-based understanding of totalitarianism—the "great mobilizing and unifying concept of the Cold War," to quote Abbott Gleason.[66] Both Nazi Germany and the Soviet Union had demonstrated the hideous susceptibility of humanity to the dark arts of propaganda and opinion manipulation, and the great "brainwashing scare" of the mid- to late 1950s had made a "powerful impression" on Americans, "suggesting to people in variously sophisticated ways that totalitarianism was at bottom the effort of a conspiratorial elite to achieve total control of the human individual." Works like Riesman's *The Lonely Crowd* and Packard's *The Hidden Persuaders*, with their additional suggestion to American citizens that within their own society "hidden forces were attempting to control them, for their own sinister purposes," had merely added to the widespread feeling that the "individual was . . . under siege," Gleason maintains.[67] (In another context, this sense of individualism under threat functioned as one of the key animating forces of postwar American conservatism, the argument being that ever since the New Deal had worked its malign collectivist magic on the American people, the United States had been heading recklessly down the wrong historical path.)

The veritable patron saint of twentieth-century antitotalitarianism and antipropaganda politics was the English novelist and essayist George Orwell, and despite his lifelong socialist beliefs, Orwell's neologistic but historically rooted notions of "Big Brother," the "Ministry of Truth," "doublethink," and "Newspeak"—from his 1949 satire, *Nineteen Eighty-Four*—were so powerful and so evocative that they were warmly embraced and frequently cited by Robert Welch and other members of the Birch Society (as well as countless other political activists of varying and frequently conflicting political hues).[68] "An image of the future, if and when the Communist tyrants succeed in taking over the whole planet and consolidating their power, has been well painted by George Orwell. He pictures that future as a booted heel trampling on a human face—forever," Welch wrote in the December 1959 issue of the *Bulletin*, for ex-ample.[69] More frequently, though, Welch and other Birchers invoked Orwell's slogans and ideas to support their identification of themselves as the purveyors of "truth" who would lead Americans away from their misguided wanderings in the contemporary "labyrinths of epistemology," as Welch memorably expressed it.[70] It was hardly a great surprise, then, when in September 1965 the Society announced that it had a new phone number to accompany the new office it was opening in Washington, DC, the last four digits of which were "1-9-8-4." The United States was "drifting toward 'Big Brother' rule," the Society's spokesman Reed Benson explained.[71] But it also shouldn't be a surprise that Orwell was being used in this way, for, as Louis Menand notes, *Nineteen Eighty-Four* is a conspiratorial text, one that "taught people to imagine government as a conspiracy against liberty."[72]

The "truth I bring you is simple, incontrovertible, and deadly," Welch wrote in *The Blue Book*, seeing it as the task of the John Birch Society to get Americans to "stop living in a dream world." "Are we really so hopelessly blind, so stupefied by 'prosperity' on one side and insidious propaganda on the other, that we cannot even see the wolves devouring the carcasses of our brothers or drawing ever nearer to ourselves?" he asked.[73] McCarthy had been "destroyed by the 'image' of him" created by his enemies, Welch believed, but the Birch Society would not be trimming *its* sails "for the sake of a creating a better 'public image.'"[74] Yet for all his hostility to the artifice and the deceptions of the television age—television might be a "quick and powerful medium," but its "separate impacts" were "glancing blows of little depth, compared . . . to that of a great book which can be read again and again and which leaves an indelible impression and resolution in the mind," he stated, unashamedly flaunting his bibliophilic tendencies—the Birch Society proved itself more than adept at navigating its way through this strange new land of symbols and slogans and acting as a guide for others to follow.[75]

Reviewing Emile de Antonio's 1964 avant-garde documentary on the Army-McCarthy hearings, *Point of Order!*, for example, the Society's film critic Jack Moffitt argued that by "shunning all pretensions of graphic honesty"— without any narration and in defiance of the actual chronology of the hearings, 188 hours of television footage had been turned into a 97-minute film—de Antonio had produced "an absolutely monstrous caricature of McCarthy in its advertisements." "A 'documentary' is sold to the public as unvarnished film truth," Moffitt noted, when in reality, it was "just another (and more pernicious) form of screen fiction in which the film editor as well as the sound man distort the material for desired effects." One may not wish to go so far as to describe *Point of Order!* as an example of what Moffitt called "Hollywood brainwashing," and his objections to the film were obviously motivated by his—and the Society's—desire to defend the memory of Senator McCarthy, but his demystifying analysis of the filmmaker's art was accurate enough.[76] (The Marxist de Antonio defended his portrait of McCarthy by arguing—in his own inimitable style—that the film "moves freely through all the material to make its points. The Form and the Truth are our Form and Truth," although he allowed that "Senator Goldwater's might be much different.")[77]

Finally, there is the possibility that the Birch Society's constant, highly charged and overstated emphasis on the conspiratorial might not always have been intended to be taken literally. Welch, it is worth emphasizing, was of a decidedly literary and poetic bent—a man who opened each issue of the *Bulletin* with an allusive epigram; who cited Longfellow, Emerson, Whittier, Keats, and Kipling in his political discourse; who issued comprehensive reading lists to his followers; and who seemed to believe that all that was really necessary for the communist advance to be stopped (or Earl Warren to be impeached) was for people to read the right books.[78] The liberal Fund for the Republic's 1962 report on the American right wing, authored by Ralph Ellsworth and Sarah Harris, rejected such an assessment completely: "A great many conservative writers and readers believe absolutely that this country is in the grip of a savage, ruthless, and even supernatural conspiracy; that disciplined known men, not abstract nouns, are the foreign agents of this conspiracy, and that these agents, under specific directives from their masters, control every single key point in American life and policy."[79] This is not an inaccurate picture: Welch, and no doubt many other Birchers (although it is difficult to know precisely how many), were certainly "true believers" in the communist conspiracy as much as, say, J. Edgar Hoover was—there is less certainty about Senator McCarthy's commitment to the cause—but this does not mean that Welch might not have also knowingly exaggerated, inflated, and overdramatized the nature of the conspiracy for political (and poetic) effect.

Welch, after all, was the kind of leader who wrote "fables" for fellow conservatives and issued "imaginary directives" for his followers.[80] After recounting a story about runaway inflation in Germany during the 1920s, he commented that "we do not vouch for the truth or the accuracy of the story, but we do vouch for the validity of the point it makes."[81] This was also the defense he made of the supposedly "confidential directive" issued by "Communist International Headquarters" in January 1968. It was "imaginary in form, but completely factual in its substance," he asserted.[82]

In addition, as Lisa McGirr has pointed out, the very term "anti-communism" also needs a little unpacking, subsuming as it does a "host of concerns . . . about the state's regulation of the economy and national life, changing cultural mores, and racial egalitarianism" in the United States during the 1950s and 1960s.[83] This was the certainly the view of the Society's own "hidden persuader," the national director of public relations John Rousselot, who, in the aftermath of the 1964 presidential election, argued that the organization had realized for some time that "the battle to re-establish the concepts of constitutional government" was a "long-range program," one that would not be "accomplished overnight" because "the forces of collectivism have been working to undermine our free society for better than 70 years."[84]

Writing back in 1961, Welch had attempted to bring together the literal and the metaphoric, the practical and the imaginary, in turning back the seemingly relentless advances of collectivism and communism within the United States. "Faith without works, poetic vision without prosaic plans, dreams without the drudgery to make them real"—none of these alone, he said, would "rout the Communists, nor contribute solid bricks to the building of a better world."[85]

The Illuminati and the Decline of the John Birch Society

Whatever it offered the Society's members, and irrespective of how it was connected to or supported by broader cultural and political trends within the United States, the organization's conspiracism also undoubtedly contributed to its decline. This was especially so after November 1966 when Welch published an essay entitled "The Truth in Time," initially in *American Opinion* and later as a pamphlet in its own right.[86] (In an apparent recognition of the increasing importance of the visual vis-à-vis the textual, a seventy-three-minute, sixteen-millimeter film of Welch—stiffly and uncomfortably—reading the essay was also made for home viewing.)[87] In "The Truth in Time," Welch revealed his discovery of a "master conspiracy," one older, grander, and even more fiendish than that of the communists:

> But the Communist movement is only a tool of the total conspiracy. As secret as the Communist activities and organizations generally appear, they are part of an open book compared to the secrecy enveloping some higher degree of this diabolic force. The extrinsic evidence is strong and convincing that by the beginning of the *Twentieth* century there had evolved an inner core of conspiratorial power, able to direct and control subversive activities which were worldwide in their reach, incredibly cunning and ruthless in their nature, and brilliantly farsighted and patient in their strategy. Whether or not this increasingly all-powerful hidden command was due to an unbroken continuation of [Adam] Weishaupt's Illuminati, or was a distillation from the leadership of this and other groups, we do not know. Some of them may never have been Communists, while others were. To avoid as much dispute as possible, therefore, let's call this ruling clique simply the INSIDERS.[88]

With his invocation of the Illuminati, Welch had tapped into one of the mother lodes of conspiracism both within the United States and around the world. Weishaupt, a canon law professor in Bavaria, had formed the organization on May 1, 1776, with the aim of freeing the world "from all established religious and political authority." Secretive and ritualistic, the organization—which at its peak in the 1780s had about 2,500 members—lasted until 1787.[89] Thanks, however, to the likes of John Robison's *Proofs of a Conspiracy* (1798) and Abbé Barruel's *Memoirs, Illustrating the History of Jacobinism* (1803)—both of which held the organization responsible for the French Revolution—as well as Nesta Webster's enormously influential *Secret Societies and Subversive Movements* (1924) and the American evangelist Gerald Winrod's *Adam Weishaupt, a Human Devil* (1935), fear of the Illuminati and a belief in its continuing existence never really went away. Indeed, Richard Hofstadter regarded the Illuminati "panic" that took hold of New England at the end of the eighteenth century as one of the grounding points for the "paranoid style" in American history.[90] Welch seems to have become aware of the Illuminati through Webster's and Winrod's work—although he rejected the anti-Semitism that was integral to their understanding of the global conspiracy—most likely due to the influence of Revilo Oliver, who had published an article on the Bavarian organization in *American Opinion* in 1962.[91] Welch's first public mention of the Illuminati—but not yet the "Insiders"—came in his "More Stately Mansions" speech, delivered before a crowd of 1,700 at the Conrad Hilton in Chicago on June 5, 1964.[92] (He told his biographer that although he had been studying the subject for a number of years prior to this, he understood that "you couldn't start putting it all out" in one go because "nobody would believe you." Instead, he'd endeavored to lead the Birch Society's members "little by little . . . to where they would be interested.")[93]

Despite these concerns, Welch's idea of the "Insiders" was quickly incorporated into the Society's official worldview, with Birch writers like Medford Evans musing about whether Dean Rusk was the "Insiders' quarterback," for example.[94] But, just as often, the conspirators continued to be identified as "the Communists," "the Liberals," "the Establishment," "the Liberal Establishment," or simply "the Conspiracy." The seeming interchangeability of the terms reflected the fact that, appearances to the contrary notwithstanding, Welch's turn to the Illuminati hadn't really changed his basic analysis. The "conspirators" were still responsible for all the world's woes, from—to attempt a summary of the argument in "The Truth in Time"—the writing of *The Communist Manifesto* and the revolutions of 1848, through Bismarck's workmen's compensation scheme, the creation of the Federal Reserve System, a graduated income tax, and the direct election of senators in the United States, to the First World War, the rise of the Soviet Union, the Second World War, Korea, and "the latest Medicare monstrosity under Lyndon Johnson." Alongside their aim of world rule, the "constant thread" of the conspirators' "hidden purpose" remained "to reduce the responsibilities and rights of individual citizens, while steadily increasing the quantity, the reach, and the potential tyranny of governments," Welch said.[95]

Indeed, to a considerable extent, Welch's creation of the Insiders seemed much like an exercise in re-branding. Through his researches, he had realized, Edward Griffin wrote in his biography, that "the term 'Communist' no longer was able to satisfy the available facts. It referred only to the lower, activist part of the Conspiracy and not to the small, controlling group of wealthy, urbane, elegantly tailored power-lusters at the top. And so the term *Insiders* was born." Had *The Politician* been written in 1966, Griffin added, it was very likely that Welch "would have described Eisenhower as an *Insider* instead of as a Communist agent."[96] If this were the case, the Founder would have been better advised sticking with the previous—and thoroughly market-tested—label.

The "internal" communist conspiracy argument may not have had the same cultural purchase in the mid-1960s it had had in the mid-1950s, but it was relatively easy to understand, and had the added advantage of speaking to and calling upon well-established traditions in American life. The same could not be said for the inchoate and rather colorless "Insiders." And if the intention had been to attract new recruits to the cause, the opposite occurred, with some thirty thousand Birchers leaving the organization between 1967 and 1968, close to a third of the membership.[97] The Society's conspiratorial shift of emphasis was not the only thing responsible for its declining numbers or receding influence, of course. Indeed, the most important factor of all—the one that most likely persuaded Welch he had little left to lose in making his Illuminati-based research public—was the organization's expulsion from the mainstream conservative movement in the aftermath of Goldwater's defeat in 1964. It was this event that also led some of its most important backers to withdraw their financial support for the Society, to which Welch responded by launching a fund-raising campaign he christened "A Stick of Dynamite"—to "blast" apathetic minds—and holding $25-to-$50-a-plate testimonial dinners around the country.[98] Nineteen sixty-six also saw the resignation of some key figures in the Society, including Revilo Oliver, Slobodan Draskovich, and T. Coleman Andrews. Both Oliver and Draskovich claimed they had become disillusioned with Welch's leadership, although Oliver's "resignation" seemed to have more to do with Welch's desire to distance the Society from the classics professor's increasingly virulent and public anti-Semitism.[99]

The resignations were nonetheless a clear indication that all was not well in the upper reaches of the organization, and Lisa McGirr has further argued that the Society's hierarchical, "top-down" structure also substantially contributed to its decline, especially as the concerns of conservatives shifted to new cultural and social issues such as abortion, sex education, school prayer, pornography, women's rights, the family, and so on, during the 1970s—and indeed beyond—because it made it more difficult for the organization's leadership to respond to the needs and interests of its grassroots supporters.[100] The irony is that the Birch Society should have been well placed to capitalize on these shifting concerns. Welch and the other Birch leaders had always emphasized the importance of "morality" and "traditional values" in their political pronouncements, and they had a ready-made nationwide infrastructure to call upon. But rather than attempting to shed their "extremist" image, Welch had in effect doubled down on it. When his old nemesis Richard Nixon finally became the president of the United States in 1968, Welch, perhaps inevitably, saw it as just one more victory for the forces of conspiracy. "The insiders think they can accomplish far more for the Communist movement, far more safely, with an Eisenhower-type Administration, this time under Richard Nixon, than they could with a Kennedy or a Humphrey as President," he argued in the run-up to the election.[101] The more things changed, it seemed, the more they remained darkly the same.

Afterword

The John Birch Society did not disappear after 1968. It survived the presidency of Richard Milhous Nixon and continued to offer its conspiratorial assessments throughout the remainder of the twentieth century and indeed on into the twenty-first, even undergoing a revival of sorts with the rise of the Tea Party in the United States in the aftermath of the "Great Recession" of 2007–2008 and the election of Barack Obama. It continued when Robert Welch eventually relinquished his leadership of the organization in 1983—he was replaced by the Georgia congressman Larry McDonald, who was killed shortly thereafter, shot down, along with 269 others, by a Soviet fighter plane, while traveling onboard Korean Air Lines Flight 007, which set in motion a whole slew of new conspiracy theories within the Society.[1] (McDonald was "the only U.S. Congressman lost to the communists during the Cold War," notes the Society's website.)[2] It continued after Welch's death on January 6, 1985, aged eighty-five—his last public appearance had been at the Society's twenty-fifth anniversary celebration in 1983.[3] And it continued after its 1989 move to Appleton, Wisconsin, the hometown and final resting place of Senator McCarthy.

Looking back at the first decade of the Society's existence during its tenth anniversary dinner in Indianapolis, the place where it had all begun—for a supposedly "secret organization," it was "quite a sizable dinner," Welch quipped—the Founder clearly had some meaningful and substantive achievements he could point to as a reward for his ten years of work. The Society had grown from twelve men in a room to a network of four thousand chapters spread out across the length and breadth of the country, for example. It had opened over four hundred American Opinion libraries, established its own book-publishing division—Western Islands, the name a homage to Keats's sonnet "On First Looking into Chapman's Homer"—and founded a new weekly, the *Review of the News*, to accompany its monthly magazine, *American Opinion* (together they had a circulation of fifty thousand). It had a weekly radio program, *Are You Listening, Uncle Sam?*, which was heard on more than one hundred stations across the United States, and its speakers bureau was, according to Welch at least, "almost certainly the largest in the world." It had demonstrated the ability to effectively organize "fronts"—or "ad hoc committees," as they had been rechristened—such as the Committee Against Summit Entanglements (CASE), the Movement to Impeach Earl Warren, the Truth About Civil Turmoil committee (TACT), the committee To Restore American Independence Now

(TRAIN), and Support Your Local Police committees. And it had certainly harnessed the "great energy and enthusiasm" of its members for various petitions, protests, and letter-writing campaigns.[4]

Yet for all the Society's considerable endeavors, to employ one of its own favorite metaphors: what, really, was the "score" in 1968? Earl Warren was still the chief justice of the United States. Barry Goldwater had not been elected president. General Walker had been marginalized, the civil rights and voting rights bills had both become law, Fidel Castro was still in power, no victory had been secured in Vietnam, and the Cold War showed no signs of abating.

Nor, more parochially, had the Society come anywhere near to reaching its goal of recruiting a million members, which it had set for itself back in 1958. At a press conference on December 7, 1968, Welch explained that because of the distinctive qualities and selfless dedication of those who had become Birchers—people who devoted "half their lives" to the Society—the organization no longer needed such numbers; its new goal, he said, was four hundred thousand, but even this seemed overly optimistic given that current membership was estimated to be somewhere between sixty thousand and seventy thousand.[5]

Welch believed, though, that the Society had "played quite a role in preventing a more rapid Communist advance" in the United States. It had made "hundreds of thousands of patriotic Americans aware of the differences between a republic and a democracy," made "millions" aware of "the Communist plans and hands behind the so-called 'civil rights' movement," and of the "background, purposes, methods, and menace of the whole international Conspiracy." Just keeping going in the face of the "infinitely varied and unbelievably extensive efforts to destroy us" and having "tens of thousands of Conservative individualists working together, despite all of the reasons they can find, or which can be found for them, to split into hundreds of fragments" was an "accomplishment of which every faithful member can well be proud," he said. "When the Communists, acting on orders from Moscow, began their campaign in February of 1961 to destroy The John Birch Society, they had no idea that we could long survive the attacks which were planned," Welch boasted, defiantly.[6]

Some wounds had not healed, however. Defending the Society's practical, non-"ivory-tower approach"—its insistence that the struggle with the communists was more than "an ideological dispute over competing philosophies of political and economic science"—had led to it being "given the cold shoulder by many of those who ought to be . . . our friends," Welch lamented. While "our compatriots on the ideological battle ground have been accorded by the Left all the respect and privileges of a 'loyal opposition,'" the Birch Society had been subjected to a "constant barrage of poisoned arrows," he went on. Indeed, so anxious were the nation's enemies "to have what is happening [in the United States] blamed on the doctrinal follies of Liberalism, rather than on the subtly moving hands of a criminal conspiracy, that if there had been no Bill Buckley on the scene for the past twenty years, the Communists would have had to invent one," Welch said, pointing his accusatory finger in a very specific direction.[7]

If the Society's ostracism from the mainstream of the conservative movement seemed complete by 1968, this did not mean that Welch and his colleagues had made no contribution to it. On the contrary, they had played an essential role in the revitalization of conservatism both as a political philosophy and as a vehicle for the attainment of practical political power in the United States. Alongside other groups and figures, both "fringe" and "mainstream," including but not limited to, Rev. Billy James Hargis's Christian Crusade, Dr. Fred Schwarz's Christian Anti-Communism Crusade, Young Americans for Freedom, the Young Republicans, Phyllis Schlafly, Barry Goldwater, and, yes, Buckley and his associates at *National Review*, the Birch Society had demonstrated that there was a large, active, and highly motivated constituency for conservatism even in the midst—or perhaps because of—liberalism's seeming ascendancy. The Society had shown how to reach this constituency, how to navigate and exploit the new media landscape, how to raise funds and launch (seemingly endless) programs and campaigns, and how to bring considerable pressures to bear on opponents and sympathizers alike. For sure, the Birchers may not have won all—or even most—of their battles, but they had illustrated to a generation of conservatives how they might fight, and that lesson was not lost on those who came after them.

The Society also made a significant and lasting contribution to America's Cold War and conspiracy cultures, often simply by embodying and exemplifying already-existing tensions in both. Over the course of its first ten years, the organization had endeavored to educate Americans about, and to guide them through, the "fantastic times" they were living in.[8] It had identified—or so it maintained—the hidden source of all the United States' ills and proposed what it saw as the solutions to those ills, the public exposure of the conspirators, together with all their sympathizers and unwitting enablers, being chief among them. In doing so, the Society had given voice not only to fears and concerns present in the life and death struggle of the Cold War, but also to those with much deeper roots in the nation's history and political psyche. The Birchers had made the conduct of U.S. foreign policy more difficult during the 1960s, revived disturbing memories of McCarthyism, and raised troubling questions about the place of extremism, fascism, and the role of the military in American society. Far from being consigned to the margins of American life or American politics, to enter the world of the John Birch Society in the years between 1958 and 1968 was to find oneself at the very heart of some of the most telling, significant, and consequential events, issues, and controversies of the period.

Notes

INTRODUCTION

1. See G. Edward Griffin, *The Life and Words of Robert Welch: Founder of the John Birch Society* (Thousand Oaks, CA: American Media, 1975), 240. When the manuscript of *The Politician* was officially published as a book in 1963, Welch altered the text. No longer was the president described as a "dedicated, conscious agent of the Communist conspiracy." The corresponding section now stated that Eisenhower "has been sympathetic to ultimate Communist aims, realistically and even mercilessly willing to help them achieve their goals, knowingly receiving and abiding by Communist orders, and consciously serving the Communist conspiracy, for all of his adult life"—a distinction without much discernable difference, one might reasonably object. See Robert Welch, *The Politician* (Belmont, MA: Belmont Publishing, 1963), 278.

2. Benjamin R. Epstein and Arnold Forster, *The Radical Right: Report on the John Birch Society and Its Allies* (New York: Vintage, 1967), 218.

3. On the membership numbers of the Society, see, for example, Epstein and Forster, *Radical Right*, 195; Robert Alan Goldberg, *Enemies Within: The Culture of Conspiracy in Modern America* (New Haven, CT: Yale University Press, 2001), 48; and John George and Laird Wilcox, *American Extremists: Militias, Supremacists, Klansmen, Communists, and Others* (Amherst, NY: Prometheus Books, 1996), 192.

4. The goal of recruiting a million members can be found in Robert Welch, *The Blue Book of the John Birch Society* (Belmont, MA: Western Islands, 1961), 152. On the revision to four hundred thousand, see Douglas E. Kneeland, "Birch Society, Age 10, Vows Red Rout," *New York Times*, December 8, 1968. The critic in question was the Democratic Wisconsin senator Gale McGee ("They Believe the Unbelievable," *Congressional Record*, March 3, 1964, 4,199).

5. James McEvoy III, *Radicals or Conservatives: The Contemporary Radical Right* (Chicago: Rand McNally, 1971), 12. See also Alan F. Westin, "The John Birch Society: Fundamentalism on the Right," *Commentary* 32, no. 2 (August 1961): 93.

6. McEvoy, *Radicals or Conservatives*, 12.

7. The phrase was popularized by Godfrey Hodgson in his book *America in Our Time: From World War Two to Nixon* (London: Macmillan, 1977), 67–98. He used it to describe the way in which most conservatives accepted the "liberal" domestic policies of the welfare state—an outgrowth of the political success of Franklin D. Roosevelt's New Deal—and almost all liberals agreed with the "conservative" foreign policy of Cold War containment during the 1950s and early 1960s.

8. Welch, *Blue Book*, 21.

9. Ibid., 3.

10. Ibid., 60–61. Emphasis in original.

11. As a consequence of its black binding, and perhaps because it added an additional layer

of intrigue or mystery to the organization, *The Politician* was also referred to as "The Black Book" of the Society.

12. On the various members of the radical or anticommunist Right of this period, see, for example, Daniel Bell, ed., *The Radical Right: "The New American Right," Expanded and Updated* (Garden City, NY: Doubleday, 1963); Epstein and Forster, *Radical Right*; George Thayer, *The Farther Shores of Politics: The American Political Fringe Today*, 2nd ed. (New York: Simon and Schuster, 1968), 174–278; William W. Turner, *Power on the Right* (Berkeley, CA: Ramparts Press, 1971); Richard Gid Powers, *Not without Honor: The History of American Anticommunism* (New York: Free Press, 1995), 273–318; Chip Berlet and Matthew N. Lyons, *Right-Wing Populism in America: Too Close for Comfort* (New York: Guildford Press, 2000), 200–202; and Donald T. Critchlow, *The Conservative Ascendancy: How the Republican Right Rose to Power in Modern America*, 2nd. ed. (Lawrence: University Press of Kansas, 2011), 32–37.

13. See, for example, Landon R. Y. Storrs, *The Second Red Scare and the Unmaking of the New Deal Left* (Princeton, NJ: Princeton University Press, 2012); David M. Oshinsky, *A Conspiracy So Immense: The World of Joe McCarthy* (New York: Oxford University Press, 2005); Ted Morgan, *Reds: McCarthyism in Twentieth-Century America* (New York: Random House, 2003); Ellen Schrecker, *Many Are the Crimes: McCarthyism in America* (Boston: Little, Brown, 1998); Griffin Fariello, *Red Scare: Memories of the American Inquisition* (New York: Norton, 1995); and David Caute, *The Great Fear: The Anti-Communist Purge under Truman and Eisenhower* (New York: Simon and Schuster, 1978).

14. This biographical sketch is drawn primarily from Griffin's *Life and Words*, together with George Barrett's "Close-Up of the Birchers' 'Founder,'" *New York Times*, May 14, 1961; J. Allen Broyles's *The John Birch Society: Anatomy of a Protest* (Boston: Beacon Press, 1964); and Robert D. McFadden's "Robert Welch Jr. Dead at 85; John Birch Society's Founder," *New York Times*, January 8, 1985.

15. Griffin, *Life and Words*, 67–68.

16. The "Oscar" phrase is Griffin's, in *Life and Words*, 111.

17. Courtney Sheldon, "Conservative Seeks GOP Nomination for Lieutenant Governor," *Christian Science Monitor*, October 4, 1949, quoted in Samuel L. Brenner, "Shouting at the Rain: The Voices and Ideas of Right-Wing Anti-Communist Americanists in the Era of Modern American Conservatism, 1950–1974" (PhD dissertation, Brown University, 2009), 104–5.

18. Robert Welch, quoted in Griffin, *Life and Words*, 139–40.

19. Ibid., 155. Emphasis added.

20. Ibid., 160. Emphasis in original.

21. Welch, *Blue Book*, 112. The importance of the 1952 Republican convention to Welch's conspiratorial worldview is discussed in more detail in Chapter 6.

22. Robert Welch, *May God Forgive Us* (Chicago: Henry Regnery, 1952), 9. The book is written in the form of one of Welch's favorite literary devices, a long letter, and was reported to have sold almost two hundred thousand copies in 1952 alone (Broyles, *John Birch Society*, 31).

23. Griffin, *Life and Words*, 190; and Robert Welch, *The Life of John Birch: In the Story of One American Boy, the Ordeal of His Age* (Chicago: Henry Regnery, 1954), v–vi.

24. On Birch's life and death, see, for example, "Young John Birch Stirred a Furor," *New York Times*, April 23, 1961; Broyles, *John Birch Society*, 22–25; Maochun Yu, *OSS in China: Prelude to Cold War* (New Haven, CT: Yale University Press, 1996); and Welch, *Life of John Birch*, quote on 65.

25. Welch, *Life of John Birch*, 119. Samuel Brenner notes that the circumstances of John

Birch's death were discussed several times before the Senate Armed Services Committee and the Foreign Relations Committee in 1951, but that otherwise his story had indeed been "relatively unknown" until Welch stumbled upon it ("Shouting at the Rain," 111n166).

26. Welch, *Politician*, vii–viii. The controversies surrounding the manuscript are discussed more fully in the following chapter.

27. Griffin, *Life and Words*, 257–58. See also Welch, *Blue Book*, vii–viii and appendix; and Broyles, *John Birch Society*, 48–52.

28. On the Koch brothers, see Jane Mayer, "Covert Operations: The Billionaire Brothers Who Are Waging a War against Obama," *New Yorker*, August 30, 2010, 45–55. On Scott, see Griffin, *Life and Words*, 257–58.

29. Welch, *Blue Book*, appendix. Another example of the Founder's sense of humor can be found in the biographical notes of the book, in which he recounts that he has "one wife, two sons, a Golden Retriever dog, and fourteen golf clubs—none of which he understands, but all of which he loves" (167).

30. Ibid., 146–47. In the "fight immediately ahead, we cannot stop for parliamentary procedures or a lot of arguments among ourselves," Welch believed.

31. Ibid., 151–52.

32. Ibid., 153.

33. Ibid., 64–96. The "fantastic cost" of the medium, a bibliophile's preference for the textual, and an initial emphasis on reaching the nation's "opinion-molders" had led to an aversion on Welch's part to using television.

34. Ibid., 56.

35. Ibid., 125 and 127. Emphasis in original.

36. On these issues, see also James A. Hijiya, "The Conservative 1960s," *Journal of American Studies* 37, no. 2 (2003): 201–27; Lisa McGirr, *Suburban Warriors: The Origins of the New American Right* (Princeton, NJ: Princeton University Press, 2001), especially 168–76; and Charles J. Stewart, "The Master Conspiracy of the John Birch Society: From Communism to the New World Order," *Western Journal of Communication* 66, no. 4 (Fall 2002): 428–30.

37. On this assessment of the Society, see also Eckard V. Toy Jr., "The Right Side of the 1960s: The Origins of the John Birch Society in the Pacific Northwest," *Oregon Historical Society* 105, no. 2 (2004): 279–80; and McGirr, *Suburban Warriors*, 222–23.

38. Fred W. Grupp Jr., "The Political Perspectives of Birch Society Members," in *The American Right Wing: Readings in Political Behavior*, ed. Robert A. Schoenberger (New York: Holt, Rinehart and Winston, 1969), 109–10. Eighteen percent of respondents, making up the next highest category, said that they had joined the Society to "associate with like-minded people," and 11 percent said that it was to "become informed." See also Fred W. Grupp Jr., "Personal Satisfaction Derived from Membership in the John Birch Society," *Western Political Quarterly* 24, no. 1 (March 1971): 79–83; and Stephen Earl Bennett, "Modes of Resolution of a 'Belief Dilemma' in the Ideology of the John Birch Society," *Journal of Politics*, 33, no. 3 (August 1971): 735–72.

39. Barbara S. Stone, "The John Birch Society: A Profile," *Journal of Politics* 36, no. 1 (February 1974): 184 and 195.

40. The "irrationality" or "social strain" theory of the Birch Society's appeal can be found in the essays collected by Daniel Bell in *The Radical Right*. See also Roy V. Peel, "The WACKACOBI: Extremists of Our Own Times," *Western Political Quarterly* 16, no. 3 (September 1963): 569–97; Richard Hofstadter, "The Paranoid Style in American Politics," in *The Paranoid Style in American Politics and Other Essays* (Cambridge, MA: Harvard University Press, 1965), 3–40; and Seymour Martin Lipset and Earl Raab, *The*

Politics of Unreason: Right-Wing Extremism in America, 1790–1977, 2nd ed. (Chicago: University of Chicago Press, 1978), 248–337.

41. Clyde Wilcox, "Sources of Support for the Old Right: A Comparison of the John Birch Society and the Christian Anti-Communism Crusade," *Social Science History* 12, no. 4 (Winter 1988): 445–46.

42. On the geographical distribution of the Society, see, for example, Wilcox, "Sources of Support," 435–36; Toy, "Right Side," 265; and McGirr, *Suburban Warriors*.

43. Wilcox, "Sources of Support," 432–33.

44. In what was a fairly typical month, the "agenda" for May 1961 urged Birchers to help promote the filmstrip *Communism on the Map*; to get four friends to read Fred Koch's booklet *A Businessman Looks at Communism*; to write a letter to Mr. B. T. Fullerton of Cleveland, Ohio, to congratulate him on his company's "excellent and long-continued advertising on behalf of the American Free Enterprise System"; and otherwise to do "all you can that is practicable to help and support other anti-Communist groups, large and small." Robert Welch, "Agenda for the Month," *Bulletin*, May 1961, 21–22.

45. Welch, *Blue Book*, xiii and 156.

46. Robert Welch, "Foreword," *Bulletin*, April 1965, 1–2, quoted in Grupp, "Personal Satisfaction," 80.

47. Alan Brinkley, "The Problem of American Conservatism," *American Historical Review* 99 (1994): 409; McGirr, *Suburban Warriors*; Jonathan M. Schoenwald, *A Time for Choosing: The Rise of Modern American Conservatism* (New York: Oxford University Press, 2001); Toy, "Right Side"; Rick Perlstein, *Before the Storm: Barry Goldwater and the Unmaking of the American Consensus* (2001; New York: Nation Books, 2009); Geoffrey Kabaservice, *Rule and Ruin: The Downfall of Moderation and the Destruction of the Republican Party, from Eisenhower to the Tea Party* (New York: Oxford University Press, 2012); and Michelle M. Nickerson, *Mothers of Conservatism: Women and the Postwar Right* (Princeton, NJ: Princeton University Press, 2012), especially 138–48. In recent years, a number of dissertations have also examined the Society and its activities. See, for example, Brenner, "Shouting at the Rain"; and Arron Max Berkowitz, "Mr. Khrushchev Goes to Washington: Domestic Opposition to Nikita Khrushchev's 1959 Visit to America" (PhD dissertation, University of Illinois at Chicago, 2010).

48. McGirr, *Suburban Warriors*, 4.

49. Schoenwald, *Time for Choosing*, 9 and 98.

50. Kim Phillips-Fein, "Conservatism: A State of the Field," *Journal of American History* 98, no. 3 (December 2011): 736.

51. See, for example, Kate Zernike, *Boiling Mad: Inside Tea Party America* (New York: Times Books, 2010); Theda Skocpol and Vanessa Williamson, *The Tea Party and the Remaking of Republican Conservatism* (New York: Oxford University Press, 2012); Sean Wilentz, "Confounding Fathers: The Tea Party's Cold War Roots," *New Yorker*, October 10, 2010, 32–39; David Welch, "Where Have You Gone, Bill Buckley?" *New York Times*, December 3, 2012; and Adam Gopnik, "The John Birchers' Tea Party," *New Yorker Blog*, October 11, 2013, *www.newyorker.com*.

CHAPTER 1

1. Robert Welch, "Dear Reader," *American Opinion*, December 1959, i. The Committee Against Summit Entanglements is examined in detail in Chapter 5.

2. Robert Welch, "An Aside to the Squeamish," *Bulletin*, June 1960, 6–9.

3. The offending quotation appeared on page 267 of the "manuscript" or "letter" version of *The Politician*. See G. Edward Griffin, *The Life and Words of Robert Welch: Founder of the John Birch Society* (Thousand Oaks, CA: American Media, 1975), 240.

4. Jack Mabley, "Bares Secrets of 'Red-Haters': They Think Ike Is a Communist," *Chicago Daily News*, July 25, 1960; and Jack Mabley, "Strange Threat To Democracy: Anti-Red Group Hits Leaders," *Chicago Daily News*, July 26, 1961.

5. Robert Welch, "Foreword," *Bulletin*, August 1960, 1. On the other "attacks" against the Birch Society in the press, see, for example, "Wisconsin Group Reportedly Views Ike as Red, Traitor," *Chicago Sun-Times*, August 1, 1960.

6. Robert Welch, "Newspaper Attacks," *Bulletin*, August 1960, 5–6. Emphasis in original.

7. Ibid., 6–7. Emphasis in original.

8. Ibid., 7–8. Emphasis in original.

9. Ibid., 8–9.

10. Ibid., 9–11.

11. Ibid., 11.

12. Hans Engh, "John Birch Society: What Is It, Why?" *Santa Barbara News-Press*, January 22, 1961; and Hans Engh, "Birch Society Members Discuss Anti-Red Aims," *Santa Barbara News-Press*, January 23, 1961. See also Robert Welch, "Agenda for the Month," *Bulletin*, September 1960, 27.

13. The allusion was not lost on the paper's readers, however. As Margaret Lord put it, in a letter in response to the *News-Press*'s coverage of the Birch Society: "Is Robert Welch carrying on where the late Joe McCarthy left off? It is so true that 'the evil that men do lives after them.'" See "Our Readers Comment," reproduced in *Congressional Record*, March 20, 1961, 4,278.

14. Thomas M. Storke, "Statement of Principles," *Santa Barbara News-Press*, February 26, 1961.

15. Gene Blake, "The John Birch Society: What Are Its Purposes?" *Los Angeles Times*, March 5, 1961; Gene Blake, "Blue Book Guides Anti-Red Society—Required Reading for Members of Birch Group Minces No Words," March 6, 1961; Gene Blake, "Birch Society's Program Outlined—Membership of Million Set as Goal in Plans of Organization," March 7, 1961; Gene Blake, "Birch Program in Los Angeles Outlined—Thousands Reportedly Belong to Chapters in Southland," March 7, 1961; and "Birch Members Reply to Critics—Founder's Early Writings Not Connected With Society," March 7, 1961.

16. Blake, "The John Birch Society: What Are Its Purposes?"

17. Blake, "Blue Book Guides."

18. Otis Chandler, "Peril to Conservatives," *Los Angeles Times*, March 12, 1961.

19. Ibid.

20. The Movement to Impeach Earl Warren, as the campaign was called, is examined in detail in Chapter 4.

21. "The Americanists," *Time*, March 10, 1961. *Newsweek* caught up the following month when it published "Wide-Swinging Bitter-Enders of the Right" on April 10 and "Birch Bark" on April 24.

22. Milton Young, "The John Birch Society," *Congressional Record*, March 8, 1961, 3,446–48, quotes on 3,446. On March 20, Young apologized for referring to the Society's chapters as "cells," but this was "one of the problems one encounters with an organization operating in a secret manner," he explained (*Congressional Record*, March 20, 1961, 4,268).

23. Young, "John Birch Society," 3,446–47.

24. Ibid., 3,447.

25. Ibid.

26. "Senator Scores Group Calling Eisenhower a Red," *New York Times*, March 9, 1961.

27. Ibid. See also Associated Press, "Cleric Denounces John Birch Group," *New York Times*,

March 20, 1961; John D. Morris, "Inquiry Is Sought on Birch Society," *New York Times*, March 31, 1961; United Press International, "Catholic Editors Scold Birch Unit," *New York Times*, April 8, 1961; and Irving Spiegel, "Rabbis Urge Inquiry into John Birch Society," *New York Times*, April 19, 1961.

28. Richard Nixon, letter to the editor, *Los Angeles Times*, March 18, 1961, quoted in "Nixon Is Critical of Birch Society," *New York Times*, March 19, 1961.

29. "Birch Group Stirs Dispute on Coast: Right-Wing Society Drawing Sharper Criticism—Inquiry Ordered in California," *New York Times*, March 26, 1961; and "Birch Inquiry Begins: California Legislators Study Ultra-Conservative Group," *New York Times*, March 29, 1961.

30. See "The John Birch Society," *Congressional Record*, March 28, 1961, 4,958–64, quote on 4,964.

31. See "The John Birch Society," *Congressional Record*, March 30, 1961, 5,330–31; and "Javits Urges Inquiry," *New York Times*, April 9, 1961. On the outpouring of newspaper articles on the Society at this time just in the nation's capital, see Ralph McGill, "Time for Belief in Americanism," *Washington Evening Star*, March 22, 1961; George E. Sokolsky, "The Conservative Ground Swell," *Washington Post*, March 25, 1961; James E. Clayton, "John Birch 'Antis' Point Unwelcome Spotlight," *Washington Post*, March 26, 1961; Marquis Childs, "Rightists Threaten 'Silence of Fear,'" *Washington Post*, March 28, 1961; and Barbara Bundschu, "Reds Everywhere: John Birch Society Would Repeal the 20th Century," *Washington Daily News*, March 29, 1961.

32. The exchange of correspondence between Reuss and Walter can be found in Henry Reuss, "Nothing Funny about the John Birch Society," *Congressional Record*, April 12, 1961, 5,666.

33. John D. Morris, "Birch Unit Pushes Drive on Warren: Chief Justice Attacked Anew—Robert Kennedy Views Society with 'Concern,'" *New York Times*, April 1, 1961.

34. Morris, "Inquiry."

35. John H. Rousselot, quoted in "Rousselot a Member: California Republican Tells of Joining Birch Group," *New York Times*, April 1, 1961.

36. Morris, "Inquiry."

37. Robert Welch, quoted in "Birch Group Stirs Dispute."

38. Robert Welch, "General Comments," *Bulletin*, January 31, 1961, 12.

39. "Text of Telegram," *New York Times*, April 2, 1961.

40. James O. Eastland, quoted in "John Birch Society Is Held 'Patriotic,'" *New York Times*, March 21, 1961.

41. Edith Green, "Hatemongers," *Congressional Record*, April 24, 1961, 6,627–30, quote on 6,630.

42. In response to a question from Senator Young in March 1961, J. Edgar Hoover said that he had "not endorsed [the John Birch Society] or its activities in any fashion whatsoever" (*Congressional Record*, March 28, 1961, 4,961). In fact, both the FBI and to a lesser extent the CIA—despite the fact that the CIA was restricted from domestic activities—investigated and monitored the Society, although as Jonathan Schoenwald notes, such surveillance paled into comparison with that of the New Left and black power movements during the 1960s and 1970s (*A Time for Choosing: The Rise of Modern Conservatism* [New York: Oxford University Press, 2001], 94–96).

43. Brooks Atkinson, "Structure of American Society Provides It and Birch Society with Certain Rights," *New York Times*, April 25, 1961.

44. "Senator Cautions Birch Unit's Foes: Goldwater Predicts Inquiry Could Embarrass Some—Says Democrats Belong," *New York Times*, April 6, 1961.

45. Milton Young, "John Birch Society: Fascist Group," *Congressional Record*, April 3, 1961,

5,427–29. Welch responded to Young's attacks on the Society in the June issue of the *Bulletin*. It was "an unfortunate mistake on his part that set him off," Welch said; he had received some critical correspondence from someone who he believed to be a Birch Society member, but the "man in question" had never been so, and the Society had "nothing whatsoever" to do with his complaints about the senator. Young had drifted too far toward Modern Republicanism for Welch's taste, he said, but in part because Young had had the "wisdom and courage" to vote against the Senate censure of Joe McCarthy, Welch was "not even tempted to fight back at the criticisms" he was making of the Society ("Agenda for the Month," 19).

46.   Anthony Lewis, "Robert Kennedy Mocks Birch Unit," *New York Times*, April 7, 1961. For more on Hart, see Michael O'Brien, *Philip Hart: Conscience of the Senate* (East Lansing: Michigan State University Press, 1996).

47.   Ibid. Eugene McCarthy also denied the need for a congressional investigation but he did think the Justice Department "should keep an eye on" the Society ("Birch Enquiry Opposed: Senator McCarthy Denies Need for Congress Action," *New York Times*, April 10, 1961).

48.   William Ryan, "Protection of Democratic Institutions under the Constitution of the United States," *Congressional Record*, April 19, 1961, 6,315.

49.   Emmanuel Rackman, quoted in Irving Spiegel, "Rabbis Urge Inquiry into John Birch Society: Council Charges a Violation of American Ideals," *New York Times*, April 19, 1961. This was also the view of William Bohn in a letter to the *Times* on July 20. The "Nazis, too, in their time were anti-liberal 'superpatriots'" Bohn explained.

The Justice Department's list of organizations thought to be dangerous to the United States was established in 1941, but it became a much more prominent weapon in the state's arsenal for dealing with subversives, after a new version was drawn up in 1947, at the very start of the Second Red Scare. See Robert Justin Goldstein, *American Blacklist: The Attorney General's List of Subversive Organizations* (Lawrence: University Press of Kansas, 2008).

50.   Percival E. Jackson, letter to the editor, *New York Times*, April 11, 1961.

51.   Lewis, "Robert Kennedy Mocks Birch Unit."

52.   Arthur Krock, "The Best Weapon against Extremism," *New York Times*, April 7, 1961.

53.   Both cartoons were reproduced in the *New York Times* on April 9, 1961.

54.   "Other Side of the Coined Word," *St. Louis Post-Dispatch*, April 17, 1961.

55.   "The Talk of the Town: News and Comment," *New Yorker*, April 15, 1961, 31. Murrow had ended "A Report on Senator Joseph R. McCarthy" on *See It Now* (March 9, 1954) with the following: "This is no time for men who oppose Senator McCarthy's methods to keep silent, or for those who approve. We can deny our heritage and our history, but we cannot escape responsibility for the result. There is no way for a citizen of a republic to abdicate his responsibilities. . . . The actions of the junior senator from Wisconsin have caused alarm and dismay amongst our allies abroad, and given considerable comfort to our enemies. And whose fault is that? Not really his. He didn't create this situation of fear; he merely exploited it—and rather successfully. Cassius was right. 'The fault, dear Brutus, is not in our stars, but in ourselves.'" Murrow's report can be viewed on YouTube. com, but see also Thomas Doherty, *Cold War, Cool Medium: Television, McCarthyism, and American Culture* (New York: Columbia University Press, 2003), 174–75.

56.   A. J. Liebling, "The Candy Kid," *New Yorker*, May 20, 1961, 156–64.

57.   See, for example, Brian O'Doherty, "Art: Clusters of Purism and Realism," *New York Times*, March 3, 1962; Milton Esterow, "Satirical Review Changes Floors," *New York Times*, July 13, 1962; and Robert Welch, "Carl Sandburg," *Bulletin*, August 1962, 10–12.

58.   Ronald Cohen suggests that the trio were fed the song by their arranger Milt Okun as a

means to tap into the hot "topical song" market of the time. As well as being a hit on the folk scene, the song reached ninety-nine on the pop charts. Ronald D. Cohen, *Rainbow Quest: The Folk Music Revival and American Society, 1940–1970* (Amherst: University of Massachusetts Press, 2002), 190.

59.   Chad Mitchell Trio, *The Chad Mitchell Trio at The Bitter End*, 1962 (Kapp Records, KL-1281). The trio had formed in 1958 after Joe Frazier, Chad Mitchell, and Mike Kobluk met at Gonzaga University in Spokane, Washington. They were joined for their recording at The Bitter End by a future member of the Byrds, Jim McGuinn, on guitar.

60.   The complete lyrics of Michael Brown's "The John Birch Society" can be found at the Digital Tradition Mirror, accessed October 14, 2013, *sniff.numachi.com*.

61.   On "Talkin' John Birch Society Blues," see Clinton Heylin, *Revolution in the Air: The Songs of Bob Dylan, 1957–1973* (Chicago: Chicago Review Press, 2009), 70–71. On *Broadside* magazine, see Cohen, *Rainbow Quest*, 179–83.

62.   The full lyrics of "Talkin' John Birch Paranoid Blues" can be found at the Official Bob Dylan Site, *www.bobdylan.com* (Sony Music Entertainment; accessed October 14, 2013). In the August 1961 issue of the *Bulletin*, Welch complained about the "baseless and malicious" but "widespread" articles that were being published with "my picture alongside that of Rockwell, founder of the so-called American Nazi Party" ("Foreword," 4). These articles presumably were what Dylan was drawing upon for the song.

63.   On these issues, see, for example, Cohen, *Rainbow Quest*, 67–92; and David King Dunaway and Molly Beer, *Singing Out: An Oral History of America's Folk Music Revivals* (New York: Oxford University Press, 2010), 76–106.

64.   *American Opinion*, quoted in Dunaway and Beer, *Singing Out*, 79. Pete Seeger's manager Harold Leventhal describes Seeger as being a "constant target . . . for the John Birch people" (quoted in Dunaway and Beer, *Singing Out*, 80). "For years," he recalled in a 1977 interview, "there was hardly a concert which was not picketed, whether by the Legion, or the Birch, or whatever, local so-called anti-Communist groups. He was the guy, he was the leader they were after. He 'poisoned the minds of young people'" (ibid., 80–81). See also Brooks Atkinson, "In View of America's Solidity, The Fear of Subversive Hootenannies Is Unhealthy," *New York Times*, October 25, 1963; and Jere Real, "Folk Music and the Red Tubthumpers," *American Opinion*, December 1964, 19–24, in which Real describes Dylan's songs in particular as "filled with the bitter polemic which characterizes the Communist folk song" (24).

65.   Heylin, *Revolution in the Air*, 141. A contrasting view of the story, which blames CBS lawyers rather than Columbia Records for the pressure to exclude "Talkin' John Birch Society Blues," can be found in Robert Shelton's *No Direction Home: The Life and Music of Bob Dylan* (New York: Ballantine Books, 1987), 175. Heylin notes that copies of the album with the song on it are now worth "at least five figures."

66.   See SOFA Entertainment, "Bob Dylan on the Ed Sullivan Show," *The Official Ed Sullivan Site*, accessed October 14, 2013, *www.edsullivan.com*.

67.   Heylin, *Revolution in the Air*, 70. The song was first officially released as "Talkin' John Birch Paranoid Blues" on *The Bootleg Series, Vol. 1–3: Rare and Unreleased, 1961–1991* (Columbia, 468086 2). Live versions can be found on *The Bootleg Series, Vol. 6: Bob Dylan Live, 1964* (Columbia, 512358 2) and *Bob Dylan in Concert: Brandeis University, 1963* (Columbia, 888697 79455 2).

68.   Martin A. Cohen, Dennis M. Altman, and Robert E. Natkin, *The John Birch Coloring Book* (Chicago: Serious Products Company, 1962). The book was "respectfully dedicated to Dwight D. Eisenhower, and to the many other loyal Americans who have been maligned by extremist groups," and contains a fictitious epigraph from General Walker:

"To the rear, march!" On the wider coloring book phenomenon of the time, see Milton Bracker, "These Are Coloring Books: Gold Is the Color," *New York Times*, August 11, 1962.

69.   Welch, "Agenda," *Bulletin*, July 1961, 14–17, quote on 14. Emphasis in original.

70.   Welch may have been referring to the activities of the American Security Council (ASC), one of the leading anticommunist organizations of the 1950s and a key part of the anticommunist network of the time. The *New York Times* reported in 1958 that the organization had gathered files on a million "subversives" in the United States and was collecting additional names at the rate of twenty thousand a month. See "Group Lists Data on 'Subversives,'" *New York Times*, July 10, 1958, quoted in Sara Diamond, *Roads to Dominion: Right-Wing Movements and Political Power in the United States* (New York: Guildford Press, 1995), 46–47. Nor was the ASC alone in this; the collection of this kind of material was a key part of the anticommunist network in the United States, both by private groups and agencies of the state.

71.   Welch, "Agenda," July 1961, 14–15.

72.   Ibid., 15–17. Emphasis in original.

73.   "I've Got a Little List," *New York Times*, July 14, 1961.

74.   Robert Welch, "About the Research Project," *Bulletin*, August 1961, 12.

75.   Ibid., 12.

76.   Ibid., 12–13.

77.   Ibid., 13. Emphasis in original.

78.   John Wicklein, "Faiths Focusing on Brotherhood," *New York Times*, February 24, 1962.

79.   Bradley Morison, "Song of a Modern Vigilante," quoted in Wicklein, "Faiths."

80.   Echoing the views of Robert Kennedy, who was cited approvingly in the report, Mosk told the governor that "the Birch Society has equal right with the Prohibitionists, the Vegetarians, the Republicans, the Democrats, or, for that matter, with any American, acting singly or in a group to an expression of its views; and no official, no matter how highly placed, can say them nay. In America, preposterousness prevents the acceptance but not the expression of ideas." Stanley Mosk, *Report to the Governor on the John Birch Society* (Sacramento: California Department of Justice, 1961), 13–14.

81.   Mosk wrote in a covering memorandum appended to the report (August 1, 1963) that it had "experienced a larger readership than we had envisioned. It was printed by metropolitan newspapers from coast to coast and by a national magazine. In addition, it has been quoted in numerous articles and books" (E740J6C34, Documents Department, Department of Justice, State of California). See, for example, Stanley Mosk and Howard H. Jewel, "The Birch Phenomenon Analyzed: A Report by the California Attorney General's Office Examines the Methods and Speculates on the Motives of the Controversial John Birch Society," *New York Times*, August 20, 1961. The report was entered into the *Congressional Record* by James Roosevelt (D-CA), FDR's eldest son, on August 15, 1961 (15,869–72).

82.   Mosk, *Report to the Governor*, quotes on 1, 4 and 11.

83.   Ibid., especially 4–5 and 7–11. As the Mosk Report put it: "The Birch Society is a monolithic authoritarian organization with the policy dictated from above and no dissent permitted in its ranks. The Communist Party is a monolithic authoritarian organization with the policy dictated from above and no dissent permitted in its ranks" (10). The fear that the Birch Society would "take over" the Republican Party is addressed in detail in Chapter 3.

84.   In typical Welchian style, the statement's opening paragraph explained that it was being "offered as an effort to pierce, by at least a tiny beam of truth, some of the incredible fog

of falsehood now being so widely circulated about me." The statement can be found in full in "Birch Group Head Disclaims Charge," *New York Times*, April 1, 1961.

85. "Pamphlet Listing Birch Council Is Released," *New York Times*, April 1, 1961.

86. Robert Welch, "Foreword," *Bulletin*, August 1961, 3–4.

87. Robert Welch, "The Movement to Impeach Earl Warren," *Bulletin*, October 1961, 4.

88. Mendel Rivers, "Earl Warren's Fellow Travelers Smear John Birch Society," *Congressional Record*, March 22, 1961, 4,604–07. Rivers's support of the Society was later "unearthed" by Republicans and used to attack him in 1966, when he was chairman of the Armed Services Committee; see Jack Anderson, "Rivers Supports Birchites," *Ocala Star-Banner*, January 5, 1966. It was warmly welcomed at the time by the Birch Society itself. In an addendum to the April 1961 issue of the *Bulletin*, Welch thanked Rivers for his "many kind words about our efforts and purposes." The support of "so able a member of our Congress is deeply appreciated," he said (4).

89. John Rousselot, quoted in "Birch Group Head Called a 'Hitler,'" *New York Times*, April 4, 1961.

90. Daniel J. Dowling, letter to the editor, *New York Times*, May 6, 1961. Dowling failed to identify the spy concerned.

91. In the September 1960 issue of the *Bulletin*, for example, Welch referred to the "massive smear campaign" that he believed was then ongoing against the Society ("Foreword," 1).

92. Robert Welch, "General Comment," *Bulletin*, March 1961, 21–22. Emphasis in original.

93. Robert Welch, "Foreword," *Bulletin*, April 1961, 1.

94. Robert Welch, "The Comrades Give the Signal," *Bulletin*, April 1961, 6–12.

95. As for Otis Chandler's editorials against the Society, Welch put them down largely to "misunderstandings" and clearly regarded the newspaper owner and himself as fighting the same enemy. Indeed, Welch had accepted an invitation to lunch with Chandler the next time he was in LA, Welch informed his readers. "In accepting his kind invitation I have assured him . . . that I shall check my horns in the coatroom before entering his office or the dining room," he joked. Ibid., 12–13.

96. Ibid.

97. Robert Welch, "About the Recent Speaking Engagements," *Bulletin*, May 1961, 9.

98. Robert Welch, "A Report, Continued," *Bulletin*, December 1961, 19–20.

99. "Enter (from Stage Right) the John Birch Society," *People's World*, February 25, 1961, 2.

100. Robert Welch to Fred Schwarz, September 6, 1960, 3. The letter was discovered by the freelance researcher Ernie Lazar and is available on his website, Documentary History of John Birch Society, at *sites.google.com/site/ernie1241a/home* (accessed October 14, 2013).

101. Ibid., 3–4.

102. Ibid., 5–7. Emphasis in original.

103. Ibid., 9.

104. See Robert Welch, "Agenda for August," *Bulletin*, August 1961, 5; John Wicklein, "Birch Society Will Offer $2,300 [*sic*] for Impeach Warren Essays," *New York Times*, August 5, 1961; and Cabell Phillips, "Head of American Bar Association Stresses Role of International Law," *New York Times*, August 8, 1961. The essay competition is examined in more detail in Chapter 4.

105. Robert Welch, "And a Report," *Bulletin*, December 1961, 9, 21–22.

106. See Dennis McDougal, *Privileged Son: Otis Chandler and the Rise and Fall of the LA Times Dynasty* (New York: Da Capo Press, 2001), 230–31; and James Sterngold, "A Family Struggle for the Soul of Times Mirror," *New York Times*, November 27, 1995. Otis Chandler had taken over the running of the *Times* from his father in 1960, having seen off the challenge of his uncle, Philip Chandler, who was a committed supporter of the Birch Society.

107. This was evident in Young's first address on the Society on March 8, 1961, but see also Russell Baker, "Senator Who Brought Birch Unit to Public Notice Fears Reprisal," *New York Times*, April 18, 1961. As it turned out, Young not only won reelection in 1962, he continued to be senator until his retirement in 1980.

108. For example, John Rousselot appeared on David Susskind's *Open End* to debate Dr. John Bennett, dean of the faculty of Union Theological Seminary, on April 23, and Welch was a guest on NBC's *Meet the Press* on May 21, 1961.

109. "Editor Honored for Birch Expose," *New York Times*, November 6, 1961. John F. Kennedy was among those who sent messages of congratulation to Storke. See also the editorial "A Courageous Editor," *New York Times*, November 2, 1961; and Thomas M. Storke's *I Write for Freedom* (Santa Barbara: News-Press Publishing Company, 1963).

110. Thomas M. Storke, "The *News-Press* Stand on John Birch Society," *Santa Barbara News-Press*, February 26, 1961. In 1962, Storke also won a Pulitzer for his anti-Birch editorials. See "Thomas More Storke Is Dead: Editor Attacked Birch Society," *New York Times*, October 13, 1971.

111. Barry Goldwater, quoted in Krock, "Best Weapon."

CHAPTER 2

1. "Military Channels Used to Push Birch Ideas," *Overseas Weekly*, April 16, 1961. Although dated April 16, the issue actually appeared on newsstands on April 14.

2. William Fulbright, "Memorandum Submitted to Department of Defense on Propaganda Activities of Military Personnel," *Congressional Record*, August 2, 1961, 14,433-39.

3. "Military Channels Used." See also Sydney Gruson, "Birch Unit Ideas Put to U.S. Troops—General Walker Indoctrinates Men in Europe Division," *New York Times*, April 14, 1961.

4. Associated Press, "General Walker Denies Charge of Link to John Birch Society," *New York Times*, April 15, 1961.

5. Edgar Hiestand, "Maj. Gen. Edwin A. Walker," *Congressional Record*, April 19, 1961, 6,317.

6. Walker had been the commander of the federalized National Guard units and the 101st Airborne Division deployed to enforce the desegregation of the Little Rock schools, following the Supreme Court's *Brown v. Board of Education* decision in 1954. Walker's involvement at Little Rock and his wider views on the civil rights movement in the United States are addressed in Chapter 4.

7. Alford, "Maj. Gen. Edwin A. Walker," 6,316-17.

8. Ibid. See also the call by Senator Styles Bridges (R-NH) for the House and Senate Armed Services Committees to investigate the affair on Walker's behalf (*Congressional Record*, May 16, 1961, 8,035-37). The Senate Armed Services Committee was receiving fifteen to twenty letters per day in support of Walker at this time. See United Press International, "Telegram Drive Supports Walker," *New York Times*, May 1, 1961.

9. Ovie Fisher, "Notorious Overseas Weekly Attacks Anticommunist Pro-Blue Americanism Program of Gen. Edwin A. Walker," *Congressional Record*, May 24, 1961, 8,848-51. Although the *Overseas Weekly* certainly published salacious material and was often a thorn in the side of the military establishment, it also had a reputation for generally getting its facts right, as well as being on the side of the ordinary GI. At the time of the Walker affair, it had a press run of fifty thousand copies a week, the largest circulation of any privately owned newspaper in Europe. See Charles C. Moskos, *The American Enlisted Man* (New York: Russell Sage Foundation, 1970), 102-3. Von Rospach was the widow of a former State Department and army information officer; an interesting account of her by one of her reporters can be found in Tad Bartimus et al.,

War Torn: Stories of War from the Women Reporters Who Covered Vietnam (New York: Random House, 2002), 36–37.

10. "Walker Is Relieved of Command While Army Checks Birch Ties," *New York Times*, April 18, 1961.

11. William Proxmire, "Needed: Education for Freedom as Well as against Communism," *Congressional Record*, April 14, 1961, 5,933–34.

12. "Transcript of the President's News Conference on World and Domestic Affairs," *New York Times*, April 22, 1961.

13. "John Birch Fantasies," *New York Times*, April 22, 1961.

14. This was also the explanation given in a letter from the wife of a serviceman serving under Walker in Europe reprinted in the *Arkansas Democrat* on April 23, 1961 ("Serviceman's Wife Raps Walker Attack as 'False, Malicious'"). Other sources used in the Pro-Blue program in addition to Welch's *The Life of John Birch* included J. Edgar Hoover's *Masters of Deceit*, Anthony Bouscaren's *A Guide to Anti-Communist Action*, Eugene Kinkead's *In Every War but One*, Edward Hunter's *The Story of Mary Liu*, and the "Index" prepared by Americans for Constitutional Action, which analyzed the voting records of every congressman to see if they could be classified as conservative or liberal. Full details of the program can be found in Edwin A. Walker, *Censorship and Survival* (New York: Bookmailer, 1961), 29–53.

15. Russell Baker, "Walker Is Rebuked for Linking Public Figures to Communism," *New York Times*, June 13, 1961. Walker's own accounts of the affair can also be found in *Pro Blue* (Dallas, TX: American Eagle Publishing, 1965) and *Walker Speaks Unmuzzled!* (Dallas, TX: American Eagle Publishing, 1962), the latter a collection of three of his speeches (given in Dallas, Los Angeles, and Chicago).

16. Edgar Hiestand and Frank Kowalski, quoted in United Press International, "Birchite Is Disturbed," *New York Times*, June 13, 1961.

17. Cabell Phillips, "Right-Wing Officers Worrying Pentagon," *New York Times*, June 17, 1961. See also Jonathan M. Schoenwald, *A Time for Choosing: The Rise of Modern American Conservatism* (New York: Oxford University Press, 2001), 102–4.

18. On the anticommunist activities of these groups and their seminars and educational programs, see, for example, Donald T. Critchlow, *The Conservative Ascendancy: How The Republican Right Rose to Power in Modern America*, 2nd ed. (Lawrence: University Press of Kansas, 2011), 32–37.

19. See Randall Bennett Woods, *Fulbright: A Biography* (New York: Cambridge University Press, 1995). Fulbright also created the enormously successful educational exchange program that bears his name, of course.

20. Ibid., 278.

21. Ibid., 278–79.

22. Ibid., 279. See also Lee Riley Powell, *J. William Fulbright and His Time: A Political Biography* (Memphis: Guild Bindery Press, 1996), 192–95; Tristram Coffin, *Senator Fulbright: Portrait of a Public Philosopher* (New York: Dutton, 1966), 151–62; and Richard Gid Powers, *Not without Honor: The History of American Anticommunism* (New York: Free Press, 1995), 297–303.

23. Fulbright, "Memorandum," 14,433–36.

24. Ibid., 14,433.

25. Ibid., 14,434.

26. Ibid. Cabell Phillips's *New York Times* article on the 1958 NSC directive was reproduced verbatim for the benefit of Kennedy and McNamara in the memo. It is not entirely clear whether Fulbright acted as a "source" for Phillips's article or the article was a source for the memo, but they certainly reinforced each other's main points and arguments.

27. Fulbright, "Memorandum," 14,434.

28. Ibid.

29. Details of the memo were first published in Marquis Childs, "Birchites Finding Allies in Military," *Washington Post*, June 28, 1961.

30. As Thurmond's biographer Joseph Crespino comments, Thurmond's involvement in the issue "transformed" his political profile: "He was no longer merely a regional figure defending white southern interests but a serious conservative critic on issues of national security. Thurmond joined in spirit, if not quite yet in party identification, a small but feverish clan that was remaking the Republican Party, one whose influence on national politics was just beginning to be felt" (*Strom Thurmond's America* [New York: Hill and Wang, 2012], 161). See also David Burnham, "Study Asserts Military Rightists Raise Obstacles to Kennedy Program," *Washington Post*, July 21, 1961; and Cabell Phillips, "U.S. Curbs Officers in Rightwing Talks," *New York Times*, July 21, 1961.

31. "Statement by Senator Strom Thurmond, Democrat, of South Carolina, on Senate Foreign Relations Committee Memorandum about Curbing Military Speakers on the Subject of Communism, July 21, 1961." Thurmond's news release is reproduced in the *Congressional Record*, July 26, 1961, 13,608.

32. See "Military Anticommunist Seminars and Statements," *Congressional Record*, July 26, 1961, 13,594–618; and "Military Anti-Communist Seminars and Statements," *Congressional Record*, July 29, 1961, 13,998–14,014, quotes on 13,998 and 13,999.

33. Slightly differing versions of the encounter can be found in the *Congressional Record*, July 26, 1961, 13,608, and August 4, 1961, 14,724–25; Woods, *Fulbright*, 284; and Coffin, *Senator Fulbright*, 158–59. Thurmond later explained in a letter to Fulbright that he had not intended any offense in his request; the apparent urgency—which Fulbright called "impertinent" on the floor of the Senate—was merely the result of him getting ready to leave Washington for the weekend.

34. Karl Mundt, *Congressional Record*, July 29, 1961, 14,006; and Barry Goldwater, "Military Anti-Communist Seminars and Statements," *Congressional Record*, July 31, 1961, 14,173–74. This was particularly the case, Goldwater said, when the United States was faced with an enemy who said things like "'We will bury you' and 'Your children will live under socialism,'" and he suggested that "if the scouts of the New Frontier are so frightened that they want to hide behind their squaws' skirts" then the "chief should get rid of them in a hurry."

35. Fulbright, "Memorandum," 14,433.

36. Strom Thurmond, "Military Anti-Communist Seminars and Statements," *Congressional Record*, August 4, 1961, 14,724–25.

37. Ibid., 14,725–26. Fulbright's shift from his "elitist" approach of the early 1960s—and before—to a more flexible and critical view of foreign policy-making, as a consequence of the Vietnam War, is one of the themes explored in Lee Riley Power's biography of the senator. On Thurmond, see Jack Bass and Marilyn W. Thompson, *Strom: The Complicated Personal and Political Life of Strom Thurmond*, rev. ed. (New York: Public Affairs, 2006); and Crespino, *Strom Thurmond's America*, especially 142–62.

38. Fulbright had "performed a service in sending his viewpoint to the Department of Defense," President Kennedy said, and he hoped that "every member of the Senate [would] continue to give the administration the benefit of their judgment" (quoted in the *Washington Post*, August 11, 1961).

39. Editorial, "Mr. Thurmond's 'Fundamentals,'" *New York Times*, August 4, 1961.

40. See "General Walker's Mistake," *New York Times*, September 9, 1961. Thurmond had inserted some of these new directives into the *Congressional Record* back in July. See

Congressional Record, July 26, 1961, 13,605–6. His response to McNamara's testimony can be found in the *Congressional Record*, September 18, 1961, 19,980–92.

41. U.S. Senate, *The Use of Military Personnel and Facilities to Arouse the Public to the Menace of the Cold War and to Inform and Educate Armed Services Personnel on the Nature and Menace of the Cold War: Report by the Special Preparedness Subcommittee of the Committee on Armed Services*. 87th Cong., 2nd Sess. (Washington, DC: Government Printing Office, 1962).

42. Woods, *Fulbright*, 288; and E. W. Kenworthy, "Alford Scores Fulbright's Memo and Urges Voters to Defeat Him," *New York Times*, August 9, 1961. On the wider coverage of the story, see also E. W. Kenworthy, "Fulbright Becomes a National Issue," *New York Times Magazine*, October 1, 1961; Frederick W. Collins, "Military Indoctrination of Civilians," *New Republic*, June 26, 1961; "Are We Muzzling Those Who Know Red Tactics Best?" *Saturday Evening Post*, November 4, 1961; "Fair Play for General Walker," *Life*, October 6, 1961; "Thunder on the Right," *Newsweek*, December 4, 1961; and "Crackpots: How They Help Communism," *Life*, December 1, 1961.

43. See, for example, "What Price Glory? Major General Edwin A. Walker," *Dan Smoot Report* 7, no. 35 (August 28, 1961): 273–80, emphasis in original. For more on Dan Smoot, whose activities were initially funded by the oil magnate H. L. Hunt, see Harry and Bonaro Overstreet, *The Strange Tactics of Extremism* (New York: Norton, 1964), 127–42.

44. Billy James Hargis, quoted in Woods, *Fulbright*, 286. On the Courtneys, see George Thayer, *The Farther Shores of Politics: The American Political Fringe Today*, 2nd ed. (New York: Simon and Schuster, 1968), 198–206; Schoenwald, *Time for Choosing*, 109–10; and Kent and Phoebe Courtney, *The Case of General Edwin A. Walker* (New Orleans, LA: Conservative Society of America, 1961).

45. "Let the Generals Beware," *National Review*, July 1, 1961, 406–7. The other articles were "Ten-Shun!," an anonymous letter from a member of Walker's Twenty-Fourth Infantry Division about the Pro-Blue program, published on May 6, 1961 (which was also reprinted in the May issue of the Birch Society's *Bulletin*); "Out: Not with a Whimper, but a Bang," about Walker's resignation from the army, published on November 18, 1961; and an interview with the general conducted by Medford Evans for the December 16 issue. A fifth article entitled "General Walker, Stage II" about Walker's later political activities, discussed further below, appeared in the October 23, 1962, issue.

46. Schoenwald, *Time for Choosing*, 111–12. Buckley and the *National Review*'s contentious relationship with the Birch Society is addressed in the following chapter.

47. Robert Welch, "Agenda for the Month," *Bulletin*, May 1961, 17–20; and Robert Welch, "Agenda for the Month," *Bulletin*, June 1961, 11–13.

48. Robert Welch, "Agenda for the Month," *Bulletin*, September 1961, 10–16.

49. Robert Welch, "The Fulbright Memorandum," *Bulletin*, October 1961, 5–9. "By the very nature of things," Welch wrote, "it is not possible for many of our concerted efforts to have measurable results. We simply have to keep right on working, taking such encouragement as we can from intangible evidences of our impact and influence. So it is good when we can, sometimes, take note of a definite victory which we have helped to win."

50. Ibid.

51. Jack Raymond, "Walker Resigns from the Army," *New York Times*, November 3, 1961. Walker's statement is reprinted in *Censorship and Survival*, 1–25. It can also be found in U.S. Senate, *Military Cold War Education and Speech Review Policies: Hearings Before the Special Preparedness Subcommittee of the Committee on Armed Services*, 87th Cong., 2nd Sess. (Washington, DC: Government Printing Office, 1962), 4: 1,405–12.

52. Walker, *Censorship and Survival*, 1.

53. Ibid., 3 and 23.

54. Ibid., 12 and 4.

55. Ibid., 15.

56. Ibid., 1.

57. The other subcommittee members were Stuart Symington (D-MO), Henry Jackson (D-WA), E. L. Bartlett (D-AK), Leverett Saltonstall (R-MA), and Margaret Chase Smith (R-ME). Senator Bridges died before the hearings could take place, and his replacement, Francis Case (R-SD), followed him before the final report was prepared.

58. U.S. Senate, *Military Cold War Education*, 4: 1,430.

59. Ibid., 1,447–49.

60. U.S. Senate, *Use of Military Personnel*, 2–13. Bartlett's views can be found on 43–45 and Thurmond's on 46–203.

61. Robert Welch, "If You Want It Straight," *American Opinion*, January 1963, 1–4.

62. On Washington's "extraordinary" decision to resign as commander in chief of the American forces at the conclusion of the Revolutionary War—the "greatest act of his life," according to Gordon Wood—see *The Radicalism of the American Revolution* (New York: Vintage, 1991), 205–6. On the wider issue of civilian-military relations in the United States, see Samuel Huntington, *The Soldier and the State: The Theory and Politics of Civil-Military Relations* (1957; Cambridge, MA: Belknap Press, 1981); and Peter D. Feaver and Richard H. Kohn, eds., *Soldiers and Civilians: The Civil-Military Gap and American National Security* (Cambridge, MA: MIT Press, 2001). For a comparative perspective on the issue, see S. E. Finer, *The Man on Horseback: The Role of the Military in Politics*, 2nd. ed. (London: Penguin, 1975).

63. U.S. Senate, *Use of Military Personnel*, 3, 9–10.

64. William Fulbright, quoted in Coffin, *Senator Fulbright*, 159–62.

65. Eisenhower's address ("Military-Industrial Complex Speech, Dwight D. Eisenhower, 1961") can be found at *The Avalon Project: Documents in Law, History, and Diplomacy*, Yale Law School, Lillian Goldman Law Library, accessed October 14, 2013, *avalon.law. yale.edu/20th_century/eisenhower001.asp*. An earlier articulation of these concerns can be found in C. Wright Mills, *The Power Elite* (New York: Oxford University Press, 1956), especially 198–224. See also Fred J. Cook, *The Warfare State* (New York: Macmillan, 1962).

66. John F. Kennedy, quoted in Waldemar A. Nielsen, "Huge, Hidden Impact of the Pentagon," *New York Times Magazine*, June 25, 1961. See also Nielsen's subsequent article, "Soldiers in Politics: A Growing Issue," *New York Times Magazine*, October 22, 1961.

67. On Kennedy's difficulties with air force chief of staff General Curtis LeMay in particular, see Robert Dallek, *An Unfinished Life: John F. Kennedy, 1917–1963* (New York: Little, Brown, 2003), 344–45 and 556–57; and Richard Rhodes, "The General and World War III," *New Yorker*, June 19, 1995: 47–59.

68. Powers, *Not without Honor*, 298.

69. Pentagon official, quoted in Phillips, "Rightwing Officers."

70. Henry Reuss, "Nothing Funny about the John Birch Society," *Congressional Record*, April 12, 1961, 5,666; Irving Spiegel, "Rabbis Urge Inquiry into John Birch Society," *New York Times*, April 19, 1961; and John Aspinwall Roosevelt, quoted in "G.O.P. Leader Says Mayor Shirks Jobs," *New York Times*, April 20, 1961.

71. Milton Young, "John Birch Society Leaders Use Tactics Hindering Fight against Communism," *Congressional Record*, July 14, 1961, 12,552. Young's previous denunciations of the Birch Society as a fascist organization can be found in the *Congressional Record*, April 3, 1961, 5,427–29; and April 20, 1961, 6,369–70.

72. On the "Brown scare" of the late 1930s and early 1940s, when the activities of William Dudley Pelley, Gerald B. Winrod, Gerald L. K. Smith, and Father Charles Coughlin in particular first led to fears about the rise of fascism in the United States, see Leo P. Ribuffo, *The Old Christian Right: The Protestant Far Right from the Great Depression to the Cold War* (Philadelphia: Temple University Press, 1983), especially 178–224.

73. These men were all members of the National Council. Bunker was also the former personal aide to Douglas MacArthur, providing another tantalizing "link" in the chain of those searching for evidence of the possibility of a domestic coup d'état. An interesting discussion of the role of the NAM in the politics of this period can be found in Jonathan Soffer, "The National Association of Manufacturers and the Militarization of American Conservatism," *Business History Review* 75, no. 4 (Winter 2001): 775–805.

74. Mike Newberry, *The Fascist Revival: The Inside Story of the John Birch Society* (New York: New Century Publishers, 1961), 7, 10–13, and 18. Newberry found an explanation for the fascist revival in a capitalism in crisis: "Big business' most warlike and rampageous elements hope to solve the crisis of capitalism—their own historically outmoded and bankrupt policies have created—by the demagogy of fascism. It is the demagogy of frightened men who are victims of their own political paranoia" (41). See also his *The Yahoos* (New York: Marzani and Munsell, 1964).

75. Gus Hall, "The Ultraright, Kennedy and the Role of the Progressive," *Worker*, July 16, 1961. See also the editorial on the Fulbright memo, "The Generals," in *Worker*, July 30, 1961.

76. Norman Thomas, introduction to *The American Ultras: The Extreme Right and the Military-Industrial Complex*, by Irwin Suall, 2nd ed. (New York: New America, 1962), 2.

77. Socialist Labor Party, *"Rightism" Is American Fascism!*, n.d. The pamphlet describes the Birch Society as the "most formidable" of the "current reactionary movements" vying for supremacy in the United States, including Fred Schwarz's Christian Anti-Communism Crusade and George Lincoln Rockwell's American Nazi Party.

78. Thomas notes in his introduction, for example, that the information contained in it has been submitted to the "proper agencies of government," including President Kennedy and New York governor Nelson Rockefeller, so that "appropriate action" can take place (*American Ultras*, 2). This is not something one imagines was the case with *The Fascist Revival*. See also Murray Illson, "Norman Thomas Hits Birch Group," *New York Times*, April 20, 1961.

79. Suall, *American Ultras*, 3–4 and 60–61.

80. Ibid., 62 and 65. Suall would go on to become the national director of fact-finding for the Anti-Defamation League in 1967.

81. John Smith, as told to Stanhope T. McReady, *Birch Putsch Plans for 1964* (n.p.: Domino Publications, 1963).

82. Ibid., 4.

83. Ibid., 95. An admittedly unreliable Internet site attributes the book to a "black propaganda" operation of the KGB intended to help prevent Barry Goldwater winning the presidency. See "Stanislav Levchenko," KeyWiki, accessed October 14, 2013, *keywiki.org*.

84. The "objectives of the Minutemen are to abandon wasteful, useless efforts and begin immediately to prepare for the day when Americans will once again fight in the streets for their lives and their liberty," declared the pamphlet *A Short History of the Minutemen* (n.p.: ca. 1960). See also the twenty-page booklet *The "Minutemen": America's Last Line of Defense against Communism* (Norborne, MO: ca. 1960).

85. Associated Press, "Police Seize Arms of '61 'Minutemen,'" *New York Times*, October

22, 1961. See also "Minutemen's Soft-Sell Leader: Robert B. DePugh," *New York Times*, November 12, 1961; and Steve Underwood, "Bands of Minutemen across the Country Whet for Communist Threat," *Kansas City Star*, December 3, 1961.

86. John F. Kennedy, quoted in Tom Wicker, "Kennedy Asserts Far-Right Groups Provoke Disunity," *New York Times*, November 19, 1961. Welch imagines what he would do if he were the "'man on the white horse' on our side in this war" in *The Blue Book of the John Birch Society* (Belmont, MA: Western Islands, 1961), 64. Kennedy was also responding to criticism that had been directed at him by E. M. Dealey, the publisher of the *Dallas Morning News*. During a White House luncheon the previous month, Dealey had told Kennedy, "We need a man on horseback to lead this nation and many people in Texas and the Southwest think that you are riding Caroline's tricycle" (quoted in "Kennedy Slaps Birch Society," *Kansas City Star*, November 19, 1961).

87. United Press International, *New York Times*, November 20, 1961. This issue is addressed more fully in the following chapter.

88. Bill Becher, "Homes of Critics of Right Bombed," *New York Times*, February 2, 1962. Paul Talbert, a Beverly Hills–based leader of the Birch Society, denied its involvement in the bombings. Neither he nor the Society as a whole "believes in this sort of thing," he stated. "We do not advocate bombing or violence of any kind." Kuchel's remarks, alongside those of Hubert Humphrey and Jacob Javits, can be found in the *Congressional Record*, February 2, 1962, 1,464–66.

89. John George and Laird Wilcox, *American Extremists: Militias, Supremacists, Klansmen, Communists, and Others* (Amherst, NY: Prometheus Books, 1996), 222. The most detailed account of the Minutemen and the group's early activities can be found in J. Harry Jones Jr., *The Minutemen* (New York: Doubleday, 1968). A recent interview with DePugh can be found in Eric Beckemeier's *Traitors Beware: A History of Robert DePugh's Minutemen* (Hardin, MO: privately printed, 2007), 118–43.

90. "Mr. DePugh has made the most continuous and determined effort to bring about the extensive collaboration of the Minutemen with the John Birch Society that we have ever experienced with any other group," Welch explained to the *Kansas City Star* on the occasion of DePugh's expulsion from the Society (quoted in George and Wilcox, *American Extremists*, 239). See also Harry Jones Jr., "Welch as Jealous of the Minutemen," *Kansas City Star*, August 28, 1964.

91. Milton Young, "Danger on the Right," *Saturday Evening Post*, January 13, 1962. The Minutemen were used as supporting evidence of the fascist nature of the Birch Society in both Suall's *American Ultras* (57–58) and Smith's *Birch Putsch Plans for 1964* (51–52). Characteristically, Suall noted that while the Minutemen's "guerrilla development" was the "logical culmination" of the Ultras' ideology, most Ultras were not Minutemen.

92. U.S. Senate, *The New Drive Against the Anti-Communist Program: Hearing Before the Subcommittee to Investigate the Administration of the Internal Security Act and Other Internal Security Laws of the Committee on the Judiciary*, 87th Cong., 1st Sess. (Washington, DC: Government Printing Office, 1961), 77. Hunter's significant contribution to the "brainwashing" debate of this period is discussed further below.

93. A. J. MacDonald, *Kangaroo Court versus The John Birch Society* (Los Angeles: A. J. MacDonald and Associates, 1963), 6–7. MacDonald was also the author of *The Belmont Brotherhood* (1963), which argued that the Birch Society was just a "front" group for the Freemasons.

94. California Senate, *Twelfth Report of the Senate Factfinding Subcommittee on Un-American Activities* (Sacramento: Senate of the State of California, 1963), 62. The Birch Society liked the subcommittee's findings so much that it republished the report as a

pamphlet of its own entitled *The California Report on the John Birch Society*, complete with commentary and explanatory footnotes by Welch.

95.   From the vast literature on fascism, I found the following sources most useful for the purposes of this discussion: Roger Eatwell, *Fascism: A History* (New York: Penguin, 1995); Roger Griffin, *The Nature of Fascism* (London: Routledge, 1993); Noel O'Sullivan, *Fascism* (London: J. M. Dent and Sons, 1983); Alan Brinkley, *Voices of Protest: Huey Long, Father Coughlin and the Great Depression* (New York: Vintage, 1983), 269–83; and Ribuffo, *Old Christian Right*, 19–24. An excellent primer on the subject is Kevin Passmore, *Fascism: A Very Short Introduction* (New York: Oxford University Press, 2002). An interesting contemporary discussion of the phenomenon with respect to both the Birchers and the Minutemen can be found in John Weiss, *The Fascist Tradition* (New York: Harper and Row, 1967).

96.   Brinkley, *Voices of Protest*, 281.

97.   See, for example, Robert Welch's critique and dismissal of charges of anti-Semitism made against the Society in the *Bulletin*, April 1961, 16–21; and his pamphlet *The Neutralizers* (Belmont, MA: John Birch Society, 1963), as well as George and Wilcox, *American Extremists*, 193–94; Robert Alan Goldberg, *Enemies Within: The Culture of Conspiracy in Modern America* (New Haven, CT: Yale University Press, 2001), 45–46; and Arthur Goldwag, *The New Hate: A History of Fear and Loathing on the Populist Right* (New York: Pantheon Books, 2012), 132.

98.   Newberry, *Fascist Revival*, 6.

99.   George Michael, *Willis Carto and the American Far Right* (Gainesville: University Press of Florida, 2008), 47–49. "Virtually to a man, these disgruntled former members renounced the JBS as a Zionist-led operation that confuses well-meaning patriots and leads them down a blind alley," Michael notes (255). See also Martin Durham, *White Rage: The Extreme Right and American Politics* (London: Routledge, 2007), 115–17; and Eckard V. Toy Jr., "The Right Side of the 1960s: The Origins of the John Birch Society in the Pacific Northwest," *Oregon Historical Society* 105, no. 2 (2004): 280.

100.   See Lisa McGirr, *Suburban Warriors: The Origins of the New American Right* (Princeton, NJ: Princeton University Press, 2001); and George and Wilcox, *American Extremists*, 192–93.

101.   The classic account of the Eichmann trial is Hannah Arendt's *Eichmann in Jerusalem: A Report on the Banality of Evil* (New York: Viking, 1963), which was based on her reports for the *New Yorker* at the time.

102.   See Les K. Adler and Thomas G. Paterson, "Red Fascism: The Merger of Nazi Germany and Soviet Russia in the American Image of Totalitarianism, 1930s–1950s," *American Historical Review* 75, no. 4 (April 1970): 1,046–64; and Abbott Gleason, *Totalitarianism: The Inner History of the Cold War* (New York: Oxford University Press, 1995). These issues are examined further in Chapter 6.

103.   See Victor G. Reuther, *The Brothers Reuther and the Story of the UAW* (Boston: Houghton Mifflin, 1976), 437–40. Reuther published the text of the memorandum in an appendix to his memoir (491–500; hereafter "Reuther memo"). Victor describes his brother as "the whipping boy of the extreme right" (437).

104.   Reuther memo, 491.

105.   Ibid., 495.

106.   Ibid., 495–96.

107.   In the long run, private agencies—the press, television, church, labor, civic, political, and other groups—could do more than the government to identify, expose, and ultimately contain the radical Right, the Reuthers and Rauh contended, but that was not the

purpose of the recommendations they had been asked to provide. However, it was also the case that "affirmative Administration policies and programs" would "set the backdrop against which private activity is most likely to succeed" (ibid., 494).

108. Ibid., 496–99.

109. Ibid., 499–500.

110. Phillip Finch, *God, Guts and Guns: A Close Look at the Radical Right* (New York: Seaview/Putnam, 1983), 119.

111. Jonathan Weisman and Matthew L. Wald, "I.R.S. Focus on Conservatives Gives G.O.P. an Issue to Seize On," *New York Times*, May 12, 2013.

112. Robert Justin Goldstein, *Political Repression in Modern America: From 1870 to 1976* (Urbana: University of Illinois Press, 1978), 425.

113. John A. Andrew III, *Power to Destroy: The Political Uses of the IRS from Kennedy to Nixon* (Chicago: Ivan R. Dee, 2002), 18–24 and 29–30. Jonathan Schoenwald supports Goldstein's assessment, arguing that the Kennedy administration "did little more than accept the memo and hope the [radical right-wing] problem would go away" (*Time for Choosing*, 117).

114. The Reuther memo had predicted as much. Implementing its recommendations, it said, would "evoke immediate charges of softness on Communism. But this is not a problem that can be swept under the rug. The Administration can no more combat the radical right by being 'tough on domestic Communism' or appeasing radical right Generals than the [Eisenhower] Republican Administration was able to fight McCarthyism by its own excesses in this area" (500).

115. Robert DePugh, in a fundraising letter circulated to potential supporters in the mid-1970s, for example, was still attributing his 1966 indictment on various firearms, bomb possession, and kidnapping charges to the Reuther memorandum ("Robert B. DePugh—Patriot" [n.d.], Wilcox Collection of Contemporary Political Movements, University of Kansas [RHWLEPH 2123.4]). The memorandum was also reproduced in full in the February 1, 1964, issue of the Minutemen newsletter, *On Target*.

Birch Society writer Jere Real tried to expose the "true" nature of Walter Reuther in his article "This Is Walter Reuther," published in the January 1963 issue of *American Opinion*, 5–12. On the broader conservative hostility to Reuther for his union activities, see Rick Perlstein, *Before the Storm: Barry Goldwater and the Unmaking of the American Consensus* (New York: Hill and Wang, 2001), especially 30–32 and 36–39.

116. Fletcher Knebel and Charles W. Bailey II, *Seven Days in May* (New York: Harper and Row, 1962). See also Michael Coyne, "*Seven Days in May*: History, Prophecy and Propaganda," in *Windows on the Sixties: Exploring Key Texts of Media and Culture*, ed. Anthony Aldgate, James Chapman, and Arthur Marwick (London: I. B. Tauris, 2000), 70–90; and "Military Control: Can It Happen Here?" *Look*, September 11, 1962.

117. Knebel and Bailey, *Seven Days*, 118–19.

118. Colonel John R. Broderick runs ECOMCON, the secret military unit Scott has created to carry out the coup. Jiggs describes him as "fine Fascist son-of-a-bitch" (ibid., 56), and another character refers to him as an "out-and-out Fascist" (237).

Michael Coyne sees him as the Walker surrogate in the book, but Scott also seems to incorporate many of Walker's characteristics. It hardly seems coincidental that "Code Blue" is the general's personal code, for example (123). Interestingly, Coyne regards another character, Senator Raymond Clark—one of Lyman's closest supporters and confidants—as a "composite" of two real-life senators: William Fulbright and George A. Smathers (D-FL); Smathers was JFK's closest personal friend in the Senate ("History, Prophecy and Propaganda," 78).

The other notable filmic military character of this time who was at least partly based on General Walker is General Jack D. Ripper (Sterling Hayden) in Stanley Kubrick's *Dr. Strangelove, or How I Learned to Stop Worrying and Love the Bomb* (1964); the other model for Ripper was Curtis LeMay.

119. Knebel and Bailey, *Seven Days*, 72–73.

120. "MacPherson" was changed to "McPherson" in the film. *Seven Days in May* (dir. John Frankenheimer, 1964). On the film, see also J. Hoberman, *The Dream Life: Movies, Media and the Mythology of the Sixties* (New York: New Press, 2003), 66–67 and 89–90; and Stephen J. Whitfield, *The Culture of the Cold War*, 2nd ed. (Baltimore: Johns Hopkins University Press, 1996), 213–14.

121. Coyne, "History, Prophecy and Propaganda," 80. Goldwater blamed the film of *Seven Days in May*—along with *On the Beach* (dir. Stanley Kramer, 1959) and *Fail Safe* (dir. Sidney Lumet, 1964)—for increasing the American public's "almost hysterical, unreasoned attitude toward nuclear war" in his 1979 memoir, *With No Apologies: The Personal and Political Memoirs of United States Senator Barry M. Goldwater* (New York: Morrow, 1979), 149.

122. *The Manchurian Candidate* (dir. John Frankenheimer, 1962); Richard Condon, *The Manchurian Candidate* (1959; Harpenden, Hertfordshire, UK: No Exit Press, 1993). On these issues in both the film and book, see Hoberman, *Dream Life*, 69–76; Whitfield, *Culture of the Cold War*, 211–13; David Seed, *Brainwashing: The Fictions of Mind Control; A Study of Novels and Films since World War II* (Kent, OH: Kent University Press, 2004), 107–33; Margot A. Henriksen, *Dr. Strangelove's America: Society and Culture in the Atomic Age* (Berkeley: University of California Press, 1997), 265–70; Susan L. Carruthers, "Redeeming the Captives: Hollywood and the Brainwashing of America's Prisoners of War in Korea," *Film History* 10 (1998): 275–94; and Michael Paul Rogin, *"Ronald Reagan," the Movie, and Other Episodes in Political Demonology* (Berkeley: University of California Press, 1987), 236–71.

123. J. Hoberman, "When Dr. No Met Dr. Strangelove," *Sight and Sound*, December 1993, 18. This is how the scene is described in the script: "In the audience [of the Spring Lake Garden Club] sit a mass of white, middle-class, little old ladies in paisley dresses and flowered hats" (George Axelrod, *The Manchurian Candidate* [Eye, Suffolk, UK: ScreenPress Publishing, 2002], 16).

124. Edward Hunter, *Brainwashing in Red China* (New York: Vanguard Press, 1951); Edward Hunter, *Brainwashing: From Pavlov to Powers* (1956; Linden, NJ: Bookmailer, 1965); and Joost A. M. Meerloo, *The Rape of the Mind* (New York: World Publishing, 1956), especially 27–28. Anthony Burgess's novel *A Clockwork Orange* (London: Heinemann, 1962) also addresses the brainwashing anxieties of the time.

125. Eugene Kinkead, "A Reporter at Large: The Study of Something New in History," *New Yorker*, October 26, 1957, 114–69. See also his book *In Every War but One* (New York: Norton, 1959). On these issues, see also Susan L. Carruthers, *Cold War Captives: Imprisonment, Escape and Brainwashing* (Berkeley: University of California Press, 2009), especially 174–16; Gleason, *Totalitarianism*, 88–107; and Ron Robin, *The Making of the Cold War Enemy: Culture and Politics in the Military-Intellectual Complex* (Princeton, NJ: Princeton University Press, 2001), 162–81.

126. As one of his division officers put it, Walker was deeply interested in "what went wrong with some of our fighting men in Korea" (quoted in Baker, "Walker Is Rebuked"). In a speech in Dallas on December 12, 1961, Walker talked about the problem of "BUG OUT" by American soldiers during the war and for the need for effective psychological training to help combat it. See *Walker Speaks Unmuzzled*, 17–18.

127. U.S. Senate, *Military Cold War Education*, 3: 1,162 and 1,223. Others who testified on these Korean War issues during the hearings included General Barksdale Hamlett, vice chief of staff, U.S. Army; Major General A. H. Luehman, director of the Office of Information, U.S. Air Force; Brigadier General S. L. A. Marshall, U.S. Army Reserve; a former POW, Major Ward M. Millar, U.S. Air Force; and Under Secretary of State George W. Ball.

128. Hunter, *Brainwashing: From Pavlov to Powers*, 309.

129. U.S. Senate, *Military Cold War Education*, 3: 1,223. Hunter's views on the subject can be found in chapter 10 of *Brainwashing: From Pavlov to Powers*, entitled "How It Can Be Beat," 265–303.

130. Proxmire, "Needed," 5,934. Emphasis added.

131. Carruthers, *Cold War Captives*, 212. "Totalitaria" was another neologism of Joost Meerloo; see *Rape of the Mind*, 105–24.

132. Robert Welch, "And Yet More Introduction," *Bulletin*, February 1960, 4; and Robert Welch, "Foreword," *Bulletin*, January 1961, 4.

133. Robert Welch, *The Politician* (Belmont, MA: Belmont Publishing, 1963), 175; Robert Welch, "The Research Department," *Bulletin*, February 1960, 7; and Robert Welch, *Blue Book*, 80.

134. Elizabeth Linington, *Come to Think of It*—(Belmont, MA: Western Islands, 1965), 92–93. On her career, see Mary Jean DeMarr, "Elizabeth Linington/Anne Blaisdell/Dell Shannon/Lesley Egan," in *Great Women Mystery Writers: Classic to Contemporary*, ed. Kathleen Gregory Klein (Westport, CT: Greenwood Press, 1994), 192–97.

135. Ibid., 115. *Invasion of the Body Snatchers* (dir. Don Siegel, 1956). The fact that the film has been remade three times, in 1978 (dir. Philip Kaufman), 1993 (dir. Abel Ferrara), and 2007 (dir. Oliver Hirschbiegel), suggests that it speaks to profound issues in the American psyche. For an interesting discussion of the original film, see J. Hoberman, *An Army of Phantoms: American Movies and the Making of the Cold War* (New York: New Press, 2011), 305–13; and Henriksen, *Dr. Strangelove's America*, 141–47.

    Fears about brainwashing have been revived in the post-9/11 world of suicide bombers and John Walker Lindh–like al-Qaida terrorists. On this, see, for example, Carruthers, *Cold War Captives*, 233–37; and Kathleen Taylor, "On Brainwashing," in *The Barbarisation of Warfare*, ed. George Kassimeris (London: Hurst, 2006), 238–53.

136. "Ex-General Walker Enters Texas Race for Governor," *New York Times*, February 3, 1962.

137. Clive Webb, *Rabble Rousers: The American Far Right in the Civil Rights Era* (Athens: University of Georgia Press, 2010), 144. Webb also examines the political careers of Navy rear admiral John G. Crommelin and lieutenant general Pedro del Valle in the far Right politics of the period.

    Away from the spotlight, Walker was apparently quite different, as the journalist George Thayer discovered. "Walker . . . has the reputation as the right's worst public speaker, often becoming incoherent when he mounts the podium," Thayer noted in his book. "But in private this is not so; he is fairly articulate and not given to the monosyllabic anti-Communist clichés he sometimes uses in public" (*Farther Shores*, 231).

138. "Walker Enters Texas Race." Walker remained a member of the Society until 1972.

139. "Walker Is Facing 4 Federal Counts," *New York Times*, October 2, 1962; and Associated Press, "Psychiatric Testing Ordered for Walker," *New York Times*, October 3, 1962. It is also perhaps worth noting in this respect that on April 5, 1962, on his way out of the Senate caucus room, after his testimony before the Senate Preparedness Subcommittee, Walker punched a *Washington Daily News* reporter in the face for asking him about

the American Nazi Party. See John W. Finney, "Walker Challenges Rusk and Rostow on Loyalty," *New York Times*, April 6, 1962.

140. Eric Pace, "Gen. Edwin Walker, 83, Is Dead; Promoted Rightist Causes in 60's," *New York Times*, November 2, 1993.

141. See, for example, Ion Mihai Pacepa, *Programmed to Kill: Lee Harvey Oswald, the Soviet KGB, and the Kennedy Assassination* (Chicago: Ivan R. Dee, 2007), xv and 134–42; Michael L. Kurtz, *The JFK Assassination Debates: Lone Gunmen versus Conspiracy* (Lawrence: University Press of Kansas, 2006), 152–56; Gerald Posner, *Case Closed: Lee Harvey Oswald and the Assassination of JFK* (New York: Random House, 1994), 99–121; and David Kaiser, *The Road to Dallas: The Assassination of John F. Kennedy* (Cambridge, MA: Belknap Press, 2008), 181–86.

142. *Report of the President's Commission on the Assassination of President John F. Kennedy* (Washington, DC: Government Printing Office, 1964), 404–6.

143. On Oswald, see John Loken, *Oswald's Trigger Films: The Manchurian Candidate, We Were Strangers, Suddenly?* (Ann Arbor, MI: Falcon Books, 2000), especially 2–17. On the withdrawal of the film, see Hoberman, *Dream Life*, 73–74. Hoberman notes that, as with *Seven Days in May*, Kennedy supported the turning of *The Manchurian Candidate* into a film (54).

144. Richard Gid Powers has written that Senator Fulbright's fears of "a plot by right-wing military officers allied to the extreme right to stage a coup, perhaps to bring General Douglas MacArthur to power as an American De Gaulle" were "as bizarre as any conspiracy theory spun by the radical right," for example (*Not without Honor*, 299).

CHAPTER 3

1. Anthony Lewis, "The Issues," *New York Times*, August 30, 1964.

2. "If my vote is misconstrued, let it be, and let me suffer its consequences," Goldwater said at the time. Quoted in Robert Alan Goldberg, *Barry Goldwater* (New Haven, CT: Yale University Press, 1995), 197. While presented as a matter of principle and constitutionality, political considerations also played a part in Goldwater's stand, as he knew he needed to win the South if he was to have any chance of winning the presidency come November. Goldwater was a member of the Arizona branch of the NAACP and he also worked for the integration of the Arizona National Guard, but in Goldberg's view, the senator was "often unable to look beyond the individual and the immediate," and, if no bigot himself, he nonetheless sometimes "acted to appease bigotry" (xi).

3. Despite its renown, the ad only aired once, on September 7, 1964. It was, though, only part of the broader attempt that was made to portray Goldwater as a dangerous extremist who would make war with the Soviet Union more likely. On the daisy ad, see Robert Mann, *Daisy Petals and Mushroom Clouds: LBJ, Barry Goldwater and the Ad That Changed American Politics* (Baton Rouge: Louisiana State University Press, 2011).

4. See Goldberg, *Goldwater*, 206–7. The phrase and Goldwater's campaign are discussed in detail later in the chapter. The issue of civil rights and the nation's nuclear policy as they pertain to the Birch Society are examined in Chapters 5 and 6 respectively.

5. On these issues, see, for example, Alan Brinkley, *The End of Reform: New Deal Liberalism in Recession and War* (New York: Knopf, 1995); and James T. Sparrow, *Warfare State: World War II Americans and the Age of Big Government* (New York: Oxford University Press, 2011).

6. George H. Nash, *The Conservative Intellectual Movement in America since 1945*, 30th anniv. ed. (Wilmington, DE: ISI Books, 2006), 400–401. The years of preparation would lead, eventually, of course, to what is generally seen as the movement's greatest triumph, Ronald Reagan's capture of the White House in 1980.

7.   The classic expression of this view can be found in the essays in Daniel Bell, ed., *The Radical Right: "The New American Right," Expanded and Updated* (Garden City, NY: Doubleday, 1963). See also Clinton Rossiter, *Conservatism in America: The Thankless Persuasion*, 2nd rev. ed. (New York: Random House, 1962). Works that have recognized the importance of the Birch Society to the conservative movement of the era include Lisa McGirr's *Suburban Warriors: The Origins of the New American Right* (Princeton, NJ: Princeton University Press, 2001), especially 75–79 and 222–23; and Jonathan M. Schoenwald's *A Time for Choosing: The Rise of Modern American Conservatism* (New York: Oxford University Press, 2001), especially 62–99. See also Kim Phillips-Fein, "Conservatism: A State of the Field," *Journal of American History* 98 (December 2011): 736.

8.   For example, Welch wrote, "Most of our Conservative critics do not yet realize that a new force has come upon the scene . . . one that is dynamic, determined, and daily growing by leaps and bounds. . . . We are rapidly becoming the rallying point for . . . thousands and then ten thousands and then hundreds of thousands of our fellow Americans who share our fears and our determination," in "The Movement to Impeach Earl Warren," *Bulletin*, March 1961, 10.

      Even George Nash, who spent little time on the Birchers and other members of the radical Right in his book because "their contribution to conservatism as an intellectual force was negligible," recognized that they were "often energetic" during the late 1950s and early 1960s (*Conservative Intellectual Movement*, xvii).

9.   Alan F. Westin, "The John Birch Society: Fundamentalism on the Right," *Commentary* 32, no. 2 (August 1961): 93. Based on financial statements submitted to the Massachusetts attorney general, Benjamin R. Epstein and Arnold Forster put the number of Society members closer to 24,000 in 1961, in *Danger on the Right* (New York: Random House, 1964), 11. By 1967, in a follow-up report, they gave figures of 50,000 to 60,000; see *The Radical Right: Report on the John Birch Society and Its Allies* (New York: Random House, 1967), 195. They also estimated that *American Opinion* was read by 43,000 Americans a month, and the *Bulletin* by 75,000 to 85,000, with another 5,800 or so reading the Society's weekly *Review of the News* (ibid., 11). But the truth is that there are no exact figures for the membership of the Society or the readership of its publications.

10.   See John B. Judis, *William F. Buckley Jr.: Patron Saint of the Conservatives* (New York: Simon and Schuster, 1988), 191; Jerome L. Himmelstein, *To The Right: The Transformation of American Conservatism* (Berkeley: University of California Press, 1990), 26–27; and Martin Durham, "On American Conservatism and Kim Phillips-Fein's Survey of the Field," *Journal of American History* 98 (December 2011): 757–58. The other most prominent "conservative" of the time who, in Buckley's estimation at least, failed to make the grade was the Objectivist and atheist Ayn Rand. On Rand's politics, career, and influence, see Jennifer Burns, *Goddess of the Market: Ayn Rand and the American Right* (New York: Oxford University Press, 2009).

11.   The best account of Buckley and his importance to American conservatism is Judis's *William F. Buckley Jr.*, but see also Linda Bridges and John R. Coyne Jr., *Strictly Right: William F. Buckley Jr., and the American Conservative Movement* (Hoboken, NJ: Wiley, 2007); and Carl T. Bogus, *Buckley: William F. Buckley Jr. and the Rise of American Conservatism* (New York: Bloomsbury Press, 2011). For a conservative's perspective on *National Review*, see Jeffrey Hart, *The Making of the American Conservative Mind:* National Review *and Its Times* (Wilmington, DE: ISI Books, 2005).

12.   Judis, *Buckley*, 184 and 221.

13.   The phrase is Nash's, of course. The importance of *National Review* to this process of

fusion, in which a shared anticommunism played the critical role, is discussed in detail in *Conservative Intellectual Movement*, 235–86.

14. See Gregory L. Schneider, *Cadres for Conservatism: Young Americans for Freedom and the Rise of the Contemporary Right* (New York: New York University Press, 1999); John A. Andrew III, *The Other Side of the Sixties: Young Americans for Freedom and the Rise of Conservative Politics* (New Brunswick, NJ: Rutgers University Press, 1997); and Bridges and Coyne, *Strictly Right*, 72–73 and 91–93.

15. Robert Welch, *The Blue Book of the John Birch Society* (Belmont, MA: Western Islands, 1961), 127.

16. William Rusher, quoted in Geoffrey Kabaservice, *Rule and Ruin: The Downfall of Moderation and the Destruction of the Republican Party, from Eisenhower to the Tea Party* (New York: Oxford University Press, 2012), 13–14. The phrase was popularized by Arthur Larson, Eisenhower's assistant secretary of labor, in his book *A Republican Looks at His Party* (New York: Harper and Brothers, 1956). Moderation was the watchword of Modern Republicanism. As Kabaservice says, it sought to reform the New Deal rather than overthrow it, and was "as much a temperament as an ideology"—one reflective of Eisenhower's personality—in its emphasis on "balance, reasonableness, prudence and common sense" (15).

17. Judis, *Buckley*, 192.

18. William F. Buckley Jr., quoted in Schoenwald, *Time for Choosing*, 69. Welch and Buckley shared the same influential conservative publisher, Henry Regnery, and it was Regnery who first introduced them to one another in 1954. See Judis, *Buckley*, 193.

19. Buckley, quoted in Judis, *Buckley*, 194, and in Schoenwald, *Time for Choosing*, 74.

20. Russell Kirk, quoted in Bridges and Coyne, *Strictly Right*, 71.

21. Judis, *Buckley*, 194. According to Judis (157), the final straw for Schlamm, following numerous editorial disputes between he and Buckley, was Buckley's decision to give Schlamm's office, which he was only using a couple of days a week at that point, to William Rusher.

22. Ibid.

23. Ibid., 195.

24. Robert Welch, quoted in Schoenwald, *Time for Choosing*, 75. Emphasis in original.

25. In an article in the *Arizona Republic* in March 1963, discussing the political situation in California, for example, Buckley argued that "the overwhelming majority of the conservatives in California who long for conservative leadership are not Birchers," but that it was "useful in politics to bury distinctions and smooth over the broken ground." Because of the "high political stink value of Mr. Welch's aboriginal imputations of disloyalty, the enemies of conservative action in America have rushed in with a crash program of syllogistic misconstruction, by which in one dazzling swoop, leaving undistributed middles lying about all over the place, they march from the premises (1) Welch said Eisenhower is a Communist, (2) Welch founded a society, (3) John is a member of that society, (4) John supports James for Congress; to the conclusion, therefore, (5) James is the candidate of those who think Eisenhower is a commie." William F. Buckley Jr., "Public Misreads John Birch Label," *Arizona Republic*, March 17, 1963. See also William F. Buckley Jr., "The Uproar," *National Review*, April 23, 1961, 243.

26. Buckley's account of what he called the "Palm Beach plotters" appeared in *Commentary* in March 2008 under the title "Goldwater, the John Birch Society, and Me." It is available at *www.commentarymagazine.com*.

27. Barry M. Goldwater, *With No Apologies: The Personal and Political Memoirs of United States Senator Barry M. Goldwater* (New York: Morrow, 1979), 119.

28. Goldberg, *Barry Goldwater*, 137; Robert Welch *"To Prevent a Third Party": A Speech by Robert Welch, Delivered at the Unauthorized Rally in Support of Senator Barry Goldwater, at the Morrison Hotel, Chicago, July 24, 1960* (Belmont, MA: American Opinion, 1960), 1; and Robert Welch, "Agenda For May," *Bulletin*, May 1960, 7. This is how Welch described Goldwater in *The Blue Book*: "Barry Goldwater has political know-how and the painstaking genius to use that know-how with regard to infinite details. He is a superb political organizer, and inspires deep and lasting loyalty. He is absolutely sound in his Americanism, has the political and moral courage to stand by his Americanist principles, and in my opinion can be trusted to stand by them until hell freezes over. I'd love to see him president of the United States, and maybe some day we shall" (109).

29. Goldberg, *Barry Goldwater*, 137. Goldwater repeated this story on the campaign trail in 1964, when, as we shall see later in the chapter, allegations of his connection to the Birch Society were used repeatedly against him. United Press International, "'Burn Book,' Goldwater Urged Welch," *Arizona Republic*, March 30, 1964.

30. Judis, *Buckley*, 198.

31. Russell Kirk, "Conservatives and Fantastics," *America*, February 17, 1962, 644. Now that Goldwater had spoken out against such "political silliness," Kirk predicted that the "Republican Party generally will clear its skirts of Mr. Welch and presumably set its face against still odder movements." See also Russell Porter, "Catholic Editor Hits Birch Group," *New York Times*, February 8, 1962.

32. This same view was expressed by another prominent anticommunist Catholic of the time, Father John F. Cronin, in his pamphlet *Communism: Threat to Freedom* (New York: Paulist Press, 1962).

33. William F. Buckley Jr., "The Question of Robert Welch," *National Review*, February 13, 1962, 83–88. Emphasis in original.

34. Ibid.

35. For example, Congressman John Rousselot noted that he had "obvious and pointed disagreements" with Welch—again primarily over Welch's views about Eisenhower as expressed in *The Politician*—in a statement in the House on February 15 ("Robert Welch and the John Birch Society," *Congressional Record*, February 15, 1962, 2,356–57). And in the same month's issue of the *Bulletin*, Welch himself acknowledged that at meetings of the Executive Committee the previous June, there had been suggestions that he step down as the Society's leader in order to give it a new "image," and that the idea had been given a "full airing" at a National Council meeting in September. Welch used such disagreements to further counter the "misunderstandings" that existed about the Society's "monolithic" structure. He had no "martyr complex," he said, and he certainly wasn't "the indispensable man," but he would not be resigning from his position. To do so "would be nothing less than a betrayal . . . of the well understood compact between our members and myself," and he was not going to be "beguiled into abandoning such a dedicated body of the finest and most purposeful people on earth into the dissensions and frustrations" that would follow his withdrawal ("A Necessary Warning," *Bulletin*, February 1962, 7–8).

36. Arthur Radford, letter to the editor, *National Review*, February 27, 1962, 160.

37. Barry Goldwater, letter to the editor, *National Review*, February 27, 1962, 160.

38. Ronald Reagan, letter to the editor, *National Review*, March 13, 1962, 177; John Tower, letter to the editor, February 27, 1962, 161; and *Congressional Record*, February 6, 1962, 1,763–66.

39. Mrs. Kenneth L. Myers and Mrs. M. N. Fuller, letters to the editor, February 6, 1962, 161; and Mrs. Paul H. Dolan, letter to the editor, March 13, 1962, 177.

40. Judis, *Buckley*, 200. Judis argues, however, that in the longer run, Buckley's attack on the Birch Society was beneficial both for him personally and for the forces of "respectable conservatism" in the United States. Buckley expressed the same view when he looked back on the affair in 2008: "The wound we Palm Beach plotters delivered to the John Birch Society proved fatal over time. Barry Goldwater did not win the presidency, but he clarified the proper place of anti-Communism on the Right, with bright prospects to follow" ("Goldwater, the John Birch Society, and Me"). *National Review*'s renewed attack on Welch and the Society in the aftermath of Goldwater's defeat in 1964 is addressed later in the chapter.

41. Fulton Lewis Jr., "Fulton Lewis Sets the Record Straight," *Wanderer*, March 8, 1962.

42. Phoebe Courtney, "Were Goldwater and Buckley 'Booby-Trapped'?" and Kent Courtney, "In Defense of Robert Welch," *Independent American*, March 1962.

43. Robert Welch, "A Fable for Conservatives," *Bulletin*, March 1962, 3–5.

44. This particular phrase is taken from the May issue of the *Bulletin*. Robert Welch, "A Place and Time to Fight Back?" *Bulletin*, May 1962, 17.

45. Welch, "Fable," 9–10.

46. Ibid., 10–11. Emphasis in original.

47. Schoenwald, *Time for Choosing*, 18.

48. See, for example, Felix Belair Jr., "Brown Accuses Nixon of Bidding for Rightist Aid in Coast Race," *New York Times*, January 9, 1962; "Nixon Bids Parties Avoid Extremists," *New York Times*, January 10, 1963; Peter Kihss, "Politicians Eye Rightist Power," *New York Times*, March 12, 1962; and Damon Stetson, "Romney Charges 'Mess in Michigan,'" *New York Times*, August 26, 1962.

49. Welch's response to Romney can be found in "The Open Season on Birchers Is Now Closed," *Bulletin*, September, 1962, 25; and his views on Nixon in *The Blue Book*, 110 and 113. For a fascinating analysis of Nixon's place in American politics and culture, see David Greenberg, *Nixon's Shadow: The History of an Image* (New York: Norton, 2003).

50. "Domestic Issues Split Chiefs of Two Parties in TV Debate," *New York Times*, September 3, 1962.

51. John F. Fenton, "Magazine Halted by Birch Society," *New York Times*, December 17, 1963. The text of Welch's telegram and a copy of the news release the Society sent to United Press International and the Associated Press on November 22 can be found in the *Interim Bulletin*, November 30, 1963, 1–2.

52. *Interim Bulletin*, November 30, 1963, 1–2.

53. See, for example, Robert Dallek, *An Unfinished Life: John F. Kennedy, 1917–1963* (Boston: Little, Brown, 2003), 400–401; William R. Polk, *Understanding Iraq* (New York: Harper Perennial, 2006), 115–16; George C. Herring, *America's Longest War: The United States and Vietnam, 1950–1975*, 4th ed. (New York: McGraw-Hill, 2001), 122–29; and David Kaiser, *American Tragedy: Kennedy, Johnson, and the Origins of the Vietnam War* (Cambridge, MA: Belknap Press, 2000), 248–84.

54. The ad was first published in the *New York Times* on December 15, 1963.

55. Robert Welch, "Our New Stickers," *Bulletin*, December 12, 1963, 21.

56. John H. Fenton, "Birch Society Spent $35,000 on Ads Asking Funds," *New York Times*, December 18, 1963.

57. Robert Welch, "On Politics and Murder," *Bulletin*, December 12, 1963, 3.

58. Martin Dies, "Assassination and Its Aftermath," *American Opinion*, March 1964, 9.

59. Revilo P. Oliver, "Marxmanship in Dallas, Part I," *American Opinion*, February 1964, 13–28; and Revilo P. Oliver, "Marxmanship in Dallas, Part II," *American Opinion*, March 1964, 65–78, quote on 69. Emphasis added.

60.   Welch, "Politics and Murder," 8.

61.   "Correction Please," *American Opinion*, January 1964, 42; and Oliver, "Marxmanship in Dallas, Part I," 14.

62.   "Correction Please," 42.

63.   Welch, "Politics and Murder," 2.

64.   Oliver, "Marxmanship in Dallas, Part I," 16–18. Welch made essentially the same point, albeit in a much less inflammatory way, in his own reflections on Kennedy's death. Kennedy having been "converted into a martyr by the bullet of an assassin," it would be futile for any critic to "start reminding people of how happy Moscow and all of our domestic Comsymps had been with the general progress of their plans, and the increased prestige of their agents and allies, under the Kennedy regime," he wrote. Kennedy's "near-deification" also meant that "even the most honest and restrained opposition" to the late president's policies "could be construed somehow as personal criticisms of so beloved a former President himself." Welch was particularly worried in this respect about Kennedy's civil rights legislation, the passage of which, he said, was now much more likely, even though it would "most certainly bring on the greatly increased rioting, turmoil, civil strife, and racial bitterness in the South which the Communists so ardently desire" ("Politics and Murder," 4).

65.   Editorial, "The Birch Advertisement," *New York Times*, December 20, 1963.

66.   A useful cross-section of the letters received by the *Times* can be found in "Comments on Birch Ad," *New York Times*, December 20, 1963. Field's letter was published on December 25 and Aitchess's on December 18.

67.   The *Worker*, quoted in Fenton, "Magazine Halted."

68.   "Birchers Condemned in State Legislature," *Arizona Republic*, February 13, 1964; "John Birch Library Here Picket Goal," *Arizona Republic*, February 13, 1964; and Editorial, "Twisted World of the Birchers," *Milwaukee Journal*, March 1, 1964. See also Associated Press, "Birchists Hold Dim View of J.F.K.," *Kansas City Star*, February 11, 1964; Editorial, "Birch Hate-Mongers at It Again," *Arizona Journal*, February 13, 1964; and Associated Press, "'Adulation' of Kennedy Again Is Assailed," *Kansas City Star*, March 4, 1964.

69.   Austin C. Wehrwein, "Is He a Jerk or a Genius?" *New York Times*, 18 March 1964.

70.   Associated Press, "Professor at Illinois Not Punished," *Arizona Republic*, March 19, 1964.

71.   Associated Press, "Birch Head Disputes Attack on Kennedy," *New York Times*, May 14, 1964. A selection of the "hate mail" Oliver received as a result of his article was published in the April issue of *American Opinion*. It included the suggestion that Oliver "should be run out of the country" and the characterization of him as a "dirty fascist anti-Semitic hate-mongger [*sic*]" ("Dear Doctor," *American Opinion*, April 1964, 71–76).

72.   See Associated Press, "Cardinal Cushing Retracts Birch Society Endorsement," *New York Times*, April 20, 1964; "Birch Society Says Cushing Has Withdrawn Repudiation," *New York Times*, April 24, 1964; and John H. Fenton, "Cushing Explains Birch Retraction," *New York Times*, April 25, 1964.

73.   "Comments on Birch Ad." Emphasis added.

74.   Earl Warren, *The Memoirs of Earl Warren* (New York: Doubleday, 1977), 353–55. Cardinal Cushing, who had married the Kennedys, presided over the president's funeral.

75.   The text of Johnson's address can be found at the website of the Miller Center, University of Virginia, *www.millercenter.org/president/speeches/detail/3381* (accessed October 14, 2013). For a discussion of its importance in both comforting the nation and establishing the tone and agenda of the new administration, see Robert A. Caro, *The Years of Lyndon Johnson*, vol. 4, *The Passage of Power* (New York: Knopf, 2012), 399–436; Randall B. Woods, *LBJ: Architect of American Ambition* (New York: Free Press, 2006), 434–36; and

Robert Dallek, *Flawed Giant: Lyndon Johnson and His Times, 1961–1973* (New York: Oxford University Press, 1998), 56–57.

76. The text of Fulbright's speech, from December 5, is reprinted in the *Congressional Record*, December 6, 1963, 22,726–28. See also Randall Bennett Woods, *Fulbright: A Biography* (New York: Cambridge University Press, 1995), 322–23.

77. Ed Cray, *Chief Justice: A Biography of Earl Warren* (New York: Simon and Schuster, 1997), 414.

78. An interesting contemporary article on the subject is "Dallas Asks Why It Happened; Worry over 'Image' Is Voiced," *New York Times*, November 24, 1963. See also Rick Perlstein, *Before the Storm: Barry Goldwater and the Unmaking of the American Consensus* (New York: Nation Books, 2009), 248–49.

79. Dallas United Nations Association president, quoted in Paul Crowell, "Pickets Jeer Warren Here and Hurl Placards at Him," *New York Times*, October 30, 1963. Warren received similar treatment from seventy-five picketers who were shouting for his impeachment as he left a meeting of the New York City Bar Association in New York City on October 29. Although the protest's organizer, Walter Zaleski, denied he was affiliated with the Birch Society, Crowell reported that the leaflets the picketers were hurling at the chief justice urged the purchase of "anti-Warren, anti-Supreme Court publications obtainable by mail from American Opinion, Belmont 78, Mass."

80. Byron Skelton, quoted in Dallek, *Unfinished Life*, 693.

81. John F. Kennedy, quoted in Dallek, *Unfinished Life*, 693.

82. Richard Nixon, quoted in Perlstein, *Before the Storm*, 247.

83. "Slugs Fired into Birch Quarters," *Arizona Republic*, November 23, 1963; and "Suit Asks John Birch Damage Pay," *Arizona Republic*, January 1, 1964. After his conviction, a civil suit was launched against Thompson for the damage his shooting had caused to a desk and two windows in the Birch office. See also Perlstein, *Before the Storm*, 248.

84. Welch, "Politics and Murder," 8.

85. See Caro, *Passage of Power*, 440–51; Dallek, *Flawed Giant*, 51–52; and Woods, *LBJ*, 438–39.

86. See, for example, James T. Patterson, *Grand Expectations: The United States, 1945–1974* (New York: Oxford University Press, 1996), 518–22; and Michael L. Kurtz, *The JFK Assassination Debates: Lone Gunman versus Conspiracy* (Lawrence: University Press of Kansas, 2006), especially 51–102. Strictly speaking, the Warren Commission only found that it had seen no "evidence" that there was any wider conspiracy behind the president's death.

87. Tim Weiner, *Enemies: A History of the FBI* (New York: Random House, 2012), 237.

88. The following political and biographical sketch is drawn primarily from Goldwater's *No Apologies*, Goldberg's *Barry Goldwater*, and Perlstein's *Before the Storm*.

89. Barry Goldwater, quoted in Goldberg, *Barry Goldwater*, 120.

90. John Micklethwait and Adrian Wooldridge, *The Right Nation: Conservative Power in America* (New York: Penguin, 2004), 56. There are many examples of Goldwater's eccentricities, but perhaps the most amusing was his response to a would-be supporter and budding entrepreneur who was selling a canned soft drink called "Gold Water" during the primary campaign of 1964. Having taken a sip of the "Right Drink for the Conservative Taste," Goldwater spat it out with the declaration: "This tastes like piss! I wouldn't drink it with gin!" See Perlstein, *Before the Storm*, 333.

91. See, for example, Goldwater, *No Apologies*, 160–61, and Goldberg, *Barry Goldwater*, 178–79. Goldwater and Kennedy respected each other and had even discussed running an "old style" political campaign in which they would go around the country together

focusing just on the issues. But this mutual respect should not disguise the fact the Kennedy was looking forward to running against Goldwater, whom he thought he could beat easily enough in the 1964 election. See Dallek, *Unfinished Life*, 689–90.

92. "Russ Radio Uses Barry as Example," *Arizona Republic*, April 20, 1964.

93. Goldwater, *No Apologies*, 160. See also Allen J. Matusow, *The Unraveling of America: A History of Liberalism in the 1960s* (New York: Harper and Row, 1986), 131; and Donald T. Critchlow, *The Conservative Ascendancy: How the Republican Right Rose to Power in Modern America*, 2nd ed. (Lawrence: University Press of Kansas, 2011), 67.

94. In support of this view, see Schoenwald, *Time for Choosing*, 138; and Allan J. Lichtman, *White Protestant Nation: The Rise of the American Conservative Movement* (New York: Atlantic Monthly Press, 2008), 237.

95. "Transcript of Goldwater's News Conference on His Entry into Presidential Race," *New York Times*, January 4, 1964. In an apparent portent of the troubled times to come, Goldwater made his announcement shortly after having had surgery on his right foot, which was now encased in a cast, as he shuffled about on crutches.

96. See Goldberg, *Barry Goldwater*, 138.

97. McGirr, *Suburban Warriors*, 112.

98. Critchlow, *Conservative Ascendancy*, 69–70.

99. Mary C. Brennan, *Turning Right in the Sixties: The Conservative Capture of the GOP* (Chapel Hill: University of North Carolina Press, 1995), 63. Goldwater acknowledged the inexperience of his team in his autobiography but characteristically took responsibility for the campaign's "errors" and "shortcomings" (*No Apologies*, 164–65).

100. Associated Press, "Goldwater in Slashing Form," *Kansas City Star*, November 18, 1961. For the Birch Society's view of the ADA, see, for example, Clarence Carson, "I Was an Extremist for the A.D.A.," *American Opinion*, April 1963, 45–47.

101. Barry Goldwater, quoted in Tom Wicker, "Goldwater Hits Extremism Issue," *New York Times*, March 18, 1964.

102. Goldwater, quoted in Charles Mohr, "Goldwater Calls Rival 'Extremist,'" *New York Times*, March 14, 1964.

103. Goldwater, quoted in "Governor Assails Goldwater's Tactics," *New York Times*, March 17, 1964.

104. Harry Keaton, quoted in Lawrence E. Davis, "Republicans Pick Birch Supporter," *New York Times*, February 18, 1963. See also "Young GOP Battles over Birchers," *Arizona Republic*, February 19, 1963; and "The Birchers Come Back Strong," *People's World*, February 23, 1963.

105. Bill Becker, "California Unionist Is Elected as GOP Moderates Triumph," *New York Times*, February 25, 1963. See also "California GOP Leader Says Birch Types Afoot, Angrily Calls Recess," *Arizona Republic*, February 24, 1963; and Sam Kushner, "How Birchers Made Their Bid," *People's World*, March 2, 1963.

106. Thomas Kuchel, quoted in "Opening Round," *New York Times*, February 26, 1963.

107. Thomas Kuchel, "The Fright Peddlers," *Congressional Record*, May 2, 1963, 7,636–41. See also the extensive reaction to Kuchel's "fright peddlers" speech in the *Congressional Record*, May 28, 1963, 9,684–702; and his article in the *New York Times*, "A PLOT!! To OVERTHROW America!!!," July 21, 1963.

108. "Far Right Grabs for GOP," *Democrat* 3, no. 14 (July 22, 1963).

109. Peter Kihss, "Rockefeller Says Rightists Imperil G.O.P and Nation," *New York Times*, July 15, 1963; and Richard Hunt, "Rockefeller Bids Goldwater Act," *New York Times*, July 20, 1963.

110. Kabaservice, *Rule and Ruin*, 48–49.

111. Ibid., 42. Kabaservice's detailed account of these different factions can be found on 18–26.
112. Ibid., 49–50. "We need disciplined pullers at the oars, not passengers in the boat," Welch wrote in *The Blue Book*, and if such a statement put readers in mind "of the Communist principle of 'the dedicated few,' as enunciated by Lenin," this was all to the good, he said, because the Society "was willing to draw on all successful human experience in organizational matters, so long as it does not involve any sacrifice of morality in the means used to achieve an end" (153).
113. Perlstein, *Before the Storm*, 221. Perlstein points out that Syndicate delegations required their members to swear affidavits confirming that they didn't belong to the Society. See also Kabaservice, *Rule or Ruin*, 64–65. Allan Lichtman argues that Goldwater's supporters were not executing a "coup" against the Republican Party, because the GOP "was already solidly conservative in its activist core" (*White Protestant Nation*, 246).
114. A good summary of the campaign can be found in Schoenwald, *Time for Choosing*, 126–29; and Brennan, *Turning Right*, 65–68. For a couple of the participants' own, more detailed versions, see F. Clifton White and William J. Gill, *Suite 3505* (New Rochelle, NY: Arlington House, 1967); and William A. Rusher, *The Rise of the Right* (New York: Morrow, 1984).
115. Welch, *Blue Book*, 95.
116. Robert Welch, "Agenda for the Month—The Conventions," *Bulletin*, July 1960, 7. See also "Be a Good Citizen, Always," *Bulletin*, August 1962, 5, when Welch urged members to "put as much hard work . . . as you can" into the campaigns of any "Conservative candidate, for any office, who is deserving of your support," without identifying exactly which candidates members should work hard for.
117. See, for example, Associated Press, "John Birch Society Neutral," *Kansas City Times*, July 3, 1964. Similarly, John Rousselot explained away the $2,000 Welch had contributed to Goldwater's 1958 senatorial campaign as a "personal gift" that had nothing to do with the Birch Society ("Goldwater Gift by Welch, Not Society, Says Rousselot," *Arizona Republic*, March 21, 1964).
118. Welch, *Blue Book*, 94–95.
119. Robert Welch, "What's Past Is Prologue," *Bulletin*, December 12, 1963, 18.
120. There are numerous accounts of the convention and of Goldwater's presidential campaign. See, for example, Theodore H. White, *The Making of the President, 1964* (New York: Atheneum, 1965); J. William Middendorf II, *A Glorious Disaster: Barry Goldwater's Campaign and the Origins of the Conservative Movement* (New York: Basic Books, 2006); Rusher, *Rise of the Right*, 119–24; Goldberg, *Barry Goldwater*, 181–209; Perlstein, *Before the Storm*, 371–405; and Kabaservice, *Rule and Ruin*, 111–22.
121. Anthony Lewis, "Scranton Forcing Goldwater Fight over Two Planks," *New York Times*, July 7, 1964.
122. "Transcript of the Keynote Address by Gov. Hatfield at G.O.P. Convention," *New York Times*, July 14, 1964.
123. Rockefeller, quoted in Kabaservice, *Rule or Ruin*, 113. See also Perlstein, *Before the Storm*, 383–84.
124. Goldberg, *Barry Goldwater*, 205–6; Richard Nixon, quoted in Kabaservice, *Rule or Ruin*, 116.
125. On these questions, see, for example, Goldberg, *Barry Goldwater*, 206–7; Perlstein, *Before the Storm*, 392; and Brennan, *Turning Right*, 78–79.
126. "Rockefeller's Statement," *New York Times*, July 18, 1964; Pat Brown, quoted in Perlstein, *Before the Storm*, 392; Martin Luther King Jr., quoted in Critchlow, *Conservative*

Ascendancy, 71; Richard Hofstadter, "The Long View: Goldwater in History," *New York Review of Books*, October 8, 1964; and Chad Mitchell Trio, quoted in "Concert Offers Social Comment," *New York Times*, September 28, 1964.

127. "Text of Democratic Party Platforms Domestic Section as Approved by Committee," *New York Times*, August 25, 1964. In contrast, and still reflecting Goldwater's equation of extremism only with the Left, the Republican plank on the topic read: "Such leaders [as those who have charted the Democrats' course] are Federal extremists—impulsive in the use of national power, improvident in the management of public funds, thoughtless as to the long-term effects of their acts on individual freedom and creative, competitive enterprise. Men so recklessly disposed cannot be safely entrusted with authority over their fellow citizens" ("Platform Planks Compared," *New York Times*, August 30, 1964).

   In the view of the *New York Times*, it had "required no vast courage" on the part of the Democrats to add the Birch Society to its list of extremist organizations; it was, the paper said, "merely an exercise in one-upmanship over Senator Goldwater's repudiation of the Ku Klux Klan" (Editorial, "Pallid Platform," August 25, 1964).

128. E. W. Kenworthy, "Humphrey Scores G.O.P. Birch Stand," *New York Times*, September 24, 1964. See also E. W. Kenworthy, "Humphrey Scores Forces of Hatred," *New York Times*, October 3, 1964; and Joseph A. Loftus, "Humphrey Warns of 'Radical Right,'" *New York Times*, October 21, 1964.

129. Editorial, "The Issue: The Vice-Presidency," *New York Times*, October 29, 1964.

130. Lyndon Johnson, quoted in Fendall W. Yerka, "President in West," *New York Times*, October 13, 1964.

131. These ideas of Goldwater's are recounted in Lichtman, *White Protestant Nation*, 251–52; and Micklethwait and Wooldridge, *Right Nation*, 56.

132. Godfrey Hodgson, *The World Turned Right Side Up: A History of the Conservative Ascendancy in America* (Boston: Houghton Mifflin, 1996), 104.

133. William F. Buckley Jr., "The Vile Campaign," *National Review*, October 6, 1964, 353. See also Lionel Lokos, *Hysteria 1964: The Fear Campaign against Barry Goldwater* (New Rochelle, NY: Arlington House, 1967), especially 27–39 and 111–168.

134. Micklethwait and Wooldridge, *Right Nation*, 56.

135. Brennan, *Turning Right*, 96.

136. On these post-election assessments, see, for example, Himmelstein, *To the Right*, 68–70; Hodgson, *World Turned*, 106–14; Brennan, *Turning Right*, 100–19; and Schoenwald, *Time for Choosing*, 156–61.

137. Goldberg, *Barry Goldwater*, 219. See also Thomas Crawford, *Thunder on the Right: The "New Right" and the Politics of Resentment* (New York: Pantheon Books, 1980); and Richard Viguerie, *The New Right: We're Ready to Lead* (Falls Church, VA: Viguerie, 1981).

138. Lichtman, *White Protestant Nation*, 244.

139. Geoffrey Vincent, "New Pamphleteers," *New York Times*, January 10, 1965. See also Phyllis Schlafly, *A Choice Not an Echo* (Alton, IL: Pere Marquette Press, 1964); Phyllis Schlafly and Chester Ward, *The Gravediggers* (Alton, IL: Pere Marquette Press, 1964); J. Evetts Haley, *A Texan Looks at Lyndon: A Study in Illegitimate Power* (Canyon, TX: Palo Duro Press, 1964); and John A. Stormer, *None Dare Call It Treason* (Florisssant, MO: Liberty Bell Press, 1964). For an analysis of Schlafly's work in particular, see Kabaservice, *Rule or Ruin*, 89–90; and Donald T. Critchlow, *Phyllis Schlafly and Grassroots Conservatism: A Woman's Crusade* (Princeton, NJ: Princeton University Press, 2005).

140. Schoenwald, *Time for Choosing*, 156.

141. Robert Welch, "If You Want It Straight," *American Opinion*, December 1964, 1–12. The

article was reproduced with the title "Reflections on the Elections" as an insert for the December *Bulletin*.

142. Ibid. There was a glimmer of good news in the election results for the Birch Society when John G. Schmitz, a thirty-four-year-old professor of American government and philosophy at Santa Ana College, became the first known Bircher to be elected to the California legislature. Even this must have been tempered, though, by the defeats of the other eight Birchers running at the state and federal level who had made public their membership of the Society. See "3 Neophytes Capture House Seats in California," *New York Times*, November 8, 1964. John Wayne joined the Birch Society in 1960, but left after the 1964 election, during which, as Welch notes, he was an enthusiastic Goldwater supporter. On the Duke's association with the Society, see Randy Roberts and James S. Olson, *John Wayne: American* (New York: Free Press, 1995), 568–69.

143. Earl Mazo, "Scranton Insists on Birch Ouster," *New York Times*, December 13, 1964.

144. United Press International, "Conservative Body Elects Rep. Bruce As First Chairmen," *New York Times*, December 22, 1964. See also Lichtman, *White Protestant Nation*, 261; and Judis, *Buckley*, 233.

145. Tom Wicker, "Goldwater Forms Group for Political Education," *New York Times*, June 18, 1965. See also Goldberg, *Barry Goldwater*, 243. The FSA was disbanded in 1969.

146. "Birch Society Scored By G.O.P.," *New York Times*, October 1, 1965.

147. "The John Birch Society and the Conservative Movement," *National Review*, October 19, 1964, 914–16.

148. Frank S. Meyer, "The Birch Malady," *National Review*, October 19, 1965, 919–20. See also James Burnham, "Get US Out!," *National Review*, October 19, 1965, 925–27.

149. Richard Hofstadter, "The Paranoid Style in American Politics," in *The Paranoid Style in American Politics and Other Essays* (Cambridge: Harvard University Press, 1965), 29–30 and 40. Emphasis in original. See also Hofstadter's essay on "Goldwater and Pseudo-Conservative Politics," in the same volume, 93–141.

150. See, for example, John H. Bunzel, *Anti-Politics in America: Reflections on the Anti-Political Temper and Its Distortions of the Democratic Process* (New York: Vintage, 1970), 32–37, 79–86, and 217–18; Seymour Martin Lipset and Earl Raab, *The Politics of Unreason: Right-Wing Extremism in America, 1790–1970* (Chicago: University of Chicago Press, 1978), 288–337; Epstein and Forster, *Radical Right*; and Robert A. Rosenstone, *Protest from the Right* (Beverly Hills, CA: Glencoe Press, 1968).

151. For an account of the Manhattan meeting, see "1,200 Pay $4 Each for Birch Meeting," *New York Times*, June 2, 1963.

152. Wallace Turner, "Union Gets Views of Birch Society," *New York Times*, July 21, 1963.

153. John H. Fenton, "Rousselot Named as Birch Publicist," *New York Times*, July 3, 1964.

154. Peter Bart, "Goldwater Regrets That G.O.P. Didn't Attack Extremism in '64," *New York Times*, October 15, 1965.

155. Ronald Reagan, quoted in J. Hoberman, *An Army of Phantoms: American Movies and the Making of the Cold War* (New York: New Press, 2011), 307.

156. Peter Bart, "Reagan Enters Gubernatorial Race in California," *New York Times*, January 5, 1966; United Press International, "Reagan Suggests Congress 'Clear Air' on Birch Society," *New York Times*, January 10, 1966. See also Gladwin Hill, "Reagan Accused of Bircher Links," *New York Times*, August 12, 1966. This didn't stop Welch from claiming that the work of individual Birchers had been instrumental in Reagan's victory. See Associated Press, "Welch Says Reagan Won with Birch Aid," *New York Times*, December 9, 1966. On Reagan's association and disassociation with the Birch Society, see, for example, Lou Cannon, *Ronnie and Jessie: A Political Odyssey* (New York: Doubleday, 1969), especially 73–76; J. Allen Broyles, *The John Birch Society: Anatomy of a Protest* (Boston:

Beacon Press, 1964), 66–67; Garry Wills, *Reagan's America: Innocents at Home* (London: Heinemann, 1988), 287, 292, and 311; and Jules Tygiel, *Ronald Reagan and the Triumph of American Conservatism*, 2nd ed. (New York: Pearson Longman, 2006), 97 and 113.

157. Brennan, *Turning Right*, 119.

158. Dan T. Carter, *The Politics of Rage: George Wallace, the Origins of the New Conservatism, and the Transformation of American Politics* (New York: Simon and Schuster, 1995), 343.

159. Patterson, *Grand Expectations*, 704.

160. Ibid., 702.

CHAPTER 4

1. Robert Welch, "A Letter to the South: On Segregation," *One Man's Opinion*, September 1956, 28–37. Reprinted in pamphlet form by American Opinion (Belmont, MA), in March 1964 (ninth printing), from which all subsequent references are taken. Emphasis in original.

2. *Brown v. Board of Education of Topeka*, 347 U.S. 483 (1954), which was followed by *Brown v. Board of Education of Topeka*, 349 U.S. 294 (1955).

3. Welch, "Letter to the South." Emphasis in original.

4. Ibid. Emphasis in original.

5. Ibid. Emphasis in original.

6. Harry Truman, quoted in Robert H. Terte, "College Training of Foreigners Hit," *New York Times*, November 14, 1961. In contrast to Truman, George Thayer argued that the "difference between a Bircher and a Klansman is important," not just in terms of ideology but with respect also to their societal and economic position. A Bircher could be found "anywhere in the social and economic system and is—or feels he is—in a state of flux," he wrote, whereas a Klansman "feels he is trapped between the Negro below him and the white power structure above him. I never met a really rich Klansman . . . nor one that had been successful before he joined the organization. This, of course, is not true among Birchers" (*The Farther Shores of Politics: The American Political Fringe Today*, 2nd ed. [New York: Simon and Schuster, 1968], 176–77).

7. Alan F. Westin, "The John Birch Society: Fundamentalism on the Right," *Commentary* 32, no. 2 (August 1961), especially 99, 101, and 103.

8. Seymour Martin Lipset and Earl Raab, *The Politics of Unreason: Right-Wing Extremism in America, 1790–1977*, 2nd ed. (Chicago: University of Chicago Press, 1978), 269; Sara Diamond, *Roads to Dominion: Right-Wing Movements and Political Power in the United States* (New York: Guildford Press, 1995), 86. On the question of the Society's racial attitudes and lack of overt racism, see also Jonathan M. Schoenwald, *A Time for Choosing: The Rise of American Conservatism* (New York: Oxford University Press, 2001), 89–90; and Martin Durham, *White Rage: The Extreme Right and American Politics* (London: Routledge, 2007), 115–17.

9. See Robert Welch, *The Blue Book of the John Birch Society* (Belmont, M: Western Islands, 1961), 19, for example; and Robert Welch, *The Politician* (Belmont, MA: Belmont Publishing, 1963), 267, where Welch refers back to his 1956 "Letter to the South: On Segregation."

10. Robert Welch, "Agenda for the Month," *Bulletin*, January 1961, 5–20; quote on12. Welch gave "sole billing" to the movement to impeach Warren because "if we are to get this drive off to a proper start, every hour of time and every ounce of energy that each member can contribute had far better be put into this one purpose than scattered elsewhere."

11. The Committee Against Summit Entanglements is discussed in more detail in the following chapter.

12. Welch, "Agenda for the Month," *Bulletin*, January 1961, 6–7.

13. Ibid., 9–11. Emphasis in original.

14. Ibid., 11.

15. Welch uses "the most brazen and flagrant usurpation . . . jurisprudence" passage to describe the *Brown* decision both in the January 1961 "Agenda for the Month" (16) and his "Letter to the South: On Segregation." The other decisions Welch discussed were *Pennsylvania v. Nelson*, 350 U.S. 497 (1956); *Konigsberg v. State Bar*, 33 U.S. 252 (1957); *Watkins v. United States*, 354 U.S. 178 (1957); and *Sweezy v. New Hampshire*, 354 U.S. 234 (1957). Welch's analysis of these cases was clearly based on Rosalie M. Gordon's *Nine Men against America: The Supreme Court and Its Attack on American Liberties*, rev. ed. (New York: Devin-Adair, 1960), especially 56–63. The discussion of them that follows is drawn from Bernard Schwartz, *Super Chief: Earl Warren and His Supreme Court—A Judicial Biography* (New York: New York University Press, 1983), 204–52; Ed Cray, *Chief Justice: A Biography of Earl Warren* (New York: Simon and Schuster, 1997), 329–41; and Jim Newton, *Justice for All: Earl Warren and the Nation He Made* (New York: Riverhead Books, 2006), 345–57.

16. A later but also influential book for Birch Society members was Warren Jefferson Davis's *Law of the Land* (New York: Carlton Press, 1962). An extensive and laudatory review of Davis's book by Revilo P. Oliver can be found as "The Warren Gang," *American Opinion*, December 1962, 23–36.

17. Earl Warren, quoted in Cray, *Chief Justice*, 334–35.

18. *Yates v. United States*, 354 U.S 298 (1957). See Schwartz, *Super Chief*, 230–34, for a detailed discussion of *Yates*. A fourth case, *Service v. Dulles* (354 U.S. 363 [1957]), placed restrictions on loyalty-security dismissals. According to Geoffrey R. Stone, the four decisions handed down on Red Monday "marked the end of the Cold War in the Supreme Court" (*Perilous Times: Free Speech in Wartime, from the Sedition Act of 1798 to the War on Terrorism* [New York: Norton, 2004], 413).

19. Joe McCarthy and James O. Eastland, both quoted in Schwartz, *Super Chief*, 183.

20. Dwight D. Eisenhower and *Chicago Tribune* both quoted in Cray, *Chief Justice*, 336–37. See also David Caute, *The Great Fear: The Anti-Communist Purge under Truman and Eisenhower* (New York: Simon and Schuster, 1978), 207–9; and Schoenwald, *Time for Choosing*, 35–40.

21. See Cray, *Chief Justice*, 338.

22. Gordon, *Nine Men*, preface (n.p), 10, and 70–71.

23. Robert Welch, "Agenda for the Month," *Bulletin*, July 1961, 3.

24. Robert Welch, "Agenda for the Month," *Bulletin*, April 1961, 24; and Robert Welch, "Agenda," July 1961, 3.

25. Welch, "Agenda," January 1961, 19–20. The January date was announced in the May issue of the *Bulletin*. See "Agenda for the Month," *Bulletin*, May 1961, 13–15; and "Agenda," July 1961, 4–5.

26. Thomas Kuchel, quoted in Marquis Childs, "Rightists Threaten 'Silence of Fear,'" *Washington Post*, March 28, 1961.

27. Milton Young, "John Birch Society: Fascist Group," *Congressional Record*, April 3, 1961, 5,428.

28. John Shelley, "The John Birch Society," *Congressional Record*, April 24, 1961, 6,627.

29. Henry Reuss, "Nothing Funny about the John Birch Society," *Congressional Record*, April 12, 1961, 5,666.

30. Young, "John Birch Society," 5,428.

31. Editorial, "How to Stop Communism," *Chicago Sun-Times*, April 9, 1961.

32. Earl Warren, *The Memoirs of Earl Warren* (New York: Doubleday, 1977), 304–5. See also Cray, *Chief Justice*, 390–92.

33. Mendel Rivers, "Earl Warren's Fellow Travelers Smear John Birch Society," *Congressional Record*, March 22, 1961, 4,604; and Barry Goldwater, quoted in "Senator Cautions Birch Unit's Foes," *New York Times*, April 6, 1961.

34. Robert Welch, "Agenda for August," *Bulletin*, August 1961, 5–6. The contest was open to any undergraduate enrolled in any American college in the fall term of 1961. The essays were required to be typed, to be no longer than three thousand words, and to be postmarked no later than November 11, 1961. The committee of judges comprised Thomas Anderson, editor and publisher of *Farm and Ranch*; J. Bracken Lee, the former governor of Utah; Doane Lowery, president of the Flintridge Preparatory School for Boys in Pasadena, California; M. T. Phelps, former chief justice of the Arizona Supreme Court; and professor of American history Charles Tansill. $1,000 was to be awarded as the first prize, $500 for second, $300 for third, and $200 for fourth; there were five more prizes of $100 each.

35. Whitney North Seymour, quoted in Cabell Phillips, "Head of American Bar Association Stresses Role of International Law," *New York Times*, August 8, 1961. See also John Wicklein, "Birch Society Will Offer $2,300 [*sic*] for Impeach Warren Essays," *New York Times*, August 5, 1961.

36. Roscoe Drummond, "The $2,300 [*sic*] John Birch Society," *Washington Post*, August 13, 1961; and Associated Press, "Contest Offered to Answer Welch," *Arizona Republic*, August 10, 1961. On Warren's friendship with Storke, see Warren, *Memoirs*, 305–6.

37. Cray, *Chief Justice*, 392. The reaction to the contest was so negative that Welch told potential entrants that if they were worried about their identities being revealed, the winning essays could be published with a pseudonym attached ("Agenda for the Month," *Bulletin*, November 1961, 7).

38. "The Unveiling," *Time*, February 16, 1962, 23. See also Associated Press, "Student at U.C.L.A. Wins Birch Contest," *New York Times*, February 6, 1962.

39. Robert Welch, "The Movement to Impeach Earl Warren," *Bulletin*, June 1962, 11–12.

40. Welch, "Agenda," January 1961, 18; and Welch, "Movement," June 1962, 22.

41. See, for example, the photographs reproduced in the following issues of the *Bulletin*: July 1962, 12; April 1963, 12; September 1964, 6; and December 1964, 6–7. In his memoirs, Warren describes these "Impeach Earl Warren" billboards as "ludicrous." "I never was inflamed by them," he says, "and in passing one . . . I could even smile as I surveyed the surroundings and speculated as to why it was placed at that particular site" (*Memoirs*, 305). See also Newton, *Justice for All*, 385–87.

42. See, for example, the accounts of Warren's appearance at Emory Law School in Atlanta, Georgia, and at a meeting of the New York City Bar Association in, respectively, Claude Sitton, "Warren Asks Modern View of Law," *New York Times*, February 13, 1963, and Paul Crowell's "Pickets Jeer Warren Here and Hurl Placards," *New York Times*, October 30, 1963.

43. "Priest Is Censured for Warren Action," *New York Times*, November 9, 1963. As late as March 1968, impeaching Warren was the third step—after informing the people about the continuing communist threat facing the nation and "untying" congressional committees—Welch said he would take within the United States were he to become president ("If I Were President," *Bulletin*, March 1968, 27–28).

44. The fullest account of these events is William Doyle, *An American Insurrection: The Battle of Oxford, Mississippi, 1962* (New York: Doubleday, 2001). See also John Dittmer, *Local People: The Struggle for Civil Rights in Mississippi* (Urbana: University of Illinois Press, 1994), 138–42; Paul J. Scheips, *The Role of Federal Military Forces in Domestic Disorders, 1946–1992* (Washington, DC: Center of Military History, United States Army, 2005), 80–135; and Taylor Branch, *Parting the Waters: America in the King Years,*

1954–63 (New York: Simon and Schuster, 1988), 633–72. Meredith's personal account of the events is given in James H. Meredith, *Three Years in Mississippi* (Bloomington: Indiana University Press, 1966).

45. "Walker Is Facing Four Federal Counts," *New York Times*, October 2, 1962; and Associated Press, "Psychiatric Testing Ordered for Walker," *New York Times*, October 3, 1962.

46. John F. Kennedy, quoted in Robert Dallek, *An Unfinished Life: John F. Kennedy, 1917–1963* (New York: Little, Brown, 2003), 517.

47. Edwin Walker, quoted in Clive Webb, *Rabble Rousers: The American Far Right in the Civil Rights Era* (Athens: University of Georgia Press, 2010), 141. See also Scheips, *Domestic Disorders*, 17–68.

48. "An Address by Edwin A. Walker, Jackson, Miss., 29 Dec. 1961," in *The American Eagle Weapons for Freedom* (n.p.: ca. 1961), 4–5. Emphasis in original. See also Doyle, *American Insurrection*, 97. The weapons Walker had in mind were not military weapons, he said; they were "the Holy Bible, our state sovereignty, our constitutional rights, and our national independence" ("Address"). Webb notes that Walker's speech in Jackson was such a hit that the Citizens' Councils "used parts of it in a thirty minute propaganda film . . . distributed to television stations across the country" (*Rabble Rousers*, 145).

49. Edwin Walker, quoted in Webb, *Rabble Rousers*, 145.

50. Robert Welch, "A Postscript: At the Beginning (October 2, 1962)," *Bulletin*, September 1962, 33–34. Emphasis in original. Walker's arrest also caused consternation for some members of Congress. See, for example, the statements of Bruce Alger (R-TX), *Congressional Record*, October 2, 1962, 21,790–91; Spessard Holland (D-FL), *Congressional Record*, October 8, 1962, 22,783; Strom Thurmond (D-SC), *Congressional Record*, October 9, 1962, 22,882–88; and Fred Hall (Democratic Farmer-Labor Party-MN), *Congressional Record*, October 10, 1962, 23,109–11.

  Some congressmen were less than charitable, however. "I think it is high time that the authorities see to it that former Maj. Gen. Edwin Walker is promptly committed to a lunatic asylum; or, if he is proved to be sane, that he be tried and imprisoned for an interminable period for insurrection," was the view of John Rooney (D-NY), for instance (*Congressional Record*, October 1, 1962, 21,508).

51. Welch, "Postscript," 34.

52. Associated Press, "Birch Member Scores Walker," *New York Times*, October 4, 1962.

53. Robert Welch, "Defend the State's Rights of Mississippi," *Bulletin*, October 1962, 15.

54. Ibid. Emphasis in original.

55. Welch, "Defend the State's Rights of Mississippi," and "Federal Troops To: Cuba, Si—Mississippi, No!" *Bulletin*, October 1962, 15–16. The Birch Society's response to the crisis in Cuba is discussed in detail in the following chapter.

56. See, for example, Dallek, *Unfinished Life*, 516–18; Branch, *Parting the Waters*, 670–672 and 918–19; James T. Patterson, *Grand Expectations: The United States, 1945–1974* (New York: Oxford University Press, 1996), 474–78; and Adam Fairclough, *Better Day Coming: Blacks and Equality, 1890–2000* (London: Penguin, 2001), 263–66.

57. Harvard Sitkoff, *The Struggle for Black Equality, 1954–1992*, rev. ed. (New York: Hill and Wang, 1993), 115. For over a year, beginning in November 1961, the citizens of Albany engaged in an unsuccessful campaign of civil disobedience in an attempt to desegregate the city.

58. Martin Luther King Jr., quoted in Branch, *Parting the Waters*, 672.

59. Bob Dylan, "Oxford Town," *The Freewheelin' Bob Dylan* (Columbia, CL 2105, 1963). The full lyrics of the song can be read on Dylan's website, *www.bobdylan.com* (accessed

October 14, 2013). See also Clinton Heylin, *Revolution in the Air: The Songs of Bob Dylan, 1957–1973* (Chicago: Chicago Review Press, 2009), 107–9. Dylan would record another significant protest song, about the murder of NAACP field secretary Medgar Evers, in 1963. It was entitled "Only a Pawn in Their Game" and it can be found on the album *The Times They Are A-Changin'* (Columbia, CDCBS, 32390, 1964).

60. See Thomas Buckley, "Way Cleared Earlier," *New York Times*, October 7, 1962; and Eric Pace, "Gen. Edwin Walker, 83, Is Dead: Promoted Rightist Causes in 60's," *New York Times*, November 2, 1993.

61. Webb, *Rabble Rousers*, 147.

62. Ibid., 148. Although Operation Midnight Right often drew large and enthusiastic crowds, Walker's poor public speaking skills again let him down. "While Hargis was an 'emotional spellbinder,' the tongue-tied performances of Walker dampened the flames lit by the evangelist," Webb notes (149).

63. Earl Lively Jr., *The Invasion of Mississippi* (Belmont, MA: American Opinion, 1963); and Massachusetts State Legislature, *The Occupation of the Campus of the University of Mississippi, September 30, 1962, by the Department of Justice of the United States*, Report by the General Legislative Investigating Committee to the Massachusetts State Legislature, May 8, 1963 (Belmont, MA: American Opinion, 1964).

64. Massachusetts State Legislature, *Occupation*, 8. The General Legislative Investigating Committee was composed of Representatives Russell L. Fox, W. Luther Sims, and Walter M. Hester, and Senators George M. Yarbrough, Frank D. Barber, and Dennis M. Baker.

65. Sitkoff, *Black Equality*, 120–21.

66. Ibid., 131. See also Branch, *Parting the Waters*, 673–845; Fairclough, *Better Day*, 273–79; and David J. Garrow, *Bearing the Cross: Martin Luther King, Jr., and the Southern Christian Leadership Conference* (New York: Vintage, 1988), 231–86.

67. Patterson, *Grand Expectations*, 480; Fairclough, *Better Day*, 274, Branch, *Parting the Waters*, 803–45; and Sitkoff, *Black Equality*, 134–44.

68. Martin Luther King Jr., "Letter from Birmingham Jail," April 16, 1963, in David Howard-Pitney, *Martin Luther King Jr., Malcolm X and the Civil Rights Struggle of the 1950s and 1960s: A Brief History with Documents* (Boston: Bedford/St. Martin's, 2004), 84.

69. See Patterson, *Grand Expectations*, 480–81; Dallek, *Unfinished Life*, 594–600; Sitkoff, *Black Equality*, 147; and Fairclough, *Better Day*, 279–82.

70. Patterson, *Grand Expectations*, 482–83. See also Branch, *Parting the Waters*, 846–87.

71. Alan Stang, "The New Plantation," *American Opinion*, June 1963, 37–57; and Alan Stang, *It's Very Simple: The True Story of Civil Rights* (Belmont, MA: Western Islands, 1965).

72. James Baldwin, *The Fire Next Time* (London: Michael Joseph, 1963). The book had begun as an article in the *New Yorker* entitled "Letter from a Region in my Mind," November 17, 1962, 59–144.

73. Stang, "New Plantation," 38.

74. Ibid., 38–40.

75. Ibid., 39.

76. Ibid., 41.

77. Ibid., 40.

78. Ibid., 45. The conspiratorial rationale of the Birch Society is examined in detail in Chapter 6.

79. Stang, "New Plantation," 46.

80. Martin Gansberg, "Birch Rally Here Attended by 1,400: Speakers Tell of Communist 'Betrayal' of Rights Cause," *New York Times*, August 20, 1964; John Rousselot, "Civil Rights: Communist Betrayal of a Good Cause," *American Opinion*, February 1964, 1–11;

Medford Evans, "Mississippi: The Long Hot Summer," *American Opinion*, November 1964, 7–18, quote on 7; Ross R. Barnett, "The Rape of Our Constitution and Civil Rights," *American Opinion*, September 1963, 20–23, quote on 22; Martin Dies, "Negroes and the Problems America Faces," *American Opinion*, May 1965, 33–39, quote on 37; and Gary Allen, "The Summer of Communist Malcontents," *American Opinion*, September 1966, 1–20, quote on 3, emphasis added. See also Gary Allen, *Communist Revolution in the Streets* (Belmont, MA: Western Islands, 1967).

81. See, for example, Jim Lucier, "King of Slick," *American Opinion*, November 1963, 1–11; and Alan Stang, "The King and His Communists," *American Opinion*, October 1965, 1–14.

82. Robert Welch, "Dear Governor Rockefeller," *Bulletin*, August 1963, 1–32, quotes on 25–27 and 29; John Pepper, *American Negro Problems* (New York: Workers Library Publishers, 1928), quotes on 7 and 11–12, emphasis in original; and James W. Ford and James S. Allen, *The Negroes in a Soviet America* (New York: Workers Library Publishers, 1935). See also Robert Welch, *Two Revolutions at Once* (Belmont, MA: American Opinion, 1965).

83. On these issues, see, for example, Tim Weiner, *Enemies: A History of the FBI* (New York: Random House, 2012), 197–201 and 230–33; David J. Garrow, *The FBI and Martin Luther King Jr.: From "Solo" to Memphis* (New York: Norton, 1981); Curt Gentry, *J. Edgar Hoover: The Man and His Secrets* (New York: Norton, 1991); Kenneth O'Reilly, *Racial Matters: The FBI's Secret File on Black America, 1960–1972* (New York: Free Press, 1989); and Jay Feldman, *Manufacturing Hysteria: A History of Scapegoating, Surveillance, and Secrecy in Modern America* (New York: Pantheon Books, 2011), 262–70.

84. Fairclough, *Better Day*, 143. See also Theodore Draper, *American Communism and Soviet Russia* (1960; New Brunswick, NJ: Transaction Publishers, 2003), 315–56; and Nikhil Pal Singh, *Black Is a Country: Race and the Unfinished Struggle for Democracy* (Cambridge, MA: Harvard University Press, 2004), 109–19.

85. Michael Kazin, *American Dreamers: How the Left Changed a Nation* (New York: Knopf, 2011), 166.

86. Ibid., 192–93.

87. Weiner, *Enemies*, 233–35.

88. See Branch, *Parting the Waters*, 121, 853–54; and Garrow, *Bearing the Cross*, 150–153. "Hundreds of thousands of copies of the [King] picture littered the South and crowded its billboards," Richard M. Fried notes in *Nightmare in Red: The McCarthy Era in Perspective* (New York: Oxford University Press, 1990), 177.

89. Branch, *Parting the Waters*, 853.

90. See Fairclough, *Better Day*, 236–38; Branch, *Parting the Waters*, 850–58; Garrow, *Bearing the Cross*, 195–96 and 200–201; and Weiner, *Enemies*, 230–32. Levison was a particular target of Hoover's attention.

91. Draper, *American Communism*, 341.

92. Ibid., 346–47.

93. Ibid., 352–56. See also Fairclough, *Better Day*, 142–43.

94. As far back as May 1958, the Society had published an article by the black history professor and future American presidential candidate for the Independent Afro-American Party Clennon King. See "Negro Americans Back to Africa?" in *American Opinion*, May 1958, 21–26. See also George Schuyler, "For America: Let Negroes Give Thanks," *American Opinion*, November 1965, 11–16; and George Schuyler, "The Hangover: Negro Masses Are Turning from the Revolution," *American Opinion*, March 1967, 29–34.

95. Welch, "Dear Governor Rockefeller," 28–29, emphasis in original; and Manning Johnson, *Color, Communism and Common Sense* (New York: Alliance, 1958). The importance of the ex-communist to the anticommunist network of the Second Red Scare period is discussed in Ellen Schrecker's *The Age of McCarthyism: A Brief History with Documents*, 2nd ed. (Boston: Bedford/St. Martin's, 2002), 16–17. On the issue of the repentant insider in dissident political movements more broadly, see Richard Hofstadter, "The Paranoid Style in American Politics," in *The Paranoid Style in American Politics and Other Essays* (Cambridge, MA: Harvard University Press, 1965), especially 30–36.

96. Charles C. Diggs Jr., "Birchite Misrepresentation," *Congressional Record*, June 3, 1965, 12,577–78.

97. The Birch Society's instructions to its members to try and stop the bill can be found in the *Interim Bulletins* of August 8 and August 30, 1963, as well as that of February 8, 1964.

98. Robert Welch, "Foreword," *Bulletin*, July 1964, 1. The epigraph for the issue was John Paul Jones's "I have not yet begun to fight." See also Welch's "More Stately Mansions" speech, which was delivered at the Conrad Hotel in Chicago on June 5, 1964, and reproduced in *The New Americanism and Other Speeches and Essays* (Belmont, MA: Western Islands, 1976), 115–52.

99. On the events of Selma, see, for example, David Garrow, *Protest at Selma: Martin Luther King, Jr., and the Voting Rights Act of 1965* (New Haven, CT: Yale University Press, 1978); Garrow, *Bearing the Cross*, 357–430; Patterson, *Grand Expectations*, 579–85; Fairclough, *Better Day*, 289–93; and Sitkoff, *Black Equality*, 174–83.

100. Scott Stanley, "Revolution: The Assault on Selma," *American Opinion*, May 1965, 1–10, quotes on 1, 2, and 3.

101. Jim Lucier, "Civil Rites: Who Should Vote?" *American Opinion*, June 1965, 17–30, quotes on 30.

102. Medford Evans, "The Sheriff: Jim Clark of Selma," *American Opinion*, February 1966, 1–10, quotes on 4.

103. Peniel E. Joseph, *Waiting 'Til The Midnight Hour: A Narrative History of Black Power in America* (New York: Holt, 2006), 121.

104. On the events of Watts and the other riots and civil disturbances of this time, see also Allen J. Matusow, *The Unraveling of America: A History of Liberalism in the 1960s* (New York: Harper and Row, 1986), 360–75; Fairclough, *Better Day*, 296–300; and Patterson, *Grand Expectations*, 588–89.

105. This was not an explanation that was acceptable to Sam Yorty, the mayor of Los Angeles. He dismissed the charges of police brutality as a cause of the Watts riot as a "Communist conspiracy" (Joseph, *Midnight Hour*, 121).

106. William Parker, quoted in Rick Perlstein, *Nixonland: The Rise of a President and the Fracturing of a Nation* (New York: Scribner, 2008), 70–71.

107. Ronald Reagan, quoted in Perlstein, *Nixonland*, 71.

108. Critics of the report pointed out that such a thesis simply wasn't credible, as surveys of the rioting revealed at least thirty thousand people taking part and another eighty thousand acting as "supporters." There was also much pushback on the notion that the rioters had been purposeless. See Matusow, *Unraveling*, 361; and Fairclough, *Better Day*, 296.

109. A penetrating analysis of the mystique associated with the idea of "The Revolution" at this time can be found in Todd Gitlin's *The Sixties: Years of Hope, Days of Rage* (New York: Bantam Books, 1987), 345–48.

110. Gary Allen and Bill Richardson, "Los Angeles: Hell in the City of Angels," *American Opinion*, September 1965, 1–15, quotes on 2 and 10. A year later, the Birch Society

published another account of life in the Watts area of L.A., purportedly written by a law enforcement officer working there and predicting more riots to come: Christopher Martin [pseudonym], "Watts: The Fire Next Time," *American Opinion*, May 1966, 1–12.

111. Gary Allen, "The Plan: To Burn Los Angeles," *American Opinion*, May 1967, 31–40, quotes on 31 and 39–40.

112. From the vast literature on the black power movement and key figures like Carmichael, Brown, and Newton, see, for example, Joseph, *Midnight Hour*; Jeffrey O. G. Ogbar, *Black Power: Radical Politics and African American Identity* (Baltimore: Johns Hopkins University Press, 2004); William L. Van Deburg, *New Day in Babylon: The Black Power Movement and American Culture, 1965–1975* (Chicago: University of Chicago Press, 1992); and Stokely Carmichael and Charles Hamilton, *Black Power: The Politics of Liberation in America* (New York: Random House, 1967).

113. "When you talk of black power," Stokely Carmichael, the chairman of SNCC, had declared in 1967, "you talk of building a movement that will smash everything Western civilization has created" (quoted in Sitkoff, *Black Equality*, 203). Members of the Birch Society were not the only ones troubled by the black power movement and its rhetoric, of course. It aroused a generally negative reaction within American society. In the view of Roy Wilkins of the NAACP, for example, "No matter how endlessly they try to explain it, the term 'black power' means anti-white power. . . . It is a reverse Mississippi, a reverse Hitler, a reverse Ku Klux Klan" (quoted in Fairclough, *Better Day*, 314).

114. Gary Allen, "Black Power: American Opinion Goes to a Berkeley Rally," *American Opinion*, January 1967, 1–14, quote on 12.

115. E. Merrill Root, "On War: Of the Racial Keys," *American Opinion*, November 1966, 79–87, quote on 86.

116. Schuyler, "Hangover," 34.

117. Robert Welch, *To the Negroes of America* (Belmont, MA: American Opinion, 1967), 8. Emphasis in original.

118. Advertisement, *American Opinion*, October 1965, 104; and Schoenwald, *Time for Choosing*, 90.

119. Gladwin Hill, "Welch Reports the John Birch Society Is Thriving," *New York Times*, March 3, 1968.

120. Robert Welch, "Support Your Local Police," *Bulletin*, July 1963, 12–14.

121. Robert Welch, "Agenda for the Month," *Bulletin*, September 1967, 13.

122. On the Wallace and Nixon campaigns, see Dan T. Carter, *The Politics of Rage: George Wallace, the Origins of the New Conservatism, and the Transformation of American Politics* (New York: Simon and Schuster, 1995), 348–49; and Perlstein, *Nixonland*, 202–3. For a broader perspective on these issues, see Thomas J. Sugrue, *Sweet Land of Liberty: The Forgotten Struggle for Civil Rights in the North* (New York: Random House, 2008).

123. On the situation in Santa Ana and Philadelphia, see, for example, Associated Press, "Bircher Policemen Called Disruptive," *New York Times*, November 6, 1964; and William G. Weart, "Philadelphia Finds Birchers in Police," *New York Times*, November 14, 1964.

124. Eric Pace, "Leary to Allow Birchers in Force," *New York Times*, February 23, 1966.

125. John Lindsay, quoted in Eric Pace, "Mayor Denounces the Birch Society," *New York Times*, February 25, 1966.

126. Roy Wilkins, quoted in Pace, "Mayor Denounces."

127. Floyd McKissick, quoted in Richard E. Rustin, "Birchers and Policemen," *Wall Street Journal*, May 12, 1966; and "Booth Urges Leary to Bar Assignment of Birch Society Policemen at Rights Demonstrations," *New York Times*, March 14, 1966.

128. Alan W. Miller, letter to the editor, *New York Times*, March 5, 1966.

129. "Mayor Rejects Birch Aide's Offer of City Police Membership List," *New York Times*, March 1, 1966.

130. John Donahue, quoted in Eric Pace, "Policeman Happy in Birch Society," *New York Times*, March 11, 1966.

131. Editorial, "The Police Have Rights Too," *New York Times*, February 25, 1966; Eric Pace, "Lindsay Enters Birchers Dispute," *New York Times*, February 24, 1966; and William F. Buckley Jr., "Policemen Can Join Birchers, but Duty to Law Comes First," *Arizona Republic*, March 24, 1966.

132. "Police Have Rights Too."

133. Eric Pace, "Rule on Birchers Displeases Leary," *New York Times*, May 28, 1966.

134. Patterson, *Grand Expectations*, 685–86; and Matusow, *Unraveling*, 396 and 409–10.

135. Susan Huck, "Insurrection: Is America Sleeping through Civil War," *American Opinion*, June 1968, 1–25, quote on 1.

136. Gary Allen, "America, 1968: Why the Score Is So High," *American Opinion*, July-August 1968, 1–20, quotes on 20, 4, and 11.

137. Huck, "Insurrection," 25; and Allen, "America, 1968," 17.

138. A sampling of Birch Society views on these subjects can be found in Gary Allen and John Rousselot, "Sunset Strip: Dope, Kooks, Kids and Communists," *American Opinion*, April 1967, 1–12; E. Merrill Root, "Pornography: Rats' Feet Tinkling over Broken Glass," *American Opinion*, June 1965, 65–76; Jere Real, "The 'S.D.S.': Students for A Democratic Society," *American Opinion*, February 1966, 73–80; and Bill Richardson, "The Press and the Vietniks," *American Opinion*, January 1966, 1–14.

CHAPTER 5

1. Robert Welch, *The Blue Book of the John Birch Society* (Belmont, MA: Western Islands, 1961), 24. Emphasis in original.

2. John F. Kennedy, quoted in Martin Walker, *The Cold War and the Making of the Modern World* (London: Vintage, 1994), 132. Kennedy had been given top-secret intelligence by the Eisenhower administration that showed that the "missile gap" actually favored the United States. On this, see, for example, Campbell Craig and Fredrik Logevall, *America's Cold War: The Politics of Insecurity* (Cambridge, MA: Belknap Press, 2009), 191–92.

3. Robert Welch, *May God Forgive Us* (Chicago: Henry Regnery, 1952); and Robert Welch, *The Life of John Birch: In the Story of One American Boy, the Ordeal of His Age* (Chicago: Henry Regnery, 1954). This was also the role Welch saw for *American Opinion*: to be "a leading authority on international affairs and on all aspects of the Cold War" ("Agenda for the Month," *Bulletin*, December 1960, 8). *May God Forgive Us* was republished by the Birch Society with the addition of Welch's 1957 "biographical sketch" of Chiang Kai-shek as *Again, May God Forgive Us!* in 1972.

4. Welch, *Blue Book*, 15. On Welch's visits to South Korea and West Germany, see G. Edward Griffin, *The Life and Words of Robert Welch: Founder of the John Birch Society* (Thousand Oaks, CA: American Media, 1975), 179–87.

5. Welch, *Blue Book*, 15–16. Emphasis added.

6. Ibid., 148. On the importance of Matthews to the anticommunist Right in the United States, see Richard Gid Powers, *Not without Honor: The History of American Anticommunism* (New York: Free Press, 1995), 104–6, 125–26, 230–33, and 241. On his brief official involvement with McCarthy's subcommittee, see David M. Oshinsky, *A Conspiracy So Immense: The World of Joe McCarthy* (New York: Oxford University Press, 2005), 318–20. The appointment came to an abrupt end in July 1953 when Matthews published an article in the *American Mercury* claiming that the "largest single group

supporting the Communist apparatus in the United States is composed of Protestant clergymen" (quoted in Oshinsky, *Conspiracy*, 319).

7. *America's Retreat from Victory* was the title McCarthy gave to the published version of his extraordinary attack on George Marshall as one of the principal U.S. enablers of Moscow's drive for world domination, which he delivered in the Senate on June 14, 1951. Joseph R. McCarthy, *America's Retreat from Victory: The Story of George Marshall* (New York: Devin-Adair, 1954).

8. Welch, *Blue Book*, 2–3.

9. Harry Overstreet and Bonaro Overstreet, *The Strange Tactics of Extremism* (New York: Norton, 1964), 73–74.

10. Welch, *Blue Book*, 4–5.

11. Welch, *May God Forgive Us*, 73.

12. Arthur Bliss Lane was the U.S. ambassador to Poland between 1944 and 1947 and a prominent Cold War crusader thereafter. For his views on the "appeasement" and "surrender to Stalin" of Yalta, see *I Saw Poland Betrayed* (Indianapolis: Bobbs-Merrill, 1948), especially 77–88. His wider Cold War career is discussed in Robert Szmczak's "Cold War Crusader: Arthur Bliss Lane and the Private Committee to Investigate the Katyn Massacre, 1949–1952," *Polish American Studies* 67, no. 2 (Autumn 2010): 5–33; and Robert Szmczak, "Hopes and Promises: Arthur Bliss Lane, the Republican Party, and the Slavic-American Vote, 1952," *Polish American Studies* 45, no. 1 (Spring 1988): 12–28.

13. The two most predominant myths of Yalta are that Stalin broke clear promises he had given to Roosevelt and Churchill about the fate of Eastern Europe and that the ailing Roosevelt had simply "sold out" Poland and other nations to the Soviets. Diplomatic historians tend to point out that the United States and Great Britain in actuality had little leverage over the Soviet Union at Yalta and that the agreements themselves were simply open to multiple interpretations. See Athan G. Theoharis, *The Yalta Myths: An Issue in U.S. Politics, 1945–1955* (Columbia: University Press of Missouri, 1970); George C. Herring, *From Colony to Superpower: U.S. Foreign Relations since 1776* (New York: Oxford University Press, 2008), 584–86; and Craig and Logevall, *America's Cold War*, 41–43.

14. Theoharis argues that there were actually three factions of the Republican Party—the "extremists," the "moderates," and the "partisans"—all seeking to use the Yalta issue between 1945 and 1955. Taft and McCarthy he regarded as firmly in the "extremist" camp (*Yalta Myths*, 5). See also Julian E. Zelizer, *Arsenal of Democracy: The Politics of National Security—From World War II to the War on Terrorism* (New York: Basic Books, 2010), 65–66.

15. Theoharis, *Yalta Myths*, 142–43.

16. Welch, *Blue Book*, 6–9.

17. Welch, *May God Forgive Us*, 9. Emphasis added.

18. Three of the most prominent figures in the China Lobby were Senator William Knowland (R-CA); the publisher of *Time* and *Life* magazines, Henry Luce; and the businessman Alfred Kohlberg. See Ross H. Koen, *The China Lobby in American Politics* (New York: Harper and Row, 1974); and Stanley D. Bachrack, *The Committee of One Million: "China Lobby" Politics, 1953–1971* (New York: Columbia University Press, 1976).

19. Dean Acheson, quoted in Powers, *Not without Honor*, 228. See also Robert L. Beisner, *Dean Acheson: A Life in the Cold War* (New York: Oxford University Press, 2009), 185–89.

20. Although this was not how it was generally understood, as Craig and Logevall note, even

at the time many of America's senior foreign policy analysts, including the "godfather" of containment, George Kennan, argued that the "loss" of China did not endanger the basic Cold War strategy of the U.S., which was to prevent the USSR dominating the Eurasian landmass. *America's Cold War*, 118–19.

21. Welch, *May God Forgive Us*, 9–17.

22. On these issues, see, for example, Robert Kagan, *Dangerous Nation: America's Foreign Policy from Its Earliest Days to the Dawn of the Twentieth Century* (New York: Vintage, 2006); William Pfaff, *The Irony of Manifest Destiny* (New York: Walker, 2010); Andrew J. Bacevich, *The Limits of Power: The End of American Exceptionalism* (New York: Holt, 2008); and Peter Beinart, *The Icarus Syndrome: A History of American Hubris* (New York: HarperCollins, 2010).

23. The idea that communism was a virus was a commonly employed metaphor of the time. See, for example, J. Edgar Hoover's testimony before HUAC on March 26, 1947, in Ellen Schrecker, *The Age of McCarthyism: A Brief History with Documents*, 2nd ed. (Boston: Bedford/St. Martin's, 2002), 133.

24. On these issues, see, for example, John E. Haynes, *Red Scare or Red Menace? American Communism and Anticommunism in the Cold War Era* (Chicago: Ivan R. Dee, 1996), especially 137–62; David H. Bennett, *The Party of Fear: The American Far Right from Nativism to the Militia Movement*, rev. ed. (New York: Vintage, 1995), 273–15; Powers, *Not without Honor*, 191–233; and Oshinsky, *Conspiracy So Immense*, 95–102.

25. An excellent introduction to the significance of the Hiss case in American political culture is Susan Jacoby's *Alger Hiss and the Battle for History* (New Haven, CT: Yale University Press, 2009). See also Sam Tanenhaus, *Whittaker Chambers: A Biography* (New York: Random House, 1997), 203–439.

26. "Web of subversion" is James Burnham's phrase, taken from his book *Web of Subversion: Underground Networks in the U.S. Government* (New York: John Day, 1954). Welch's description of Hiss's influence at Yalta can be found in *May God Forgive Us*, 28.

27. See, for example, Robert Welch, "United Nations—Get US Out!" *Bulletin*, April 1963, 14–15. An interesting account of opposition to the UN within the United States during the mid-1950s can be found in Gene Martin's "The U.N. Haters: Death Rattlers in San Francisco," *Nation*, May 14, 1955, 419–21.

28. Robert Welch, *The Politician* (Belmont, MA: Belmont Publishing, 1963), 169–70.

29. Ibid., 6.

30. McCarthy, *Retreat from Victory*, 168.

31. Khrushchev's 1956 speech at the Twentieth Party Congress in Moscow denouncing Stalin's crimes and his "cult of personality" was secret but its contents were deliberately leaked to the Western press. As for the inevitability of war between communist and capitalist nations, Stalin had reiterated this staple of Marxist-Leninist thought in a speech at the Bolshoi Theater in Moscow in 1946 at the very start of the Cold War. On these issues, as well as on Khrushchev's foreign policy in general during this period, see Walker, *Cold War*, 103–11; Craig and Logevall, *America's Cold War*, 183–87; and Aleksandr Fursenko and Timothy Naftali, *Khrushchev's Cold War: The Inside Story of an American Adversary* (New York: Norton, 2006).

32. Welch, *Politician*, 156–57. "Phrase-making is a far more important part of the Communist arsenal in the Communist-style war they are now fighting, than rockets or submarines," Welch maintained in the December 1959 issue of *American Opinion*. "'Containment,' when what is planned is exactly the opposite of holding the Communist tyranny within its current boundaries; 'peaceful coexistence,' when what is intended is the subversion and swallowing up, by aggressive trouble-making that is exactly the

opposite of 'peaceful,' the non-Communist countries in this 'coexistence'; these and a dozen other catch phrases carry us and the rest of the still free world nearer every day towards the grave in which the Kremlin expects to bury us" ("If You Want It Straight," 26–27).

33. Useful introductions to Eisenhower's foreign policy, including his covert overthrow of the governments of Mohammed Mossadeqh in Iran and Jacobo Arbenz Guzman in Guatemala, can be found in Craig and Logevall, *America's Cold War*, 139–76; Herring, *From Colony to Superpower*, 651–701; and Stephen E. Ambrose, *Eisenhower*, vol. 2, *The President* (New York: Simon and Schuster, 1984), especially 109–12, 171–72, 192–97, and 224–26.

34. Unlike other *National Review* editors, Burnham also believed that Khrushchev's "thaw," although "modest," was nonetheless "real," as did another prominent anticommunist and *National Review* contributor, Whittaker Chambers. Chambers resigned from the magazine in September 1960 over the issue. On Burnham and Chambers's thinking, as well as their conflicts within *National Review*, see George H. Nash, *The Conservative Intellectual Movement in America since 1945*, 30th anniv. ed. (Wilmington, DE: ISI Books, 2006), 139–60; John B. Judis, *William F. Buckley, Jr.: Patron Saint of the Conservatives* (New York: Simon and Schuster, 1988), 144–58 and 174–78; Tanenhaus, *Whittaker Chambers*, 512–13; James Burnham, *The Struggle for the World* (New York: John Day, 1947); and James Burnham, *Containment or Liberation? An Inquiry into the Aims of United States Foreign Policy* (New York: John Day, 1953).

35. Robert Welch, "A Letter to Khrushchev," March 3, 1958, in *The New Americanism and Other Speeches and Essays* (Belmont, MA: Western Islands, 1976), 17–55.

36. Lyndon Johnson, quoted in Paul Dickson, *Sputnik: The Shock of the Century* (New York: Walker, 2001), 113–17. See also Robert A. Divine, *The Sputnik Challenge* (New York: Oxford University Press, 1993); and Fursenko and Naftali, *Khrushchev's Cold War*, 138–57.

37. *Washington Post*, December 20, 1957, quoted in Walker, *Cold War*, 115. Although the commission was chaired by H. Rowland Gaither Jr., Paul Nitze (the author of NSC 68) was the primary author of its report, which contained similar recommendations for a massive military buildup by the United States. See Divine, *Sputnik*, 37.

38. Welch, "Letter to Khrushchev," 25–26.

39. Contrasting views of Reagan's role in bringing about the end of the Cold War can be found in Raymond Garthoff, *The Great Transition: American-Soviet Relations and the End of the Cold War* (Washington, DC: Brookings Institution Press, 1984); Peter Schweizer, *Reagan's War: The Epic Story of His Forty-Year Struggle and Final Triumph over Communism* (New York: Doubleday, 2002); Paul Kengor, *The Crusader: Ronald Reagan and the Fall of Communism* (New York: Regan, 2006); and Frances Fitzgerald, *Way Out There in the Blue: Reagan, Star Wars and the End of the Cold War* (New York: Simon and Schuster, 2000).

40. Fursenko and Naftali, *Khrushchev's Cold War*, 243 and 256.

41. Craig and Logevall, *America's Cold War*, 175.

42. Welch, "Letter to Khrushchev," 19. Malenkov had "resigned" as Soviet premier in February 1955 as result of the machinations of Khrushchev and the Soviet foreign minister, Vyacheslav Molotov. He was replaced by Marshal Nikolai Bulganin; Khrushchev would not formally assume the position until March 27, 1958. In doing so, he became the first person since Stalin to be both premier of the Soviet Union and first secretary of the Communist Party.

43. Welch, "Letter to Khrushchev," 26-27 and 24.

44. Ibid., 43–44. Emphasis in original.

45. Ibid., 47–49.

46. The occupation of West Berlin by France, Great Britain, and the United States did not just represent a symbolic problem for the Soviets—Western forces nestled deep within the Eastern bloc—it was also a practical one, in that it provided an escape route for thousands of skilled East German workers. See Fursenko and Naftali, *Khrushchev's Cold War*, 185–213; and Herring, *From Colony to Superpower*, 695–96.

47. Welch, *Blue Book*, 79; and Griffin, *Life and Words*, 278. Kohlberg was also a member of the Birch Society's National Council. On the Committee of One Million, see Bachrack, *Committee of One Million*, especially 51–81. Another likely source of influence would have been Ten Million Americans Mobilizing for Justice, the committee formed to protest the censure of Joe McCarthy in 1954.

48. "Petition: Please, Mr. President, Don't Go!," *American Opinion*, August 1959, 60.

49. "The President's News Conference of August 3, 1959," in *Public Papers of the Presidents of the United States: Dwight D. Eisenhower, 1959* (Washington, DC: Government Printing Office, 1960), 560–65. Keen to improve relations with the United States so that he could divert resources from the Soviet Union's military budget to the economy, Khrushchev had first floated the idea of visiting the USA in a meeting with American governors on July 7, 1959. Eisenhower was also interested in the idea of disarmament talks, not least because he had begun to see the limitations and dangers of his policy of massive retaliation. But the invitation itself arose from a slight misunderstanding. The president had wanted to make it conditional on progress being made in the foreign ministers' meetings going on in Geneva over the situation in Berlin, but it was not issued with sufficient specificity and Khrushchev was able to accept it at face value. See Ambrose, *Eisenhower*, 535. The number of CASE's petitions is given in Arron Max Berkowitz, "Mr. Khrushchev Goes to Washington: Domestic Opposition to Nikita Khrushchev's 1959 Visit to America" (PhD dissertation, University of Illinois at Chicago, 2010), 111.

50. "Petition: Please, President Eisenhower, Don't!," insert, *Blue Book*. The records are incomplete, but at least 6,927 of these petitions were received at the White House between August 24 and September 24, 1959 (Gary Tocchet, "September Thaw: Khrushchev's Visit to America, 1959" [PhD dissertation, Stanford University, 1995], quoted in Berkowitz, "Mr. Khrushchev," 114).

51. "Petition: Please, President Eisenhower, Don't!"

52. "Goldwater Denies Knowing He Joined Birch Front Group," *New York Times*, October 19, 1964; and Robert Welch, "Agenda for the Month," *Bulletin*, June 1961, 20. In January 1962, Goldwater joined another Birch front group, the American Committee for Aid to Katanga Freedom Fighters, which supported anticommunist secessionists in the Congo, although Robert Goldberg suggests in this case Goldwater may not have known it was an organization run by the Birch Society. See Robert Alan Goldberg, *Barry Goldwater* (New Haven, CT: Yale University Press, 1995), 159.

53. Carl T. Bogus, *Buckley: William F. Buckley Jr. and the Rise of American Conservatism* (New York: Bloomsbury Press, 2011), 183–84. CASE was a classic letterhead organization, and there is little evidence that the members of the Executive Committee or the National Board did anything more than lend their names to it.

54. See, for example, "Eisenhower Falls to the Summit," *National Review*, August 15, 1959, 262–65; "What Khrushchev Intends," *National Review*, August 29, 1959, 293–94; "Triumphal March," *National Review*, September 12, 1959, 318–19; and Gary Wills, "Nero in Our Camp," *National Review*, September 12, 1959, 332–33. See also Jonathan M. Schoenwald, *A Time for Choosing: The Rise of Modern American Conservatism* (New York: Oxford University Press, 2001), 40–45.

55. Peter Kihss, "2500 Anti-Communists Rally; Mayor and President Scored," *New York Times*, September 18, 1959; and Schoenwald, *Time for Choosing*, 42.

56. Bogus, *Buckley*, 186. Emphasis in original. The text of Buckley's address can be found in "The Damage We Have Done," *National Review*, September 25, 1959, 349–51.

57. Committee for Freedom of All Peoples, "A Call for National Mourning," advertisement, *National Review*, September 12, 1959, 323; "Americans Exhorted to Greet Khrushchev with 'Civil Silence,'" *New York Times*, August 24, 1959; Schoenwald, *Time for Choosing*, 42; and Fursenko and Naftali, *Khrushchev's Cold War*, 233–35.

58. "One reason I was suspicious was that I remembered in the early years after the Revolution, when contacts were first being established with the bourgeois world, a Soviet delegation was invited to a meeting held in someplace called Prince's Island. It came out in the newspapers that it was to these islands that stray dogs were sent to die. . . . I was afraid maybe this Camp David was the same sort of place, where people who were mistrusted could be kept in quarantine," Khrushchev recalled. Quoted in Fursenko and Naftali, *Khrushchev's Cold War*, 227–28.

59. On the Camp David discussions, see Craig and Logevall, *America's Cold War*, 186–87; and Ambrose, *Eisenhower*, 542–45.

60. Copies of the postcards and advertisements to which the slogans were attached can be found in the appendix to the *White Book of the John Birch Society* (Belmont, MA: John Birch Society, 1961).

61. Robert Welch, "Agenda for January," *Bulletin*, December 1959, 11. See also Robert Welch, "Get the Summit Postponed Again," *Bulletin*, February 1960, 16–21; and Robert Welch, "Letter Writing for May," *Bulletin*, May 1960, 15–23.

62. The fullest account of the U-2 affair is Michael Beschloss's *Mayday: Eisenhower, Khrushchev and the U-2 Affair* (New York: Harper and Row, 1988).

63. Robert Welch, "General Comment," *Bulletin*, June 1960, 2–6.

64. Ibid., 3–4. Emphasis in original. Oddly, Edward Griffin's account of CASE in his biography of Welch does not even mention the U-2 incident. In his telling, Eisenhower's failure to visit the Soviet Union was due to his need to "look after his grandchildren" (*Life and Words*, 279).

65. Dwight D. Eisenhower, quoted in Fursenko and Naftali, *Khrushchev's Cold War*, 289; Khrushchev's beliefs about Dulles are discussed on 271, 278, and 286. Powers was tried in August 1960, and sentenced to three years in prison with an additional sentence of seven years hard labor. He returned to the United States as part of a spy swap in February 1962.

66. Carl Bogus suggests that CASE was created simply as a "recruiting vehicle" for the Society, but this is to dismiss Welch and his colleagues' genuine concern about the impact the summits would have on American interests and national security. There is no reason to think that the Birchers' concerns in this regard were any less real than Buckley's and Goldwater's were, for example. See Bogus, *Buckley*, 182. As an example of the fund-raising ability of the campaign, as well as an indication of the still infant state of the Birch Society's organization, Welch recalled in the 1961 edition of *The Blue Book* how at one point in the campaign against Khrushchev's visit, the Society "had on hand what later proved to be about twenty thousand dollars which we were unable to use for three full days, because nobody could get to the job of processing the hundreds of small checks that were involved, so that they could be deposited" (*Blue Book*, 99).

67. The phrase is Welch's, from "Foreword," *Bulletin*, March 1961.

68. The following discussion is drawn from Thomas G. Paterson, *Contesting Castro: The United States and the Triumph of the Cuban Revolution* (New York: Oxford University Press, 1994); Fursenko and Naftali, *Khrushchev's Cold War*; Ambrose, *Eisenhower*; and

Herring, *Colony to Superpower*. Two very useful biographies of Castro are Tad Szulc's *Fidel: A Critical Portrait* (New York: Morrow, 1986); and Volker Skierka's *Fidel Castro: A Biography* (Cambridge: Polity, 2004).

69. On Nixon, see Fursenko and Naftali, *Khrushchev's Cold War*, 299; on the CIA's advice to Eisenhower, see Ambrose, *Eisenhower*, 527.

70. John F. Kennedy, quoted in Fursenko and Naftali, *Khrushchev's Cold War*, 339.

71. On the Bay of Pigs invasion, see, for example, Howard Jones, *The Bay of Pigs* (New York: Oxford University Press, 2008); and Aleksandr Fursenko and Timothy Naftali, *"One Hell of a Gamble": Khrushchev, Castro and Kennedy, 1958–1964* (New York: Norton, 1997), 77–100.

72. Robert Welch, "If You Want It Straight," *American Opinion*, December 1959, 21. See also James Burnham, "Is Fidel Castro a Communist?" *National Review*, August 15, 1959, 268.

73. Kennedy was attacked for his "barbarism" by the Left and for his "spinelessness" by the Right—especially over his failure to authorize American military airstrikes that might have saved the invaders. Yet, for all the criticism, it is often forgotten that there was also a great deal of support for the president, at least in terms of his plans to remove Castro, if not their execution. The United States was "engaged in an all-out struggle to save the Western Hemisphere for democracy and freedom," ran a supportive editorial in the *New York Times*, for example, while the *Washington Post* worried that the invasion's failure would make it appear to the world that the USSR had saved its "Cuban stooges by intimidating the United States." That, it said, was the "unlovely prospect that may confront this country unless the effort to deliver Cuba from the Communists quickly catches hold." *New York Times*, April 20, 1961, and *Washington Post*, April 19, 1961, both quoted in Walker, *Cold War*, 149–50. See also Herring, *From Colony to Superpower*, 706–7.

74. Robert Welch, "Agenda for the Month," *Bulletin*, June 1961, 6.

75. Ibid., 5. Welch had been on a speaking tour of the West Coast at the time of the invasion, and he claimed to have predicted how it would turn out in response to a question from the floor even before it began. See "6,000 Hear Welch in Coast Address," *New York Times*, April 12, 1961.

76. Welch, *Politician*, xvii.

77. Ibid., xvii–xviii. Anthony Kubek also stressed the importance of this in "Fidel Castro on Tour," *American Opinion*, October 1963, 1–12.

78. Welch, *Politician*, xviii–xix.

79. Ibid., xix–xxi. Emphasis in original.

80. Ibid., xxi. Welch may have removed the most damning claims against Eisenhower, but the official publication of *The Politician* also made it difficult for him to maintain the argument that the manuscript had nothing to do with the Birch Society. In an erratum to the fifth printing of the book, Welch noted that the "only error anybody has ever been able to find in any published version of *The Politician*" was his mistaken reference to Milton Eisenhower—who served as the president's expert on Latin America—having had a secret meeting with Castro in the Cuban hills just six weeks before the capture of Havana. It now appeared that the president's brother had "exchanged messages" with the Cuban leader, Welch said (xviii).

81. Wallace Carroll, "President Tells Nation Struggle with Reds Will Last Decade," and "Transcript of the President's News Conference on World and Domestic Affairs," *New York Times*, April 22, 1961; and Tom Wicker, "President Finds Deficit Spending Aids New Budget," *New York Times*, January 2, 1962.

82. The transcript of Case's address can be found in the *Congressional Record*, January 23, 1962, 681–82.

83. It was a point on which the Society's critics seemed able to agree upon. As discussed in Chapter 2, this theme was also one of the chief avenues of attack of Gus Hall and Irwin Suall, and also formed the basis of Walter Reuther's recommendations to the Kennedy administration in the Reuther memorandum.

84. Robert Welch, "Dear Reader," *American Opinion*, May 1962, foreword. The situation also put the Founder in mind of a poem about the nineteenth-century theologian and master of Oxford University's Balliol College, which runs:

> My name is Benjamin Jowett,
> I'm Master of Balliol College;
> Whatever is knowledge I know it,
> And what I don't know isn't knowledge.

85. Ibid.

86. "Welch, on L.I., Calls U.S. Soft on Reds," *New York Times*, June 19, 1962.

87. There is an extremely rich literature on the Cuban missile crisis. The discussion that follows is drawn in particular from Fursenko and Naftali, *"One Hell of a Gamble"*; Dallek, *Unfinished Life*, 535–75; Michael Beschloss, *The Crisis Years: Kennedy and Khrushchev, 1960–1963* (New York: HarperCollins, 1991); Thomas G. Paterson, "Fixation with Cuba: The Bay of Pigs, Missile Crisis, and Covert War against Cuba," in *Kennedy's Quest for Victory: American Foreign Policy, 1961–1963*, ed. Thomas G. Paterson (New York: Oxford University Press, 1989), 123–55; and Sheldon M. Stern, *The Week the World Stood Still: Inside the Secret Cuban Missile Crisis* (Stanford, CA: Stanford University Press, 2005). See also Michael Dobbs, *One Minute to Midnight: Kennedy, Khrushchev, and Castro on the Brink of Nuclear War* (New York: Knopf, 2008); and Max Frankel, *High Noon in the Cold War* (New York: Presidio Press, 2004).

88. Robert Welch, "Cuba," *Bulletin*, December 1962, 27.

89. Richard Nixon, quoted in Beschloss, *Crisis Years*, 557. The Democrats won four seats in the Senate and suffered only a net loss of two in the House, "the best midterm showing of any party holding the White House since 1934," Beschloss notes, although he argues that civil rights and other domestic matters were actually the key issues in the elections.

90. Welch, "Cuba," 27–28. Emphasis in original.

91. There was in fact some degree of ambiguity about Kennedy's noninvasion pledge. In his November 20, 1963, press conference, for example, the president explained that since the preconditions for the pledge had not been met, including onsite inspections and various verification procedures, he was not able to issue the "guarantee" formally. He did say, though, that provided offensive weapons were kept out of Cuba and Castro ended "the export of aggressive Communist purposes," there would be "peace in the Caribbean" (Stern, *World Stood Still*, 210).

    The Taiwan crises had arisen over the tiny Quemoy-Matsu island chain in the strait, which Chiang had hoped to use to launch his re-takeover of China and which Mao claimed belonged to the mainland. During the first crisis of 1954–1955, the Eisenhower administration had threatened nuclear retaliation if the Chinese tried to invade the islands. But during the second, it made a distinction, saying that it would come to the defense of Taiwan if it was attacked by China, but not the islands alone. See Craig and Logevall, *America's Cold War*, 150–53 and 180–83.

92. Welch, "Cuba," 28. Emphasis in original. This is not the view of most historians, needless to say. As Fursenko and Naftali point out, once the missiles were gone, the Soviet premier was no closer to strategic parity with the United States and still had no deal on Berlin (*Khrushchev's Cold War*, 492).

93. Welch, "Cuba," 29.

94. Slobodan M. Draskovich, "The Ventriloquist and the Dummy," *American Opinion*,

January 1963, 41–48. Emphasis in original. See also Slobodan M. Draskovich, *Tito: Moscow's Trojan Horse* (Chicago: Henry Regnery, 1957).

95.   Robert Welch, "Cuba Free—In '63," *Bulletin*, January 1963, 20–21. According to Welch, the idea of the "Cuba Free" campaign had come from a Birch chapter in a city in a southern state, but he didn't specify where exactly.

96.   On opposition to the Test Ban Treaty and disarmament in general, see Robert Welch, "To All Chapter Leaders," *Interim Bulletin*, August 8, 1963, 1–2; and John Rousselot, "Disarmament," *American Opinion*, February 1963, 11–17.

97.   Robert Welch, "Cuba Free—In '63," *Bulletin*, September 1963, 99–100. See also Robert Welch, "Free Cuba," *Bulletin*, November 1963, 9–11.

98.   Welch, *Politician*, 145–46. The literature on the Vietnam War, both academic and general, is overwhelming. Useful—and relatively brief—introductions to the subject can be found in George C. Herring, *America's Longest War: The United States and Vietnam, 1950–1975*, 4th ed. (Boston: McGraw-Hill, 2001); Marilyn Young, *The Vietnam Wars, 1945–1990* (New York: Harper, 1991); Robert Schulzinger, *A Time for War* (New York: Oxford University Press, 1997); and James S. Olson and Randy Roberts, *Where the Domino Fell: America and Vietnam, 1945–1995*, rev. 5th ed. (Malden, MA: Wiley-Blackwell, 2008).

99.   Robert Welch, "If You Want It Straight," *American Opinion*, December 1965, 1–2.

100. Hilaire du Berrier, "About South Vietnam," *American Opinion*, February 1958, 7–12. The article was actually a republication of a December 1957 piece du Berrier had written for the National Economic Council of New York.

101. See, for example, Hilaire du Berrier, *Background to Betrayal: The Tragedy of Vietnam* (Belmont, MA: Western Islands, 1965); and Hilaire du Berrier, "From Saigon: Our Correspondent on Tu Do Street," *American Opinion*, January 1967, 15–16.

102. Detailed information on du Berrier's remarkable life is not easy to locate. The biographical sketch in this chapter is based on his own "About the Author" account in *Background to Betrayal*, 298–306; James P. Lucier's "Hilaire du Berrier: Spy from North Dakota," *Insight on the News*, January 4, 1991, 21; and Richard Harris Smith's book, *OSS: The Secret History of America's First Central Intelligence Agency* (Berkeley: University of California Press, 1972).

103. Welch, *May God Forgive Us*, 3.

104. Du Berrier, quoted in Smith, *OSS*, 18.

105. On the Eisenhower administration's involvement in Vietnam and support for Diem, see David Anderson, *Trapped by Success: The Eisenhower Administration and Vietnam, 1953–1961* (New York: Columbia University Press, 1991); George McT. Kahin, *Intervention: How America Became Involved in Vietnam* (New York: Anchor Books, 1986); and Herring, *Longest War*, 45–87.

106. Du Berrier, "About South Vietnam," 12. Italics in original.

107. Hilaire du Berrier, "The Diem Myth," *American Opinion*, October 1963, 55–59, quotes on 59 and 55.

108. On the Kennedy administration's conduct of the war, see, for example, Fredrik Logevall, *Choosing War: The Lost Chance for Peace and the Escalation of the War in Vietnam* (Berkeley: University of California Press, 1999); David Kaiser, *American Tragedy: Kennedy, Johnson and the Origins of the Vietnam War* (Cambridge, MA: Belknap Press, 2000); and Herring, *Longest War*, 89–129.

109. Du Berrier, *Background to Betrayal*, 273–74. *National Review* had been a major supporter of the Diem regime, for example, and struggled to come to terms with what Diem's death meant for U.S. policy in Vietnam. See Bogus, *Buckley*, 311–13.

110. Du Berrier, *Background to Betrayal*, 284.

111. Ibid.

112. Ibid., 284–85.

113. The "whiz kids" was the name used to describe business leaders and academics like McNamara, McGeorge Bundy, and Walt Rostow, who were brought into the Kennedy administration. See David Halberstam, *The Best and the Brightest* (New York: Random House, 1972).

114. A. F. Canwell, "Robert McNamara: Strange Is His Middle Name," *American Opinion*, September 1963, 1–10; and Jack Moffitt, "Moffitt on Films," *American Opinion*, June 1963, 57–58. "The 'Revolution in the Pentagon' is proceeding smoothly," Canwell wrote. "The graven image which has replaced God for the Socialists who are entrenched there is the Red Dove of Peace. The thirty-three battle paintings in the Department of Defense have already been removed and replaced with paintings of the tranquil majesty of the High Sierras. We wait now to hear the strains of the *Internationale* in pianissimo" (10). Moffitt actually seemed to like *The Ugly American*. It was "definitely not pro-Communist," he said, and there were some "stunning scenes of locations in Bangkok and some exciting riot scenes," but neither the film nor book made it clear "how America was to win a cold war or a hot war while handicapped by a State Department dedicated to a 'no-win' policy or by an Administration determined to merge the sovereignty of the United States into a socialistic world state dominated by the Soviets" (58). The historian Charles Callan Tansill also took the whiz kids to task in "The President . . . Up with Which We Will Not Put," *American Opinion*, November 1963, 31–38.

115. On other, similar conservative critiques of the United States' conduct of the war in Vietnam, see, for example, Goldberg, *Goldwater*, 191–92 and 243–44; Bogus, *Buckley*, 290–327; and Mary C. Brennan, *Turning Right in the Sixties: The Conservative Capture of the GOP* (Chapel Hill: University of North Carolina Press, 1995), 116–17. An excellent broader examination of the issue can be found in Tom Englehardt's *The End of Victory Culture: Cold War America and the Disillusioning of a Generation* (Amherst: University of Massachusetts Press, 1995).

116. On Johnson's escalation of the war, see, for example, Logevall, *Choosing War*, 300–374; Herring, *Longest War*, 131–96; Brian VanDeMark, *Into the Quagmire: Lyndon Johnson and the Escalation of the Vietnam War* (New York: Oxford University Press, 1991); Larry Berman, *Lyndon Johnson's War* (New York: Norton, 1989); and Robert McNamara, *In Retrospect: The Tragedy and Lessons of Vietnam* (New York: Random House, 1995).

117. Earl Lively Jr., "Limited War: The War We Are Supposed to Lose," *American Opinion*, October 1964, 25–30. See also Earl Lively Jr., "McNamara: Four Years of Catastrophe," *American Opinion*, April 1965, 57–63.

118. Lively, "Limited War," 28-30. Emphasis in original. This was also the theme of E. Merrill Root's "Vietnam: A Letter to Our Soldiers There," *American Opinion*, February 1966, 31–40. Quoting MacArthur's famous admonition that in war "there is no substitute for victory," Root told the soldiers that their devotion and sacrifices obligated the Johnson administration to really commit to victory—to "strike the enemy where he lives . . . bomb his industries, his harbors, his central hornet-nests of power" (40).

119. Lively, "Limited War," 30. Coincidently, October 1964 was the month of China's first successful atomic bomb test, but the production of nuclear—and later thermonuclear—warheads would not begin until 1968.

120. Martin Luther King Jr., quoted in Harvard Sitkoff, *King: Pilgrimage to the Mountaintop* (New York: Hill and Wang, 2008), 215. On Fulbright, see Randall Bennett Woods, *Fulbright: A Biography* (New York: Cambridge University Press, 1995), 418–20. On the antiwar movement in general, see Charles DeBenedetti and Charles Chatfield, *An*

American Ordeal: The Anti-War Movement of the Vietnam Era (Syracuse, NY: Syracuse University Press, 1990); and Tom Wells, *The War Within: America's Battle over Vietnam* (Berkeley: University of California Press, 1994).

121. For an overview of the New Left and the Vietnam War, see Terry H. Anderson, *The Movement and the Sixties: Protest in America from Greensboro to Wounded Knee* (New York: Oxford University Press, 1995); and Todd Gitlin, *The Sixties: Years of Hope, Days of Rage* (New York: Bantam Books, 1987), especially 261–304.

122. Bill Richardson and Ken Granger, "The Press and the Vietniks," *American Opinion*, January 1966, 1–13, quotes on 8, 13 and 4.

123. Staughton Lynd and Tom Hayden's account of their visit to North Vietnam is *The Other Side* (New York: New American Library, 1966). See also Gitlin, *Sixties*, 261–68. Fonda's visit to North Vietnam is discussed in fascinating detail in Jerry Lembcke's *Hanoi Jane: War, Sex and Fantasies of Betrayal* (Amherst: University of Massachusetts Press, 2010).

124. Jere Real, "The 'S.D.S.': Students for a Democratic Society," *American Opinion*, February 1966, 73–80, quotes on 75 and 80.

125. See Wells, *War Within*, 195–203; and Norman Mailer, *The Armies of the Night* (London: Weidenfeld and Nicolson, 1968).

126. Robert Dallek, *Flawed Giant: Lyndon Johnson and His Times, 1961–1973* (New York: Oxford University Press, 1998), 485–88.

127. Susan L. M. Huck, "The Vietniks: 'American' Vietcong Assault the Pentagon," *American Opinion*, January 1968, 1–22, quotes on 20 and 22. Emphasis in original.

128. Richard Helms, quoted in Dallek, *Flawed Giant*, 489. Emphasis in original. On Hoover, see Tim Weiner, *Enemies: A History of the FBI* (New York: Random House, 2012), especially 264–65 and 271–73. See also Gitlin, *Sixties*, 263–64.

129. Herring, *Longest War*, 210.

130. Ibid., 209.

131. "Anti-Defamation Unit Hits Birch Group over Vietnam," *New York Times*, June 4, 1967. See also "Anti-Defamation League Reports Klan Gaining and Birch Shifting," *New York Times*, September 20, 1967.

132. Benjamin R. Epstein and Arnold Forster, *The Radical Right: Report on the John Birch Society and Its Allies* (New York: Vintage, 1967), 195–96.

133. Speaking before a crowd of 2,013 at the Manhattan Center in New York on March 10, 1967, for example, Welch had claimed that the Johnson administration had not the "slightest intention or desire to win [the war in Vietnam], or to end it, but only to make it larger and longer and a more overwhelming obsession in the minds of the American people." "Welch Says U.S. Is Not Trying to Win or End War in Vietnam," *New York Times*, March 11, 1967.

134. Robert Welch, *The Truth about Vietnam* (Belmont, MA: American Opinion, 1967), 20. See also Robert Welch, *More Truth about Vietnam* (Belmont, MA: American Opinion, 1967). Epstein and Forster's discussion of the former can be found in *Radical Right*, 121–27.

135. Robert Welch, "Agenda for the Month," *Bulletin*, July 1967, 21.

136. On the need to write five letters a week to senators, congressmen, editors, broadcasters, and so on, see Robert Welch, "Agenda for the Month—Temporary Projects," *Bulletin*, July 1967, 3. On the Birch Society's Vietnam petitions—which in October 1967 Welch claimed had generated more than twenty thousand signatures per week—see Welch, "Foreword," *Bulletin*, November 1967, 1–2. On visiting wounded veterans, see Welch, "Visit Veterans Hospitals," *Bulletin*, June 1966, 30. On TRAIN's activities, see, for example, Welch, "Agenda for the Month—Temporary Projects," *Bulletin*, June 1968, 13–14.

See also the article by one of TRAIN's coordinators, Wallis W. Wood, "Vietnam: While Brave Men Die," *American Opinion*, June 1967, 1–16.

137. Robert Welch, "Foreword," *Bulletin*, December 1967, 1–2. Emphasis in original.

138. Robert Welch, "The Scoreboard for 1960," *American Opinion*, September 1960, 1.

139. This is the theme of Julian Zelizer's book *Arsenal of Democracy*.

140. Lyndon Johnson, quoted in VanDeMark, *Into the Quagmire*, 25. The importance of a fear of a renewed bout of McCarthyism to the foreign policy of the Kennedy administration is also discussed in Craig and Logevall, *America's Cold War*, 221–22.

141. On this point, see Craig and Logevall, *America's Cold War*, 167–68.

142. Robert Welch, "Foreword," *Bulletin*, January 1963, 5–6.

143. A revealing collection of essays on Henry Luce's famous 1941 pronouncement of "The American Century" can be found in *The Short American Century: A Postmortem*, ed. Andrew J. Bacevich (Cambridge, MA: Harvard University Press, 2012).

CHAPTER 6

1. On the issues of fluoridation, gun control, and Johnson's "war on poverty" programs, see, for example, F. B. Exner, "The Real Issue behind Fluoridation," *American Opinion*, May 1962, 9–14; Robert Welch, "Oppose the Firearm Registration Bills," *Bulletin*, April 1964, 26–28; and Hans Sennholz, "Poverty: Mr. Johnson's War," *American Opinion*, December 1964, 13–18.

2. Associated Press, "Youth Death's Suicide: Father Said Communists Had Hanged Boy on Coast," *New York Times*, April 15, 1962. See also "Mystery Hanging of SDS Student Baffles Police," *San Diego Union*, April 1, 1962.

3. Robert Welch, "The Murder in San Diego," *Bulletin*, May 1962, 3–5.

4. Ibid. Monies collected by the fund were to be used, Welch said, "as circumstances may require, for a continuing effort to protect the Society and its members—and in some cases other anti-Communists—from all of the ruthless tactics the Comsymps and their dupes and allies may use against us; and to help established authorities to bring to justice those who carry their malice against the Society and its members to the point of criminal action."

5. Bill Becker, "Rightists Stirred by Youth's Death," *New York Times*, July 15, 1962.

6. Gale McGee, "They Believe the Unbelievable," *Congressional Record*, March 3, 1964, 4,199; Anthony Lewis, "Kuchel Scores Birch Society as 'Fright Peddlers,'" *New York Times*, May 3, 1963 (see also Thomas H. Kuchel, "A PLOT!! To OVERTHROW America!!!" *New York Times*, July 21, 1963); Milton Young, "John Birch Society," *Congressional Record*, April 20, 1961, 6,369–70; and George McGovern, "The Mad Hatter and the Looking-Glass House," *Congressional Record*, June 8, 1964, 12,972–73.

7. Stanley Mosk, *Report to the Governor on the John Birch Society* (Sacramento: California Department of Justice, 1961), 12.

8. Irwin Suall, *The American Ultras: The Extreme Right and the Military-Industrial Complex*, 2nd ed. (New York: New America, 1962), 61–62.

9. Richard Hofstadter, "Pseudo-Conservatism Revisited," in *The Radical Right: "The New American Right," Expanded and Updated*, ed. Daniel Bell (Garden City, NY: Doubleday, 1963), 100.

10. Richard Hofstadter, "The Paranoid Style in American Politics," in *The Paranoid Style in American Politics and Other Essays* (Cambridge, MA: Harvard University Press, 1965), especially 27–29.

11. See, for example, Seymour Martin Lipset and Earl Raab, *The Politics of Unreason: Right-Wing Extremism in America, 1790–1977*, 2nd ed. (Chicago: University of Chicago Press,

1978), 248–337; Benjamin R. Epstein and Arnold Forster, *The Radical Right: Report on the John Birch Society and Its Allies* (New York: Vintage, 1967); George Thayer, *The Farther Shores of Politics: The American Political Fringe Today*, 2nd ed. (New York: Simon and Schuster, 1968), 174–98; John H. Bunzel, *Anti-Politics in America: Reflections on the Anti-Political Temper and Its Distortions of the Democratic Process* (New York: Vintage, 1970), especially 32–90; George Johnson, *Architects of Fear: Conspiracy Theories and Paranoia in American Politics* (Los Angeles: Jeremy P. Tarcher, 1983), 125–38; David H. Bennett, *The Party of Fear: The American Far Right from Nativism to the Militia Movement*, rev. ed. (New York: Vintage, 1995), 315–23; John E. Haynes, *Red Scare or Red Menace? American Communism and Anticommunism in the Cold War Era* (Chicago: Ivan R. Dee, 1996), 184–85; and Arthur Goldwag, *The New Hate: A History of Fear and Loathing on the Populist Right* (New York: Pantheon Books, 2012).

Less generally hostile treatments of the Birchers' conspiracism can be found in Robert S. Robins and Jerrold M. Post, *Political Paranoia: The Psychopolitics of Hatred* (New Haven, CT: Yale University Press, 1997), 190–94; Robert Alan Goldberg, *Enemies Within: The Culture of Conspiracy in Modern America* (New Haven, CT: Yale University Press, 2001), 37–51; and Charles J. Stewart, "The Master Conspiracy of the John Birch Society: From Communism to the New World Order," *Western Journal of Communication* 66, no. 4 (Fall 2002): 424–47.

12. Jack Z. Bratich, *Conspiracy Panics: Political Rationality and Popular Culture* (Albany: State University of New York, 2008), 25. See also Mark Fenster, *Conspiracy Theories: Secrecy and Power in American Culture* (Minneapolis: University of Minnesota Press, 1999).

13. "John Birch Fantasies," *New York Times*, April 22, 1961. See also "Transcript of the President's News Conference on World and Domestic Affairs," *New York Times*, April 22, 1961.

14. Alan Westin, quoted in Irving Spiegel, "Birch Unit Scored as 'Least Useful,'" *New York Times*, June 23, 1961.

15. John F. Cronin, *Communism: Threat to Freedom* (New York: Paulist Press, 1962), 32 and 36.

16. See Stephen Earl Bennett, "Modes of Resolution of a 'Belief Dilemma' in the Ideology of the John Birch Society," *Journal of Politics* 33, no. 3 (August 1971): 735–72; Peter Knight, *Conspiracy Culture: From Kennedy to the X-Files* (London: Routledge, 2000), especially 1–22; and D. J. Mulloy, *American Extremism: History, Politics and the Militia Movement* (New York: Routledge, 2004), 169–74.

17. Michael Barkun, *A Culture of Conspiracy: Apocalyptic Visions in Contemporary America* (Berkeley: University of California Press, 2003), 178.

18. The phrase is taken from Edward Shils, *The Torment of Secrecy: The Background and Consequences of American Security Politics* (Glencoe, IL: Free Press, 1956). On the development of the U.S. national security state in the aftermath of the Second World War, see Michael J. Hogan, *A Cross of Iron: Harry S. Truman and the Origins of the National Security State, 1945–1954* (Cambridge: Cambridge University Press, 1998).

19. The best account of this way of thinking is Gordon S. Wood's "Conspiracy and the Paranoid Style: Causality and Deceit in the Eighteenth Century," *William and Mary Quarterly* 39 (1982): 401–41. However, as Wood moves away from the eighteenth century, he moves closer to the dominant Hofstadter/Lipset and Raab approach, arguing that conspiracy theories are "so out of place" in the modern world that they "can be accounted for only as mental aberrations, as a paranoid style symptomatic of psychological disturbance" (441).

20. Robert Welch, *The Blue Book of the John Birch Society* (Belmont, MA: Western Islands, 1961), 117.

21. See, for example, Bernard Bailyn, *The Ideological Origins of the American Revolution* (Cambridge, MA: Harvard University Press, 1967); Gordon S. Wood, *The Creation of the American Republic* (Chapel Hill: University of North Carolina Press, 1969); Gordon S. Wood, "Conspiracy and the Paranoid Style"; David Brion Davis, ed., *The Fear of Conspiracy: Images of Un-American Subversion from the Revolution to the Present* (Ithaca, NY: Cornell University Press, 1971); Richard O. Curry and Thomas M. Brown, eds., *Conspiracy: The Fear of Subversion in American History* (New York: Holt, Rinehart and Winston, 1972); Michael Paul Rogin, *"Ronald Reagan," the Movie, and Other Episodes in Political Demonology* (Berkeley: University of California Press, 1987); and Kathryn S. Olmsted, *Real Enemies: Conspiracy Theories and American Democracy, World War I to 9/11* (New York: Oxford University Press, 2009).

22. Daniel T. Rodgers, *Contested Truths: Keywords in American Politics since Independence* (New York: Basic Books, 1987), 215.

23. Harry S. Truman, "Special Message to Congress on Greece and Turkey," March 12, 1947, in *Public Papers of the Presidents of the United States: Harry S. Truman, 1947* (Washington, DC: Government Printing Office, 1963), 176–80. The full text of the speech is also available online in various locations. See, for example, *www.americanrhetoric.com*.

24. George Kennan, quoted in Martin Walker, *The Cold War and the Making of the Modern World* (London: Vintage, 1994), 40; and NSC 68, quoted in Ernest R. May, *American Cold War Strategy: Interpreting NSC 68* (Boston: Bedford/St. Martin's, 1993), 27 and 52.

25. Arnold A. Offner, "Liberation or Dominance?: The Ideology of U.S. National Security Policy," in *The Long War: A New History of U.S. National Security Policy since World War II*, ed. Andrew Bacevich (New York: Columbia University Press, 2007), 14.

26. Anders Stephanson, "Liberty or Death: The Cold War as US Ideology," in *Reviewing the Cold War: Approaches, Interpretations, Theory*, ed. Odd Arne Westad (London: Frank Cass, 2000), 84 and 91.

27. Welch, *Blue Book*, 28. Emphasis in original. See also Goldberg, *Enemies Within*, 39–40.

28. Robert Welch, "Some General Comments," Supplement to the *Bulletin*, February 1961, 13. Compare this also with the preamble to the Internal Security Act of 1950—more widely known as the McCarran Act—which, as David Caute points out, contained the legislative conclusion that "World Communism had as its one purpose the establishment of a totalitarian dictatorship in America, to be brought about by treachery, infiltration, sabotage and terrorism" (*The Great Fear: The Anti-Communist Purge under Truman and Eisenhower* [New York: Simon and Schuster, 1978], 38).

29. Susan L. Carruthers, *Cold War Captives: Imprisonment, Escape and Brainwashing* (Berkeley: University of California Press, 2009), 151. On the broader cultural response to the Cold War in the United States, see also Richard M. Fried, *The Russians Are Coming! Pageantry and Patriotism in Cold-War America* (New York: Oxford University Press, 1998); Lisle A. Rose, *The Cold War Comes to Main Street: America in 1950* (Lawrence: University Press of Kansas, 1999); and Stephen J. Whitfield, *The Culture of the Cold War*, 2nd ed. (Baltimore: Johns Hopkins University Press, 1996).

30. Robert Welch, "Foreword," *Bulletin*, August 1961, 5.

31. Thayer, *Farther Shores*, 187. For a similar critique, see also George Barrett's profile of Welch, "Close-Up of the Birchers' 'Founder,'" *New York Times*, May 14, 1961. The principle is set out most clearly by Welch in "Through All the Days to Be," a speech he delivered at the Shrine Auditorium in Los Angeles on April 11, 1961; it is reprinted in

Welch, *The New Americanism and Other Speeches and Essays* (Belmont, MA: Western Islands, 1976), 56–88. An account of the speech, which apparently "evoked dozens of bursts of applause" during its one hour and forty-minute length—it was Welch's standard address at the time—can be found in "6,000 Hear Welch in Coast Address," *New York Times*, April 12, 1961.

32. This was the idea, taken from Aesop's Fables, that communists used "protective" language to hide their real intentions, which had originated with Lenin's attempts to escape the attentions of Tsarist officials during the Russian Revolution. Eleven leaders of the Communist Party were charged with violating the 1940 Smith Act, which prohibited the "teaching and advocating" of the overthrow of the government of the United States by "force and violence," and part of the evidence against them was this "cursed Aesopian language," as Hoover called it; Ellen Schrecker, *The Age of McCarthyism: A Brief History with Documents*, 2nd ed. (Boston: Bedford/St. Martin's, 2002), 48–57, 130, and 197–208. See also J. Edgar Hoover, *The Masters of Deceit: The Story of Communism in America and How to Fight It* (New York: Holt, 1958), 307; Hoover's "Testimony before HUAC," March 26, 1947, in Schrecker, *Age of McCarthyism*, 129–30; Caute, *Great Fear*, 185–99; and Richard Gid Powers, *The Life of J. Edgar Hoover: Secrecy and Power* (New York: Free Press, 1987), 292–97.

33. Haynes, *Red Scare*, 200 and 185.

34. Robert Robins and Jerrold Post get close to this formulation in their analysis of the Birch Society. "A core of reality underlay the central ideology of the John Birch Society," they write. "A reading of Lenin and Stalin provided ample support for belief in the aggressively expansionist aims of the Soviet Union during the height of the Cold War. The Soviet Union's attempts to penetrate Western governments through espionage are well documented. But the paranoid ideology of the John Birch Society expanded dramatically from this rational foundation. The ideology identifies an international Communist conspiracy as the cause of nearly all of America's problems, foreign and domestic" (*Political Paranoia*, 193). "More than two decades after the fall of the Soviet Union, much of the material in Welch's *Blue Book* reads like dated Cold War propaganda," writes Jonathan Kay in *Among the Truthers: A Journey into the Growing Conspiracist Underground of 9/11 Truthers, Birthers, Armageddonites, Vaccine Hysterics, Hollywood Know-Nothings and Internet Addicts* (New York: HarperCollins, 2011), 40.

35. John F. Kennedy, quoted in Walker, *Cold War*, 132.

36. Ibid., 150–51.

37. Offner, "Liberation or Dominance," 19.

38. Arthur Vandenberg, quoted in Campbell Craig and Fredrik Logevall, *America's Cold War: The Politics of Insecurity* (Cambridge, MA: Belknap Press, 2009), 79.

39. Walter P. Reuther, Victor G. Reuther, and Joseph L. Rauh Jr., Reuther memorandum, quoted in Victor G. Reuther, *The Brothers Reuther and the Story of the UAW* (Boston: Houghton Mifflin, 1976), 499. The Reuther memorandum is discussed more fully in Chapter 2.

40. Recognizing this helps to explain why Sara Diamond regards the Birch Society as "system supportive" rather than "extremist." "Though . . . grassroots anticommunists [such as the Birch Society] took an oppositional stance toward politicians deemed 'soft' on communism, overall the Right reinforced prevailing state and corporate prerogatives during the Cold War era," she writes in *Roads to Dominion: Right-Wing Movements and Political Power in the United States* (New York: Guildford Press, 1995), 58. Similarly, writing in 1964, J. Allen Broyles argued that "[Americans] are in a social setting characterized by hatred of communism, by anomie, and by extensive alteration

of our social structure. In such a social setting, one of the major appeals of the rigid and invulnerable ideology of the Society is in its provision of a basis for certainty. The ideology of the Society provides certainty of understanding because it is a fairly simple framework of interpretation through which to view world and national events" (*The John Birch Society: Anatomy of a Protest* [Boston: Beacon Press, 1964], 151).

41. Ronald Reagan, quoted in Jonathan Martin Kolkey, *The New Right, 1960–1968, with Epilogue, 1969–1980* (Washington, DC: University Press of America, 1983), 77.

42. Jules Tygiel, *Ronald Reagan and the Triumph of American Conservatism*, 2nd ed. (New York: Pearson Longman, 2006), 97. During this time, as Tygiel notes, Reagan also appeared at Christian Anti-Communism Crusade rallies with Fred Schwarz and accepted public service awards from Governors Ross Barnett of Mississippi and Orville Faubus of Arkansas.

43. Barry Goldwater, *The Conscience of a Conservative* (1960; London: Fontana, 1964), 85. Emphasis added.

44. On Schlafly, see Geoffrey Kabaservice, *Rule and Ruin: The Downfall of Moderation and the Destruction of the Republican Party, from Eisenhower to the Tea Party* (New York: Oxford University Press, 2012), 89–90.

45. Jerome L. Himmelstein, *To the Right: The Transformation of American Conservatism* (Berkeley: University of California Press, 1990), 68. See also Lisa McGirr, *Suburban Warriors: The Origins of the New American Right* (Princeton, NJ: Princeton University Press, 2001), 55–56.

46. Corey Robin, *The Reactionary Mind: Conservatism from Edmund Burke to Sarah Palin* (New York: Oxford University Press, 2011), 173. For a critical review of Robin's book, see Mark Lilla, "Republicans for Revolution," *New York Review of Books*, January 12, 2012, 12–16. See also their exchange of letters in "The Reactionary Mind: An Exchange," *New York Review of Books*, February 23, 2012, 53.

47. See James T. Patterson, *Mr. Republican: A Biography of Robert A. Taft* (Boston: Houghton Mifflin, 1972); Michael Bowen, *The Roots of Modern Conservatism: Dewey, Taft, and the Battle for the Soul of the Republican Party* (Chapel Hill: University of North Carolina Press, 2011); Kabaservice, *Rule and Ruin*, 5–13; and Donald T. Critchlow, *The Conservative Ascendancy: How the Republican Right Rose to Power in Modern America*, 2nd ed. (Lawrence: University Press of Kansas, 2011), 37–40.

48. Patterson, *Mr. Republican*, 514 and 536.

49. Critchlow, *Conservative Ascendancy*, 39.

50. Robert Taft, quoted in Bowen, *Roots of Modern Conservatism*, 151.

51. Welch, *Blue Book*, 112.

52. Ibid.

53. Welch, "Through All the Days to Be," 71–72.

54. Ibid., 72–74.

55. Robert Welch, *The Politician* (Belmont, MA: Belmont Publishing, 1963), 87.

56. Welch, quoted in Associated Press, "Senator Scores Group Calling Eisenhower a Red," *New York Times*, March 9, 1961.

57. Robert Welch, "Foreword," *Bulletin*, November 1959, 1, quoted in Lipset and Raab, *Politics of Unreason*, 255. Lipset and Raab note that references to the supposed murder of McCarthy were also common in conservative and extreme right-wing circles at the time.

58. Thomas Doherty, *Cold War, Cool Medium: Television, McCarthyism, and American Culture* (New York: Columbia University Press, 2003), 96–97.

59. J. Hoberman, *An Army of Phantoms: American Movies and the Making of the Cold War* (New York: New Press, 2011), 204.

60. Vance Packard, *The Hidden Persuaders* (New York: Pocket Books, 1958), 1. Packard

believed Richard Nixon (164) to be the contemporary politician most adept in the new techniques of "symbol manipulation" and "depth analysis." He also described the GOP's 1956 convention in San Francisco as providing a "showcase" for the image age, in which even "the ministers in their opening and closing intonations (over TV) worked in key GOP slogans" and the "man supervising the production—he was called the 'producer' of the show—was George Murphy, the Hollywood actor and public-relations director of M-G-M" (167).

61. Daniel J. Boorstin, *The Image: A Guide to Pseudo-Events in America*, 25th anniversary ed. (New York: Atheneum, 1987), 3 and 248–49. The book's title when it was first published (1961) was *The Image, or Whatever Happened to the American Dream?*

62. David Riesman, with Nathan Glazer and Reuel Denney, *The Lonely Crowd: A Study of Changing American Character* (New York: Doubleday, 1950); Theodore H. White, *The Making of the President, 1960* (New York: Atheneum Publishers, 1961); and Marshall McLuhan, *Understanding Media: The Extensions of Man* (London: Sphere Books, 1964).

63. Hoberman, *Army of Phantoms*, 334. Concerns about television's negative impact on the political process in particular are likewise much in evidence in John Frankenheimer's two paranoid thrillers of the 1960s—discussed in Chapter 2—*The Manchurian Candidate* (1962) and *Seven Days in May* (1964), although it should be noted that this also had much to do with fears about the negative impact television was having on the cinema.

64. Alfred W. McCoy, *A Question of Torture: CIA Interrogation from the Cold War to the War on Terror* (New York: Holt, 2006), 25.

65. Ibid., 28–31.

66. Abbott Gleason, *Totalitarianism: The Inner History of the Cold War* (New York: Oxford University Press, 1995), 3.

67. Ibid., 103. See also Eric Hoffer, *The True Believer: Thoughts on the Nature of Mass Movements* (1951; New York: HarperCollins, 2002).

68. In addition to *Nineteen Eighty-Four* (1949; London: Penguin, 1988), the other texts most frequently relied upon in this regard are the allegorical novel *Animal Farm* (1945; London: Penguin, 1988), and the essays "Politics and the English Language" and "Propaganda and Demotic Speech," both of which can be found in *All Art Is Propaganda: Critical Essays*, complied by George Packer (New York: Harcourt, 2008), 270–86 and 223–31. An excellent essay on Orwell's reputation and the uses to which it has been put is Louis Menand's "Honest, Decent, Wrong: The Invention of George Orwell," *New Yorker*, January 27, 2003, 84–91. A more detailed study is John Rodden's *George Orwell: The Politics of Literary Reputation*, rev. ed. (Piscataway, NJ: Transaction Publishers, 2002). On the deployment of Orwell's work during the Cold War in particular, see Frances Stonor Saunders, *The Cultural Cold War: The CIA and the World of Arts and Letters* (New York: New Press, 1999), 293–301.

69. Robert Welch, "Foreword," *Bulletin*, December 1959, 1.

70. Robert Welch, "Foreword," *Bulletin*, April 1962, 3. The use of Orwellian concepts like the slogans "War Is Peace," "Freedom Is Slavery," and "Big Brother Is Watching You" can be found in two successive articles in the October 1963 issue of *American Opinion*, E. Merrill Root's "Bad Seed" (25–32) and Richard Jennett's "Robert Kennedy" (43–54).

71. "John Birch Group Opens New Office in Washington, D.C.," *New York Times*, September 18, 1965.

72. Menand, "Honest, Decent, Wrong," 91. In *The Hidden Persuaders*, Packard also invoked Orwell, arguing that the United States was increasingly moving into the "chilling world of George Orwell and his Big Brother" (2).

73. Welch, *Blue Book*, 1 and 28; and Robert Welch, "Some General Comments," 14.

74. Robert Welch, "Agenda for the Month," *Bulletin*, July 1961, 13; and Robert Welch, "A Necessary Warning," *Bulletin*, February 1962, 6. In *The Politician*, Welch referred to the Army-McCarthy hearings as a "factitious proceeding" that had been "cooked up inside the White House," and an "artificial storm and fury" (86).

75. Welch, *Blue Book*, 70.

76. Jack Moffitt, "Documentaries: Deception by Film," *American Opinion*, September 1964, 65–67. Moffitt also objected to Stanley Kubrick's *Dr. Strangelove, or How I Learned to Stop Worrying and Love the Bomb* (1964), for its "gratuitous smear against the late Senator McCarthy." See "Moffitt on the Arts," *American Opinion*, April 1964, 70.

77. Emile de Antonio, "The Point of View in *Point of Order*" (1964), in *Emile de Antonio: A Reader*, ed. Douglas Kellner and Dan Streible (Minneapolis: University of Minnesota Press, 2000), 150. See also Doherty, *Cold War, Cool Medium*, 244–48.

78. A fascinating and instructive examination of Welch's poetic inclinations is James Darcy's "Prophecy as Poetry: The Romantic Vision of Robert Welch," in *The Prophetic Tradition and Radical Rhetoric in America* (New York: New York University Press, 1997), 151–74.

79. Ralph E. Ellsworth and Sarah M. Harris, *The American Right Wing: A Report to the Fund for the Republic* (Washington, DC: Public Affairs Press, 1962), 35.

80. Robert Welch, "A Fable for Conservatives," *Bulletin*, March 1962, 3–5; Robert Welch, "A Confidential Directive—January 1, 1968," *Bulletin*, January 1968, 3–22.

81. Robert Welch, "In Conclusion," *Bulletin*, December 31, 1959, 24.

82. Welch, "Confidential Directive," 2.

83. McGirr, *Suburban Warriors*, 176.

84. John Rousselot, quoted in "Bircher Sees Long Battle to 'Re-establish' Philosophy," *New York Times*, November 6, 1964.

85. Robert Welch, "Agenda for the Month," *Bulletin*, July 1961, 3.

86. Robert Welch, "The Truth in Time," *American Opinion*, November 1966, 1–25.

87. G. Edward Griffin, *The Life and Words of Robert Welch: Founder of the John Birch Society* (Thousand Oaks, CA: American Media, 1975), 247. The Birch Society transferred the film of Welch reading his essay to video in 1995. It was uploaded to *YouTube.com* as "The Truth in Time by Robert Welch.flv" by Hal Shurtleff (a regional field director for the John Birch Society) on June 12, 2011.

88. Welch, "Truth in Time," 3. Emphasis in original.

89. Barkun, *Culture of Conspiracy*, 46–47.

90. Hofstadter, "Paranoid Style," 10–14.

91. Revilo P. Oliver, "A Review of Reviews," *American Opinion*, June 1962, 31–37. See also Goldberg, *Enemies Within*, 46; Lipset and Raab, *Politics of Unreason*, 252; and Epstein and Forster, *Radical Right*, 110–12 and 117–19.

92. Robert Welch, "More Stately Mansions" in *The New Americanism and Other Speeches and Essays* (Belmont, MA: Western Islands, 1976), 115–52. See also "If You Want It Straight," *American Opinion*, June 1964, 41–46.

93. Griffin, *Life and Words*, 246.

94. Medford Evans, "Dean Rusk: Is He the Insiders' Quarterback?" *American Opinion*, March 1968, 81–91. Later works to emphasize the importance of the Insiders include Gary Allen's *None Dare Call It Conspiracy* (New York: Buccaneer Books, 1976) and John F. McManus's *The Insiders* (Belmont, MA: John Birch Society, 1983).

95. Welch, "Truth in Time," 5.

96. Griffin, *Life and Words*, 248.

97. See Goldberg, *Enemies Within*, 47–48. "Anybody who even starts to point out the truth

is mercilessly ridiculed as a believer in the 'conspiratorial theory of history,'" Welch lamented in his "Truth in Time" essay (20).

98. See Thayer, *Farther Shores*, 193; Benjamin R. Epstein and Arnold Forster, *Report on the John Birch Society* (New York: Random House, 1966), 64–69; and McGirr, *Suburban Warriors*, 221–22.

99. "The Mr. Welch who founded the society was a man in whom I had great confidence," Oliver said in his resignation statement. "Since then, however, changes which have taken place internally, in the organization and in its policies leave me no alternative but to disassociate myself from it" (quoted in Thomas Buckley, "A Birch Society Founder Quits; Pressure by Welch Is Reported," *New York Times*, August 16, 1966). See also John H. Fenton, "Birch Society Is Shaken by 'Acrimonious Disputes,'" *New York Times*, August 28, 1966. In the words of Epstein and Forster, Oliver had given a speech "replete with open and unmistakable anti-Semitism" during a Fourth of July rally in Boston, which may have been the final straw for Welch (*Radical Right*, 112–14).

The Society had been rocked by internal disputes before. Back in 1963, rumors had circulated that Welch was being forced to relinquish his control of the Society, for example. See Jack Langguth, "Welch Replaced as Birch Leader," *New York Times*, October 12, 1963. Welch's response can be found in "General and Miscellaneous Comments," *Bulletin*, November 1963, 19–20; quoting Mark Twain, he said that rumors of his ousting were "greatly exaggerated."

100. McGirr, *Suburban Warriors*, 221.

101. Robert Welch, quoted in Warren Weaver, "Welch Calls a Nixon Election Boon to Pro-Reds," *New York Times*, October 16, 1968.

AFTERWORD

1. See Robert Alan Goldberg, *Enemies Within: The Culture of Conspiracy in Modern America* (New Haven, CT: Yale University Press, 2001), 54; Robert S. Robins and Jerrold M. Post, *Political Paranoia: The Psychopolitics of Hatred* (New Haven, CT: Yale University Press, 1997), 192; and Seymour Hersh, *"The Target Is Destroyed": What Really Happened to Flight 007* (New York: Random House, 1986).

2. "Rep. Larry McDonald," John Birch Society, accessed October 14, 2013, *www.jbs.org/rep-larry-mcdonald*.

3. Robert D. McFadden, "Robert Welch Jr. Dead at 85; John Birch Society's Founder," *New York Times*, January 8, 1985.

4. Robert Welch, "Looking Ahead: A Speech Delivered at the Tenth Anniversary Dinner of the John Birch Society," Indianapolis, December 7, 1968, reproduced in the *Bulletin*, December 1968, 9–32, quotes on 9, 23 and 20. See also Douglas E. Kneeland, "Birch Society, Age 10, Vows Red Rout," *New York Times*, December 8, 1968. Kneeland reported that few of the Society's "knowledgeable critics" took "serious issue" with the figures and numbers Welch had presented during his speech.

5. Kneeland, "Birch Society, Age 10."

6. Welch, "Looking Ahead," 20, 24–27.

7. Ibid., 17–18.

8. Robert Welch, *The Blue Book of the John Birch Society* (Belmont, MA: Western Islands, 1961), 96.

Bibliography

Primary Sources

JOHN BIRCH SOCIETY PERIODICALS, PAMPHLETS, AND SPEECHES

American Opinion, 1958–1968.

Bulletin, 1958–1968.

Review of the News, 1965–1968.

Draskovich, Slobodan M. "The John Birch Society: A Threat to Whom?" Belmont. MA: John Birch Society, ca. 1961.

John Birch Society. *Ad Hoc Committee Functions and Objectives*. Belmont, MA: John Birch Society, 1964, n.d.

———. *The Coming Church Establishment*. Belmont, MA: John Birch Society, 1962.

———. *Current Communist Goals*. San Marino, CA: T.R.A.I.N. Committee, n.d.

———. *From Our Mail: Appreciation and Encouragement*. Belmont, MA: John Birch Society, 1961.

———. *Have You Had Enough?* Belmont, MA: John Birch Society, n.d.

———. *The Heartbeat of the Americanist Cause*. Belmont, MA: John Birch Society, n.d.

———. *The Innocents Defiled: Sex Education in the Schools; A Documentary Filmstrip on Sex Education in the Schools*. San Marino, CA: John Birch Society, 1969.

———. *The John Birch Society: A Report*. Newspaper advertisement insert. Belmont, MA: John Birch Society, n.d.

———. *Let's Stop Kidding Ourselves about the United Nations*. Baltimore, MD: T.R.A.I.N. Committee, n.d.

———. *Our Action Programs Include*. Belmont, MA: John Birch Society, n.d.

———. *The Pink Book of the John Birch Society*. Belmont, MA: John Birch Society, 1963.

———. *The Principles and Purposes of the Movement to Restore Decency*. Belmont, MA: John Birch Society, 1969.

———. *Responsible Leadership through the John Birch Society*. San Marino, CA: John Birch Society, n.d.

———. *Robert Welch Testimonial Dinner* (September 25). Phoenix, AZ: n.p., 1965. Wilcox Collection of Contemporary Political Movements, University of Kansas.

———. *Support Your Local Police*. Belmont, MA: John Birch Society, 1963.

———. *This Is It!* Belmont, MA: American Opinion, 1967.

———. *The Time Has Come*. Belmont, MA: John Birch Society, 1964.

———. *TRAIN (To Restore American Independence Now): Statement of Principles*. Belmont, MA: John Birch Society, n.d.

———. *Victory in Vietnam*. Belmont, MA: John Birch Society, 1969.

———. *Why Join the John Birch Society*. 1961. Belmont, MA: John Birch Society, 1968.

———. *What the United Nations Is Up To Now*. Belmont, MA: John Birch Society, n.d.

Welch, Robert. *A Letter to the South: On Segregation*. 1956. Belmont, MA: American Opinion, 1964.

———. *More Truth about Vietnam*. Belmont, MA: American Opinion, 1967.

———. *The Neutralizers*. Belmont, MA: John Birch Society, 1963.

———. *To the Negroes of America*. Belmont, MA: American Opinion, 1967.

———. *"To Prevent a Third Party": A Speech by Robert Welch, Delivered at the Unauthorized Rally in Support of Senator Barry Goldwater, at the Morrison Hotel, Chicago, July 24, 1960.* Belmont, MA: American Opinion, 1960.

———. *The Truth about Vietnam*. Belmont, MA: American Opinion, 1967.

———. *Two Revolutions at Once*. Belmont, MA: American Opinion, 1965.

———. *What Is Communism?* Belmont, MA: American Opinion, 1970.

———. *What Is the John Birch Society?* Belmont, MA: American Opinion, 1970.

———. *White Book of the John Birch Society*. Belmont, MA: John Birch Society, 1961.

———. *Wild Statements*. Belmont, MA: American Opinion, 1965.

WEBSITE

The John Birch Society, *www.jbs.org*.

BOOKS

Allen, Gary. *Communist Revolution in the Streets*. Boston: Western Islands, 1967.

———. *None Dare Call It Conspiracy*. New York: Buccaneer Books, 1976.

Berrier, Hilaire du. *Background to Betrayal: The Tragedy of Vietnam*. Belmont, MA: Western Islands, 1965.

Griffin, G. Edward. *The Life and Words of Robert Welch: Founder of the John Birch Society*. Thousand Oaks, CA: American Media, 1975.

———. *This Is the John Birch Society: An Invitation to Membership*. Thousand Oaks, CA: American Media, 1972.

Linington, Elizabeth. *Come to Think of It—*. Belmont, MA: Western Islands, 1965.

Lively, Earl, Jr. *The Invasion of Mississippi*. Belmont, MA: American Opinion, 1963.

McManus, John, F. *The Insiders*. Belmont, MA: John Birch Society, 1983.

Stang, Alan. *It's Very Simple: The True Story of Civil Rights*. Belmont, MA: Western Islands, 1965.

Welch, Robert. *Again, May God Forgive Us!* Belmont, MA: Belmont Publishing, 1972.

———. *The Blue Book of the John Birch Society*. Belmont, MA: Western Islands, 1961.

———. *The Life of John Birch: In the Story of One American Boy, the Ordeal of His Age*. Chicago: Henry Regnery, 1954.

———. *May God Forgive Us*. Chicago: Henry Regnery, 1952.

———. *The New Americanism and Other Speeches and Essays*. Belmont, MA: Western Islands, 1966.

———. *The Politician*. Belmont, MA: Belmont Publishing, 1963.

NEWSPAPERS AND PERIODICALS

Arkansas Democrat

America

Arizona Journal

Arizona Republic

Boston Herald

Chicago Daily News

Chicago Sun-Times

Good Housekeeping
Independent American
Kansas City Star
Life
Look
Los Angeles Times
Milwaukee Journal
Nation
National Review
New Republic
Newsweek
New Yorker
New York Times
New York Review of Books
Ocala Star-Banner
Overseas Weekly
People's World
Santa Barbara News-Press
Saturday Evening Post
St. Louis Post-Dispatch
Time
Wall Street Journal
Wanderer
Washington Daily News
Washington Evening Star
Washington Post
Worker

OFFICIAL DOCUMENTS AND REPORTS

California Senate. *Twelfth Report of the Senate Factfinding Subcommittee on Un-American Activities*. Sacramento: Senate of the State of California, 1963.

Congressional Record, 1958–1968.

Massachusetts State Legislature. *The Occupation of the Campus of the University of Mississippi, September 30, 1962, by the Department of Justice of the United States*. Report by the General Legislative Investigating Committee to the Massachusetts State Legislature, May 8, 1963. Belmont, MA: American Opinion, 1964.

Mosk, Stanley. *Report to the Governor on the John Birch Society*. Sacramento: California Department of Justice, 1961.

Public Papers of the Presidents of the United States: Harry S. Truman, 1947. Washington, DC: Government Printing Office, 1963.

Public Papers of the Presidents of the United States: Dwight D. Eisenhower, 1959. Washington, DC: Government Printing Office, 1960.

Report of the President's Commission on the Assassination of President John F. Kennedy. Washington, DC: Government Printing Office, 1964.

U.S. Senate. *Military Cold War Education and Speech Review Policies: Hearings Before the Special Preparedness Subcommittee of the Committee on Armed Services*. Parts 1–8. 87th Cong., 2nd sess. Washington, DC: Government Printing Office, 1962.

———. *The New Drive against the Anti-Communist Program: Hearing Before the Subcommittee to Investigate the Administration of the Internal Security Act and Other Internal Security*

Laws of the Committee on the Judiciary. 87th Cong., 1st sess., July 11, 1961. Washington, DC: Government Printing Office, 1961.

———. *The Use of Military Personnel and Facilities to Arouse the Public to the Menace of the Cold War and to Inform and Educate Armed Services Personnel on the Nature and Menace of the Cold War.* Report by the Special Preparedness Subcommittee of the Committee on Armed Services. 87th Cong., 2nd sess. Washington, DC: Government Printing Office, 1962.

Secondary Sources

Adler, Les K., and Thomas G. Paterson. "Red Fascism: The Merger of Nazi Germany and Soviet Russia in the American Image of Totalitarianism, 1930s–1950s." *American Historical Review* 75, no. 4 (April 1970): 1046–64.

Ambrose, Stephen E. *Eisenhower.* Vol. 2, *The President.* New York: Simon and Schuster, 1984.

Anderson, David. *Trapped by Success: The Eisenhower Administration and Vietnam, 1953–1961.* New York: Columbia University Press, 1991.

Anderson, Terry H. *The Movement and the Sixties: Protest in America from Greensboro to Wounded Knee.* New York: Oxford University Press, 1995.

Andrew, John A., III. *The Other Side of the Sixties: Young Americans for Freedom and the Rise of Conservative Politics.* New Brunswick, NJ: Rutgers University Press, 1997.

———. *Power to Destroy: The Political Uses of the IRS from Kennedy to Nixon.* Chicago: Ivan R. Dee, 2002.

Arendt, Hannah. *Eichmann in Jerusalem: A Report on the Banality of Evil.* New York: Viking, 1963.

———. *The Origins of Totalitarianism.* 1951. New York: Harcourt Brace Jovanovich, 1973.

Axelrod, George. *The Manchurian Candidate.* Eye, Suffolk, UK: ScreenPress Publishing, 2002.

Bacevich, Andrew J. *The Limits of Power: The End of American Exceptionalism.* New York: Holt, 2008.

———, ed. *The Short American Century: A Postmortem.* Cambridge, MA: Harvard University Press, 2011.

Bachrack, Stanley D. *The Committee of One Million: "China Lobby" Politics, 1953–1971.* New York: Columbia University Press, 1976.

Bailyn, Bernard. *The Ideological Origins of the American Revolution.* Cambridge, MA: Harvard University Press, 1967.

Baldwin, James. *The Fire Next Time.* London: Michael Joseph, 1963.

Barkun, Michael. *A Culture of Conspiracy: Apocalyptic Visions in Contemporary America.* Berkeley: University of California Press, 2003.

Bartimus, Tad, Denby Fawcett, Jurate Kazickas, Edith Lederer, Ann Bryan Mariano, Anne Morrissy Merick, Laura Palmer, Kate Webb, and Tracy Wood. *War Torn: Stories of War from the Women Reporters Who Covered Vietnam.* New York: Random House, 2002.

Bass, Jack, and Marilyn W. Thompson. *Strom: The Complicated Personal and Political Life of Strom Thurmond.* Rev. ed. New York: Public Affairs, 2006.

Beckemeier, Eric. *Traitors Beware: A History of Robert DePugh's Minutemen.* Hardin, MO: privately printed, 2007.

Beinart, Peter. *The Icarus Syndrome: A History of American Hubris.* New York: HarperCollins, 2010.

Beisner, Robert L. *Dean Acheson: A Life in the Cold War.* New York: Oxford University Press, 2009.

Bell, Daniel, ed. *The Radical Right: "The New American Right," Expanded and Updated*. Garden City, NY: Doubleday, 1963.

Bennett, David H. *The Party of Fear: The American Far Right from Nativism to the Militia Movement*. Rev. ed. New York: Vintage, 1995.

Bennett, Stephen Earl. "Modes of Resolution of a 'Belief Dilemma' in the Ideology of the John Birch Society." *Journal of Politics* 33, no. 3 (August 1971): 735–72.

Berkowitz, Arron Max. "Mr. Khrushchev Goes to Washington: Domestic Opposition to Nikita Khrushchev's 1959 Visit to America." PhD diss., University of Illinois at Chicago, 2010.

Berlet, Chip, and Matthew N. Lyons. *Right-Wing Populism in America: Too Close for Comfort*. New York: Guildford Press, 2000.

Berman, Larry. *Lyndon Johnson's War*. New York: Norton, 1989.

Beschloss, Michael. *The Crisis Years: Kennedy and Khrushchev, 1960–1963*. New York: HarperCollins, 1991.

———. *Mayday: Eisenhower, Khrushchev and the U-2 Affair*. New York: Harper and Row, 1988.

Bogus, Carl T. *Buckley: William F. Buckley Jr. and the Rise of American Conservatism*. New York: Bloomsbury Press, 2011.

Boorstin, Daniel J. *The Image: A Guide to Pseudo-Events in America*. 25th anniv. ed. New York: Atheneum, 1987.

Bowen, Michael. *The Roots of Modern Conservatism: Dewey, Taft, and the Battle for the Soul of the Republican Party*. Chapel Hill: University of North Carolina Press, 2011.

Branch, Taylor. *Parting the Waters: America in the King Years, 1954–63*. New York: Simon and Schuster, 1988.

Bratich, Jack Z. *Conspiracy Panics: Political Rationality and Popular Culture*. Albany: State University of New York, 2008.

Brennan, Mary C. *Turning Right in the Sixties: The Conservative Capture of the GOP*. Chapel Hill: University of North Carolina Press, 1995.

Brenner, Samuel L. "Shouting at the Rain: The Voices and Ideas of Right-Wing Anti-Communist Americanists in the Era of Modern American Conservatism, 1950–1974." PhD diss., Brown University, 2009.

Bridges, Linda, and John R. Coyne Jr. *Strictly Right: William F. Buckley Jr., and the American Conservative Movement*. Hoboken, NJ: Wlley, 2007.

Brinkley, Alan. *The End of Reform: New Deal Liberalism in Recession and War*. New York: Knopf, 1995.

———. "The Problem of American Conservatism." *American Historical Review* 99 (1994): 409–29.

———. *Voices of Protest: Huey Long, Father Coughlin and the Great Depression*. New York: Vintage, 1983.

Broyles, J. Allen. *The John Birch Society: Anatomy of a Protest*. Boston: Beacon Press, 1964.

Bunzel, John H. *Anti-Politics in America: Reflections on the Anti-Political Temper and Its Distortions of the Democratic Process*. New York: Vintage, 1970.

Burgess, Anthony. *A Clockwork Orange*. London: Heinemann, 1962.

Burnham, James. *Containment or Liberation? An Inquiry into the Aims of United States Foreign Policy*. New York: John Day, 1953.

———. *The Struggle for the World*. New York: John Day, 1947.

———. *Web of Subversion: Underground Networks in the U.S. Government*. New York: John Day, 1954.

Burns, Jennifer. *Goddess of the Market: Ayn Rand and the American Right*. New York: Oxford University Press, 2009.

Cannon, Lou. *Ronnie and Jessie: A Political Odyssey*. New York: Doubleday, 1969.

Carmichael, Stokely, and Charles Hamilton. *Black Power: The Politics of Liberation in America*. New York: Random House, 1967.

Caro, Robert A. *The Years of Lyndon Johnson*. Vol. 4, *The Passage of Power*. New York: Knopf, 2012.

Carter, Dan T. *The Politics of Rage: George Wallace, the Origins of the New Conservatism, and the Transformation of American Politics*. New York: Simon and Schuster, 1995.

Carruthers, Susan L. *Cold War Captives: Imprisonment, Escape and Brainwashing*. Berkeley: University of California Press, 2009.

———. "Redeeming the Captives: Hollywood and the Brainwashing of America's Prisoners of War in Korea." *Film History* 10 (1998): 275–94.

Caute, David. *The Great Fear: The Anti-Communist Purge under Truman and Eisenhower*. New York: Simon and Schuster, 1978.

Coffin, Tristram. *Senator Fulbright: Portrait of a Public Philosopher*. New York: Dutton, 1966.

Cohen, Martin A., Dennis M. Altman, and Robert E. Natkin. *The John Birch Coloring Book*. Chicago: Serious Products Company, 1962.

Cohen, Ronald D. *Rainbow Quest: The Folk Music Revival and American Society, 1940–1970*. Amherst: University of Massachusetts Press, 2002.

Condon, Richard. *The Manchurian Candidate*. 1959. Harpenden, Hertfordshire, UK: No Exit Press, 1993.

Cook, Fred J. *The Warfare State*. New York: Macmillan, 1962.

Courtney, Kent, and Phoebe Courtney. *The Case of General Edwin A. Walker*. New Orleans, LA: Conservative Society of America, 1961.

Coyne, Michael. "*Seven Days in May*: History, Prophecy and Propaganda." In *Windows on the Sixties: Exploring Key Texts of Media and Culture*, ed. Anthony Aldgate, James Chapman, and Arthur Marwick, 70–90. London: I. B. Tauris, 2000.

Craig, Campbell, and Fredrik Logevall. *America's Cold War: The Politics of Insecurity*. Cambridge, MA: Belknap Press, 2009.

Crawford, Thomas. *Thunder on the Right: The "New Right" and the Politics of Resentment*. New York: Pantheon Books, 1980.

Cray, Ed. *Chief Justice: A Biography of Earl Warren*. New York: Simon and Schuster, 1997.

Crespino, Joseph. *Strom Thurmond's America*. New York: Hill and Wang, 2012.

Critchlow, Donald T. *The Conservative Ascendancy: How the Republican Right Rose to Power in Modern America*. 2nd ed. Lawrence: University Press of Kansas, 2011.

———. *Phyllis Schlafly and Grassroots Conservatism: A Woman's Crusade*. Princeton, NJ: Princeton University Press, 2005.

Cronin, John F. *Communism: Threat to Freedom*. New York: Paulist Press, 1962.

Curry, Richard O., and Thomas M. Brown, eds. *Conspiracy: The Fear of Subversion in American History*. New York: Holt, Rinehart and Winston, 1972.

Dallek, Robert. *Flawed Giant: Lyndon Johnson and His Times, 1961–1973*. New York: Oxford University Press, 1998.

———. *An Unfinished Life: John F. Kennedy, 1917–1963*. New York: Little, Brown, 2003.

Darcy, James. *The Prophetic Tradition and Radical Rhetoric in America*. New York: New York University Press, 1997.

Davis, David Brion, ed. *The Fear of Conspiracy: Images of Un-American Subversion from the Revolution to the Present*. Ithaca, NY: Cornell University Press, 1971.

Davis, Warren Jefferson. *Law of the Land*. New York: Carlton Press, 1962.

DeBenedetti, Charles, and Charles Chatfield. *An American Ordeal: The Antiwar Movement of the Vietnam Era*. Syracuse, NY: Syracuse University Press, 1990.

DeMarr, Mary Jean. "Elizabeth Linington/Anne Blaisdell/Dell Shannon/Lesley Egan." In *Great Women Mystery Writers: Classic to Contemporary*, ed. Kathleen Gregory Klein, 192–97. Westport, CT: Greenwood Press, 1994.

Diamond, Sara. *Roads to Dominion: Right-Wing Movements and Political Power in the United States*. New York: Guildford Press, 1995.

Dickson, Paul. *Sputnik: The Shock of the Century*. New York: Walker, 2001.

Dittmer, John. *Local People: The Struggle for Civil Rights in Mississippi*. Urbana: University of Illinois Press, 1994.

Divine, Robert A. *The Sputnik Challenge*. New York: Oxford University Press, 1993.

Dobbs, Michael. *One Minute to Midnight: Kennedy, Khrushchev, and Castro on the Brink of Nuclear War*. New York: Knopf, 2008.

Dochuk, Darren. *From Bible Belt to Sun Belt: Plain-Folk Religion, Grassroots Politics and the Rise of Evangelical Conservatism*. New York: Norton, 2011.

Doherty, Thomas. *Cold War, Cool Medium: Television, McCarthyism, and American Culture*. New York: Columbia University Press, 2003.

Doyle, William. *An American Insurrection: The Battle of Oxford, Mississippi, 1962*. New York: Doubleday, 2001.

Draper, Theodore. *American Communism and Soviet Russia*. 1960. New Brunswick, NJ: Transaction Publishers, 2003.

Draskovich, Slobodan M. *Tito: Moscow's Trojan Horse*. Chicago: Henry Regnery, 1957.

Dunaway, David King, and Molly Beer. *Singing Out: An Oral History of America's Folk Music Revivals*. New York: Oxford University Press, 2010.

Durham, Martin. "On American Conservatism and Kim Phillips-Fein's Survey of the Field." *Journal of American History* 98 (December 2011): 757–58.

———. *White Rage: The Extreme Right and American Politics*. London: Routledge, 2007.

Eatwell, Roger. *Fascism: A History*. New York: Penguin, 1995.

Ellsworth, Ralph E., and Sarah M. Harris. *The American Right Wing: A Report to the Fund for the Republic*. Washington, DC: Public Affairs Press, 1962.

Englehardt, Tom. *The End of Victory Culture: Cold War America and the Disillusioning of a Generation*. Amherst: University of Massachusetts Press, 1995.

Epstein, Benjamin R., and Arnold Forster. *Danger on the Right*. New York: Random House, 1964.

———. *The Radical Right: Report on the John Birch Society and Its Allies*. New York: Vintage, 1967.

———. *Report on the John Birch Society*. New York: Random House, 1966.

Fairclough, Adam. *Better Day Coming: Blacks and Equality, 1890–2000*. London: Penguin, 2001.

Fariello, Griffin. *Red Scare: Memories of the American Inquisition*. New York: Norton, 1995.

Feaver, Peter D., and Richard H. Kohn, eds. *Soldiers and Civilians: The Civil-Military Gap and American National Security*. Cambridge, MA: MIT Press, 2001.

Feldman, Jay. *Manufacturing Hysteria: A History of Scapegoating, Surveillance, and Secrecy in Modern America*. New York: Pantheon Books, 2011.

Fenster, Mark. *Conspiracy Theories: Secrecy and Power in American Culture*. Minneapolis: University of Minnesota Press, 1999.

Finch, Phillip. *God, Guts and Guns: A Close Look at the Radical Right*. New York: Seaview/ Putnam, 1983.

Finer, S. E. *The Man on Horseback: The Role of the Military in Politics*. 2nd ed. London: Penguin, 1975.

Fitzgerald, Frances. *Way Out There in the Blue: Reagan, Star Wars and the End of the Cold War*. New York: Simon and Schuster, 2000.

Ford, James W., and James S. Allen. *The Negroes in a Soviet America*. New York: Workers Library Publishers, 1935.

Frankel, Max. *High Noon in the Cold War*. New York: Presidio Press, 2004.

Fried, Richard M. *Nightmare in Red: The McCarthy Era in Perspective*. New York: Oxford University Press, 1990.

———. *The Russians Are Coming! Pageantry and Patriotism in Cold-War America*. New York: Oxford University Press, 1998.

Fursenko, Aleksandr, and Timothy Naftali. *Khrushchev's Cold War: The Inside Story of an American Adversary*. New York: Norton, 2006.

———. *"One Hell of a Gamble": Khrushchev, Castro and Kennedy, 1958–1964*. New York: Norton, 1997.

Garrow, David J. *Bearing the Cross: Martin Luther King, Jr., and the Southern Christian Leadership Conference*. New York: Vintage, 1988.

———. *The FBI and Martin Luther King Jr.: From "Solo" to Memphis*. New York: Norton, 1981.

———. *Protest at Selma: Martin Luther King, Jr., and the Voting Rights Act of 1965*. New Haven, CT: Yale University Press, 1978.

Garthoff, Raymond. *The Great Transition: American-Soviet Relations and the End of the Cold War*. Washington, DC: Brookings Institution Press, 1984.

Gentry, Curt. *J. Edgar Hoover: The Man and His Secrets*. New York: Norton, 1991.

George, John, and Laird Wilcox. *American Extremists: Militias, Supremacists, Klansmen, Communists, and Others*. Amherst, NY: Prometheus Books, 1996.

Gitlin, Todd. *The Sixties: Years of Hope, Days of Rage*. New York: Bantam Books, 1987.

Gleason, Abbott. *Totalitarianism: The Inner History of the Cold War*. New York: Oxford University Press, 1995.

Goldberg, Robert Alan. *Barry Goldwater*. New Haven, CT: Yale University Press, 1995.

———. *Enemies Within: The Culture of Conspiracy in Modern America*. New Haven, CT: Yale University Press, 2001.

Goldstein, Robert Justin. *American Blacklist: The Attorney General's List of Subversive Organizations*. Lawrence: University Press of Kansas, 2008.

———. *Political Repression in Modern America: From 1870 to 1976*. Urbana: University of Illinois Press, 1978.

Goldwag, Arthur. *The New Hate: A History of Fear and Loathing on the Populist Right*. New York: Pantheon Books, 2012.

Goldwater, Barry. *The Conscience of a Conservative*. 1960. London: Fontana, 1964.

———. *Why Not Victory? A Fresh Look at American Foreign Policy*. New York: McGraw-Hill, 1962.

———. *With No Apologies: The Personal and Political Memoirs of United States Senator Barry M. Goldwater*. New York: Morrow, 1979.

Gordon, Rosalie M. *Nine Men against America: The Supreme Court and Its Attack on American Liberties*. Rev. ed. New York: Devin-Adair, 1960.

Greenberg, David. *Nixon's Shadow: The History of an Image*. New York: Norton, 2003.

Griffin, Roger. *The Nature of Fascism*. London: Routledge, 1993.

Grupp, Fred W., Jr. "Personal Satisfaction Derived from Membership in the John Birch Society." *Western Political Quarterly* 24, no. 1 (March 1971): 79–83.

———. "The Political Perspectives of Birch Society Members." In Schoenberger, *American Right Wing*, 83–118.

Halberstam, David. *The Best and the Brightest*. New York: Random House, 1972.

Haley, J. Evetts. *A Texan Looks at Lyndon: A Study in Illegitimate Power*. Canyon, TX: Palo Duro Press, 1964.

Hardisty, Jean. *Mobilizing Resentment: Conservative Resurgence from the John Birch Society to the Promise Keepers*. Boston: Beacon Press, 1999.

Hargis, Billy James. *Billy James Hargis' Complete Vietnam Report, December 13-21, 1968*. Tulsa, OK: Christian Crusade Publications, 1968.

———. *The Death of Freedom of Speech in the U.S.A.* Tulsa, OK: Christian Crusade Publications, 1967.

———. *Tells It Like It Is!* Tulsa, Oklahoma: Christian Crusade Publications, 1969.

———. *That Chicago Revolution!* Tulsa, OK: Christian Crusade Publications, 1968.

Hart, Jeffrey. *The Making of the American Conservative Mind: National Review and Its Times*. Wilmington, DE: ISI Books, 2005.

Haynes, John E. *Red Scare or Red Menace? American Communism and Anticommunism in the Cold War Era*. Chicago: Ivan R. Dee, 1996.

Henriksen, Margot A. *Dr. Strangelove's America: Society and Culture in the Atomic Age*. Berkeley: University of California Press, 1997.

Herring, George C. *America's Longest War: The United States and Vietnam, 1950–1975*. 4th ed. Boston: McGraw-Hill, 2001.

———. *From Colony to Superpower: U.S. Foreign Relations since 1776*. New York: Oxford University Press, 2008.

Hersh, Seymour. *"The Target Is Destroyed": What Really Happened to Flight 007*. New York: Random House, 1986.

Heylin, Clinton. *Revolution in the Air: The Songs of Bob Dylan, 1957–1973*. Chicago: Chicago Review Press, 2009.

Himmelstein, Jerome L. *To The Right: The Transformation of American Conservatism*. Berkeley: University of California Press, 1990.

Hijiya, James A. "The Conservative 1960s." *Journal of American Studies* 37, no. 2 (2003): 201–27.

Hoberman, J. *An Army of Phantoms: American Movies and the Making of the Cold War*. New York: New Press, 2011.

———. *The Dream Life: Movies, Media and the Mythology of the Sixties*. New York: New Press, 2003.

———. "When Dr. No Met Dr. Strangelove." *Sight and Sound*, December 1993, 16–21.

Hodgson, Godfrey. *America in Our Time: From World War Two to Nixon*. London: Macmillan, 1977.

———. *The World Turned Right Side Up: A History of the Conservative Ascendancy in America*. Boston: Houghton Mifflin, 1996.

Hoffer, Eric. *The True Believer: Thoughts on the Nature of Mass Movements*. 1951. New York: HarperCollins, 2002.

Hofstadter, Richard. "The Long View: Goldwater in History." *New York Review of Books*, October 8, 1964.

———. *The Paranoid Style in American Politics and Other Essays*. Cambridge, MA: Harvard University Press, 1965.

———. "Pseudo-Conservatism Revisited: A Postscript." In Bell, *Radical Right*, 97–103.

Hogan, Michael J. *A Cross of Iron: Harry S. Truman and the Origins of the National Security State, 1945–1954*. Cambridge: Cambridge University Press, 1998.

Hoover, J. Edgar. *The Masters of Deceit: The Story of Communism in America and How to Fight It*. New York: Holt, 1958.

Howard-Pitney, David. *Martin Luther King Jr., Malcolm X and the Civil Rights Struggle of the 1950s and 1960s: A Brief History with Documents*. Boston: Bedford/St. Martin's, 2004.

Hunter, Edward. *Brainwashing: From Pavlov to Powers*. 1956. Linden, NJ: Bookmailer, 1965.

———. *Brainwashing in Red China*. New York: Vanguard Press, 1951.

Huntington, Samuel. *The Soldier and the State: The Theory and Politics of Civil-Military Relations*. 1957. Cambridge, MA: Belknap Press, 1981.

Jacoby, Susan. *Alger Hiss and the Battle for History*. New Haven, CT: Yale University Press, 2009.

Johnson, George. *Architects of Fear: Conspiracy Theories and Paranoia in American Politics*. Los Angeles: Jeremy P. Tarcher, 1983.

Johnson, Manning. *Color, Communism and Common Sense*. New York: Alliance, 1958.

Jones, Howard. *The Bay of Pigs*. New York: Oxford University Press, 2008.

Jones, J. Harry, Jr. *The Minutemen*. New York: Doubleday, 1968.

Joseph, Peniel E. *Waiting 'til the Midnight Hour: A Narrative History of Black Power in America*. New York: Holt, 2006.

Judis, John B. *William F. Buckley, Jr.: Patron Saint of the Conservatives*. New York: Simon and Schuster, 1988.

Kabaservice, Geoffrey. *Rule and Ruin: The Downfall of Moderation and the Destruction of the Republican Party, from Eisenhower to the Tea Party*. New York: Oxford University Press, 2012.

Kagan, Robert. *Dangerous Nation: America's Foreign Policy from Its Earliest Days to the Dawn of the Twentieth Century*. New York: Vintage, 2006.

Kahin, George McT. *Intervention: How America Became Involved in Vietnam*. New York: Anchor Books, 1986.

Kaiser, David. *American Tragedy: Kennedy, Johnson, and the Origins of the Vietnam War*. Cambridge, MA: Belknap Press, 2000.

———. *The Road to Dallas: The Assassination of John F. Kennedy*. Cambridge, MA: Belknap Press, 2008.

Kay, Jonathan. *Among the Truthers: A Journey into the Growing Conspiracist Underground of 9/11 Truthers, Birthers, Armageddonites, Vaccine Hysterics, Hollywood Know-Nothings and Internet Addicts*. New York: HarperCollins, 2011.

Kazin, Michael. *American Dreamers: How the Left Changed a Nation*. New York: Knopf, 2011.

Kellner, Douglas, and Dan Streible, eds. *Emile de Antonio: A Reader*. Minneapolis: University of Minnesota Press, 2000.

Kengor, Paul. *The Crusader: Ronald Reagan and the Fall of Communism*. New York: Regan, 2006.

King, Martin Luther, Jr. "Letter from Birmingham Jail," April 16, 1963. In David Howard-Pitney, *Martin Luther King Jr., Malcolm X and the Civil Rights Struggle of the 1950s and 1960s: A Brief History with Documents*, 84. Boston: Bedford/St. Martin's, 2004.

Kinkead, Eugene. *In Every War but One*. New York: Norton, 1959.

———. "A Reporter at Large: The Study of Something New in History." *New Yorker*, October 26, 1957, 114–69.

Knebel, Fletcher, and Charles W. Bailey II. *Seven Days in May*. New York: Harper and Row, 1962.

Knight, Peter. *Conspiracy Culture: From Kennedy to the X-Files*. London: Routledge, 2000.

Koen, Ross H. *The China Lobby in American Politics*. New York: Harper and Row, 1974.

Kolkey, Jonathan Martin. *The New Right, 1960–1968, with Epilogue, 1969–1980*. Washington, DC: University Press of America, 1983.

Kurtz, Michael L. *The JFK Assassination Debates: Lone Gunman versus Conspiracy*. Lawrence: University Press of Kansas, 2006.

Lane, Arthur Bliss. *I Saw Poland Betrayed*. Indianapolis: Bobbs-Merrill, 1948.

Larson, Arthur. *A Republican Looks at His Party*. New York: Harper and Brothers, 1956.

Lembcke, Jerry. *Hanoi Jane: War, Sex and Fantasies of Betrayal*. Amherst: University of Massachusetts Press, 2010.

Lichtman, Allan J. *White Protestant Nation: The Rise of the American Conservative Movement*. New York: Atlantic Monthly Press, 2008.

Lipset, Seymour Martin, and Earl Raab. *The Politics of Unreason: Right-Wing Extremism in America, 1790–1977*. 2nd ed. Chicago: University of Chicago Press, 1978.

Logevall, Fredrik. *Choosing War: The Lost Chance for Peace and the Escalation of the War in Vietnam*. Berkeley: University of California Press, 1999.

Loken, John. *Oswald's Trigger Films: The Manchurian Candidate, We Were Strangers, Suddenly?* Ann Arbor, MI: Falcon Books, 2000.

Lokos, Lionel. *Hysteria 1964: The Fear Campaign against Barry Goldwater*. New Rochelle, NY: Arlington House, 1967.

Lynd, Staughton, and Tom Hayden. *The Other Side*. New York: New American Library, 1966.

MacDonald, A. J. *Kangaroo Court versus The John Birch Society*. Los Angeles: A. J. MacDonald and Associates, 1963.

Mailer, Norman. *The Armies of the Night*. London: Weidenfeld and Nicolson, 1968.

Mann, Robert. *Daisy Petals and Mushroom Clouds: LBJ, Barry Goldwater and the Ad That Changed American Politics*. Baton Rouge: Louisiana State University Press, 2011.

Matusow, Allen J. *The Unraveling of America: A History of Liberalism in the 1960s*. New York: Harper and Row, 1986.

May, Ernest R. *American Cold War Strategy: Interpreting NSC 68*. Boston: Bedford/St. Martin's, 1993.

Mayer, Jane. "Covert Operations: The Billionaire Brothers Who Are Waging a War against Obama." *New Yorker*, August 30, 2010, 45–55.

McCarthy, Joseph R. *America's Retreat from Victory: The Story of George Marshall*. New York: Devin-Adair, 1954.

———. *McCarthyism: The Fight for America*. New York: Devin-Adair, 1952.

McCoy, Alfred W. *A Question of Torture: CIA Interrogation from the Cold War to the War on Terror*. New York: Holt, 2006.

McDougal, Dennis. *Privileged Son: Otis Chandler and the Rise and Fall of the LA Times Dynasty*. New York: Da Capo Press, 2001.

McEvoy, James, III. *Radicals or Conservatives: The Contemporary Radical Right*. Chicago: Rand McNally, 1971.

McGirr, Lisa. *Suburban Warriors: The Origins of the New American Right*. Princeton, NJ: Princeton University Press, 2001.

McLuhan, Marshall. *Understanding Media: The Extensions of Man*. London: Sphere Books, 1964.

McNamara, Robert. *In Retrospect: The Tragedy and Lessons of Vietnam*. New York: Random House, 1995.

Meerloo, Joost A. M. *The Rape of the Mind*. New York: World Publishing, 1956.

Menand, Louis. "Honest, Decent Wrong: The Invention of George Orwell." *New Yorker*, January 27, 2003, 84–91.

Meredith, James H. *Three Years in Mississippi*. Bloomington: Indiana University Press, 1966.

Michael, George. *Willis Carto and the American Far Right*. Gainesville: University Press of Florida, 2008.

Micklethwait, John, and Adrian Wooldridge. *The Right Nation: Conservative Power in America*. New York: Penguin, 2004.

Middendorf, J. William, II. *A Glorious Disaster: Barry Goldwater's Campaign and the Origins of the Conservative Movement*. New York: Basic Books, 2006.

Mills, C. Wright. *The Power Elite*. New York: Oxford University Press, 1956.

Minutemen. *The "Minutemen": America's Last Line of Defense against Communism*. Norborne, MO: ca. 1960.

———. *A Short History of the Minutemen*. N.p.: ca. 1960.

Morgan, Ted. *Reds: McCarthyism in Twentieth-Century America*. New York: Random House, 2003.

Moskos, Charles C. *The American Enlisted Man*. New York: Russell Sage Foundation, 1970.

Mulloy, D. J. *American Extremism: History, Politics and the Militia Movement*. New York: Routledge, 2004.

Nash, George H. *The Conservative Intellectual Movement in America since 1945*. 30th anniv. ed. Wilmington, DE: ISI Books, 2006.

Newberry, Mike. *The Fascist Revival: The Inside Story of the John Birch Society*. New York: New Century Publishers, 1961.

———. *The Yahoos*. New York: Marzani and Munsell, 1964.

Newton, Jim. *Justice for All: Earl Warren and the Nation He Made*. New York: Riverhead Books, 2006.

Nickerson, Michelle M. *Mothers of Conservatism: Women and the Postwar Right*. Princeton, NJ: Princeton University Press, 2012.

Offner, Arnold A. "Liberation or Dominance? The Ideology of U.S. National Security Policy." In *The Long War: A New History of U.S. National Security Policy since World War II*, ed. Andrew Bacevich, 1–52. New York: Columbia University Press, 2007.

Ogbar, Jeffrey O. G. *Black Power: Radical Politics and African American Identity*. Baltimore: Johns Hopkins University Press, 2004.

Olmsted, Kathryn S. *Real Enemies: Conspiracy Theories and American Democracy, World War I to 9/11*. New York: Oxford University Press, 2009.

Olson, James S., and Randy Roberts. *Where the Domino Fell: America and Vietnam, 1945–1995*. Rev. 5th ed. Malden, MA: Wiley-Blackwell, 2008.

O'Reilly, Kenneth. *Racial Matters: The FBI's Secret File on Black America, 1960–1972*. New York: Free Press, 1989.

Orwell, George. *All Art Is Propaganda: Critical Essays*. Complied by George Packer. New York: Harcourt, 2008.

———. *Animal Farm*. 1945. London: Penguin, 1988.

———. *Nineteen Eighty-Four*. 1949. London: Penguin, 1988.

Oshinsky, David M. *A Conspiracy So Immense: The World of Joe McCarthy*. New York: Oxford University Press, 2005.

O'Sullivan, Noel. *Fascism*. London: J. M. Dent and Sons, 1983.

Overstreet, Harry, and Bonaro Overstreet. *The Strange Tactics of Extremism*. New York: Norton, 1964.

Pacepa, Ion Mihai. *Programmed to Kill: Lee Harvey Oswald, the Soviet KGB, and the Kennedy Assassination*. Chicago: Ivan R. Dee, 2007.

Packard, Vance. *The Hidden Persuaders*. New York: Pocket Books, 1958.

Passmore, Kevin. *Fascism: A Very Short Introduction*. New York: Oxford University Press, 2002.

Paterson, Thomas G. *Contesting Castro: The United States and the Triumph of the Cuban Revolution*. New York: Oxford University Press, 1994.

———. "Fixation with Cuba: The Bay of Pigs, Missile Crisis, and Covert War against Cuba." In *Kennedy's Quest for Victory: American Foreign Policy, 1961–1963*, ed. Thomas G. Paterson, 123–55. New York: Oxford University Press, 1989.

Patterson, James T. *Grand Expectations: The United States, 1945–1974*. New York: Oxford University Press, 1996.

———. *Mr. Republican: A Biography of Robert A. Taft*. Boston: Houghton Mifflin, 1972.

Peel, Roy V. "The WACKACOBI: Extremists of Our Own Times." *Western Political Quarterly* 16, no. 3 (September 1963): 569–97.

Pepper, John. *American Negro Problems*. New York: Workers Library Publishers, 1928.

Perlstein, Rick. *Before the Storm: Barry Goldwater and the Unmaking of the American Consensus*. 2001. New York: Nation Books, 2009.

———. *Nixonland: The Rise of a President and the Fracturing of a Nation*. New York: Scribner, 2008.

Pfaff, William. *The Irony of Manifest Destiny*. New York: Walker, 2010.

Phillips-Fein, Kim. "Conservatism: A State of the Field," *Journal of American History* 98, no. 3 (December 2011): 723–43.

———. *Invisible Hands: The Making of the Conservative Movement from the New Deal to Reagan*. New York: Norton, 2009.

Polk, William R. *Understanding Iraq*. New York: Harper Perennial, 2006.

Posner, Gerald. *Case Closed: Lee Harvey Oswald and the Assassination of JFK*. New York: Random House, 1994.

Powell, Lee Riley. *J. William Fulbright and His Time: A Political Biography*. Memphis: Guild Bindery Press, 1996.

Powers, Richard Gid. *The Life of J. Edgar Hoover: Secrecy and Power*. New York: Free Press, 1987.

———. *Not without Honor: The History of American Anticommunism*. New York: Free Press, 1995.

Reuther, Victor G. *The Brothers Reuther and the Story of the UAW*. Boston: Houghton Mifflin, 1976.

Ribuffo, Leo P. *The Old Christian Right: The Protestant Far Right from the Great Depression to the Cold War*. Philadelphia: Temple University Press, 1983.

Riesman, David, with Nathan Glazer and Reuel Denney. *The Lonely Crowd: A Study of Changing American Character*. New York: Doubleday, 1950.

Roberts, Randy, and James S. Olson. *John Wayne: American*. New York: Free Press, 1995.

Robin, Corey. *The Reactionary Mind: Conservatism from Edmund Burke to Sarah Palin*. New York: Oxford University Press, 2011.

Robin, Ron. *The Making of the Cold War Enemy: Culture and Politics in the Military-Intellectual Complex*. Princeton, NJ: Princeton University Press, 2001.

Robins, Robert S., and Jerrold M. Post. *Political Paranoia: The Psychopolitics of Hatred*. New Haven, CT: Yale University Press, 1997.

Rodden, John. *George Orwell: The Politics of Literary Reputation*. Rev. ed. Piscataway, NJ: Transaction Publishers, 2002.

Rodgers, Daniel T. *Contested Truths: Keywords in American Politics since Independence*. New York: Basic Books, 1987.

Rogin, Michael Paul. *"Ronald Reagan," the Movie, and Other Episodes in Political Demonology*. Berkeley: University of California Press, 1987.

Rose, Lisle A. *The Cold War Comes to Main Street: America in 1950*. Lawrence: University Press of Kansas, 1999.

Rosenstone, Robert A. *Protest from the Right*. Beverly Hills, CA: Glencoe Press, 1968.

Rossiter, Clinton. *Conservatism in America: The Thankless Persuasion*. 2nd rev. ed. New York: Random House, 1962.

Rusher, William A. *The Rise of the Right*. New York: Morrow, 1984.

Saunders, Frances Stonor. *The Cultural Cold War: The CIA and the World of Arts and Letters*. New York: New Press, 1999.

Scheips, Paul J. *The Role of Federal Military Forces in Domestic Disorders, 1946–1992*. Washington, DC: Center of Military History, United States Army, 2005.

Schlafly, Phyllis. *A Choice Not an Echo*. Alton, IL: Pere Marquette Press, 1964.

Schlafly, Phyllis, and Chester Ward. *The Gravediggers*. Alton, IL: Pere Marquette Press, 1964.

Schneider, Gregory L. *Cadres for Conservatism: Young Americans for Freedom and the Rise of the Contemporary Right*. New York: New York University Press, 1999.

Schoenberger, Robert A., ed. *The American Right Wing: Readings in Political Behavior*. New York: Holt, Rinehart and Winston, 1969.

Schoenwald, Jonathan M. *A Time for Choosing: The Rise of Modern American Conservatism*. New York: Oxford University Press, 2001.

Schrecker, Ellen. *The Age of McCarthyism: A Brief History with Documents*. 2nd ed. Boston: Bedford/St. Martin's, 2002.

———. *Many Are the Crimes: McCarthyism in America*. Boston: Little, Brown, 1998.

Schulzinger, Robert. *A Time for War*. New York: Oxford University Press, 1997.

Schwartz, Bernard. *Super Chief: Earl Warren and His Supreme Court—A Judicial Biography*. New York: New York University Press, 1983.

Schwarz, Fred. *The Christian Answer to Communism*. Long Beach, CA: Christian Anti-Communism Crusade, 1961.

———. *Communism: Diagnosis and Treatment*. Los Angeles: World Vision, n.d.

———. *The Heart, Mind and Soul of Communism*. 23rd ed. Long Beach, CA: Christian Anti-Communism Crusade, 1952.

———. *You Can Trust the Communists (to be Communists)*. Englewood Cliffs, NJ: Prentice-Hall, 1960.

Schweizer, Peter. *Reagan's War: The Epic Story of His Forty-Year Struggle and Final Triumph over Communism*. New York: Doubleday, 2002.

Seed, David. *Brainwashing: The Fictions of Mind Control; A Study of Novels and Films since World War II*. Kent, OH: Kent University Press, 2004.

Shelton, Robert. *No Direction Home: The Life and Music of Bob Dylan*. New York: Ballantine Books, 1987.

Sherwin, Mark. *The Extremists*. New York: St. Martin's Press, 1963.

Shils, Edward. *The Torment of Secrecy: The Background and Consequences of American Security Politics*. Glencoe, IL: Free Press, 1956.

Singh, Nikhil Pal. *Black Is a Country: Race and the Unfinished Struggle for Democracy*. Cambridge, MA: Harvard University Press, 2004.

Sitkoff, Harvard. *King: Pilgrimage to the Mountaintop*. New York: Hill and Wang, 2008.

———. *The Struggle for Black Equality, 1954–1992*. Rev. ed. New York: Hill and Wang, 1993.

Skierka, Volker. *Fidel Castro: A Biography*. Cambridge: Polity, 2004.

Skocpol, Theda, and Vanessa Williamson. *The Tea Party and the Remaking of Republican Conservatism*. New York: Oxford University Press, 2012.

Skousen, W. Cleon. *The Naked Communist*. Cutchogue, NY: Buccaneer Books, 1958.

Smith, John, as told to Stanhope T. McReady. *Birch Putsch Plans for 1964*. N.p.: Domino Publications, 1963.

Smith, Richard Harris. *OSS: The Secret History of America's First Central Intelligence Agency*. Berkeley: University of California Press, 1972.

Smoot, Dan. "What Price Glory? Major General Edwin A. Walker." *Dan Smoot Report* 7, no. 35 (August 28, 1961): 273–80.

Socialist Labor Party. *"Rightism" Is American Fascism!* N.p.: n.d.

Soffer, Jonathan. "The National Association of Manufacturers and the Militarization of American Conservatism." *Business History Review* 75, no. 4 (Winter 2001): 775–805.

Sparrow, James T. *Warfare State: World War II Americans and the Age of Big Government*. New York: Oxford University Press, 2011.

Stephanson, Anders. "Liberty or Death: The Cold War as US Ideology." In *Reviewing the Cold War: Approaches, Interpretations, Theory*, ed. Odd Arne Westad, 81–100. London: Frank Cass, 2000.

Stern, Sheldon M. *The Week the World Stood Still: Inside the Secret Cuban Missile Crisis*. Stanford, CA: Stanford University Press, 2005.

Stewart, Charles J. "The Master Conspiracy of the John Birch Society: From Communism to the New World Order." *Western Journal of Communication* 66, no. 4 (Fall 2002): 424–47.

Stone, Barbara S. "The John Birch Society: A Profile." *Journal of Politics* 36, no. 1 (February 1974): 184–97.

Stone, Geoffrey R. *Perilous Times: Free Speech in Wartime, from the Sedition Act of 1798 to the War on Terrorism*. New York: Norton, 2004.

Storke, Thomas M. *I Write for Freedom*. Santa Barbara, CA: News-Press Publishing Company, 1963.

Storrs, Landon R. Y. *The Second Red Scare and the Unmaking of the New Deal Left*. Princeton, NJ: Princeton University Press, 2012.

Stormer, John A. *None Dare Call It Treason*. Florisssant, MO: Liberty Bell Press, 1964.

Suall, Irwin. *The American Ultras: The Extreme Right and the Military-Industrial Complex*. 2nd ed. New York: New America, 1962.

Sugrue, Thomas J. *Sweet Land of Liberty: The Forgotten Struggle for Civil Rights in the North*. New York: Random House, 2008.

Szulc, Tad. *Fidel: A Critical Portrait*. New York: Morrow, 1986.

Tanenhaus, Sam. *The Death of Conservatism*. New York: Random House, 2009.

———. *Whittaker Chambers: A Biography*. New York: Random House, 1997.

Taylor, Kathleen. "On Brainwashing." In *The Barbarisation of Warfare*, ed. George Kassimeris, 238–53. London: Hurst, 2006.

Thayer, George. *The Farther Shores of Politics: The American Political Fringe Today*. 2nd ed. New York: Simon and Schuster, 1968.

Theoharis, Athan G. *The Yalta Myths: An Issue in U.S. Politics, 1945–1955*. Columbia: University Press of Missouri, 1970.

Toy, Eckard V., Jr. "The Right Side of the 1960s: The Origins of the John Birch Society in the Pacific Northwest." *Oregon Historical Society* 105, no. 2 (2004): 260–83.

Turner, William W. *Power on the Right*. Berkeley, CA: Ramparts Press, 1971.

Tygiel, Jules. *Ronald Reagan and the Triumph of American Conservatism*. 2nd ed. New York: Pearson Longman, 2006.

Van Deburg, William L. *New Day in Babylon: The Black Power Movement and American Culture, 1965–1975*. Chicago: University of Chicago Press, 1992.

VanDeMark, Brian. *Into the Quagmire: Lyndon Johnson and the Escalation of the Vietnam War*. New York: Oxford University Press, 1991.

Viguerie, Richard. *The New Right: We're Ready to Lead*. Falls Church, VA: Viguerie, 1981.

Waldor, Milton A. *The John Birch Society: Peddlers of Fear*. Newark, NJ: Lynnross Publishing, 1966.

Walker, Edwin A. "An Address by Edwin A. Walker, Jackson, Miss., 29 Dec. 1961." In *The American Eagle Weapons for Freedom*. N.p.: ca. 1961.

———. *Censorship and Survival*. New York: Bookmailer, 1961.

———. *Walker Speaks Unmuzzled!* Dallas, TX: American Eagle Publishing, 1962.

———. *Pro Blue*. Dallas, TX: American Eagle Publishing, 1965.

Walker, Martin. *The Cold War and the Making of the Modern World*. London: Vintage, 1994.

Warren, Earl. *The Memoirs of Earl Warren*. New York: Doubleday, 1977.

Webb, Clive. *Rabble Rousers: The American Far Right in the Civil Rights Era*. Athens: University of Georgia Press, 2010.

Weiner, Tim. *Enemies: A History of the FBI*. New York: Random House, 2012.

Weiss, John. *The Fascist Tradition*. New York: Harper and Row, 1967.

Wells, Tom. *The War Within: America's Battle over Vietnam*. Berkeley: University of California Press, 1994.

Westin, Alan F. "The John Birch Society: Fundamentalism on the Right." *Commentary* 32, no. 2 (August 1961): 93–104.

White, F. Clifton, and William J. Gill. *Suite 3505*. New Rochelle, NY: Arlington House, 1967.

White, Theodore H. *The Making of the President, 1960*. New York: Atheneum, 1961.

———. *The Making of the President, 1964*. New York: Atheneum, 1965.

Whitfield, Stephen J. *The Culture of the Cold War*. 2nd ed. Baltimore: Johns Hopkins University Press, 1996.

Wilentz, Sean. "Confounding Fathers: The Tea Party's Cold War Roots." *New Yorker*, October 10, 2010, 32–39.

Wills, Garry. *Reagan's America: Innocents at Home*. London: Heinemann, 1988.

Wilcox, Clyde. "Sources of Support for the Old Right: A Comparison of the John Birch Society and the Christian Anti-Communism Crusade." *Social Science History* 12, no. 4 (Winter 1988): 429–49.

Wood, Gordon S. "Conspiracy and the Paranoid Style: Causality and Deceit in the Eighteenth Century." *William and Mary Quarterly* 39 (1982): 401–41.

———. *The Creation of the American Republic*. Chapel Hill: University of North Carolina Press, 1969.

———. *The Radicalism of the American Revolution*. New York: Vintage, 1991.

Woods, Randall Bennett. *Fulbright: A Biography*. New York: Cambridge University Press, 1995.

———. *LBJ: Architect of American Ambition*. New York: Free Press, 2006.

Young, Marilyn. *The Vietnam Wars, 1945–1990*. New York: Harper, 1991.

Zelizer, Julian E. *Arsenal of Democracy: The Politics of National Security—From World War II to the War on Terrorism*. New York: Basic Books, 2010.

Zernike, Kate. *Boiling Mad: Inside Tea Party America*. New York: Times Books, 2010.

Index

Page numbers in bold refer to illustrations. Abbreviations used in the index are those given in parentheses in main entries; for example, the John Birch Society is referred to as "JBS" throughout.